MW00526893

About Island Press

Since 1984, the nonprofit organization Island Press has been stimulating, shaping, and communicating ideas that are essential for solving environmental problems worldwide. With more than 1,000 titles in print and some 30 new releases each year, we are the nation's leading publisher on environmental issues. We identify innovative thinkers and emerging trends in the environmental field. We work with world-renowned experts and authors to develop cross-disciplinary solutions to environmental challenges.

Island Press designs and executes educational campaigns, in conjunction with our authors, to communicate their critical messages in print, in person, and online using the latest technologies, innovative programs, and the media. Our goal is to reach targeted audiences—scientists, policy makers, environmental advocates, urban planners, the media, and concerned citizens—with information that can be used to create the framework for long-term ecological health and human well-being.

Island Press gratefully acknowledges major support from The Bobolink Foundation, Caldera Foundation, The Curtis and Edith Munson Foundation, The Forrest C. and Frances H. Lattner Foundation, The JPB Foundation, The Kresge Foundation, The Summit Charitable Foundation, Inc., and many other generous organizations and individuals.

THE ECONOMICS OF SUSTAINABLE FOOD

THE ECONOMICS OF SUSTAINABLE FOOD

Smart Policies for Health and the Planet

Edited by Nicoletta Batini

A Co-publication of Island Press and the International Monetary Fund

Library of Congress Control Number: 2020944714

All Island Press books are printed on environmentally responsible materials.

Manufactured in the United States of America
10 9 8 7 6 5 4 3 2 1

Nothing contained in this book should be reported as representing the views of the IMF, its Executive Board, member governments, or any other entity mentioned herein. The views in this book belong solely to the authors.

Keywords: Agricultural industrialization, developing economies, food demand, food insecurity, food prices, food production, food supply, food system, food waste, global food shortage, Green Revolution, Intergovernmental Panel on Climate Change (IPCC), macroeconomic policy, polyfunctional farming, subsistence economies, sustainable agriculture, sustainable development, true cost of food

For Lina and Jehanne,
my small (but mighty) Mother Nature warriors.

CONTENTS

Food systems have come a long way since the era of hunting and gathering began some 1.8 million years ago, yet the undeniable advances have come at a price. While more than two thirds of the population in poor countries still work in subsistence agriculture and fishing, less than 5 percent of the population does in richer countries, where most of our food is produced, using industrial methods focused on high crop and animal productivity. Globally, the industrial food chain is extremely concentrated, with a few players dominating entire food markets vertically or horizontally.

So far, twenty-first-century macroeconomists have largely ignored food systems. This is odd, considering that the agri-food sector is both the largest, fastest-growing industry in the world and the major employer in the developing world.

Perhaps more worryingly, many macroeconomists have overlooked the fact that our current food systems pose several existential threats to people and economies. First, almost half of humanity is chronically malnourished, and most of the rest is either overweight or obese, because the food we produce is less and less nutritious and the way we distribute it globally is grossly inefficient and vulnerable to disruptions. This has huge implications for labor productivity and health expenditures and, accordingly, for private and public finances. Second, industrial food production, from intensive monocrops and confined animal operations in the Northern Hemisphere to thousands of small-scale ranchers in the Amazon serving the cattle industry, is bringing entire ecosystems to biological collapse, causing a human-made mass extinction. Crucially, the food system is the top contributor to greenhouse gas emissions and the number one degrader of natural resources, including water and air. Third, human diets have shifted progressively toward consumption of more foods derived from animals. Many of these animals are fed from birth with growth-promoting subtherapeutic dosages of antibiotics, generating conditions for the proliferation of new, untreatable superbugs resistant to known antimicrobials. Industrial animal farming operations that raise large numbers of animals in confined spaces also breed bacteria and viruses such as *Salmonella*, *Escherichia coli*, and the 2009 swine flu H1N1. Even more concerning is the spread of zoonotic diseases such as SARS-CoV, Zika, HIV, Ebola, and today's

SARS-CoV-2, as more and more pathogens confined for millennia to the animal kingdom jump species to infect ours. This spread is traceable to the increasing disturbance of wildlife, both through the consumption of wild animals for food and through the loss of wildlife habitat as more land is cleared for farming and urbanization.

The impact of each one of these threats on people and the planet is immense and is economically unbearable, making their combined adverse effects too large to conceive. The good news is that this implies that reforming food systems promises incredible opportunities to advance both human and environmental well-being. Apart from feeding us properly and conserving the natural world, well-managed food systems can secure multiple social, economic, and environmental goals, such as keeping humanity healthy and well-nourished, sustaining inclusive trade and income, and creating millions of local high-quality jobs. In this sense, reforming food systems is central to achieving the UN Sustainable Development Goals and the pledges of the Paris Climate Agreement.

As populations grow and dietary patterns shift to become progressively more caloric and protein-rich, natural resources are put under growing stress while climate change wreaks havoc on global food security. To avoid the very real risk of a human and planetary catastrophe, we need to quickly reinstate food systems in the pantheon of economic activities that macroeconomists routinely analyze and work on. And we must design and implement economic strategies to make food production more inclusive, profitable, sustainable, and nutritious.

To this end, this book identifies a portfolio of policy measures to reform food systems based on a multidisciplinary approach connecting macroeconomics, public health, and environmental sciences. Recommendations are based on the most recent scientific literature and on a large array of successful country cases.

I strongly recommend this book to all those who want to understand the importance of food systems for economies and their relationship with climate and developmental goals, as well as to those who want to design sound public policy strategies to attain those goals.

The first step is to recognize that economic health is human health is planetary health.

Nicoletta Batini
Washington, D.C., June 2020

Chapter 1

We Depend on Food, Food Depends on Nature

Nicoletta Batini

> "The truth is: the natural world is changing. And we are totally dependent on that world. It provides our food, water and air. It is the most precious thing we have and we need to defend it."
> —*David Attenborough*

At the World Economic Forum in Davos, Switzerland in 2019, delegates spoke of a "Great Energy Transformation" needed to ensure a clean and secure energy future. No less urgent for the future of the planet is what we might call a "Great Food Transformation."

While the climate implications of burning fossil fuels have received a great deal of attention, recent research by the UN's Intergovernmental Panel on Climate Change (IPCC) shows that what we eat, how we produce it, and how it gets to us exerts an even greater impact on the global environment and public health, a finding made even more evident by the emergence of the COVID-19 pandemic. Greening food production and managing food demand to ensure that it is safe and nutritious for all are crucial for meeting the UN's 2030 Agenda for Sustainable Development and the environmental pledge behind the UN's Paris Agreement (Batini 2019b).

The True Cost of Our Food

Modern industrial agriculture has been described to the public as a technological miracle. Its advanced level of specialization and mechanization, we were told, would increase food production to meet the demand of a rapidly growing global population, and its economies of scale would ensure that farming remained profitable. But something crucial was left out of this story: the price tag.

Although productivity advances in agriculture have dramatically increased the supply of food, reducing the risk of global shortages, today hundreds of millions of people still go to bed hungry each night, and 2 billion more lack essential nutrients. Moreover, the way we produce food is making diets for the rest of humanity increasingly hypercaloric, undernutritious, and unhealthy, and unsafe food containing harmful bacteria, viruses, parasites, or chemical substances is a growing global threat leading to more than half a billion cases of illness a year (WHO 2020). Crucially, science shows that the practices currently used in conventional agriculture and fishing are harming the planet beyond repair (IPCC 2019; IPBES 2019; Willett et al. 2019).

Looking forward, fears are rising that industrial agriculture and fishing may not be able to feed a growing world because we are approaching the ceiling of what can be done to expand production industrially in terms of land, water, and chemical soil fertilization (FAO 2019). These challenges are aggravated by climate change, which is eroding the fertility of the land and the vitality of the sea, as well as making rain and other seasonal patterns more volatile and extreme (IPCC 2019). That should not surprise us: Since the inception of the not-so-green "Green Revolution"[1] in the 1950s, agriculture has churned through natural resources, and we may soon reach the bottom of the bucket. As Schumacher (1973, p. 30) pointed out, "infinite growth in a finite environment is an obvious impossibility."

Importantly, agriculture, fishing, and forestry are fundamentally different from other industrial sectors in that the former deal with living substances subject to their own laws, whereas the latter do not. Altering these laws, as through synthetic fertilization or genetic manipulation of factory-raised animals, is creating biological imbalances of vast proportions, the effects of which are known to be either extremely dangerous or totally unpredictable.

The crises of the modern food system—malnutrition, diseases, and ecosystem collapse—generate incommensurate economic costs. However, the importance of developing economic policies that can help transform the system have long disappeared from the economic profession's radar screen because of the widespread belief that producing food industrially would solve global food problems. Reflecting this belief, economic analysis regularly disregards the primary sector and its interactions with the rest of the economy, and macroeconomic policy design largely abstracts from it on the grounds of the low value added and job intensity of the sector in the advanced world. Accordingly, when major developments wreak havoc on the food system, such as foodborne pandemics, mass extinctions, spikes in food prices, record crop losses, or record deforestation from abnormal wildfire seasons, they are treated as exogenous, unanticipated "shocks" even if they are the direct result of specific public or private agents' actions.

The joint health and economic crises unleashed by the coronavirus outbreak and the burning down of large sections of the Amazon rainforest in 2019–2020 demonstrate that ignoring the role played by food systems in the economy is an expensive mistake not just from a public health and environmental perspective but also from an economic point of view. This is because food systems are an integral part of economic systems and intersect with human activity in many ways. Food systems do not only feed us, influence our health, and shape the way we interact with the natural world—including climate and pathogens. They also affect employment and labor productivity, drive international trade and domestic intermediate exchanges, and via land and sea rights have traditionally spurred exploration, commerce, and financial activities, helping to build nations' wealth.

The industrialization of agriculture and fishing have not diminished the importance of food systems for people and economies but have distorted it, leading to five types of negative externalities:

- *Environmental degradation*. Scientific evidence from a variety of independent sources and fields unanimously identifies agriculture (crop and animal) as the single most important driver of climate change (IPCC 2019; Sanjo et al. 2016). Specifically, agriculture is estimated to be responsible for 21–37 percent of all greenhouse gas emissions because of the release of carbon dioxide from deforestation to claw back land for pasture and feedstock crops and from burning fossil fuels to power farm machinery and to transport, store, and cook foods; the release of methane from ruminant livestock; and the release of nitrous oxide from industrially tilled, heavily fertilized soils and liquid manure management systems (IPCC 2019). Beyond warming the atmosphere and catalyzing climate change, industrial agriculture is quickly exhausting other natural resources. It has led to the clearing of more than 40 percent of Earth's arable land, a surface area equivalent to the size of South America, and global pastures currently occupy land equivalent to the surface area of Africa. In addition, irrigation for industrial agriculture is responsible for the biggest use of water on the planet, absorbing 70–80 percent of all available freshwater. Meanwhile, fertilizers have more than doubled the levels of nitrogen and phosphorus in Earth's crust, leading to massive water degradation and pollution in the remaining water available for human consumption and other uses (Rockström et al. 2017). Likewise, commercial fishing is removing an increasingly large number of fish from the ocean, depleting key fish stocks, and many industrial fishing practices also destroy aquatic habitat, with far-reaching consequences for biodiversity, climate, and life on Earth more generally (WWF 2018).

These phenomena are bound to get worse. Hastened population growth and the shift to hypercaloric, animal-based diets, together with a ramp-up in the production of biofuels as fossil fuels run scarce, suggest that we will need to double global food production by 2050 and triple it over the following decades. Looking at livestock alone, for example, projections indicate that by 2050 animal production will increase by 80 percent compared with 2005 (Alexandratos and Bruinsma 2012), in line with estimates of the trend in the global demand for milk and meat (Fiala 2008; Thornton 2010). But these rhythms and methods of production are plainly incompatible with the sustainability of the world's future food supply, heralding the advent of a simultaneous global agricultural, food, and water crisis.

- *Jobs and income inequality*. Industrial agriculture also threatens jobs and income equality in a variety of ways. In advanced economies, as predicted by Colin Clark in 1951, the industrialization of agriculture has eliminated most agricultural jobs in the industrialized world (figure 1-1). Far more jobs have been lost in farming than in manufacturing over the past half century.

Although economy-wide unemployment did not materialize after the industrialization of agriculture, as new industries emerged and expanded, the transition between agricultural and manufacturing or service jobs had far-reaching impacts on income inequality both in rural and urban areas, with effects still vividly felt today (Judis 2016). Production is also massively concentrated vertically, with 1 percent of all companies dominating two thirds of world markets and even higher concentration in some domestic markets (figure 1-2). This has negative implications for price and wage setting and the types and quality of food and beverages produced.[2]

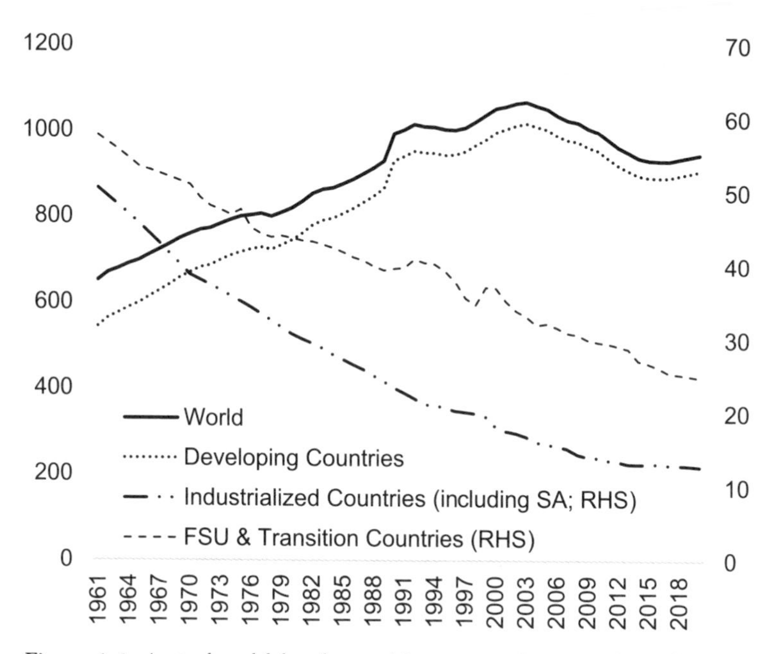

Figure 1-1. Agricultural labor by world region, 1961–2020 (in millions of persons active, 15+ years, male and female). *Sources:* ILO Model estimates, May 2018 update; USDA Economic Research Service.

In emerging and developing economies, agricultural industrialization is significantly less advanced, and agriculture in these economies still employs about 1 billion people (ILO 2019). However, if agriculture were to follow the same destiny observed in advanced economies and to be industrialized as implied by UN projections on urbanization trends (UN 2018), most of these jobs could be permanently lost, leading to a quadrupling of 2019 global unemployment. Industrial agriculture in the advanced world, on the other hand, is already a leading cause of income inequality and poverty in developing countries: Subsidies to industrial agriculture in advanced economies distort international commodity prices, making it cheaper for developing countries to import rather than continue to produce food. This not only destroys the main source of income in subsistence economies; it also makes countries dependent on imports for food (among many others, see Alam et al. 2015; Boltvinik and Mann 2016).[3] The COVID-19 pandemic is likely to affect food prices internationally and plunge developing economies into deeper debt (FAO 2020; UNSCN 2020).

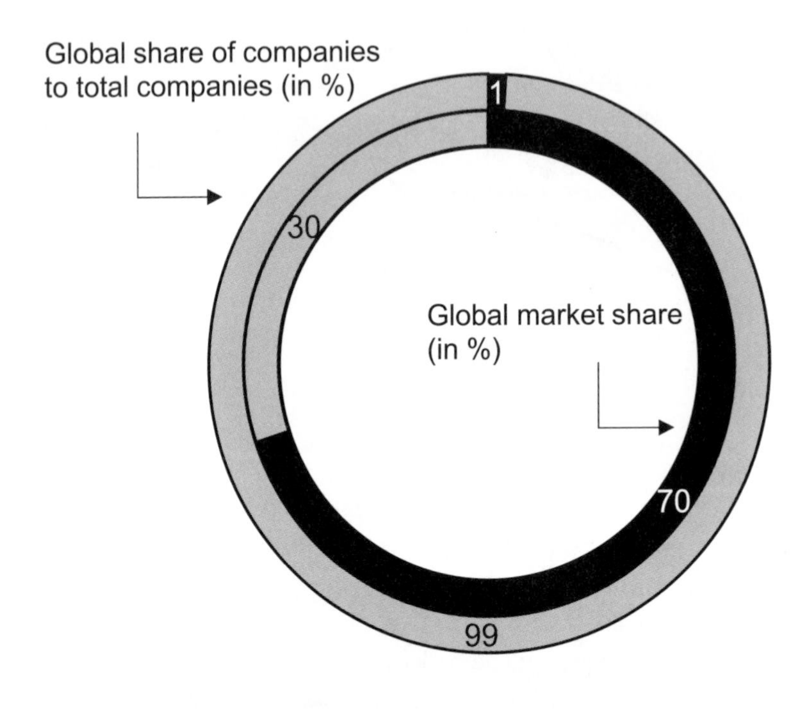

Figure 1-2. Global food industry market concentration. *Sources:* Dow Jones Factiva; Oxfam International (2013).

- *Malnutrition and food insecurity.* At the end of the eighteenth century, Malthus postulated that agricultural innovations would raise prosperity only fleetingly: By stimulating population growth, more food would lead to a fight for scarce resources, causing hunger, war, and diseases. In turn this would restrain economic growth and put a lid on population growth. Malthus's prediction has long been dismissed as spectacularly wrong, because continuous advances in food production—alongside medical advances and improvements in sanitary infrastructure—have ensured a permanent global food glut and continual growth in global longevity. But although Malthus was wrong yesterday, he probably would have been right today and tomorrow in two important respects. First, although industrial agriculture has ensured that increasing amounts of food are produced globally, this has not solved world hunger. Major distributional problems remain between and within nations, with about 2 billion people around the world overeating and 3 billion undereating. Furthermore, a third of all food produced is wasted. The misallocation of food, in turn, is a cause of persistent differentials in the levels of prosperity around the world, and thus of migration and conflicts. Second, the ecological footprint from current agricultural methods demonstrably exceeds the carrying capacity of the planet. Absent bold and globalized policy action, this is bound to hamper production soon, causing either a massive rationing of food or drastic adjustments in food prices, making food unaffordable for billions of people. To make things worse, as the current COVID-19 crisis has shown, the global food supply chain—heavily concentrated, globalized, and operating on a just-in-time supply basis—is likely to falter and fail in the case of major events such as natural disasters or pandemics, a high-probability scenario in a world of swift climate change (Batini et al. 2020; see also Blay-Palmer et al. 2020). In some cases, we do not have the ability to produce food. In other cases, we can produce it but do not have the ability to process it and package it, a limitation conducive to industrial-scale food crises. This is aggravated by the fact that large swathes of the food system rely on foreign seasonal labor, which depends on migration flows, which in turn are volatile and hinge on the resilience of international travel—gravely disrupted during the pandemic, for example—and migration policies.

- *Rural exodus and urbanization.* The industrialization of food production has contributed to a global phenomenon of rural-to-urban migration. It is estimated that the rural population represented almost two thirds of the total population of the world in the middle of the twentieth century. Since then, the percentage of people living in rural areas has been decreasing at a very fast rate. The rate of decrease remained roughly the same between 1950 and 2000, at around 2 percent every 5 years, or 0.35 percent per annum. The projections suggest that this phenomenon will accelerate in the future: In 2030, only 40 percent of the world population will live in rural settlements, reflecting a rapid rate of decrease of 0.44 percent per year projected from 2000 to 2030 (UN 2018). Different continents have different patterns of urbanization, but the consequences in the rural population are similar. They include the disappearance of rural cultures, the increased risk of economic instability and deviant behavior among rural–urban migrants, higher unemployment in urban areas, changes in fertility behavior, and cultural tensions in urban areas. Crucially, the decline in agricultural employment has led to a degradation of human skills in traditional agriculture, which may aggravate the shift to industrial agriculture. Urbanization also adds to environmental degradation on two levels. First, poor air and water quality, insufficient water availability, waste disposal problems, and high energy consumption are exacerbated by the increasing population density and demands of urban environments. Second, urban development is one of the key causes of human encroachment on natural habitats, loss of tree cover, and for wild animal populations the loss of habitat and food sources. Together with farming and hunting, urbanization simultaneously threatens species survival and increases the risk of dangerous viruses such as COVID-19 spilling over from animals to humans (Johnson et al. 2020).

- *Risks to public health.* Finally, there is compelling evidence that industrial agriculture has vast implications for public health, and the cost and risks are escalating fast. First, as animal products have become less expensive per unit of agricultural land than fruit and vegetables in most advanced and large emerging markets, and food is becoming increasingly processed, the average diet in richer countries is skewing toward protein- and cholesterol-rich, high-sugar, and nonfibrous foods, often laden with hormones, antibiotics, and chemicals used in industrial production. This has led to higher rates of noncommunicable diseases and obesity, illnesses exacerbated by the shift toward sedentary lifestyles that has accompanied the shift from agricultural economies to service-based economies and urbanization in the developing world. To this we add the human and social costs of pesticide use in industrial agriculture and its effect on the neurologic, respiratory, and reproductive systems (Nicolopoulou-Stamati et al. 2016).

Second, most livestock today are raised in concentrated animal feeding operations, more commonly known as factory farms. These industrial-scale facilities, where thousands of genetically similar animals are packed together in unsanitary, overcrowded quarters and are vulnerable to disease because of the stress placed on their immune systems by these living conditions, continuously breed lethal bacteria such as *Salmonella*, *Escherichia coli*, and, in farms at sea, *Vibrio cholerae*, as well as an array of flu viruses, such as the bird (poultry) 2006 highly pathogenic avian influenza or the swine 2009 H1N1 flu, which triggered deadly pandemics. Research shows that these farms create the perfect conditions for rapid amplification and spread of pathogens (Saenz et al. 2006). These conditions have been shown to be comparable to those in wet markets in Asia, Africa, and South America, where zoonotic viruses such as severe acute respiratory syndrome, HIV, Ebola, and now, possibly, COVID-19, spilled over to our species from stressed wild animals mixed with humans in unsanitary and crowded spaces.

Third, the overuse of subtherapeutic doses of antibiotics in factory farms for nonmedical purposes has led to antibiotic-resistant strains of bacteria that make treating human illnesses more difficult. Although the links between animal agriculture and human disease are complex and in need of additional study, evidence is strong enough for scientists and public health organizations to have repeatedly called for reduced use of antibiotics in agriculture (WHO 2017; CDC 2020). Based on current projections, if unaddressed, antimicrobial resistance will lead to more deaths than cancer by 2050 and an economic cost equivalent to 260 percent of the 2016 Global World Product (O'Neill 2016).

The current and future costs of fixing these public health challenges are enormous. Yet they are only part of the true cost of our food. By harming human health, through overnourishment or undernourishment, dysfunctional food systems erode labor productivity because they increase the number and types of workers' disabilities and, correspondingly, the number of years of work lost. By raising health spending and lowering potential output, industrial food systems pose one of the greatest menaces to fiscal sustainability in most world countries today.

Fixing Food Systems

Few issues will be more important for individual prosperity and the global economy than the way we produce our food and what food we eat. Adopting policy measures to move away from current methods of industrial agriculture and fishing and to make them sustainable, healthy, and safe is a tremendous opportunity for global policymakers to make a difference across a range of issues and in many people's lives.

Seizing this opportunity involves following three steps (figure 1-3).

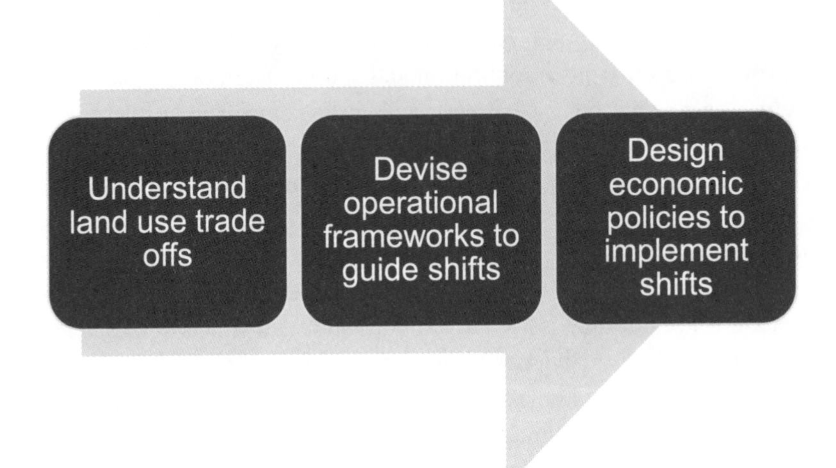

Figure 1-3. The three steps toward a Great Food Transformation.

Step One

To begin with, policymakers need to understand the public health, economic, and environmental trade-offs between using land and sea for food production and their use for competing activities: urban, extractive, industrial, recreational, and conservational. In addition, policymakers need to appreciate the different impacts of alternative food systems on natural resources, biological diversity, and greenhouse gas emissions. Farming and fishing methods that are more resource intensive eat into resources that could be used for other ends, raising the opportunity cost of producing food relative to methods that are less resource intensive. Also, policymakers need to have a clear sense of how different diets affect health. Diets that are healthier are less burdensome for people and the economy because they minimize the risk of premature death, the need for and cost of sick care and nonmedical care, and losses of work and income due to illnesses.

In recent years, researchers have come up with precise measures of these relative impacts and have arrived at three broad conclusions. First, the true cost of food produced industrially is very high for people, nature, and the economy (IPCC 2019). In contrast, regenerative agriculture and fishing follow ecological principles that can heal the environment, are more adaptive to changes in climate, and produce nutritious and safe food that is comparatively cheap (FAO 2019; FOLU 2019; UNEP 2019). Second, diets that are primarily plant based are healthier and more sustainable than diets that are heavy in animal products (Willet et al. 2019). Finally, biological diversity of both animals and plants is key to human food security because a significant diversity of organisms is necessary to protect the web of life that sustains crops and livestock. Conservation of pristine ecosystems is also essential to stabilize climate, which in turn shelters food production from an exacerbation of extreme weather events and global warming (IPBES 2019).

Step Two

Having identified the direction in which food systems must go for health and planet, society needs clear operational frameworks to guide shifts at the country or regional level. Ideally, these frameworks should reflect scenarios obtained with integrated land and sea use models calibrated nationally. These models can typically compare the environmental, dietary, and socioeconomic implications of alternative production and consumption templates given specific geographic, resource, climate, and cultural initial conditions in various places around the world. In turn, these frameworks can be weaved into larger analytical and modeling setups involving energy planning and macroeconomic variables, such as the country's international trade balance, to assess the overall environmental and socioeconomic impact of competing food supply models. Advanced geospatial models of land, food production, and trade can then be built to test policy options and develop pathways, as has been done successfully for Brazil, France, Indonesia, and the United Kingdom (Bretz, 2016; Solagro 2016; Vergara et al., 2016; Harwatt and Hayek 2019; Schmidt-Traub et al. 2019).[4]

Step Three

Finally, policymakers need to design economic policies and structural reforms that can transform food systems to meet their country's development and environmental goals. These are the actual policy levers that change food production and consumption.

Regrettably, although today we understand how to produce and eat food for the well-being of people and the planet (Step One), and these precepts are starting to be investigated more pragmatically in some countries (Step

Two), the design of economic policies to make a food transformation happen is much sketchier. Globally, only a handful of countries have announced plans to earmark modest amounts of public investment and changes in regulations or green food production and consumption. Elsewhere, reforms to promote food sustainability and health continue to be sidelined to a bilateral debate between agriculture ministries, nongovernment organizations, and the few large corporations that dominate the sector (Andersen and Kuhn 2014).

And yet macroeconomic policy is ideally suited to improve food systems. "Green" fiscal, trade, and financial policies, as well as structural reform measures used successfully to spur green transitions in other markets, such as energy, can be deployed in food markets to arrive at more sustainable production and healthier diets and reap the ensuing economic, social, and planetary gains.

The route to food system reform via well-targeted economic measures is uphill but far from impossible as food markets everywhere seem ready to embrace change. Promising trends toward greater agri-food sustainability are emerging independently, including a global acceleration in land and sea used for nonconventional, regenerative farming, a shift away among Millennials and Generation Z members from animal-based protein, and technological advancements in restorative methods of agricultural production and regenerative ocean farming. These trends are accompanied by parallel, self-directed shifts in financing, which is slowly but relentlessly becoming more engaged in funding "green," sustainable agri-food production and consumption solutions (Batini 2019c). Novel investment trends, which largely respond to emergent demand trends, include plant-based investing, alternative protein investing, and agricultural technology venture capital investing. They also include a growing class of green and sustainable bond investing that is no longer limited to green projects in the energy realm but increasingly incorporates a focus on land use.

Although the potential benefits of making global food systems sustainable are enormous, not all of them can be achieved through a business-as-usual approach. In fact, current trends in global investment do not yet reflect the potential for disruption in demand-side agri-food innovations—innovations that target and affect consumers. The lower levels of investment in food systems are due in great part to the complexity of the sector. Fragmented rural markets, poor infrastructure, high regulatory burdens, and other factors raise costs, while revenues are constrained by customers' limited ability and willingness to pay. In addition, much of the food systems' startup activity is concentrated in developed countries and on improving the production landscape, indicating both the risk of unequal access to new solutions and the opportunities for scaling in developing countries and in demand-side innovations. Coordinated efforts by policymakers, investors, educators, and others to accelerate a transformation of food systems in all regions can overcome those obstacles.

Economic Policies for the Great Food Transformation

Many science-driven plans exist to move food systems in the right direction, but we still lack a comprehensive and simple guide for economic policymakers exploring tools to nudge markets into the new era. This book fills this gap by gathering a multidisciplinary team of scientists and economic policy experts to summarize and explain the science behind the challenges posed to the environment, our economies, and public health by today's global food system, documenting the scientific dietary and food production targets needed to make food systems healthy, sustainable, and conducive to both the SDGs and the 1.5°C Paris Agreement goal; study the economic benefits of greening the agri-food sector while reviewing the environmental and public health benefits from meeting these targets; and propose a toolkit of economic and structural policies to implement the Great Food Transformation.

The book is divided into four sections, each dealing with a specific, interrelated aspect of the food system: production, consumption, food waste, and sustainable use of land and seas for ecosystem conservation, a key ingredient for sustainable food production. Throughout, real-world examples of economic and structural policies from around the globe illustrate the levers that are being used successfully, explaining which of these are most effective and how they can be combined to meet today's unique challenges.

Tailored Policies

In discussing economic policies to transform the food system, much hinges on where each country stands in terms of prevalent diets, food production, and imports, as well as on the conditions for reform. Because food choices depend on a variety of perceptions, attitudes, and norms, building effective policies for food systems' change also calls for an increasingly interactive process with consumers and producers of food.

Accordingly, the book provides a portfolio of targeted policy options. Focusing exclusively on a limited set of first–best, optimal measures would narrow choices and thus risk limiting or postponing policy action, as in the case of carbon pricing taxation in the energy sector. In most cases, effective behavior change strategies will entail combining measures across various areas of public intervention. Therefore, the book reviews measures ranging from taxes and spending to education, labor market, healthcare, and pension reforms, alongside regulatory steps to influence behavior more speedily where market incentives are unlikely to work or to work fast enough.

The book's main policy prescriptions can be summarized as follows.

To green our food supply, science shows that at a global level, we need to halve animal-based food production, replacing it with plant-based production, and shift away from conventional farming and fishing to regenerative farming. This can be achieved by raising taxes on intensive animal farms and farms growing crops destined for animal use, cutting subsidies to these operations, and redirecting subsidies to sustainable farms just as carbon taxes are being proposed and raised to shift away from fossil fuels toward sustainable energy sources. Reforms to make land cheaper for regenerative farmers or to limit land available for conventional farming can complement these measures, alongside labor market reforms promoting regenerative agro-fishing jobs and the setup of enterprises involved in small agro-business. Other measures include public investment in research and innovation and public sponsoring of food industry initiatives aimed at promoting healthy food. These policies would mostly interest developed and large emerging market economies, which are the world's top suppliers of meat and dairy, as well as the main exporters of key food commodities such as grains, sugar, and rice. In these markets, 98 percent of production is industrial, highly concentrated all along the supply chains, and heavily subsidized (chapter 2).

Greening agri-food production in less industrialized countries indicates that the challenges are great, but the opportunities exist. In some countries, regenerative farming is timidly but successfully emerging as an approach to increase income while supporting sustainability. Affordable sun-powered irrigation systems are gradually empowering farmers to take charge of their crops even during droughts, and producers are experimenting with combinations of agriculture and aquaculture to create more productive and sustainable food systems. Policymakers in those countries need to consider public health and environmental outcomes along with production goals when determining which crops and production systems receive support through research, extension, and policy (chapter 3). Everywhere, policies should sustain old and novel sustainable farming practices that include polycultural small farming (chapter 4a), urban vertical farming (chapter 4b), regenerative ocean farming (chapter 4c), and alternative-protein farming (chapter 4d).

Greening food demand requires a parallel global shift away from animal food products and, in most advanced and emerging market countries, a decline in protein and calories to bring them in line with recommended nutritional values (chapter 5). In regions and countries in the developing world that struggle with specific nutritional deficiencies, more animal protein may actually be needed. This implies that, initially at least, the heavy lifting of moving to plant-based diets should happen in the developed world, where people overeat animal foods (chapter 6). To this end, science has identified a "planetary" diet that is conducive to good health and can limit greenhouse gas emissions. The diet can be tweaked to account for differences in age, sex, cultural traditions, and regional food options.

These dietary shifts can be attained by taxing unhealthy foods and subsidizing healthy ones (especially in those developing countries where the "planetary" diet is not fully affordable) while compensating consumers for potential losses in purchasing power by redistributing net tax revenues. Recent reviews of country cases indicate that these incentive mechanisms work well and are politically viable (chapter 5). Complementary or alternative policy options include health tax bonuses, lowering taxes for people who eat well. They also include a reform of medical systems to strengthen preventive care based on healthy lifestyles and nutrition as opposed to "sick" care, because research shows that these measures can go a long way in shifting dietary patterns toward healthful and sustainable diets. Market reforms can inform consumers of dietary risks and limit unhealthy ingredients in food products, and education reforms can ensure that dietary shifts are durable (chapter 5).

Economic policy levers, as well as efforts by businesses, organizations, and consumers, can also help cut the amount of food that goes to waste. Reducing this waste, which is responsible for almost one tenth of global greenhouse gas emissions, would conserve natural resources, create economic opportunity, and feed the hungry (chapter 7). This important goal is more challenging than expected because food is wasted for different reasons in different places. In low- and middle-income countries, food waste happens largely within the supply chain, whereas in wealthier countries it occurs at the consumer level. At the same time, not all interventions to reduce food waste are equally effective or justifiable from an environmental, nutrition, or economic point of view. Yet cutting food waste is one of the lowest-hanging fruits in transforming food systems, and country cases indicate that many policies can make a dent in the amount of food that is wasted. In developing countries, strategies include public investment in weather systems to increase farming accuracy, training in quality standards and storage, removal of infrastructure constraints, and investments in cooling systems, refrigeration, improved storage, and roads to get perishable food onto the market faster. In developed countries, policies include education to foster a no-waste culture, portion sizing, food banks, and regulation for restaurants and grocery stores.

Alongside efficient use of all food and demand for sustainable food, small-scale regenerative agriculture is the backbone of global food security. And of course, wildlife-friendly farming both on land and at sea provides crucial ecosystem services.

Equally important for climate mitigation, however, is the ability of forests, other undeveloped lands, and our oceans to absorb greenhouse gases, keeping them out of the atmosphere (chapters 8 and 9). Using less land to support animal agriculture is key not just to carbon sequestration but to protecting the biological diversity that is necessary for food production (chapters 10 and 11). A barrage of economic policies and regulations can be used to incentivize private entities to engage in conservation efforts. Fiscal policies and structural reforms at the national and international level are well suited to ensure conservation of land, forests, and seas. Indeed, success stories show remarkable benefits for the economy and the environment. Mapping land and seas to account for natural capital is essential to successful conservation efforts, and innovative techniques are now available to do this accurately and globally.

Who Should Read This Book

Because the policy toolkit presented here promises multiple economic, financial, and social-ecological benefits, the book is relevant not just for economic ministries (finance, labor) and central banks but also for policymakers in the areas of health, agriculture, trade, interiors, education, and research, as well as national regulators and financial supervisors. It can help countries attain several key macroeconomic and macro-financial goals at once, including job-rich, high-productivity, sustainable growth, external balance, financial (and price) stability, sustainable public finances, public health, and climate mitigation.

The book should be particularly germane to officials working on Sustainable Development Goals and other UN deliverables, especially related to the Paris Agreement. It is also for those working in foreign development, illustrating the links between development and climate goals, as well as the importance of climate mitigation diversification. This implies redistributing decarbonization policies across all economic sectors to lessen political resistance to single, one-lever environmental solutions.

Academics researching these topics will find in this book a useful, hands-on *vade mecum* of key challenges and goals, as well as practical policy examples to aid in the design of more granular policies and to simulate policy scenarios. In this sense, the book could be used in graduate economics programs, particularly in courses specifically devoted to climate change economics.

Finally, the book provides an easy-to-navigate roadmap of policy options for international organizations that must advise countries on climate economics during this critical time of global change.

Conclusions

The IPCC's 2019 report indicates that by 2050, reforms in agriculture could mitigate up to a third of all greenhouse gas emissions, and dietary changes alone could reduce emissions by the amount currently emitted each year by the United States and India. Eliminating food waste could cut another 8–10 percent of the world's carbon emissions. Shifting production and consumption toward plant-based foods would also halt deforestation and enable conservation of critical ecosystems.

Beyond securing our planet's habitability and biological richness, the wins for current and future generations would be vast. The food we eat would be more nutritious, more varied, safer, more humanely raised, and more affordable. We would live longer and healthier lives. Savings from lower healthcare costs—one of the top expenditures for governments and households—could stabilize global finances. Labor productivity would rise with fewer work years lost because of ill health, disability, or early death. Critical progress would be made in eradicating world hunger, income inequality, and social immobility, averting mass migration due to climate change.

All in all, the promise of reforming our food systems is too great to be overlooked. To grab it, though, governments will need to act quickly and with conviction. This book shows them the way.

References

Alam, S., S. Atapattu, C. G. Gonzalez, and J. Razzaque. 2015. *International Environmental Law and the Global South*. Cambridge, UK: Cambridge University Press.

Alexandratos, N., and J. Bruinsma. 2012. "World agriculture towards 2030/2050: the 2012 revision." ESA working paper no. 12-03. Rome: FAO.

Andersen, K., and K. Kuhn. 2014. *Cowspiracy: The Sustainability Secret* [Documentary]. https://g.co/kgs/TymZ1K

Batini, N. 2019a. "Macroeconomic gains from agri-food reforms: the case of France." International Monetary Fund working paper no. 19/41. Washington, D.C.: IMF.

———. 2019b. "Reaping what we sow." International Monetary Fund, Finance and Development, December 2019. https://www.imf.org/external/pubs/ft/fandd/2019/12/farming-food-and-climate-change-batini.htm

———. 2019c. "Transforming agri-food sectors to mitigate climate change: the role of green finance." *Quarterly Journal of Economic Research* 88, no. 3: 7–42.

Batini, N., J. Lomax, and D. Mehra. 2020. "Why sustainable food systems are needed in a post-COVID world." https://blogs.imf.org/2020/07/14/why-sustainable-food-systems-are-needed-in-a-post-covid-world/

Blay-Palmer, A., R. Carey, E. Valette, et al. 2020. "Post COVID 19 and food pathways to sustainable transformation." *Agricultural and Human Values*. https://doi.org/10.1007/s10460-020-10051-7

Boltvinik, J., and S. A. Mann. 2016. *Peasant Poverty and Persistence in the Twenty-First Century: Theories, Debates, Realities and Policies*. London: Zed Books Ltd.

Bretz, Kaitlyn. 2016. "Geospasial Indonesia: the utilization of spatial data through geographic information systems across Indonesia in various environmental contexts." Independent Study Project (ISP) Collection. 2588.

Centers for Disease Control and Prevention (CDC). 2020. "Antibiotic/antimicrobial resistance. food and food animals." https://www.cdc.gov/drugresistance/food.html

Fiala, N. 2008. "Meeting the demand: an estimation of potential future greenhouse gas emissions from meat production." *Ecological Economics* 67: 412–9.

Food and Agriculture Organization (FAO). 2019. "The state of the world's biodiversity for food and agriculture." FAO Commission on Genetic Resources for Food and Agriculture Assessments. Rome: FAO.

———. 2020. "Keeping food and agricultural systems alive: analyses and solutions in a period of crises—COVID-19 pandemic." http://www.fao.org/2019-ncov/analysis/en/

Food and Land Use Coalition (FOLU). 2019. *Growing Better: Ten Critical Transitions to Transform Food and Land Use*. https://www.foodandlandusecoalition.org/wp-content/uploads/2019/09/FOLU-GrowingBetter-GlobalReport.pdf

Harwatt, H., and M. N. Hayek. 2019. "Eating away at climate change with negative emissions: repurposing UK agricultural land to meet climate goals." Cambridge, Mass.: Animal Law and Policy Program, Harvard Law School.

Intergovernmental Panel on Climate Change (IPCC). 2019. "Climate change and land: an IPCC special report on climate change, desertification, land degradation, sustainable land management, food security, and greenhouse gas fluxes in terrestrial ecosystems." Geneva, Switzerland: IPCC.

Intergovernmental Science-Policy Platform on Biodiversity and Ecosystem Services (IPBES). 2019. "Global assessment report on biodiversity and ecosystem services." Bonn, Germany: IPBES.

International Labor Organization (ILO). 2019. *World Employment and Social Outlook: Trends 2019*. Geneva, Switzerland: ILO.

International Monetary Fund (IMF). 2008. *World Economic Outlook, October 2008*. Chapter 3, Appendix 3.2. Washington D.C.: IMF.

Johnson, C. K., P. L. Hitchens, P. S. Pandit, J. Rushmore, T. Smiley Evans, C. C. W. Young, and M. M. Doyle. 2020. "Global shifts in mammalian population trends reveal key predictors of virus spillover risk." *Proceedings of the Royal Society B: Biological Sciences* 287 (1924).

Judis, J. 2016. *The Populist Explosion: How the Great Recession Transformed American and European Politics*. New York: Columbia Global Reports.

Nicolopoulou-Stamati, P., S. Maipas, C. Kotampasi, P. Stamatis, and L. Hens. 2016. "Chemical pesticides and human health: the urgent need for a new concept in agriculture." *Frontiers in Public Health* 4: 148.

O'Neill, J. 2016. "The review on antimicrobial resistance (AMR): tackling drug-resistant infections globally: final report and recommendations." A report chaired by Jim O'Neill, commissioned in 2014 by the UK Government and sponsored by the Wellcome Trust and the UK Department of Health. https://amr-review.org/

Rockström, J., O. Gaffney, J. Rogelj, M. Meinshausen, N. Nakicenovic, and H. Joachim Schellnhuber. 2017. "A roadmap for rapid decarbonization." *Science* 355, no. 6331: 1269–71.

Saenz, R. A., H. W. Hethcote, and G. C. Gray. 2006. "Confined animal feeding operations as amplifiers of influenza." *Vector Borne and Zoonotic Diseases (Larchmont, N.Y.)* 6(4): 338–46.

Sanjo, J., V. Sejian, M. Bagath, A. P. Ratnakaran, A. M. Lees, Y. A. S. Al-Hosni, M. Sullivan, R. Bhatta, and J. B. Gaughan. 2016. "Modeling of greenhouse gas emission from livestock." *Frontiers in Environmental Science* 4: 27. https://doi.org/10.3389/fenvs.2016.00027

Schmidt-Traub, G., M. Obersteiner, and A. Mosnier. 2019. "Fix the broken food system in three steps." Comment. *Nature*. 8 May.

Schumacher, E. F. 1973. *Small Is Beautiful: A Study of Economics As If People Mattered*. Chapter 3. New York: HarperCollins.

Solagro. 2016. *Afterres2050 version 2016*. Solagro Association (C. Couturier, M. Charru, S. Doublet, and P. Pointereau). https://afterres2050.solagro.org/wp-content/uploads/2020/02/Afterres2050-eng.pdf

Thornton, P. K. 2010. "Livestock production: recent trends, future prospects." *Philosophical Transactions of the Royal Society B: Biological Sciences* 365: 2853–67.

United Nations. 2018. *2018 Revision of World Urbanization Prospects*. New York: United Nations.

United Nations Environment Programme (UNEP). 2019. *Sixth Global Environment Outlook*. Cambridge, UK: Cambridge University Press.

United Nations Standing Committee on Nutrition (UNSCN). 2020. "Food environments in the COVID-19 pandemic: impacts and positive policy actions to deliver sustainable healthy diets for all." https://www.unscn.org/en/news-events/recent-news?idnews=2040

Vergara, W., L. Gallardo Lomeli, A. R. Rios, P. Isbell, S. Prager, and R. De Camino. 2016. "The economic case for landscape restoration in Latin America." Washington, D.C.: World Resource Institute.

Willett, W., J. Rockström, B. Loken, et al. 2019. "Food in the Anthropocene: the EAT-

Lancet Commission on Healthy Diets from Sustainable Food Systems." *Lancet* 393, no. 10170: 447–92.

World Health Organization (WHO). 2017. "WHO guidelines on use of medically important antimicrobials in food-producing animals." https://www.who.int/foodsafety/areas_work/antimicrobial-resistance/cia_guidelines/en/

———. 2020. "Food safety." https://www.who.int/news-room/fact-sheets/detail/food-safety

World Wildlife Fund (WWF). 2018. *Living Planet Report—2018: Aiming Higher*, ed. M. Grooten and R. E. A. Almond. Gland, Switzerland: WWF.

Endnotes

1. The Green Revolution, or Third Agricultural Revolution, occurred after World War II. and was the systematic implementation in agriculture of new technologies, including pesticides and fertilizers as well as new breeds of high-yield crops that led to a great increase in global food production.
2. For example, wages in the U.S. agricultural sector (both average and median) are below national levels, and even wages in the higher range (75th and 90th percentile) of the sector's wage distribution are approximately half the national cross-industry wages and have remained stagnant over the past 30 years. In France, the greatest agricultural producer in the European Union (EU), farmers' income has held recently, mostly due to the decline in the number of farmers and farms, and to the increase in subsidies to farmers both from the state and from the EU, but income distribution across farms has become significantly uneven, with most small farmers having to integrate farm income with other sources of income, and farmers' debt-to-income ratios continued to trend upwards in the past two decades (Batini 2019a).
3. One notable example of the economic vulnerabilities induced by food import dependencies is 2008, when a sharp rise in oil prices—that are linked to the price of fertilizers and biofuels—spilled over onto the prices of basic food commodities, driving 44 million people into poverty (IMF 2008).
4. One among a few examples is Brazil in 2015, which, ahead of the Paris Agreement, studied how alternative policies might change domestic and global demand for soya, sugarcane, beef, and timber, and thus deforestation trends. Alternative, less ambitious planning approaches can be equally effective, however. In this case, science-endorsed targets for health and sustainability are set over a desired policy horizon, and operational pathways are identified to achieve them through a series of integrated policy steps. France, for example, has launched a National Low Carbon Strategy (Stratégie National Bas-Carbone), an ambitious set of climate and energy targets within the framework of the commitments made by the European Union.

PART I

GREENING FOOD SUPPLY

Chapter 2

Greening Food Supply in Advanced Economies

Nicoletta Batini and Philippe Pointereau

> "One of the most fateful errors of our age is the belief that 'the problem of production' has been solved."—*Ernst F. Schumacher*

For centuries, agriculture was dominated by family-owned farms raising diversified crops and livestock. Today, food and agriculture, also known as the agri-food sector, is a US$6 trillion industry responsible for feeding the planet and hiring well over 40 percent of it (McKinsey 2015; FAO 2018a; Euler Hermes 2019). Following sectoral policies aimed at boosting production volumes and profits, and a hasty financialization all along the food chain (Clapp 2016; Schmidt 2016), the agri-food sector in advanced and large emerging market economies has become heavily industrialized and reliant on large-scale monoculture, a narrowing of crops, heavy use of fossil fuels and machinery, synthetic chemical applications, genetic modification, and deforestation to produce growing amounts of meat, dairy, and eggs, as well as fiber, timber, and biofuels (Willet et al., 2019) (figure 2-1). At sea, high-tech techniques such as sonar and equipment such as supertrawlers with mechanized nets make it possible to exploit deeper waters at farther-flung locations and capture fish faster than they can reproduce.

In low-income countries, poor farming and fishing practices, overreliance on nonfood crops, and climatic extremes have put communities and biodiversity at great risk. Land clearing leads to the destruction of native forests, soil erosion, and poor harvests. Local fish stocks are regularly ransacked by global commercial fishing vessels. Low sectoral productivity, because of both rising

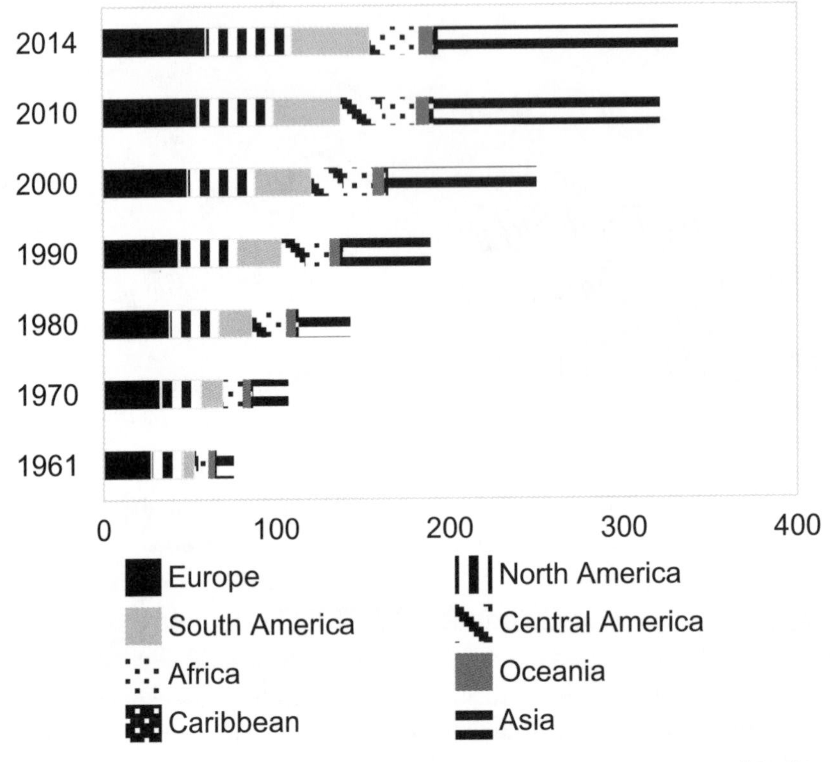

Figure 2-1. Meat production by country (in million tons). *Sources:* Roser and Ritchie (2020).

temperatures and abnormal weather events, constrains both income and food security, pushing many farmers and fishers toward poaching or charcoal production to make ends meet.[1]

The Most Polluting Sector in the World

As a result of all these transformations, the agri-food sector creates a quarter to a third of human-produced greenhouse gas (GHG) emissions, a share expected to increase to a half of all such emissions by 2050, and another 8 percent of emissions results from nonfood agriculture and deforestation, according to the IPCC's 2019 Special Report on Climate Change and Land and the EAT-Lancet Commission (figure 2-2). Thus, the agri-food industry is currently responsible for up to 37 percent of total net anthropogenic GHG

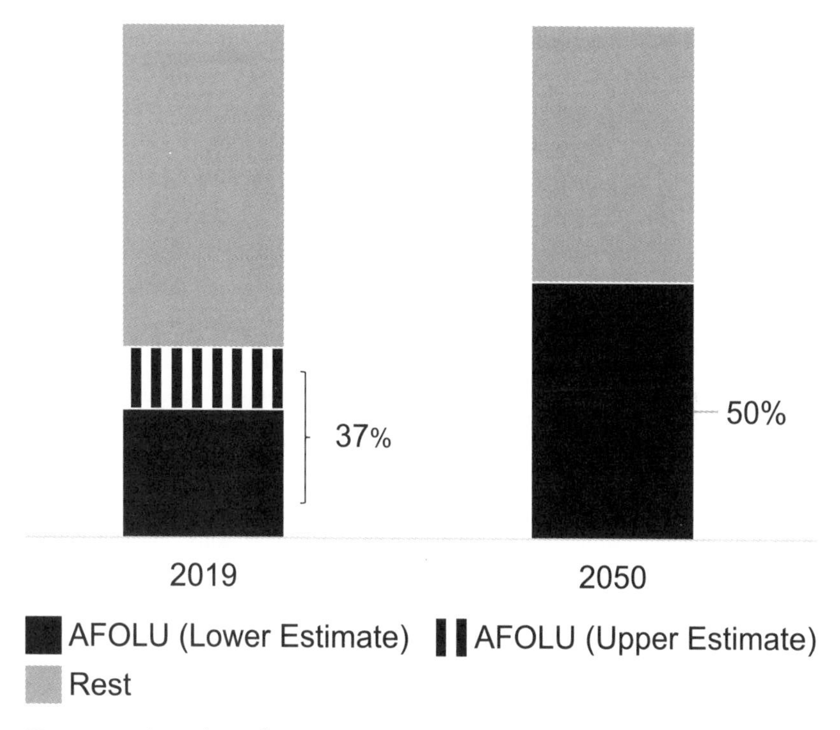

Figure 2-2. Agriculture, forestry, and other land use (AFOLU) greenhouse gas emissions (percentage of global). *Sources:* IPCC (2019), Willett et al. (2019).

emissions and is thus the number one enemy in the fight against climate change (IPCC 2019).

Cows, sheep, and goats, a major source of meat and dairy, have an outsized impact because they release methane, one of the most potent GHGs. There are about 1.5 billion cows in the world, a population second only to humans among large mammals. They can be raised anywhere: from the equator, to the Artic, on prairies, in deserts, and on mountains. Livestock account for about 15 percent of the world's GHGs each year, according to conservative estimates by the UN Food and Agriculture Organization.[2] That roughly equals the emissions from all the world's cars, trucks, trains, airplanes, and ships. Critically, emissions of methane (CH_4) and nitrous oxide (N_2O) from farmed ruminants are believed to be more important in solving the climate problem than direct CO_2 emissions. Although methane, which is the most emitted gas by cattle and is released through belching, does not linger as long in the atmosphere as carbon dioxide, it is initially far more devastating to the climate because of how effectively it absorbs heat. In the first two decades after its release, methane is eighty-four times more potent than carbon dioxide.

So it turns out that if we halted all fossil fuel burning today, we would not see a signal in global temperatures for decades because of the delay in temperature increase as the climate catches up with all the carbon that's in the atmosphere.[3] After about forty more years, the climate would stabilize at a temperature higher than what was normal for previous generations. However, if we eliminated all methane and nitrous oxide emissions from livestock today, we would dramatically increase our chances to stabilize the 1.5°C increase in temperature by 2050 as recommended by the IPCC because these GHGs have much stronger heat trapping potential over shorter horizons than carbon dioxide (Rockström 2016; IPCC 2019). Fires set in the Amazon rainforests and central Africa to make room for pasture illustrate the dramatic trade-offs between cattle ranching, monocultures (soya, palm tree), biological diversity, and the planet's decreasing ability to absorb human-emitted carbon dioxide (figure 2-3).

Beyond its direct impact on climate change, the agri-food sector uses a lot of the planet's resources, including about half the world's ice- and desert-free land and three quarters of its fresh water (figure 2-4). Farming depletes these resources because of routine discharges of pollutants, such as antibiotics, pesticides, synthetic fertilizers, and manure; discharges of genetically modified organisms and sediment to surface water and groundwater; and loss of topsoil and salinization and waterlogging of irrigated land. Current farming methods have been found to degrade soil more than 100 times faster than new soil is formed. Climate change exacerbates land degradation, particularly in low-lying coastal areas, river deltas, and drylands and in permafrost areas (IPCC 2019). Agriculture is also the prime cause of Earth's current mass extinction, according to the UN's Intergovernmental Science-Policy Platform on Biodiversity and Ecosystem Services (2019). Overall, half of current global food production vastly exceeds the capacity of the planet to sustain it (Gerten et al. 2020).

Cloudy Skies

Several global trends and natural constraints are expected to worsen this picture in coming decades, influencing the overall sustainability of global food

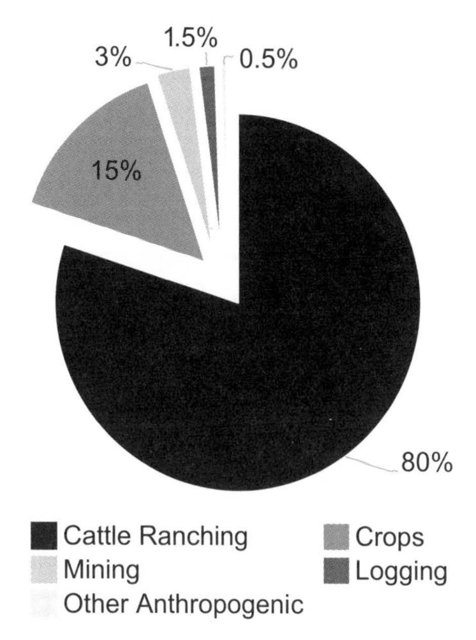

Figure 2-3. Causes of deforestation in the Amazon. *Source:* Yale School of Forestry and Environmental Studies (2019).

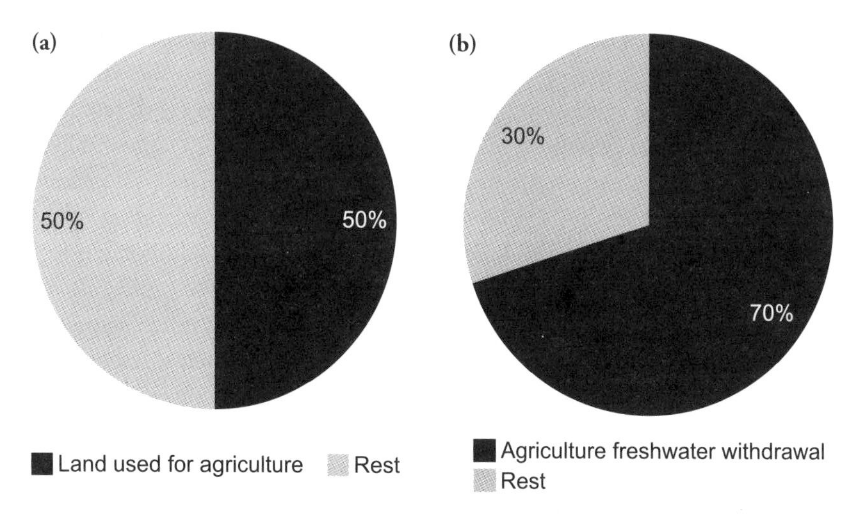

Figure 2-4. Agriculture's use of global resources. **(a)** Agriculture's use of Earth's landmass (percentage of total, excluding glaciers and barren land). **(b)** Agriculture's use of global freshwater (percentage of total freshwater). *Source:* OurWorldInData (2020), https://ourworldindata.org/agricultural-land-by-global-diets.

and agricultural systems and thus casting a dark shadow on global food security (FAO 2018a, 2019).

First, the world's population is expected to grow to almost 10 billion by 2050, boosting agricultural demand—in a scenario of modest economic growth—by some 50 percent compared with 2013 (FAO 2018b).[4] As the global population swells and more people demand animal products, achieving targets to limit climate change will become harder because income growth in low- and middle-income countries is expected to hasten a dietary transition toward higher consumption of animal protein relative to plant-based protein, requiring commensurate shifts in output and adding pressure on natural resources (Bajzelj et al. 2014; Willett et al. 2019). The expected increase of population and income levels between 2010 and 2050 could increase by 50 to 90 percent the environmental effects of the global food system (Springmann et al. 2016). And without action, by 2030 the livestock sector alone could account for 37 percent of the emissions allowable to keep warming under the 2°C target and 49 percent if the temperature goal is 1.5°C (Harwatt 2018).

Second, biodiversity is shrinking at an exponential rate, posing major risks to the future of global food and agriculture: Crop and livestock total diversity has narrowed over the past fifty years because of the expansion of industrial monoculture and global seed patenting, and consequently the composition of the diet at the global level has become more uniform at the expense of regionally important crops, as shown by a meta-study across 150 countries (Khoury et al. 2014).[5] Although 6,000 plant species are cultivated for food, just nine of them account for two thirds of all crop production. When it comes to livestock, about a quarter of breeds are at risk of extinction; just a handful provide most of the meat, milk, and eggs, and more than half of fish stocks are at risk of extinction (IPBES 2019). This lack of dietary diversity is an additional threat to food security and human health. Wild food species are also rapidly disappearing, with just under a quarter of known wild food species still in existence. In addition, species that contribute to the food ecosystem, such as pollinators, soil organisms, and natural enemies of pests, are under severe threat. Examples include bees, butterflies, bats, and birds (FAO 2019; IPBES 2019).

Finally, as the value added and employment generated by agriculture continue to decline at different speeds, the needed acceleration in productivity growth to ensure that supply keeps up with demand is in turn hampered by global warming via changes in average temperatures, rainfall, and climate extremes (e.g., heat waves) and rise in seal levels. Future climate change will probably reduce crop production in low-latitude countries, but effects in northern latitudes may be positive or negative. More favorable effects on yield tend to depend to a large extent on realization of the potentially beneficial effects of carbon dioxide on crop growth and increase of efficiency in water use. Decrease in potential yields is likely to be caused by shortening of the growing period, decrease in water availability, and poor vernalization (IPCC 2019). Beyond temperature and regional climate events, agricultural productivity is also going to be affected by the degradation of natural resources, the loss of biological diversity, and the spread of transboundary pests and diseases of plants and animals, some of which are leading to the spread of zoonotic diseases such as avian and swine flu, while others are becoming resistant to antimicrobials with potentially pandemic consequences (O'Neill 2016).[6]

Meeting increased demands on agriculture with current farming practices is expected to give rise to larger GHG emissions, fast-track climate change, intensify competition for natural resources, and exacerbate deforestation and land degradation. It follows that greening agri-food sectors and demand-managing food is scientifically recognized as a necessary condition for meeting both the 2030 UN Agenda for Sustainable Development and the environmental pledge behind the UN Paris Climate Agreement (Rockström et al. 2017; IPCC 2019).

Production 1.5°C Targets

Making food systems sustainable for a growing global population is technologically possible but involves a fundamental reconsideration of production and consumption: a Great Food Transformation (GFT).

On the supply side, three changes are necessary.

Halve Animal-Based Food Production and Increase Plant-Based Production

It is necessary to couple a sizable reduction in animal-based food production with a swift increase of plant-based food production. Fundamentally, this implies a substantial reduction in global livestock (now more than 77 billion against a global human population of 7.6 billion). Specifically, global production of red meat (especially beef and mutton) and dairy (which requires the farming of cows and sheep) will need to be cut by about 50 percent, through substitution of proteins supplied by plants (IPCC 2019).[7] Urgent action in the top three beef (United States, Brazil, European Union) and dairy (United States, India, China) producers is particularly important.

Substituting half of the nutrition we source from animals with nutrition sourced from plants is necessary for two reasons. First, farmed animals consume more food than they produce in terms of both calories and proteins, because most of the caloric energy animals consume is used to fuel their metabolism and to form bones, cartilage, feathers, fluids, and other nonedible parts. Estimated feed conversion ratios (FCRs)[8] measuring the amount of feed or crops needed to produce a unit of edible meat indicate that animals are inefficient producers of human nutrition, an inefficiency that depends on the species. For cows it is estimated at 25:1, for pigs at 9.4:1, and for chicken at 4.5:1 (Smil 2008). It follows that diets rich in red meat and dairy, such as the Western diet, are incompatible with a growing population: Animal-based diets require many more crops than feeding people directly with plant-based diets, and it is simply impossible to feed the whole future world population a diet containing meat and dairy given the planet's resources of land, water, soil, and air.

Halving meat and dairy production would free vast amounts of land to source plant-based proteins and nutrients for the world's growing population, as well as free room for environmentally sustainable forestry, primarily through preservation or restoration of natural landscapes, which promise enormous gains through carbon capture but also through afforestation or reforestation. Second, animals that are more inefficient at turning crops into protein and calories—such as cows and sheep—are also heavier GHG direct and indirect emitters, reflecting the fact that feeding them uses more resources, including land from deforestation (IPCC 2019). With so much land currently being used to raise these animals or the food to feed them, it is a constant challenge to find adequate pastureland to meet demand. This means that producers have had to create pastures where there were not any originally, with pristine forests being a popular choice. Currently, 260 million acres (and counting) of U.S. forests have been clear-cut to create land used to produce livestock feed, and 80 percent of the deforestation in the Amazon rainforest is attributed to beef production.

Shift to Organic, Regenerative Farming

We need a large-scale shift away from conventional monoculture agriculture toward practices that support biodiversity, such as organic and mixed crop–livestock farming, sustainable soil management, and ecosystem restoration. As the FAO (2018a) has stated, "Needed are innovative systems that protect and enhance the natural resource base, while increasing productivity, implying a transformative process towards 'holistic' approaches, such as agroecology, agro-forestry, climate-smart agriculture and conservation agriculture, which also build upon indigenous and traditional knowledge. Technological improvements, along with drastic cuts in economy-wide and agricultural fossil fuel use, would help address climate change and the intensification of natural hazards, which affect all ecosystems and every aspect of human life." Such a shift would contain and potentially reverse some of the hazardous dynamics that have emerged over the past few decades as a result of the spread of conventional agricultural methods. Denmark and the Netherlands were among the first countries to announce ambitious plans to transition to organics, and Austria is the present leader, with 22 percent of the utilized agricultural area engaged in organic farming in 2016. Restoring soils with regenerative practices (e.g., planting cover crops and perennials and eliminating monocultures) could lock up as much as 60 tons of carbon in soil and vegetation per acre, thus reducing levels of carbon dioxide in the atmosphere. Leading soil experts have calculated that a mere 2 percent increase in the carbon content of the planet's soils could offset 100 percent of all GHG emissions (Lal 2018).

Today, conventional agriculture is by far the predominant method of production in advanced and large emerging market countries. However, sustainable agriculture, usually described as "organic farming" (i.e., the use of scientific farming techniques that protect the environment, public health, human communities, and animal welfare) is slowly emerging in advanced and large emerging market economies alike (Ikerd 2017).

Results from 30-year side-by-side comparisons of conventional and organic farming methods at the Rodale Institute in Pennsylvania showed that, contrary to conventional wisdom, organic farming can outperform conventional farming in every measure. The Rodale trials show that after a three-year transition period, organic yields equaled conventional yields. What is more, the study showed that organic crops were more resilient. Organic corn yields were 31 percent higher than conventional crops in years of drought, for example. Drought-year yields for organic crops are remarkable when compared with genetically modified "drought-tolerant" varieties, which showed increases of only 6.7 percent to 13.3 percent over conventional (non–drought-resistant) varieties. This is of particular interest considering that climate change is likely to bring drier conditions in many areas. These findings were corroborated by a new meta-analysis that reviewed yield comparisons from 115 studies—more than three times the amount of any previous analysis published (Ponisio et al. 2015). The study reported that organic farms that practice rotational or multicropping had negligible yield gaps, between 8 and 9 percent relative to conventional yields, and these gaps inverted at times of drought or excessive precipitation.

Looking at farmers' income, multiple recent studies suggest that nonconventional agriculture is three to six times more profitable than conventional agriculture even when receiving smaller or no subsidies relative to conventional farming (Crowder and Reganold 2015; Rodale Institute 2018).[9] Part of the competitive edge of nonconventional farming comes from the premium price—driven by consumer demand—that organic farmers can get for their products. Several comparative studies find that even when profits are adjusted for 50 percent of the current organic premium, organic agriculture still comes out ahead of conventional agriculture because of a series of additional advantages. To begin with, organic agriculture not only delivers better quality but produces similar or larger quantities than conventional agriculture, because it is more resilient to climate volatility. Second, organic agriculture has lower input costs than conventional agriculture, being less dependent on fossil fuels and on expensive inputs such as pesticides or herbicides, water, and associated annual loans. This makes organic agriculture less vulnerable to financial market fluctuations even in the face of more field operations (Delbridge et al. 2011). Third, organic agriculture is a low-waste system and uses less land for the same profit. Fourth, in contrast to conventional agriculture, farms engaging in organic agriculture also accumulate "natural capital," an array of ecosystem services and resources that increase the value of the farmland. These include soil enrichment, particularly soil's ability to sequester large amounts of carbon; greater soil water retention, which can increase yields by 40 percent during droughts, providing a natural insurance against climate volatility; and biodiversity, which means a succession of blooms that can feed insect populations (and provide them with habitat) year-round. These beneficial insects reduce populations of harmful insects, reducing or eliminating the need for pesticides and providing pollination services to increase harvest yields. They also increase genetic diversity on organic vegetable and seed farms, which acts as a well-endowed gene bank for potential new varieties that will be resilient against future environmental changes, insect populations, and diseases.

These benefits allow farmers to at least partially overcome the financial constraints and lessen the initial economic risks of venturing into nonconventional methods of production, especially in years when the new organic crops or animal breeds are established (Cernansky 2018).

In 2016, the global organic farming market accounted for about 58 million hectares of organic agricultural farmland, with the United States accounting for nearly half the global market, followed by Europe (nearly a third) and China (6 percent) (Lernoud and Willer 2018). Nearly 180 countries reported organic acres in 2016, yet they accounted for a mere 1.2 percent of global agricultural land. However, production is rising in response to the sharp increase in organic consumption. Demand consistently exceeds supply in most markets as organic products have shifted from being a lifestyle choice for a small segment of consumers to being purchased at least occasionally by many. Consumers are responding to organic's nutritional health benefits, nontoxicity, and tastiness as well as socioecological benefits, including the low environmental footprint and greater protection for animal welfare.[10]

On the supply side, organic premiums and additional economic advantages have attracted capital over the past decade or so, and as a result, the organic market is going through a simultaneous process of expansion and concentration. Globally, the market, which is about half U.S.-owned and operated, is dominated by fifteen to twenty top players and is seeing growing collaboration between farmers and top food brands (Cernansky 2018). The market is expected to triple in value by 2024, to about $320 billion, reflecting a global average growth rate of nearly 15 percent per year between 2017 and 2024 (Technavio 2019). Some market analysis predicts even faster growth (Allied Market Research 2018). Both Asia-Pacific and Europe are expected to show significant market growth by expanding organic agricultural land in these regions.

Similarly to organic farming on land, regenerative ocean farming can sequester carbon and restore ecosystems. Batini et al. look at the benefits and policy options to foster regenerative ocean farming in more detail in chapter 4 of this book.

Rewild, Reforest, and Afforest Land

The creation of forest carbon funds, for the purpose of planting forests and reducing deforestation, will be an integral part of limiting climate change because intact forests sequester twice as much carbon as planted monocultures. A proposed companion pact to the Paris Agreement—a Global Deal for Nature—targets 30 percent of Earth to be formally protected and an additional 20 percent designated as climate stabilization areas by 2030 to hold global temperature increases below 1.5°C. In chapter 8 of this book, Batini looks at challenges in land and forest conservation and proposes a palette of actionable policies to redress them in line with recommendations in the Global Deal for Nature.

If sizeable and consistent, these three changes combined can slash emissions, boost carbon sequestration from arable soil, release land for crops and forests, halt biodiversity and pollinator loss, and restore global freshwater resources.

Changes in supply and land use must be accompanied by a shift in diets toward more diverse plant-based foods. In chapter 5 of this book, Batini and Fontana discuss challenges, targets, and policies to move to more plant-based diets globally.

Economic Benefits of Greening Food Supply

On the macroeconomic front, a well-designed transition to a sustainable agrifood system promises several tangible gains, including an increase in agricultural production and value-added, more numerous farm and food industry jobs, and substantial trade gains relative to a business-as-usual scenario.

Calculations of the economic benefits of the GFT are likely to vary depending on each country's level and type of agricultural production, income level, and share of agricultural employment. Simulation for a representative country where industrial farming is the norm can give a broad sense of potential economic benefits, however. Specifically, simulations conducted for France looked at the effect of a series of changes by 2050: gradual elimination of all synthetic inputs to production and their total replacement with agroecological methods; a full shift in the sector's use of energy to renewables; a reduction in the herd of cows (against unchanged pasture land) accompanied by an expansion of smaller-sized livestock herds, notably ovine; and an expansion of agroforestry production. These changes could quadruple agricultural nonfood production while maintaining current levels of primary production; raise the sector's value added by 10 percent; avert the projected deterioration of the sector's trade balance by increasing cereal exports to the Mediterranean region and the Middle East, halving exports of fodder crops to Europe, and eliminating imports of soya and France's trade deficit from commerce in forest products; increase agricultural jobs by 7–11 percent at current productivity growth levels, and by more for lower future productivity levels; and double the stock of agroecological infrastructure, with multiplicative growth effects on the rest of the economy (Solagro 2016; Batini 2019a).

Similarly, Ikerd (2018) compared the community impacts of conventional, industrial agriculture in the United States, using data from Michigan, with those of sustainable farmers who market directly to local customers. These calculations suggest that the sustainable farm contributes about four times as much to the local economy as the industrial farm. These are just the first-round economic impacts. The multiplication effect of the combined direct and indirect effects of local sustainable farming is estimated to beat the economic impact of conventional (industrial) farming 5:1; the effects on employment are estimated to be even larger, about 10:1 (Ikerd 2018). It is likely that other advanced economies would enjoy comparable economic gains.

In emerging and developing economies, the economic advantages of making agriculture and fishing sustainable domestically promise to be larger still, because agriculture in these economies still employs about 1 billion people (ILO 2019), and absent the GFT, these jobs risk being lost permanently if the sector were to follow the same path as advanced economies. Critically, a more localized, sustainable, and profitable food supply in these countries would reduce dependence on imports from other nations, increase market competition internationally, and boost their sources of income at home (Hanley 2014; Boltvinik and Mann 2016). If the price of agricultural goods became gradually less dependent on the price of fertilizers, food commodity prices would be less influenced by other highly volatile commodity prices, sheltering the income of poorer countries that depend more heavily on agricultural produce (IMF 2008).[11]

Indeed, the 2019 IPCC Report on Climate Change and Land Use shows that "sustainable land management, [and] . . . reducing and reversing land degradation, at scales from individual farms to entire watersheds, can provide cost effective, immediate, and long-term benefits to communities and support several Sustainable Development Goals (SDGs) with co-benefits for adaptation and mitigation" ("Summary for Policymakers," p. 23).

Beyond macroeconomic gains, a shift to more plant-based food production promises investors lower financial risks and higher financial returns on investment. In recent years, fossil fuel–free investing has become an important response from investors of all sizes to growing awareness of the need to bring the fossil fuel age to a close. This trend, together with the lower demand of fossil fuels as a response to climate change, is leading to a drop in energy prices, meaning that only the lowest-cost projects will deliver an economic return.

This implies that some fossil fuel extracting and refining projects risk becoming stranded assets even before they are built.[12] In a similar vein, as people take action to address the climate crisis, concerns about the climate impacts of food systems and the benefits of a plant-based diet are also increasingly coming to the fore, affecting risks and returns of the agri-food sector, as protein diversification is increasingly recognized by institutional and individual investors as socially responsible investing, impact investing, green investing, or environmental, social, and governance (ESG).

Measures of the impact of intensive livestock and fish farming are being developed to analyze the largest global meat, dairy, and aquaculture producers by combining nine ESG risk factors with the Sustainable Development Goals (SDGs).[13] The Coller FAIRR Index, for example, shows promising potential return from investing in alternative proteins. Specifically, the index classifies two thirds of industrial meat, dairy, and aquaculture companies as high risk on overall management of sustainability; three fourths of companies are classified as high risk on antibiotics management; and only five out of sixty companies in the index are prepared to capitalize on opportunities in the rapidly growing alternative (nonmeat or nondairy) protein sector (FAIRR 2018). The index also unveils that more than three fourths of companies in the index showed little or no reporting on GHG emissions, that only about a quarter of companies specifically referenced their management of animal waste, and that only one third of companies report on water use from their operations, a serious concern considering that agriculture accounts for 92 percent of global freshwater use, nearly one third of which is for animal agriculture.

ESG scores also illustrate growing investor demand for sustainable food. Plant-based investing totaled US$8.7 trillion in assets under professional management in the United States alone as of 2016, according to the Forum for Sustainable and Responsible Investing (FSRI 2018; see also Green America's Green Business Network 2019). Multiple financial instruments are available for plant-based investing. On the equity side, custom stock mixes or exchange-traded funds seemed preferred options, but some investors have resorted to mutual funds managed by leaders in animal or cruelty-free investing, primarily portfolio managers who have signed onto the FAIRR initiative.[14] In terms of returns, investing using ESG ratings has been shown to reduce risk and offer tangible financial advantages relative to unscreened investments (CSSP-South Pole Carbon Asset Management 2016; Gregory 2017; Gorte 2019; In et al., 2019; Bloomberg Intelligence 2019), promising an increase in investment bias toward those products.

Environmental Benefits of Greening Food Supply

The 2019 IPCC report estimates that changes in food production, combined with agroforestry, can reduce global GHG emissions up to 26 percent (9.6 $GtCO_2eq/year^-$) by 2050. Future land use depends, in some measure, on the desired climate outcome and the portfolio of policies enacted.

In fact, the report finds that all pathways capable of containing global warming to 1.5°C or well below 2°C require land-based mitigation and land use change, with most including different combinations of reforestation, afforestation, reduced deforestation, and bioenergy. A small number of modeled pathways achieve 1.5°C with reduced land conversion and thus reduced consequences for desertification, land degradation, and food security (IPCC 2019).

Changes in food production would be also key in eliminating price and quantity distortions and, in particular, contribute to lowering the price of plant-based foods. This would help make sustainable diets, such as the Eat-Lancet "planetary diet" (discussed in chapter 5) affordable for all.[15]

Aside from enabling us to dramatically slash GHG emissions, sustainable farming produces crops and raises animals without relying on chemical pesticides, synthetic fertilizers, genetically modified seeds, or practices that degrade soil, water, or other natural resources. By growing a variety of plants and using techniques such as crop rotation, intercropping, conservation tillage, biological control, and pasture-based livestock husbandry, sustainable farms protect biodiversity and foster healthy ecosystems, addressing all the planetary challenges posed by industrial agriculture.

Policies to Green the Food Supply

Well-targeted economic, financial, and trade policies, as well as structural reforms, can go a long way toward delivering these goals. Specifically, three sets of policy levers can be deployed to feed growing populations in a sustainable and healthy way.

Fiscal Policy

On the supply side, fiscal measures to shift supply may include adjustments to both taxes and subsidies.

- *Taxes.* Tax adjustments should focus on calibrating direct and indirect taxes and social security contributions to agri-food production and

> agri-food sales based on the level of externalities these generate. For example, net profits from conventional farming should be taxed more than net profits from organic farming, because the former's externalities are several orders of magnitude larger than the latter.

To this end, on the tax and payroll contribution front, several fiscal options are at hand.[16] Building on existing differentials in the way various agricultural products are taxed and by differences in income and payroll taxes between agriculture and other economic sectors, it is possible to modify further the way agriculture is taxed to penalize more the least sustainable agricultural activities.[17] Accounting for supply elasticities to fiscal costs, these modifications can be devised to be cumulatively fiscally neutral in the new production equilibrium.

Similar to the approach taken to promote clean energy, changing the tax structure can engineer a targeted shift in the type of farm animals bred (e.g., by reducing taxes on income generated by rearing and selling more sustainable animals such as poultry relative to the taxation levied on breeding bovines, which are much less sustainable),[18] the way farm animals are bred (e.g., by reducing the relative taxation on income from selling animals reared organically and with longer pasture exposure), the type of crops farmed (e.g., by reducing taxes on income generated from producing legumes, pulses, and cereals relative to that on income from producing less sustainable produce, such as potatoes and sugar),[19] and the type of farming practiced (promoting agroecology and regenerative farming operated through polyfunctional farms with a higher labor-to-acre ratio vis-á-vis large, monoculture, highly-mechanized farms.[20] Additionally, increases in estate taxes should be considered to prevent accumulation of intergenerational landed wealth in countries where land ownership is concentrated.

A land value tax (a tax levied on the value of unimproved land) has been proposed as a potential solution to a variety of problems, from business tax avoidance to high house prices. In theory, it is the only nondistortionary tax: Income tax reduces the incentive to work, corporate tax reduces the incentive to invest in business, stamp duty reduces the incentive to sell property, and so on, whereas land is not affected in size whether it is taxed or not. A land value tax can also help reduce land prices because economic factors other than profitability of agriculture determine land values, including capitalization of single-farm payments and business rollover tax relief. Although land overvaluation is advantageous for investors and speculators (see Batini 2019b), it complicates entry into farming and the profitability of farming businesses because prices become too removed from the potential profitability of the business.

- *Subsidies.* Currently, in many countries large amounts of taxpayers' money are spent on subsidies that encourage otherwise unprofitable, unsustainable meat and dairy production predicated on the systematic inhumane treatment of farmed animals, as well as growing monoculture commodity crops for animal feed. (According to the latest Organisation for Economic Co-operation and Development [OECD] estimates, subsidies to agriculture in fifty-three OECD member countries amounted to US$705 billion per year, or more than US$1.3 million per minute. In the 2016–2018 period, this amount is comparable to Switzerland's 2019 gross domestic product). The OECD estimates that only 1 percent of these subsidies are used to benefit the environment, whereas most go to meat and dairy production either directly or indirectly. More than half of these subsidies are distortive, a percentage that has slowly fallen over the years from higher peaks in the late 1980s, when about 90 percent of all subsidies are estimated to have been distortive. Even more taxpayers' money then goes to fixing the resulting problems: water and air pollution, animal-borne pandemics, antimicrobial resistance, and the impacts of unhealthy diets. Subsidies for unsustainable farming in advanced economies also discourage private investment in agriculture in developing economies, leaving their consumers dependent on imported food and exposed to volatile international food prices.

As in the case of taxes, subsidies to agri-food production should be recalibrated to better reflect the level of externalities its various activities generate. For example, subsidies currently destined for unsustainable farms should be redirected toward sustainable ones producing plant-based protein, innovation on alternative proteins, and smart farming technologies. In developing economies, replacing production subsidies with ecological payments to sustainable farmers could reorient industrial agriculture, increasing the climate mitigation potential while reducing negative impacts on farm incomes. Focusing efforts on women and indigenous farmers and promoting local and community collective action is particularly effective (Cook et al., 2019). Chapter 4 discusses these issues in more detail.

- *Public investment.* Climate-smart technologies and practices are emerging, including methods to expand biomass energy production from crop and food wastes, manure management, renewable energy–based farming systems, solar- or wind-powered water pumping, drip irrigation, innovative greenhouse technologies, and efficient field machinery. Still critically needed are additional public–private early warning systems for weather, crop yields, and seasonal climate events and public support for innovation in sustainable agricultural technology.

Structural Reforms

In addition to the fiscal measures previously discussed, structural reforms are necessary to fix regulatory failures. Among many possible others, these include the following:

- *Regulatory changes* aimed at simplifying the transition to a new global food system are key. Main levers include limiting the acreage per county or region that can be dedicated to monoculture crops in relation to polyculture or rotating crops; imposing cover cropping and regulating tilling; stepping up environmental regulation to prohibit industrial farming activities that damage the air, land, water, and soil by providing clear environmental thresholds to nitrogen, ammonia, and phosphorus in water, land, and air; banning concentrated animal feeding operations by introducing strict limits to the number of livestock per farm and per acre; limiting the use of antibiotics, hormones, pesticides, chemicals, and genetic manipulation of live beings, including plants; imposing automatic fines for inhumane livestock conditions, defined by strict scientific criteria; reducing the regulatory burden associated with the use of land for agricultural purposes (e.g., by introducing changes to zoning regulations); and reducing the barriers to converting to organic agriculture (Batini 2019b).[21] These changes should be accompanied by regulatory efforts to increase the compatibility and coordination of agricultural development and biodiversity conservation policies and legislation that protects the rights of farming communities as conservators of biodiversity, such as those of indigenous populations of pristine ecosystems such as the Amazon (see Scherr and McNeely 2008).

- *Land reforms* to foster agroecological food production. Land is not the same as other goods and therefore must be treated not as a commodity but as a common asset. Measures to lengthen tenancies and ensure availability of land can support projects that are sustainable and productive, create livelihoods, enhance the environment, and involve local people in making decisions about the places they care about. Land reforms should create (where missing) publicly available, comprehensive, and transparent land registries. This would enable farmers to identify and make contact with landowners and identify opportunities because, typically, land is required to be registered only when it is bought or sold. This means large historic holdings, where little may change hands for centuries, are not covered.
- *Public sponsoring* of food industry businesses initiatives to research, test, and scale up new strategies that propose and guide healthy and sustainable consumer choices in line with recommendations, such as those of the World Resource Institute's Better-Buying Lab.
- *Incentives* through conceptualization, education, training, and dedicated administrative simplification for all voluntary greening schemes.

These policies should be reinforced by supply-side structural reforms, such as the following:

- *Labor market measures* to promote farming jobs and small agricultural enterprises.
- *Training and apprenticeship programs* in sustainable and organic farming and small agricultural business administration.

Financial Policies

A number of financial constraints make it difficult to switch to organic farming. First, relative to conventional farming, organic farming requires both different equipment and other costly up-front investments and more labor, mainly to tackle weeds. Second, during the initial years, organic farming may produce reduced yields. Third, most nationally recognized organic certifications require crop rotation, which limits the crops farmers can produce in a given year, whereas a conventional producer can select a crop that appears to be most profitable that year and plant it. Likewise, agricultural infrastructure (e.g., grain storage facilities and transportation networks) is designed for conventional crops; organic farmers need to tap into a different market structure. At the same time, funding for organic research pales in comparison to conventional support, which means organic farmers have fewer tools available to them, such as improved crop varieties and strategies for battling weeds or disease, as well as fewer experts to consult.[22] Finally, the transition period to organic farming itself can be a money-losing proposition. Farmers need to keep their land free of most chemicals for a full three years before they can be certified as organic, which implies that during the transition farmers are basically farming organically but cannot get the premium.

To help farmers make the switch, in recent years some large organic companies and brands have launched "certified transitional" initiatives, which formally certify when a farmer is undergoing a shift to organic methods and secures them at least a limited premium to help get through those initial years (Cernansky 2018). However, more needs to be done. Helping farmers overcome these hurdles will require transitional technical and financial assistance, including direct loans, guarantee schemes, crop insurance, and measures to improve land and market access (see Batini 2019b). Currently a mere 1.2 percent of global agricultural land is farmed organically, a figure expected to reach only 3.2 percent by 2024 under current policies.

Also, on the financial side, changes to prudent regulation to properly account for the financial risks institutions take when they lend to nonsustainable agri-food firms would provide essential support to a GFT. A bolder approach to investment of public funds in assets associated with sustainable land use and steps to expand green and sustainable bond markets could help fund the transition (Batini 2019b).

Countries Leading the Transformation

Two small countries are making big changes to implement this transformation. In the following sections, we will examine how the Netherlands and Denmark are working to support organic agriculture and minimize environmental damage.

The Netherlands' 2030 Plant Protection Vision

Despite being a small and densely populated country, the Netherlands is the second-largest exporter of agriculture in the world, after the United States, and is leading the way in agricultural innovation. In 2017, the Netherlands exported US$111 billion worth of agricultural goods, including US$10 billion of flowers and US$7.4 billion of vegetables. Dutch farmers are pioneering ways to produce higher yields because both land and labor in their country are expensive, so they have to be more efficient than others to compete. And that competition drives innovation and technology.

Examples of sustainable, innovative agriculture adopted by small, family-run businesses include using geothermal energy to heat greenhouses and growing plants in a hydroponic vertical system to use less water. At one of the top-exporting farms, for example, the tomatoes are grown in small bags of rock wool substrate, made from spinning together molten basaltic rock into fine fibers, which contains nutrients and allows the plants to soak up water even when moisture levels are low. No pesticides are used, and the farm pipes waste CO_2 (which the plants need to grow) into the greenhouses, which reduces the carbon dioxide being released into the atmosphere. In addition, greenhouses have a double glass roof, which conserves heat, and LED lights, which mean the plants can keep growing through the night. All of this means that farming teams can produce higher yields of vegetables, in less space, using fewer resources—a technique known as precision farming, whereby farming leverages new techniques and innovations with minimum impact on the environment.

Currently, the Netherlands organic agricultural area measures about 48,000 hectares and includes about 4,000 organic operators. Over the past ten years, the organic market has experienced sustained growth, with top-selling products including milk and dairy products (4.8 percent of all milk and dairy products sold), fresh vegetables and potatoes (3.9% of all fresh vegetables and potatoes sold), meat and meat products (2.7% of all meat and meat products sold), and bread and bakery products (3.2% of all bread and bakery products sold).

To encourage even greater levels sustainability, in 2019 the Dutch government launched a new vision for the country's agriculture, which prioritizes the protection of natural resources and the reduction of the sector's environmental impact. The 2030 Plant Protection Vision is based on two principles: innovative plant breeding and precision or smart farming, which are both hot topics for the future of EU farming. The plan calls for a paradigm shift that embodies the GFT: More resilient plants and growing methods require less pesticide use, and where pesticides remain necessary, their use should be "smart" so as to minimize environmental emissions and ensure the production of crops with negligible residues. Enhancing the natural defenses of plants is at the core of the vision, with an emphasis on the development of healthy soil.

Wherever possible, growers should use the natural enemies of weeds and pests and strengthen the natural resources available in the immediate surroundings (functional agrobiodiversity). The plan's strategy for eliminating pesticides rests also on the promotion of new plant breeding techniques, namely scientific methods for the genetic engineering of plants to enhance natural traits such as drought tolerance and pest resistance.[23] Another element of the Dutch plan is mitigation of the uncertainty created by climate change through better monitoring of crops and soil to provide early warning of risks, the now widely known technique called precision farming.

The plan buttresses other general policies for stimulating rural development and sustainable agricultural production from which organic producers can benefit. Dutch organic farmers receive support under the EU's Rural Development Program, and although there is no policy or action plan at the national level, some provinces, such as Noord-Holland, have policies to stimulate conversion to organic farming. The Ministry of Economic Affairs also provides up to 60 percent of the funding for research into organic food and farming. The challenge for the coming years is to increase the area under production and to guarantee the organic quality of the products being traded.

Denmark's 2020 Økologiplan

In 2015, the Danish government announced a new strategy to double organic farming by 2020 (relative to 2007) and serve more organic food in the nation's public institutions—the world's most ambitious attempt yet to support a GFT. The government's Ministry of Food, Agriculture and Fisheries' sixty-seven–point plan, dubbed Økologiplan, aims to strengthen cooperation between municipalities, regions, and ministries to speed up the transition from conventional to organic production on publicly-owned land. A long line of new initiatives are intended to strengthen both development of and conversion to organic farming, working with alternative ownership and operation models. Critically, besides requiring organic farming on public lands, the plan also subsidizes farmers transitioning to organic and simplifies the country's organic regulations.

Through the plan, the government has committed to including more organic items on the menu of public cafeterias, hospitals, and daycare centers, targeting more than 800,000 people who use these institutions daily. Interestingly, although the Ministry of Food, Agriculture and Fisheries is behind the plan, other ministries have also pledged to do their part. The Defense

Ministry, for example, has committed to increasing the amount of organic food served at its bases. (Approximately 1.1 million kilos of food are served in military cafeterias each year.) The Ministry of Education has also committed to strengthening young people's ecological awareness. This shift is linked to Denmark's public school reform, which includes teaching students about organic farming and production in the natural sciences. Furthermore, the plan supports research into new organic solutions; creating space for new experiments; investment in new export drivers; and information to increase the sales of Danish organics nationally and globally. The government has committed a total of 400 million kroner (US$60.8 million) to its action plan.[24]

As a result of the plan, 10.5 percent of land reserved for agriculture in Denmark was transformed into organic land by 2019, and the number of organic farmers in the country is now close to 4,000.[25] Danish consumers are now the most pro-organic consumers in the world, according to Organic Denmark, an association of companies, organic farmers, and consumers. Nearly 8 percent of all food sold in Denmark is organic, the highest percentage in Europe. And Danish organic export has risen by more than 200 percent since 2007.

Conclusions

Global food production has a massive economic, social, and environmental footprint: It is the largest industry in the world, representing 10 percent of global consumer spending, 40 percent of employment, and between 21 and 37 percent of all GHG emissions—emissions expected to rise to 50 percent of the total by 2050 as the demand for food increases alongside the world's population. In recent decades, agri-food systems in advanced and large emerging market economies have become heavily industrialized and are now the number one contributor to climate change (with transportation a far distant second at 15 percent of total GHG emissions). Agri-food is also the primary cause of air, soil, water, and land degradation worldwide and the number one driver of the terrifying pace of biodiversity loss.

Making food systems sustainable for a growing global population is technologically possible but involves a fundamental reconsideration of production and consumption: a GFT. Three steps are needed: Halve animal-based food production and increasing proportionally plant-based production to attain a level of supply that is nutritionally adequate and healthy for the entire global population; shift away from conventional farming to organic, regenerative farming; rewild, reforest, and afforest the land saved.

Shifting supply in this direction requires embracing a specific set of familiar macroeconomic policy levers, notably fiscal policy and structural reforms. On the fiscal front, taxes should be recalibrated to be higher on crops and animals that are least sustainable, and agricultural subsidies should be repurposed to support sustainable farming only. These fiscally neutral measures should be accompanied by land reforms to raise the affordability and accessibility of land for sustainable farming and to limit land available for conventional farming and support agroecology. Furthermore, labor market reforms should be implemented to promote agricultural employment and the setup of startups and enterprises involved in small agrobusinesses to hasten a return to the land. Other measures include public investment in research and innovation and public sponsoring of food industry businesses initiatives to research, test, and scale up new retail strategies promoting healthy food consumption; and incentives through conceptualization, education, training, and dedicated administrative simplification for all voluntary greening schemes.

On the financial front, transitional technical and financial assistance, including direct loans, guarantee schemes, crop insurance, and measures to improve land and market access, should be provided to help farmers transition to organic practice. At the same time, changes to prudential regulation to properly account for financial risks of institutions that lend to nonsustainable agri-food firms would provide essential support to a GFT. A bolder approach to investing public funds in assets associated with sustainable land use and steps to expand green and sustainable bond markets could help fund the transition.

It is hard to overstate the environmental benefits of greening the agri-food sector. The IPCC's 2019 report indicates that by 2050, reforms of crop and livestock activities and agroforestry could mitigate up to a third of all GHG emissions. Shifting production toward plant-based foods would also halt deforestation and enable conservation of critical ecosystems and planetary resources, securing our planet's future habitability and biological richness. On the macroeconomic front, a well-designed transition to a sustainable agri-food system promises several tangible gains, including an increase in agricultural production and value-added, more numerous farm and food industry jobs, and substantial trade gains relative to a business-as-usual scenario.

References

Allied Market Research. 2018. "Organic and clean label food consumer in the United States." *Packaged Facts*. https://www.packagedfacts.com/Organic-Clean-Label-Food-Consumer-11410671/

Bajzelj, B., K., Richards, J. M. Allwood, P. Smith, J. S. Dennis, E. Curmi, and C. Gilligan. 2014. "Importance of food-demand management for climate mitigation." *Nature Climate Change* 4: 924–9.

Barbieri, P., S. Pellerin, and T. Nesme, 2017. "Comparing crop rotations between organic and conventional farming." *Scientific Reports* 7: 13761.

Batini, N. 2019a. *Macroeconomic Gains from Reforming the Agri-Food Sector: The Case of France*. IMF working paper no. 19/41. Washington, D.C.: IMF.

———. 2019b. "Transforming agri-food sectors to mitigate climate change: the role of green finance." *Quarterly Journal of Economic Research* 88, no. 3: 7–42.

Bloomberg Intelligence. 2019. "Do-good investments are smashing your emerging-market returns." https://www.bloomberg.com/professional/blog/good-investments-smashing-emerging-market-returns/?mpam-page=20568

Boltvinik, J., and S. Archer Mann, eds. 2016. *Peasant Poverty and Persistence*. London: Zed Books.

Cernansky, R. 2018. "We don't have enough organic farms. Why not?" *National Geographic* https://www.nationalgeographic.com/environment/future-of-food/organic-farming-crops-consumers/

Clapp, J. 2016. *Food*. 2nd ed. Cambridge, UK: Policy Press.

Cook, N. J., Grillos, T., and Andersson, K. P. 2019. "Gender quotas increase the equality and effectiveness of climate policy interventions." *Nature Climate Change* 9: 330–4.

Crowder, D. W., and J. P. Reganold. 2015. "Financial competitiveness of organic agriculture on a global scale." *Proceedings of the National Academies of Science of the United States of America* 112, no. 24: 7611–6.

CSSP–South Pole Carbon Asset Management. 2016. *Climate-Friendly Investment Strategies and Performance*. Study commissioned by the Swiss Federal Office for the Environ ment (FOEN).

Delbridge, T. A., J. A. Coulter, R. P. King, C. C., Sheaffer, and D. L. Wyse. 2011. "Economic performance of long-term organic and conventional cropping systems in Minnesota." *Agronomy Journal* 103: 1372–82.

Euler Hermes Global. 2019. *Agri-food Global Sector Report*. https://www.eulerhermes.com/en_global/economic-research/sector-reports/Agrifood.html

FAIRR. 2018. "Plant-based profits: investment risks and opportunities in sustainable food systems." https://www.fairr.org/article/plant-based-profits-investment-risks-opportunities-sustainable-food-systems/

Food and Agriculture Organization. 2018a. "Transforming food and agriculture to achieve the SDGs: 20 interconnected actions to guide decision-makers." Rome: FAO. http://www.fao.org/3/i9900en/i9900en.pdf

———. 2018b. "The future of food and agriculture: alternative pathways to 2050." Rome: FAO. http://www.fao.org/publications/fofa/en/

———. 2019. "The state of the world's biodiversity for food and agriculture." Rome: FAO Commission on Genetic Resources for Food and Agriculture Assessments.

Forum for Sustainable and Responsible Investing (FSRI). 2018. "Report on US sustainable, responsible and impact investing trends, 2018." https://www.ussif.org/files/Trends/Trends%202018%20executive%20summary%20FINAL.pdf

Gallup. 2019. "Nutrition and food poll 2019." https://news.gallup.com/poll/6424/nutrition-food.aspx

Gerten, D., V. Heck, J. Jägermeyr, et al., 2020. "Feeding ten billion people is possible within four terrestrial planetary boundaries." *Nature Sustainability*. doi:10.1038/s41893-019-0465-1

Gorte, J. 2019. "The financial performance of sustainability: ESG and risk. Pax World Funds. https://paxworld.com/the-financial-performance-of-sustainability-esg-and-risk/

Green America's Green Business Network. 2019. *Industrial Agriculture, Food and Climate News.*

Gregory, R. P. 2017. "Does socially responsible corporate reporting lead to less stock speculation?" http://dx.doi.org/10.2139/ssrn.3092245

Hanley, P. 2014. *Eleven*. Victoria, B.C.: Friesenpress.

Harwatt, H. 2018. "Including animal to plant protein shifts in climate change mitigation policy: a proposed three-step strategy." *Climate Policy* 19, no. 5: 533–41.

Hirvonen, K., Y. Bai, D. Headey, and W. A. Masters. 2020. "Affordability of the EAT–Lancet reference diet: a global analysis." *The Lancet Global Health* 8, no. 1: PE59–E66.

Ikerd, J. 2017. "Feeding the world intelligently—without corporate agriculture." Keynote speech at the OCM's 19th Annual Food and Agriculture Conference.

———. 2018. "Difference in local economic impacts local foods versus conventional foods" [mimeo]. University of Missouri.

Intergovernmental Panel on Climate Change (IPCC). 2019. *Climate Change and Land: An IPCC Special Report on Climate Change, Desertification, Land Degradation, Sustainable Land Management, Food Security, and Greenhouse Gas Fluxes in Terrestrial Ecosystems.* Geneva, Switzerland: IPCC.

Intergovernmental Science-Policy Platform on Biodiversity and Ecosystem Services (IPBES). 2019. *Global Assessment Report on Biodiversity and Ecosystem Services*. Bonn, Germany: IPBES.

International Labor Organization (ILO). 2019. "World employment and social outlook: trends 2019." https://www.ilo.org/global/research/global-reports/weso/2019/lang--en/index.htm

International Monetary Fund (IMF). 2008. "World economic outlook, October 2008." In *Is 'Being Green' Rewarded in the Market? An Empirical Investigation of Decarbonization and Stock Returns*, ed. S. Y. In, K. Y. Park, and A. H. B. Monk. Stanford Global Project Center working paper. https://ssrn.com/abstract=3020304

Khoury, C. K., A. D. Bjorkman, H. Dempewolf, J. Ramirez-Villegas, L. Guarino, A. Jarvis, L. H. Rieseberg, and P. C. Struik, 2014. "Increasing homogeneity in global food supplies and the implications for food security." *Proceedings of the National Academy of Sciences* 111, no. 11: 4001–6.

Lal, R. 2018. "Digging deeper: A holistic perspective of factors affecting soil organic carbon sequestration in agroecosystems." *Global Change Biology* 24, no. 8. https://doi.org/10.1111/gcb.14054

Lernoud, J., and H. Willer. 2018. *Organic Agriculture Worldwide 2016: Current Statistics.* Nuremberg, Germany: Research Institute of Organic Agriculture (FIBL). https://orgprints.org/32677/19/Willer-2018-global-data-biofach.pdf

McKinsey Global Institute. 2015. *Digital America: A Tale of Haves and Have-Mores*. A McKinsey Report by J. Manyika, S. Ramaswamy, S. Khanna, H. Sarrazin, G. Pinkus, G. Sethupathy, and A. Yaffe. https://www.mckinsey.com/industries/technology-media-and-telecommunications/our-insights/digital-america-a-tale-of-the-haves-and-have-mores

Montgomery, D. R. 2018. *Growing a Revolution: Bringing Our Soil Back to Life*. New York: WW Norton.

O'Neill, J. 2016. "The review on antimicrobial resistance (AMR): tackling drug-resistant infections globally. Final report and recommendations." A report chaired by Jim O'Neill, commissioned in 2014 by the UK Government and sponsored by the Wellcome Trust and the UK Department of Health.

Parry, I., D. Heine, E. Lis, and S. Li. 2014. *Getting Energy Prices Right. From Principles to Practice*. Washington, D.C.: International Monetary Fund.

Ponisio, L. C., L. K. M'Gonigle, K. C. Mace, J. Palomino, P. de Valpine, and C. Kremen. 2015. "Diversification practices reduce organic to conventional yield gap." *Proceedings of the Royal Society, Biological Science* 282, no. 1799.

Rockström, R. J. 2016. Video interview released at the EAT Stockholm Food Forum. https://www.youtube.com/watch?v=swHCIwUGuI0

Rockström, R. J., O. Gaffeny, et al. 2017. "A roadmap for rapid decarbonization." *Science* 355, no. 6331: 1269–71.

Rodale Institute. 2018. *Farming System Trial*. https://rodaleinstitute.org/wp-content/uploads/RI-FST-Brochure-2018.pdf

Roser, M., and H. Ritchie. 2020. "Food per person." OurWorldInData.org. https://ourworldindata.org/food-per-person

Scherr, S. J., and J. A. McNeely. 2008. "Biodiversity conservation and agricultural sustainability: towards a new paradigm of 'ecoagriculture' landscapes." *Philosophical Transactions of the Royal Society of London. Series B, Biological Sciences* 363, no. 1491: 477–94.

Schmidt, T. 2016. *The Political Economy of Food and Finance*. London: Routledge.

Smil, V. 2008. *Energy in Nature and Society General Energetics of Complex Systems*. Cambridge, Mass.: MIT Press.

Solagro. 2016. *Afterres2050 version 2016*. Solagro Association, C. Couturier, M. Charru, S. Doublet, and P. Pointereau. https://afterres2050.solagro.org/wp-content/uploads/2020/02/Afterres2050-eng.pdf

Springmann, M., H. Charles, J. Godfray, M. Rayner, and P. Scarborough. 2016. "Co-benefits of global dietary change." *Proceedings of the National Academy of Sciences* 113, no. 15: 4146–51.

Technavio. 2019. "Plant-based meat market by type and geography: forecast and analysis 2020–2024." *Global Industries Reports*. https://www.technavio.com/report/plant-based-meat-market-industry-analysis

Willett, W., J. Rockström, B. Loken, M. Springmann, et al. 2019. *Food in the Anthropocene*. Oslo, Norway: EAT–Lancet Commission on Healthy Diets from Sustainable Food Systems.

Yale School of Forestry and Environmental Studies. 2019. "Cattle ranching in the Amazon region." Global Forest Atlas. https://globalforestatlas.yale.edu/amazon/land-use/cattle-ranching

Endnotes

1. In chapter 3 of this book, DeFries looks at challenges from agri-food supply in less-advanced economies and policies to reform it.

2. Alternative estimates based on a more accurate attribution of GHGs by other sectors to the livestock sector put this figure at 51 percent of all GHGs. The key difference between the two estimates is that the larger one embeds the impact of the exponential growth in livestock production (now above 70 billion land animals per year), accompanied by large-scale deforestation and forest burning, which have dramatically accelerated the volatilization of soil carbon.
3. The IPCC estimates that even if carbon emissions stopped completely right now, as the oceans catch up with the atmosphere, Earth's temperature would rise about another 1.1°F (0.6°C). Scientists refer to this as committed warming (IPCC 2019).
4. Chapter 5 in this book discusses challenges to food systems from trends in food demand.
5. Chapters 8–11 in this book explain pressures of biological diversity and food security from current food systems.
6. Chapter 5 and the other section in this chapter discuss these trade-offs, proposing policy solutions.
7. Chapter 5 in this book explains why Western diets are also bad for human health.
8. FCRs are for crop-fed farmed animals; they indicate how much more food each animal consumes than it produces. Typical feed crops are grains and legumes: corn, soy, and wheat. These numbers are important because crop-fed, factory- or conventionally farmed animals are the norm in industrialized countries, and the global growth rate of meat consumption is alarmingly high. Intensive (factory) farming represents the overwhelming majority (>98 percent) of meat produced in countries of the Group of Twenty.
9. Crowder and Reganold (2015) analyzed the financial performance of organic and conventional agriculture from forty years of studies covering fifty-five crops grown on five continents. When actual organic premiums were applied, organic agriculture was significantly more profitable (22–35 percent) and had higher benefit/cost ratios (20–24 percent) than conventional agriculture. Although premiums were 29–32 percent, breakeven premiums necessary for organic profits to match conventional profits were only 5–7 percent, even with organic yields being 10–18 percent lower. Total costs were not significantly different, but labor costs were significantly higher (7–13 percent) with organic farming practices.
10. Recent food consumption surveys reveal that in the United States more than half of millennials actively try to include organic foods in their diets, a higher share than for other age groups, and that preferences for organic food are comparable across different income group levels (Gallup 2019).
11. For example, when the prices of agricultural products suddenly increased in 2008, in the wake of higher oil prices and speculation, overall inflation picked up in a number of emerging market and developing countries, reflecting the greater weight of rising food prices in the consumer price index (IMF 2008), and lower-income countries found themselves trapped in a higher inflation–lower growth equilibrium with a more adverse outlook for income distribution. Forty-four million people were driven into poverty by rising food prices in the second half of 2010.
12. Since 2018, oil and gas companies have spent US$50 billion (€45.3 billion) on investment projects that undermine the Paris Agreement, with a new report from think tank Carbon Tracker warning that major companies risk wasting US$2.2 trillion (€1.9 trillion) on stranded assets by 2030.

13. The index assesses sixty of the largest livestock and aquaculture companies, with a combined market cap of close to $300 billion, on behalf of the world's largest investors.
14. Organizations that have joined the FAIRR initiative—now representing US $4.1 trillion in assets—acknowledge the risk associated with factory farming.
15. Hirvonen et al. (2020) estimate that the most affordable EAT–Lancet diet would have cost a global median of US$2.84 per day in the reference year (2011), of which the largest share was the cost of fruits and vegetables (31.2%), followed by legumes and nuts (18.7%), meat, eggs, and fish (15.2%), and dairy (13.2%). This diet costs a small fraction of average incomes in high-income countries but is not affordable for the world's poor. It is estimated that the cost of an EAT–Lancet diet exceeded household per capita income for at least 1.58 billion people. The EAT–Lancet diet is also more expensive than the minimum cost of nutrient adequacy, on average, by a mean factor of 1.6). Among regions, diet cost as a fraction of mean daily per capita household income was lowest in North America (4.42%) and highest in sub-Saharan Africa (72.73%). Geographic variation was considerable even within regions.
16. On the general case for, and design of, environmental taxes, see Parry et al. (2014).
17. This would be administratively practical once production has been categorized in the base of externalities.
18. In countries where imports of bovine meat are high, these differentials in taxation between bovine and other meats are better implemented on the final product (meat), but this is not the case in France.
19. Sugar beets and citrus crops, followed by vegetables, tubers, and grains, consume the highest levels of nitrogen, phosphate, and potash fertilizer per acre of cultivation. Peas and beans need just a fraction of these fertilizers per acre, in part because they have capacity to absorb nitrogen from the air.
20. See Barbieri, Pellerin, and Nesme (2017). Comparing conventional with smaller-scale polyculture farms in the United States, Montgomery (2018) concluded that well-managed alternative farming systems nearly always use less synthetic chemical pesticides, fertilizers, and antibiotics per unit of production than conventional farms.
21. One of the main barriers for many small-scale farmers is not being able to live on the land, whether they are tenants or owners. Agroecological farming is a labor-intensive business, and the farmer is at the center of the human ecology of the farm, making agroecological farming from offsite scarcely viable. Living onsite with no additional accommodation or travel costs can be essential to a viable business plan during the initial few years. As a result, the key planning requirements for a new agricultural residence is the major need to be on onsite, which includes both functional and financial viability. In practice, many farming applicants struggle with planning permits because they do not understand the nature of agroecological farms and often make unrealistic assumptions about financial viability, given the low-profit nature of the whole sector (and the fact that established farmers often make money from alternative enterprises, including property letting).
22. A U.S.-based study of 1,800 farmers transitioning to organic agriculture pointed to mentoring and one-on-one technical assistance as both critical and hard to come by. See Cernansky (2018).
23. The discussion over new plant breeding techniques has taken center stage in Brussels since a European court ruled in July 2018 that organisms obtained by mutagenesis are genetically modified organisms (GMOs) and in principle should fall under the GMO

directive. The agri-food industry disputes the GMO classification, saying the plants obtained through these techniques might have occurred naturally or through conventional cross-breeding techniques that mimic natural processes.

24. Full details of the plan can be found here (in Danish): https://mfvm.dk/fileadmin/user_upload/FVM.dk/Dokumenter/Landbrug/Indsatser/Oekologi/OekologiplanDanmark.pdf.
25. Compared with 2017, for example, an additional 34,000 hectares of land was made organic in 2018—280,000 hectares in total in Denmark now—and the number of organic farmers in Denmark increased by 325. With almost 79,000 hectares, the region of south Jutland has the most organic farming land, followed by west and north Jutland (both about 58,000 hectares), east Jutland (almost 30,000), and west and south Zealand (just over 25,000).

Chapter 3

Greening Food Supply in Less-Advanced Economies

Ruth DeFries

"Agriculture is civilization." —*E. Emmons*

The greening of agri-food production in less-industrialized countries rests on three pillars: healthy diets and nutrition security, minimal environmental impacts, and climate-resilient production systems. The production paradigm to produce more calories has dominated agriculture for the last fifty years, which has discounted the importance of agrodiversity and production of micronutrients for human consumption. With rising recognition of the burdens of micronutrient deficiencies, increasing obesity, and adverse environmental impacts as high-input agriculture extends to less-industrialized countries, the critical need is to identify and implement policies that maximize synergies and minimize trade-offs between these three pillars. Examples of win–win–win strategies are the adoption of "nutri-cereals" by the Government of India and Bhutan's promotion of organic production.

The Pillars of Green Agri-Food Systems

Innovations in the agricultural sector in the latter twentieth century profoundly altered the course of urbanization, economic development, diets, and natural resources in less industrially advanced countries. As high-yielding varieties, irrigation, and other agricultural inputs boosted cereal production in Latin America and Asia through the Green Revolution, per capita production of calories from cereals increased faster than population growth (DeFries et al. 2015). The Green Revolution successfully averted fears about mass food shortages driven by population growth.

The legacy of the Green Revolution is mixed when viewed from multiple lenses of environment, nutrition, and social equity (Swaminathan and Kesavan 2017). On the positive side, the technological achievements to increase production rank among humanity's greatest achievements. Low food prices and trade supported a dramatic decline in the number of undernourished people, from approximately 35 percent of the population in developing countries in 1970 to 13 percent in 2015 (Roser and Ritchie 2020), although since 2015 the trend has reverted (FAO et al. 2019). On the negative side, the focus on cereal yields and calorie production rather than healthy diets leaves 2 billion—one in three of the world's population—with micronutrient deficiencies (von Grebmer et al. 2014) and a similar number of adults obese and overweight (FAO et al. 2019). Agriculture and land use change contribute approximately a quarter of anthropogenic greenhouse gas emissions and place high demands on water resources (DeFries and Rosenzweig 2010). Moreover, research focus and extension to farmers of high-yield wheat and rice varieties during the Green Revolution deemphasized locally adapted crop varieties, making agricultural systems more homogeneous and vulnerable to pests and climate shocks.

Today's agricultural sector faces the difficult challenge of providing society with sufficient and nutritious food and fodder while minimizing its environmental impact and adapting to a changing climate. In less-industrialized countries, this challenge is particularly acute for multiple reasons. Demands for agricultural products from rapid urbanization are changing traditional farming practices. Production systems are heterogeneous, with both millions of smallholder farmers and intensive, large –scale farms, often within the same country. Temperatures are increasing, and rainfall patterns are shifting with climate change.

A green agriculture sector, sometimes referred to as climate-smart agriculture, rests on three equal pillars (Lipper et al., 2014): healthy diets and food security; minimal environmental impacts, including low greenhouse gas emissions, reduced nitrogen runoff, and less demand for water and land; and production systems that are resilient to climate change and variability (figure 3-1). Many practitioners and academics recognize the need to change course from the model of high inputs and homogenization of production systems to achieve a green agricultural sector. Approaches that promote synergies between the three pillars lie at the heart of such a transition.

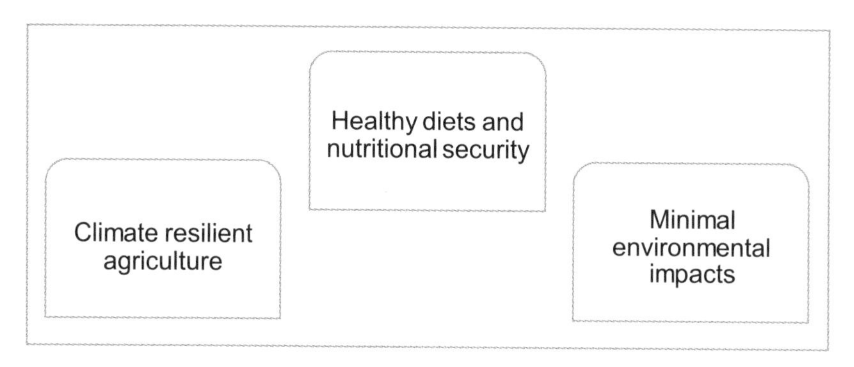

Figure 3-1. The three pillars of green agri-food production systems.

This chapter examines current major trajectories related to the three pillars of green agriculture, followed by policy and management options to achieve these goals in less-industrialized countries. The chapter focuses mainly on crops, although livestock also plays a major role in agricultural systems and its environmental impacts.

Diets and Nutritional Security

In the 1960s and 1970s, national and international investments in agriculture focused on sufficient provision of macronutrients, calories, and protein to avert famine and mass food shortages. As Demographic and Health Surveys and other measures of anthropometric measure of nutritional status began in the 1980s and 1990s, the importance of adequate micronutrients (vitamins such as vitamins A, C, E, and B complex and minerals such as iron, zinc, and magnesium) in addition to macronutrients came to the attention of the international community (Herforth 2015). Micronutrient deficiencies, or "hidden hunger," affect an estimated 2 billion people globally, with detrimental impacts on physical growth, immunity, cognitive development, and productivity. Young children and women of reproductive age in developing countries are most affected by micronutrient deficiencies (Muthayya et al. 2013).

Micronutrient deficiencies can result from poor diet diversity and quality even if macronutrients are sufficient. The increase in area devoted to the major staple cereals rice, wheat, and maize from 66 to 79 percent of all cereal area between 1961 and 2013 occurred at the expense of other nutritious cereals. Barley, oats, rye, millet, and sorghum declined from 33 to 19 percent of cereal area in the same time period. Consequently, the energy density (calories per 100 g of cereal) of the world's cereal supply remained constant, but the protein, iron, and zinc content of directly consumed cereals declined by 4, 19, and 5 percent, respectively (DeFries et al. 2015). The reduction in nutrient density is particularly consequential for less-industrialized countries, where people generally obtain a large proportion of calories from cereal staples. To compensate for the loss in nutrients, a more diverse, nutrient-dense diet, fortification or biofortification of currently consumed foods, or increased production and consumption of more nutrient-dense, traditional cereals is needed.

Echoing the trends in production toward more homogeneous production of cereals, diets have generally become more similar between countries, while they have become more diverse within countries because of imports of different products. The dominant trend is toward Westernized diets, with increasing consumption of animal foods and vegetable oils (Khoury et al. 2014). The greatest increase in the fat supply in the last fifty years comes from oil crops, which increased 196 percent in Asia's food supply between 1961 and 2013 compared with 74 percent for the world (FAOSTAT 2020).

Between 1961 and 2011, the prevalence of inadequate intake of fourteen micronutrients declined in all regions because of increased total production or imports and increased nutrient density in the food supply (the balance between domestic production, imports and exports, and changes in stock from seed, feed, manufacturing, and losses during storage and transport). The decline is weaker in South Asia and Sub-Saharan Africa and strong in East and Southeast Asia. Micronutrient density in the food supply has increased in all countries except those in Sub-Saharan Africa (Beal et al. 2017). Trade plays a major role in equalizing the distribution of nutrients between countries, but low-income countries nevertheless have inadequate supplies of calcium, iron, and folate, even assuming that nutrients are distributed evenly across the population (Wood et al. 2018) (figure 3-2).

The Hidden Hunger Index, which combines the national prevalence of stunting, anemia due to iron deficiency, and low serum retinol levels among preschool-aged children, indicates that many countries in Sub-Saharan Africa along with India and Afghanistan have the highest levels of hidden hunger. For example, stunting affects about 30 to 60 percent of preschool-aged children in the countries with the highest Hidden Hunger Index (Muthayya et al. 2013). The likely causes of hidden hunger are low-nutrient diets combined with frequent infections, which inhibit absorption of nutrients. South American countries have only mild to moderate levels of hidden hunger.

At the same time, as hidden hunger affects large segments of the population, a third of the world's population is overweight or obese. The shift in

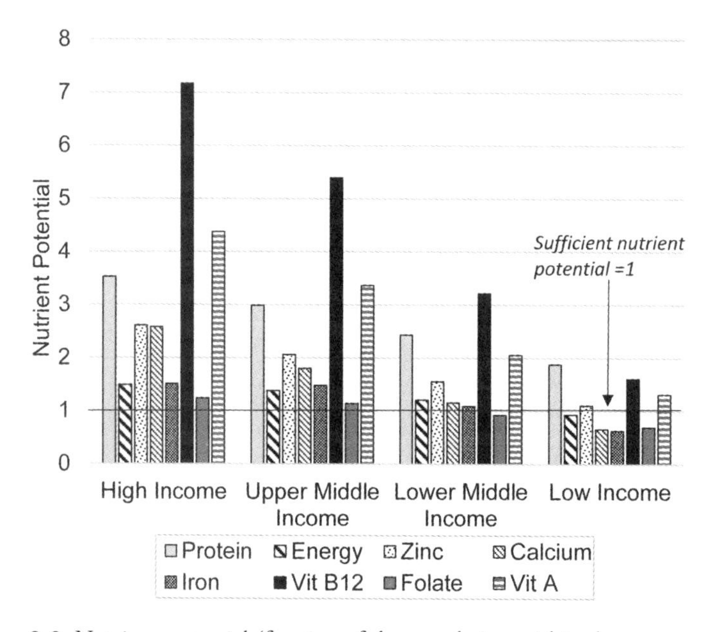

Figure 3-2. Nutrient potential (fraction of the population within the country whose nutritional needs could be potentially met from the food supply for each nutrient, not considering distributional differences within countries). *Note:* Values less than 1 (solid line) indicate an insufficient amount of the nutrition in the food supply to meet the nutritional needs of the population. *Sources:* Country income groups are from the World Bank classification; data from Wood et al. (2018, Supplementary Table 3).

the food supply, with processed foods rich in sugars and fats, is a major factor (Zobel et al. 2016). The obesity epidemic is not restricted to developed countries. Cheap vegetable oils have enabled increased energy consumption for low-income people. Although data are sparse for many countries, evidence indicates that the prevalence of obesity is rising across all low- and middle-income countries (Popkin et al. 2012).

This cursory review of trends in diets indicates both negative and positive trends. Except in Sub-Saharan Africa, national food supplies have increased their nutrient densities, mostly through imports of nutrient-dense foods. However, cereals, which make up a large proportion of calories for low-income populations, have become less nutrient dense. Moreover, increased consumption of vegetable oils plays a role in the increasing rates of obese and overweight people. With the triple burden of increasing obesity, hidden hunger, and undernutrition in less-industrialized countries, the agricultural sector plays a large role in reorienting food supplies toward nutritious diets.

The developing transition from a paradigm that maximizes production of low-nutrient foods to one that meets the nutritional needs of the population is an essential pillar of greening the agricultural sector.

Environmental Impacts

A second pillar of greening the agriculture sector in less-industrialized countries calls for minimizing environmental impacts. Impacts from agriculture range across many dimensions of the environment, including land conversion, greenhouse gas emissions, nitrogen runoff, and unsustainable water use.

The increase in cereal production in the last few decades has occurred mainly through improvements in yields and cropping intensity rather than expansion of cultivated area. Production of oil crops, including oil palm, rapeseed, and soy, has increased eightfold, more than any other crop. This increase has resulted predominantly from expanding areas, with some contribution of improved yields (Ramankutty et al. 2018). Most agricultural expansion in the 1980s and 1990s occurred at the expense of tropical forests (Gibbs et al. 2010), with pastures the main land use after deforestation in Latin America and oil palm cultivation in Southeast Asia. Most lands available for further expansion are in tropical forests, which have high environmental value for carbon sequestration and biodiversity. Peatlands in Southeast Asia contribute a disproportionately large amount of greenhouse gases when drained and used for agriculture (Carlson et al. 2017). Tropical forests in central Africa have not undergone major deforestation as in Latin America and Asia because of conflict and lack of access.

Agriculture and land use contribute 23 percent of all global anthropogenic greenhouse gas emissions (Shukla et al. 2019), with a declining proportional contribution over time as fossil fuel emissions increase at a more rapid rate than agricultural emissions (Tubiello et al. 2013). These emissions include carbon emissions from clearing forests for cropland and pasture, nitrous oxide from synthetic fertilizer and manure, and methane from rice paddies, and enteric fermentation in ruminant livestock. Greenhouse gas emissions from croplands and biomass burning make up the majority of all emissions in less-industrialized countries (approximately 73, 83, and 60 percent of all emissions in tropical countries of Latin America, Africa, and Asia) (DeFries and Rosenzweig 2010). Greenhouse gas emissions from crops per unit area increased by 126 and 29 percent between 1970 and 2007 in South and Southeast Asia and Sub-Saharan Africa, respectively, and declined by 18 percent in Central and South

America with a reduction in deforestation (Bennetzen et al. 2016). Global emissions from croplands are concentrated in Asia, with methane from rice and carbon dioxide, methane, and nitrous oxide from peatlands in China, Indonesia, and India contributing more than half of all cropland emissions (Carlson et al. 2017).

Beyond greenhouse gas emissions, increasing application of synthetic fertilizer in Asia and Latin America contributes to eutrophication of water bodies and hypoxia if excessively applied. The threat to coral reefs in the tropics, which have high environmental value because of their importance for fish nurseries, is probably underestimated (Altieri et al. 2017).

Agriculture is the largest user of freshwater. With a looming water scarcity crisis, the types of crops, where they are grown, and the water embodied in traded agricultural products (Chen et al. 2018) are critical issues for green agriculture. These multiple environmental aspects challenge farmers to increase production with efficient use of resources, a trend that is taking place with precision agriculture and decision support systems (Lindblom et al. 2017).

Ability to Adapt to a Changing Climate

Diversity of crop species, crop varieties within species, and genetic diversity within varieties are critical to adapting to climate change. These genetic resources are the foundation for breeding crops that are resilient to climate change and that can withstand pests and diseases that are likely to become more prevalent with climate change.

Agrodiversity, the genetic resources and knowledge evolved through millennia from cultural selection of desirable traits for edible species, enables plant breeders to develop drought-, heat-, and pest-resistant crop varieties. This need is particularly acute in the developing world, where scientists predict that climate change will have the greatest impact on agriculture in the coming decades (Rosenzweig et al. 2014).

With the homogenization of production systems, diversity of crops and varieties has followed a declining trend. Historically, humans used more than 7,000 plant species for food. With modern, mechanized farming, only 150 species are under cultivation and only three—wheat, rice, and maize—provide nearly 60 percent of calories that humans consume from plants (Gepts 2006). Increased production of these three staple crops has replaced coarse cereals such as millet and sorghum throughout the developing world (DeFries et al. 2015). In India, for example, the expansion of rice at the expense of coarse cereals during the Green Revolution reduced the climate resilience of cereal production because the latter are significantly less sensitive to climate extremes (Davis et al. 2019a).

In the 1970s, scientists raised concern about the genetic erosion of crops with the substitution of improved cultivars for thousands of locally adapted varieties of heirloom varieties and landraces. This erosion brings increased risks of epidemics of plant diseases and a narrower genetic pool of traits that could withstand climate change. As examples of the loss of diversity within staple crops, only 20 percent of corn types recorded in 1930 in Mexico are found today, and only 10 percent of 10,000 wheat varieties found in China in 1949 are still grown (Gepts 2006). In addition to seedbanks that provide genetic resources to plant breeders, small traditional farms collectively maintain a high diversity of varieties (Jarvis et al. 2008). These essential resources conserve genetic diversity to counter the historical decline in crop types and varieties.

Policies to Green Food Supply in Less-Advanced Countries

Policy and management options for greening the agri-food system ideally address all three pillars of healthy diets, minimal environmental impacts, and climate resilience in concert. In reality, policies that account for multiple dimensions are difficult to design and implement with siloed decision making for individual sectors. Greening agriculture requires cross-sectoral considerations to minimize trade-offs and maximize synergies across the three pillars.

Policy options that holistically address the first pillar, healthy diets and nutritional security, link agricultural production policies with public health measures to promote healthy consumption, although decision makers in these two spheres often operate separately. HarvestPlus, a program in place since 2003, is a notable exception. Plant breeders and nutritionists collectively develop biofortified varieties of staple crops with high micronutrient content. More than 20 million people in developing countries grow and consume these biofortified crops. With leadership and mainstreaming into plant breeding programs, these crops could nourish 1 billion people by 2030 (Bouis and Saltzman 2017).

No country in the world has yet been able to reverse the obesity epidemic (Popkin et al. 2012), a problem compounded by increased consumption of processed foods in developing countries. Inexpensive vegetable oils, a major ingredient in processed foods, drives this trend. One promising success is mandatory warning labels in Chile for foods high in sodium, calories, sugar, and saturated fats. After one year of implementation, consumers reported changes in purchasing habits (Correa et al. 2019). For low-income consumers with high proportions of cereals in their diets, fortification, biofortification, and emphasis on nutritious "orphan" cereals can address micronutrient deficiencies.

Regarding the second pillar, minimizing environmental impacts, agricultural technologies can reduce greenhouse gas emissions and improve efficiency of inputs. These technologies include methane inhibitors in cattle feed to reduce methane emissions, no-till agriculture to sequester soil carbon, water management in rice paddies, efficient fertilizer application, and transitioning to more efficient livestock production systems (Wollenberg et al. 2016). Systematic policies to promote these technologies through extension services and incentive programs are needed. Some success has been achieved with reducing excess use of synthetic fertilizer in the developed world, such as Walmart's initiative to reduce fertilizer use by its suppliers (Davidson et al. 2014). Bhutan's National Organic Program aims to contribute to national carbon neutrality and 100 percent organic production.

Perhaps the greatest evidence of policies that aim to minimize environmental impacts from deforestation and agricultural practices resides in the private sector. The voluntary soy moratorium, implemented in Brazil in 2006 in response to retailers and nongovernment organizations who demanded that soy be produced without new deforestation, was a major factor in reducing deforestation in Brazil in the latter half of the decade (Gibbs et al. 2015). The soy moratorium set the stage for supply chain management of other commodities including beef through the Global Roundtable for Sustainable Beef and oil palm through the Roundtable for Sustainable Palm Oil. Many companies have taken zero-deforestation pledges to remove products produced on deforested land from their supply chains. The success of these efforts is mixed, with lack of transparency and traceability, leakage, marginalization of smallholders, and selective adoption compromising the effectiveness (Lambin et al. 2018).

For the third pillar, climate resilience, farmers need to adopt climate-resilient strategies. Crop switching, change in planting dates, dissemination of climate information and weather forecasts, and crop insurance are among the approaches that extension activities and policies can include to promote climate resilient agriculture. The program on Climate Change Agriculture and Food Security has piloted these approaches throughout the developing world (Aggarwal et al. 2018). Plant breeding through modern and traditional methods plays a major role in developing climate-resilient crops. Publicly funded and community seedbanks store and provide the basic genetic material to plant breeders around the world, with the free exchange of genetic material guided by the International Treaty on Plant Genetic Resources for Food and Agriculture adopted in 2001.

These various policy and management options collectively can contribute to greening agri-food production systems (table 3-1). One example of a policy measure that simultaneously addresses all three pillars comes from the declaration of "nutri-cereals" by the Government of India.

Country Cases

India's Nutri-Cereals

On April 10, 2018 the Ministry of Agriculture and Farmer's Welfare of the Government of India issued a circular that identified millets as "climate resilient crops" that "possess unique nutritional characteristics." They declared millets as "nutri-cereals" for their high nutritive value, in stark departure from the perception of these cereals as low-status cereals of the poor.

This declaration represents a major departure. For the past fifty years, government policies and research focused mainly on increasing yields and expanding production of the rice and wheat, the Green Revolution cereals. The proportion of millets in the country's cereal basket declined substantially (DeFries et al. 2015). Because millets contain more micronutrients than rice, and cereals make up a large portion of diets, iron consumption per capita declined nationally by 21 and 11 percent in rural and urban populations, respectively, and most dramatically for the rural poor (DeFries et al. 2018). Additionally, millets use less water (Davis et al. 2018), are more resilient to climate change (Davis et al. 2019a), and produce less greenhouse gases than a rice/wheat rotation (Rao et al. 2018). Hypothetical replacement of rice with millets in strategic locations results in multiple benefits for nutrition (iron and protein), water savings, climate resilience, and reduced greenhouse gas emissions without compromising overall production of the supply of calories (Davis et al. 2019b).

Some states are working toward incorporating millets into the Public Distribution System, the world's largest food security safety net, which provides highly subsidized cereals to below-poverty-level households. In most states, the system distributes rice and wheat. The Special Programme for Promotion of Millets in Tribal Areas in the state of Odisha is reviving millets in rainfed agriculture and promoting consumption of traditionally produced and consumed

TABLE 3-1. *Examples of Policy and Management Options and Their Ability to Address the Three Pillars of Green Agri-Food Production in Less-Industrialized Countries*

	Healthy Diets and Nutritional Security	Minimal Environmental Impacts	Climate Resilience
Consumer behavior modification	X		
Supply chain management		X	
Promotion of low–greenhouse gas agricultural technologies and efficient resource use		X	X
Maintenance of genetic diversity for crop breeding	X	X	X
Promotion of climate-appropriate and nutritious crops for production and consumption	X	X	X

nutri-cereals. The program targets farmers, state nutrition programs, and ultimately the Public Distribution System. Challenges include overcoming stigma that millets are inferior cereals and promoting technologies for processing. In Karnạtaka, another state that has replaced fortified white rice with millets in some children's midday meal programs, stunting decreased and body mass index improved relative to a control group (Anitha et al. 2019). These examples demonstrate a potential win–win–win transition to a green agri-food system that improves nutrition for consumers with high micronutrient deficiencies, increases resilience to climate shocks, and provides livelihood options for farmers to participate in the revival of millets in the country.

Bhutan 2020 National Organic Program

As discussed by Batini and Pointereau in chapter 2, Denmark wants to go completely organic "as soon as possible," but at least one country has an even more ambitious plan. In 2011, Bhutan pledged to go 100 percent organic by 2020 and launched the National Organic Program in order to meet that goal. Under the plan, the government offers free training programs in organic farming to turn Bhutan's subsistence farmers, barely making a living, into successful entrepreneurs. By teaching farmers good organic farming practices, so they can earn more money by growing organic produce, and by providing financial support, Bhutan has been able to reduce waste, decrease the country's dependence on imported food, and ensure that it remains climate-neutral, producing no more climate-changing emissions each year than its forests absorb.

The switch to organic is also helping this Himalayan mountain kingdom achieve its zero waste goal. Currently, the country's carbon emission rate is a negligible 0.8 metric tons per capita, according to the World Bank. Not only is Bhutan carbon neutral, it's also a carbon sink, making it one of the few countries in the world to have negative carbon emissions. Recent figures indicate that the country emits about 1.5 million tons of carbon annually, while its forests absorb more than 6 million tons (see chapter 8). Bhutan has been hailed as one of the greenest countries on Earth.

Conclusions

Greening agri-food production in less-industrialized countries indicates that the challenges are great, but the opportunities exist. Although 2 billion people suffer from micronutrient deficiencies and agriculture has many adverse environmental impacts, successes include the improving micronutrient density of the food supply (except in Sub-Saharan Africa) and an incipient recognition of agrodiversity as a key component of green agriculture. Improvements in efficient use of agricultural inputs are also on the horizon, although they are far from widely adopted. The challenge for agricultural policymakers is to consider public health and environmental outcomes along with production goals when determining which crops and production systems will receive support through research, extension, and promotion.

References

Aggarwal, P. K., A. Jarvis, B. M. Campbell, R. B. Zougmoré, A. Khatri-Chhetri, S. Vermeulen, A. Loboguerrero Rodriguez, L. Sebastian, J. Kinyangi, and O. Bonilla Findji. 2018. "The climate-smart village approach: framework of an integrative strategy for scaling up adaptation options in agriculture." *Ecology and Society* 23.

Altieri, A. H., S. B. Harrison, J. Seemann, R. Collin, R. J. Diaz, and N. Knowlton. 2017. "Tropical dead zones and mass mortalities on coral reefs." *Proceedings of the National Academy of Sciences* 114: 3660–5.

Anitha, S., J. Kane-Potaka, T. W. Tsusaka, D. Tripathi, S. Upadhyay, A. Kavishwar, A. Jalagam, N. Sharma, and S. Nedumaran. 2019. "Acceptance and impact of millet-based mid-day meal on the nutritional status of adolescent school going children in a peri urban region of Karnataka State in India." *Nutrients* 11: 2077.

Beal, T., E. Massiot, J. E. Arsenault, M. R. Smith, and R. J. Hijmans. 2017. "Global trends in dietary micronutrient supplies and estimated prevalence of inadequate intakes." *PLoS One* 12: e0175554.

Bennetzen, E. H., P. Smith, and J. R. Porter. 2016. "Agricultural production and greenhouse gas emissions from world regions: the major trends over 40 years." *Global Environmental Change* 37: 43–55.

Bouis, H. E., and A. Saltzman. 2017. "Improving nutrition through biofortification: a review of evidence from HarvestPlus, 2003 through 2016." *Global Food Security* 12: 49–58.

Carlson, K. M., J. S. Gerber, N. D. Mueller, M. Herrero, G. K. MacDonald, K. A. Brauman, P. Havlik, C. S. O'Connell, J. A. Johnson, and S. Saatchi. 2017. "Greenhouse gas emissions intensity of global croplands." *Nature Climate Change* 7: 63–8.

Chen, B., M. Han, K. Peng, S. Zhou, L. Shao, X. Wu, W. Wei, S. Liu, Z. Li, and J. Li. 2018. "Global land–water nexus: agricultural land and freshwater use embodied in worldwide supply chains." *Science of the Total Environment* 613: 931–43.

Correa, T., C. Fierro, M. Reyes, F. R. D. Carpentier, L. S. Taillie, and C. Corvalan. 2019. "Responses to the Chilean law of food labeling and advertising: exploring knowledge, perceptions and behaviors of mothers of young children." *International Journal of Behavioral Nutrition and Physical Activity* 16: 21.

Davidson, E., J. Galloway, N. Millar, and A. Leach. 2014. "N-related greenhouse gases in North America: innovations for a sustainable future." *Current Opinion in Environmental Sustainability* 9: 1–8.

Davis, K. F., A. Chhatre, N. Rao, D. Singh, S. Ghosh-Jerath, A. Mridul, M. Poblete-Cazenave, N. Pradhan, and R. DeFries. 2019a. "Assessing the sustainability of post–Green Revolution cereals in India." *Proceedings of the National Academy of Sciences* 116, no. 50: 25034–41.

Davis, K. F., A. Chhatre, N. D. Rao, D. Singh, and R. DeFries. 2019b. "Sensitivity of grain yields to historical climate variability in India." *Environmental Research Letters* 14: 064013.

Davis, K. F., D. D. Chiarelli, M. C. Rulli, A. Chhatre, B. Richter, D. Singh, and R. DeFries. 2018. "Alternative cereals can improve water use and nutrient supply in India." *Science Advances* 4: eaao1108.

DeFries, R., A. Chhatre, K. F. Davis, A. Dutta, J. Fanzo, S. Ghosh-Jerath, S. Myers, N. D. Rao, and M. R. Smith. 2018. "Impact of historical changes in coarse cereals consumption in India on micronutrient intake and anemia prevalence." *Food and Nutrition Bulletin* 39: 377–92.

DeFries, R., J. Fanzo, R. Remans, C. Palm, S. Wood, and T. L. Anderman. 2015. "Metrics for land-scarce agriculture." *Science* 349: 238–240.

DeFries, R., and C. Rosenzweig. 2010. "Toward a whole-landscape approach for sustainable land use in the tropics." *Proceedings of the National Academy of Sciences* 107: 19627–32.

FAO, IFAD, UNICEF, WFP, and WHO. 2019. *The State of Food Security and Nutrition in the World 2019. Safeguarding against Economic Slowdowns and Downturns*. Rome: FAO.

Gepts, P. 2006. "Plant genetic resources conservation and utilization." *Crop Science* 46: 2278–92.

Gibbs, H. K., L. Rausch, J. Munger, I. Schelly, D. C. Morton, P. Noojipady, B. Soares-Filho, P. Barreto, L. Micol, and N. F. Walker. 2015. "Brazil's soy moratorium." *Science* 347: 377–8.

Gibbs, H. K., A. S. Ruesch, F. Achard, M. K. Clayton, P. Holmgren, N. Ramankutty, and J. A. Foley. 2010. "Tropical forests were the primary sources of new agricultural land in the 1980s and 1990s." *Proceedings of the National Academy of Sciences* 107: 16732–7.

Herforth, A. 2015. "Access to adequate nutritious food: new indicators to track progress and inform action." Pp. 139–64 in *The Fight against Hunger and Malnutrition: The Role of Food, Agriculture, and Targeted Policies*, ed. D. Sahn. Oxford, UK: Oxford University Press.

Jarvis, D. I., A. H. Brown, P. H. Cuong, L. Collado-Panduro, L. Latournerie-Moreno, S. Gyawali, T. Tanto, M. Sawadogo, I. Mar, and M. Sadiki. 2008. "A global perspective of the richness and evenness of traditional crop-variety diversity maintained by farming communities." *Proceedings of the National Academy of Sciences* 105: 5326–31.

Khoury, C. K., A. D. Bjorkman, H. Dempewolf, J. Ramirez-Villegas, L. Guarino, A. Jarvis, L. H. Rieseberg, and P. C. Struik. 2014. "Increasing homogeneity in global food supplies and the implications for food security." *Proceedings of the National Academy of Sciences* 111: 4001–6.

Lambin, E. F., H. K. Gibbs, R. Heilmayr, K. M. Carlson, L. C. Fleck, R. D. Garrett, Y. L. P. de Waroux, C. L. McDermott, D. McLaughlin, and P. Newton. 2018. "The role of supply-chain initiatives in reducing deforestation." *Nature Climate Change* 8: 109–16.

Lindblom, J., C. Lundström, M. Ljung, and A. Jonsson. 2017. "Promoting sustainable intensification in precision agriculture: review of decision support systems development and strategies." *Precision Agriculture* 18: 309–31.

Lipper, L., P. Thornton, B. M. Campbell, T. Baedeker, A. Braimoh, M. Bwalya, P. Caron, A. Cattaneo, D. Garrity, and K. Henry. 2014. "Climate-smart agriculture for food security." *Nature Climate Change* 4: 1068–72.

Muthayya, S., J. H. Rah, J. D. Sugimoto, F. F. Roos, K. Kraemer, and R. E. Black. 2013. "The global hidden hunger indices and maps: an advocacy tool for action." *PLoS One* 8.

Popkin, B. M., L. S. Adair, and S. W. Ng. 2012. "Global nutrition transition and the pandemic of obesity in developing countries." *Nutrition Reviews* 70: 3–21.

Ramankutty, N., Z. Mehrabi, K. Waha, L. Jarvis, C. Kremen, M. Herrero, and L. H. Rieseberg. 2018. "Trends in global agricultural land use: implications for environmental health and food security." *Annual Review of Plant Biology* 69: 789–815.

Rao, N. D., J. Min, R. DeFries, S. Ghosh-Jerath, H. Valin, and J. Fanzo. 2018. "Healthy, affordable and climate-friendly diets in India." *Global Environmental Change* 49: 154–65.

Rosenzweig, C., J. Elliott, D. Deryng, A. C. Ruane, C. Müller, A. Arneth, K. J. Boote, C. Folberth, M. Glotter, and N. Khabarov. 2014. "Assessing agricultural risks of climate change in the 21st century in a global gridded crop model intercomparison." *Proceedings of the National Academy of Sciences* 111: 3268–73.

Roser, M., and H. Ritchie. 2020. "Hunger and undernourishment." OurWorldInData.org. https://ourworldindata.org/hunger-and-undernourishment

Shukla, P., J. Skeg, E. C. Buendia, V. Masson-Delmotte, H.-O. Pörtner, D. Roberts, P. Zhai, R. Slade, S. Connors, and S. van Diemen. 2019. "Climate change and land: an IPCC special report on climate change, desertification, land degradation, sustainable land management, food security, and greenhouse gas fluxes in terrestrial ecosystems." Geneva, Switzerland: International Panel on Climate Change.

Swaminathan, M., and P. Kesavan. 2017. "The transition from green to evergreen revolution." Pp. 91–100 in *Sustainable Development of Organic Agriculture.* Palm Bay, Fla.: Apple Academic Press.

Tubiello, F. N., M. Salvatore, S. Rossi, A. Ferrara, N. Fitton, and P. Smith. 2013. "The FAOSTAT database of greenhouse gas emissions from agriculture." *Environmental Research Letters* 8: 015009.

von Grebmer, K., A. Saltzman, E. Birol, D. Wiesman, N. Prasai, S. Yin, Y. Yohannes, P. Menon, J. Thompson, and A. Sonntag. 2014. *2014 Global Hunger Index: The Challenge of Hidden Hunger.* Washington, D.C.: IFPRI Books.

Wollenberg, E., M. Richards, P. Smith, P. Havlík, M. Obersteiner, F. N. Tubiello, M. Herold, P. Gerber, S. Carter, and A. Reisinger. 2016. "Reducing emissions from agriculture to meet the 2 C target." *Global Change Biology* 22: 3859–64.

Wood, S. A., M. R. Smith, J. Fanzo, R. Remans, and R. S. DeFries. 2018. "Trade and the equitability of global food nutrient distribution." *Nature Sustainability* 1: 34–7.

Zobel, E. H., T. W. Hansen, P. Rossing, and B. J. von Scholten. 2016. "Global changes in food supply and the obesity epidemic." *Current Obesity Reports* 5: 449–55.

CHAPTER 4

Sustainable Farming Trends

The Great Food Transformation necessary to sustain our environment and health will require wide-ranging changes in agriculture, both on land and at sea. This chapter examines four innovative approaches to farming and how smart economic policy can speed their adoption. John Ikerd, Patty Cantrell, and Hanna Wernerson describe how we can level the financial and regulatory playing field for those practicing small and polyfunctional farming. Dickson Despommier and Charles Knirsch illustrate how existing programs to support sustainable agriculture can be repurposed for controlled environment farming, which reduces chemical and water use, while protecting farmers from weather fluctuations exacerbated by climate change. Nicoletta Batini and Bren Smith explore how the creation of a "blue carbon fund" and other economic and structural reforms can support restorative ocean farming. Finally, Bruce Friedrich and Stephen Kaufman look at the role governments can play in the research and development of alternative proteins, easing the environmental burdens of animal agriculture. Each of these agricultural approaches holds tremendous environmental and economic promise, and each can be practiced on a broader scale with the right policy levers.

Small and Polyfunctional Farming

John Ikerd, Patty Cantrell, and Hanna Wernerson

> "The Earth wants to give (to) us if we will treat it as a lover instead of a reluctant enemy." —*Joel Salatin*

The industrial era of economic development, including the era of agricultural industrialization, has brought dramatic increases in anthropogenic contributions to global climate change. Advocates of industrial agriculture contend that its contributions to climate change can be mitigated or reversed by modifying production practices and implementing more sophisticated agroindustrial technologies. Advocates of alternatives to industrial agriculture contend that its contributions to climate change are inherent consequences of the industrial paradigm, which, consequently, must be fundamentally changed or replaced. Both agree that meeting the challenges of climate change will require significant changes in current agricultural practices and policies, but they disagree about the nature of these changes.

Industrial economic development is a very efficient model for extracting economic value from human and natural resources, the ultimate sources of all economic value. The inevitable ecological challenge of industrial agriculture is that industrialization is a linear process, which unavoidably creates chemical and biological wastes as it transforms resources into useful products. Industrial production has no integral or internal process for neutralizing or reintegrating wastes back into the production process. In addition, the concentration of production by industrialization has a natural tendency to concentrate more waste in specific locations than natural processes are capable of neutralizing or assimilating. Nor is the industrial process capable of renewing or regenerating the productive capacity of natural resources, which is inevitably depleted during the processes of production.

Ultimately, industrial economic development destroys the productivity of the natural ecosystems in which all industries must function. These characteristics are widely recognized in industrial manufacturing operations and are addressed through government regulation such as the Clean Water Act and Clean Air Act in the United States. However, industrial agriculture remains unacknowledged as an industry and virtually unregulated as it degrades and pollutes the natural environment with agricultural chemical and biological wastes.

Monofunctional Farming Operations

Industrial farming operations may be referred to as economically monofunctional because they are motivated primarily, if not exclusively, by profits and managed for economic efficiency; they are owned and operated to perform a singularly economic function. In reality, all farms are multifunctional, rather than monofunctional, in the sense that farming invariably has economic, social, and ecological effects on the natural ecosystem, social communities, and economies in which they function. The consequences of these functions may be positive or negative.

Throughout this chapter, the concept of monofunctionality refers to the primary motivation for ownership and intention of management (Ikerd 2016). *Monofunctional farming* is most commonly used in relation to farm businesses that are economically monofunctional. However, farms can also be ecologically or socially monofunctional, if they are owned and managed primarily for noneconomic purposes (Quendler et al. 2020). Some monofunctional farms are owned and operated principally to preserve wildlife, rural landscapes, or natural ecosystems, and others function mainly as rural residences or recreational or hobby farms. In these cases, costs of operation are matters of affordability rather than profitability. Economically monofunctional farming is the primary source of concern about monofunctionality because it is inherently ecologically and socially extractive and exploitive.

As a consequence of agricultural industrialization, large numbers of small, diversified, family-owned and -operated farms have been displaced by fewer large, specialized, mechanized, homogeneous farming operations. In the same sense that industrial farming operations are monofunctional, the traditional family farms they displace are multifunctional. Traditional family farms are managed to further the social and ethical values of the farm family, as well as to meet the economic necessities of families. They are owned and managed to perform ecological, social, and economic functions for families, communities, and society as a whole. Even if changes in industrial farming practices and technologies could mitigate the negative environmental impacts of industrial agriculture, the mitigation process would not create new economic opportunities for small, individually owned and operated family farms and thus would not restore social or economic integrity to rural communities.

Polyfunctional Farming Operations

As used in this chapter, *polyfunctional* refers to the wide variety of different ecological, social, and economic functions and related outputs and roles of multifunctional farms. A Global Report, *Agricultural at a Crossroads*, reflecting the consensus of 400 scientists from fifty-eight different countries, points out that agriculture "provides food, feed, fiber, fuel, and other goods. It also has a major influence on other essential ecosystem services such as water supply and carbon sequestration or release. Agriculture plays an important social role, providing employment and a way of life. Both agriculture and its products are a medium of cultural transmission and cultural practices worldwide. Agriculturally based communities provide a foundation for local economies and are an important means for countries to secure their territories" (McIntyre et al. 2009, 2). Monofunctional farm businesses may provide food, feed, fiber, fuel, and other goods, but their main function is to create economic benefits for their owners and managers. Polyfunctional family farms are managed to provide and balance the provision of many different ecological, social, and economic benefits to the farm family, community, society, and the future of humanity. These distinctions between types of farms are critically important in meeting the challenges of climate change and the future of family farming.

Costs and Risks of Monocultures

An important consideration with respect to climate change is that monofunctional farming operations also tend to be monocultural in that they specialize in a single crop, a species of livestock or poultry, or even a single phase of production. Monocultural farming operations reflect the basic tendency of industrial agriculture toward specialization. Polyfunctional farms, on the other hand, tend to be polycultural in that they rely on diverse crop and livestock enterprises. They use integrated cropping and livestock rotations to maintain soil fertility, manage agricultural pests, and sustain their productivity. Global data verify that small farms tend to have higher species diversity and are the largest contributors to global food supplies (Ricciardi et al. 2018). By definition, monocultures lack ecological diversity and thus must depend on commercial chemical fertilizers and pesticides to maintain their productivity. As a result of these differences, small, polyfunctional farms are very different from monofunctional farms in their ability to adapt to and mitigate climate change.

Monocultures are furthermore economically risky. They lack the economic resilience that characterizes polycultural farming systems, which possess economic and ecological diversity. Diversity reduces economic risk in the face of market fluctuations and production risks induced by climate change. Generous government farm programs have long been used to mitigate the economic risks of industrial agriculture in an effort to offset its inherent lack of diversity. Commodity price supports buffer the negative market impacts of surplus production and low prices in years of unanticipated excess production. Subsidized crop insurance programs, which may insure both yields and prices, ensure monocropping profits during years of adverse weather conditions and uncontrollable outbreaks of crop pests. Government disaster payments also offset economic losses for operators of large-scale, confinement animal feeding operations whenever extreme heat or cold, flooding, or disease outbreaks destroy or sicken millions of animals in monocultural livestock or poultry operations.

The ecological costs of industrial agriculture could perhaps be reduced by adopting different farming methods and production practices or by developing and implementing new technologies. However, much of the economic efficiency advantage of industrial agriculture, as in all industrial operations, depends on their ability to extract without paying the costs for regeneration and to pollute without paying the costs of mitigation. The costs of regeneration and mitigation are not reflected in economic expenses or returns and thus are currently avoided or externalized upon society and nature. The economic value of these costs could be internalized through government policies, but the ecological and social integrity of nature and society has important values that simply cannot be expressed in monetary terms. Government programs cannot change the fundamental laws of nature nor fully compensate for the damage done in the pursuit of economic efficiency.

In summary, the contributions of industrial agriculture to global climate change can be reduced but cannot be eliminated without abandoning the linear industrial process of transforming natural resources into saleable products and waste. Agricultural contributions to climate change cannot be eliminated or reversed without replacing today's large industrial monofunctional, monocultural agricultural operations with smaller regenerative polyfunctional, polycultural farms that function in harmony with both nature and society.

Environmental Benefits of Small Polyfunctional Farms

Regenerative agricultural systems are fundamentally different from industrial agricultural systems: They are circular, rather than linear, in that wastes are returned to soil to restore productivity instead of being released into the environment to be mitigated or endured elsewhere. Plants combine atmospheric carbon and nitrogen with water and soil minerals to form carbohydrates and proteins. Excess carbon is stored in decaying plant roots and soil organic matter in biologically active soils. Mineral wastes are returned to remineralize soils, and biological wastes provide food for micro- and macro-soil organisms that in turn store carbon and make soil minerals available to plants. Solar energy is recycled and reused before it eventually dissipates through the inevitable process of entropy.

Monocultural systems are capable of sequestering carbon in soils but lack the capacity to transform organic matter into humus for long-term carbon storage. The Intergovernmental Panel on Climate Change (IPCC) acknowledged that "land-based options that deliver carbon sequestration in soil or vegetation, such as afforestation, reforestation, agroforestry, soil carbon management of mineral soils, or carbon storage in harvested wood products do not continue to sequester carbon indefinitely" (IPCC 2019, 20). Carbon in soil organic matter that is not used by plants is eventually "burnt off" through tillage or consumed by soil microorganisms and volatized into the air as carbon dioxide. Although there is some scientific uncertainty regarding the specific processes, there is general agreement that soil microorganisms interact with plant roots to exchange soil minerals for carbohydrates produced by plants and then store some of the carbon in soil humus. Only healthy, biologically active soils are capable of storing carbon in the form of soil humus, which is a biologically and chemically stable form of carbon.

Anything short of radically modifying the basic nature of industrial agriculture will only temporarily moderate its negative environmental impacts. Plants in monocropping systems acquire most of their minerals from commercial fertilizers rather than soil mineralization, which also create a toxic environment for the soil microorganisms essential for formation of humus. As a result, monocropping systems can sequester carbon but are incapable of storing it in the stable form needed to halt and potentially help reverse climate change (Wozniacka 2019). Furthermore, the IPCC report acknowledges that "there are limits to the deployment of land-based mitigation measures such as bioenergy crops or afforestation. Widespread use at the scale of several millions of km^2 globally could increase risks for desertification, land degradation, food security and sustainable development" (IPCC 2019, 21).

Greenhouse gases (GHGs) other than carbon dioxide include methane and nitrous oxide, both of which have far more potent greenhouse effects.

There is an ongoing disagreement between agricultural scientists about whether large, monocultural livestock and cropping operations emit more or less of these pollutants than small, polycultural farms while producing the similar quantities of agricultural products. Arguments in favor of monocultures hinge largely on their assumed superior productive capabilities: faster rates of gain, bigger animals, and high crop yields per acre or hectare of land. However, these basic assumptions are seriously challenged by research showing the productive potential of small, polycultural farms that are managed polyfunctionally to provide ecological, social, and economic benefits (IPES-Food 2016, 3). Regardless, it is counterintuitive to believe moving agriculture even further toward monocultures—which created the problem in the first place—is somehow a logical means of solving the problem.

A study of the potential of agroecological farming sanctioned by the Food and Agriculture Organization of the United Nations (FAO) concludes, "The biggest and most durable benefits [of changes in agriculture] will likely result from more radical agroecological measures that will strengthen the resilience of farmers and rural communities, such as diversification of agroecosystems in the form of polycultures, agroforestry systems, and crop–livestock mixed systems accompanied by organic soil management, water conservation and harvesting, and general enhancement of agrobiodiversity" (Altieri et al. 2015, 1). Regenerative polycultural farms are grounded firmly in the conceptual principles of agroecology: "Agroecology embraces a science, a set of practices, and a social movement and has evolved over recent decades to expand in scope from a focus on fields and farms to encompass whole agriculture and food systems. It now represents a transdisciplinary field that includes all the ecological, sociocultural, technological, economic and political dimensions of food systems, from production to consumption" (HLPE 2019, 2). The FAO has endorsed agroecology as a key strategy for mitigating future climate change as well as for coping with the consequences of climate change that are now inevitable (Altieri et al. 2015).

Economic Benefits of Small Polyfunctional Farms

A prevailing perception is that small polycultural farms cannot be competitive with large monocultural farms in terms of production and could not provide food security for a growing global population. However, past studies of economies of scale in advanced economies, such as the United States, have compared the productivity of large farms with that of small farms that rely primarily on the monocultural management strategies that characterize industrial agriculture. The only logical conclusion of such studies is that small farms cannot compete by using the monocultural management strategies more suitable for large farms, not that small farms cannot compete with large farms.

Polyfunctional farms tend to be smaller than their industrial counterparts because the complexity of their integrated cropping and livestock enterprises requires them to be managed intensively. This use of the term *intensive* differs from the more common usage, which typically refers to the intensity of reliance on purchased inputs or technologies, rather than management, to increase yields per acre or hectare. Industrial agricultural operations tend to be larger because routinization and mechanization simplify management processes. Large farms are management extensive because they require less management per unit of land. To summarize, management-intensive farms rely more on management and skilled labor and less on capital, in the form of purchased inputs and technologies. Management-extensive farms rely more on purchased inputs and technologies, and unskilled labor. Monocultures are easier to manage than similar sized polycultures. That is why the industrialization of agriculture has meant fewer, larger farms managing more land and capital per farm.

Studies that have compared intensively managed small farms with extensively managed large farms have often found an advantage for small farms. Small farms have consistently been shown to be highly productive in terms of their output per unit of land area, even though their productivity per unit of labor and management is sometimes lower or more variable (e.g., Barrett et al. 2010; Gollin 2018; Ricciardi et al. 2018). Yields of specific crops in small, diverse farming systems may not adequately measure their actual productivity. For example, studies in nonindustrial farming regions of the world have shown that polycultures characterizing many small farms producing grains, fruit, vegetables, animal fodder, trees, and livestock cultivated in the same field generally yield more in total than monocultures, even if the yields of each single crop are below crop yields in monocultures on larger farms. In addition, diversified polyculture systems can be more efficient than monocultures because they occupy all available growing space, thus reducing weed pressures and losses due to pests and diseases. By associating multiple species that use natural resources differently, polycultures can also make more efficient use of water and light by exploiting niche differentiation (Francis 1986; Anderson and Sinclair 1993; Cardinale et al. 2007; Prieto et al. 2015; Gollin 2018).

Studies comparing organic with conventional cropping systems in industrial agricultural areas typically show significantly lower organic yields. However, most studies have compared yields for specific commodities rather than total agricultural production of integrated whole farm systems. Some studies conducted at state universities in the United States indicate that organic yields can be comparable and economic returns higher than monocropping for well-managed organic crop rotations (Chase et al. 2006). With further research and development of regenerative farming systems, even higher yields seem likely. Thus far, farmers on small, polycultural farms have had to rely on knowledge gained through experience on their own farms, information sharing among like-minded farmers, and information gleaned from publications by preindustrial agricultural scientists.

Regardless, the challenge in advanced economies is not to increase agricultural productivity but instead to achieve agricultural sustainability. Advanced economies are turning food crops into biofuels, wasting a third of all foods produced, and exporting surpluses to countries that would be capable of providing their own food security by applying the principles of agroecology. The leader of an International Panel of Experts on Sustainability (IPES-Food 2016) concluded, "It is not a lack of evidence holding back the agroecological alternative. It is the mismatch between its huge potential to improve outcomes across food systems, and its much smaller potential to generate profits for agribusiness firms. Simply tweaking industrial agriculture will not provide long-term solutions to the multiple problems it generates. We must change the way we set political priorities" (De Shutter 2016).

Policies to Support Small Polycultural Farming

Unfortunately, there are few examples of current agricultural policies that even have the potential for incentivizing and supporting a transition from large monofunctional to small polyfunctional farms. The basic problem with current government farm policies is their myopic focus on monocultural and monofunctional farming systems as the only viable means of providing global food security. A preoccupation with commodity-based farm policies has precluded a serious study, or even consideration, of regenerative, sustainable agricultural alternatives.

Government price supports and subsidized crop insurance for specific commodities mask and mitigate the inherent risks of industrial agriculture while small, polycultural farms are left to self-manage risk through diversification. Government-guaranteed loans subsidize the construction of large confinement animal feeding operations, whereas those with small polycultural farms are left to convince skeptical local bankers to approve loans at often unfavorable interest rates. Investment tax credits and accelerated depreciation of buildings and equipment for tax purposes favor large farms that make large investments. The highest government farm policy priority to address climate change, as well as other environmental, social, and rural economic issues, ought to be to reduce and eventually phase out all government programs that subsidize the monocultural farming operations. This would not only address the problems of industrial agriculture but also free up government funds to incentivize and support the transition to regenerative, polycultural farming operations, needed to mitigate and help reverse the cumulative effects of decades of industrial agriculture.

Thus far, few government policies have been proposed to address the problems of monocultural farming. The most prominent policy proposals for addressing the challenge of climate change in the United States would simply pay farmers to sequester soil carbon. There are no requirements that carbon be sequestered in humus or other stable forms necessary to mitigate long-term climate change, something that would require biologically active and healthy soils. In addition, such policies would not address agricultural emissions of other GHGs or the other negative environmental and social impacts of industrial agriculture. Carbon markets or emission trading also has been proposed as a means of incentivizing carbon sequestration by farmers (Environmental Defense Fund 2018). Both approaches have encountered problems in quantifying carbon sequestered and enforcing government requirements or offset agreements (Song and Moura 2019). Perhaps most important, by relying on economic incentives rather than regulations, both carbon payments and carbon trading simply reinforce the economic culture of monofunctional farming, which is the root cause of excess agricultural carbon emissions.

Some current U.S. government farm programs have the potential to be modified and enhanced to incentivize and support regenerative polyfunctional farming rather than extractive monocultural commodity production. The Conservation Stewardship Program offers government payments to farmers for implementing a variety of individual conservation and natural resource protection practices (U.S. Department of Agriculture [USDA] Conservation Stewardship Program n.d.). Examples include reducing soil loss, mitigating impacts of excess water, reducing airborne soil particles and GHG emissions, improving habitat for domestic and wildlife species, and promoting energy efficiencies for on-farm activities. Again, the shortcoming of this program is that it provides economic incentives for implementing specific practices rather than transitioning to regenerative whole-farm systems. Implementation of conservation and stewardship practices may reduce the negative ecological impacts of monocultures but may actually delay the transition from monocultures to polycultures, which is essential for long-run climate change mitigation.

Another U.S. government program with potential for modification and enhancement is the Whole Farm Revenue Protection program (USDA Risk Management Agency n.d.). This program allows farmers to ensure a percentage of historic gross farm revenue, or value of sales, for the whole farming operation rather than requiring farmers to ensure individual crops. Provisions are available for basing ensured revenues on documented farm plans rather than historic performance. Although this program deals with whole farm systems, eligibility does not depend on implementing farming practices for resource conservation or stewardship.

These two programs could be modified and enhanced to incentivize and support farmers who choose to transition from current industrial monocultural farming operations to regenerative polycultural farming systems. Farmers who are willing to commit to developing and implementing regenerative, whole-farm plans could be eligible for government-subsidized whole-farm net revenue insurance to mitigate the risk of their transition (Feldman et al. 2020). Reduced premiums could be available for more diversified farming operations that more effectively and holistically address climate change and other environmental risks. The program could be available also for new farmers who want to start regenerative farms. In this case, the primary incentive would not be economic. The government-subsidized insurance would simply make the transition economically feasible.

None of these programs are currently in place in the United States. The most promising of currently existing government programs for small polycultural farms in the United States and other advanced economies seem to be those that address challenges beyond the farm level—in processing, distribution, and retailing. Many consumers in advanced economies are currently willing to pay significantly higher prices for foods produced by regenerative farmers, but farmers lack an effective means of identifying, connecting with, and getting their products to these potential customers. In addition, many more consumers prefer organic and other alternatives to industrially produced foods but cannot afford the high prices for these products in most retail food stores.

The current agri-food marketing system is designed to accommodate industrial production: large-scale, specialized production and mass distribution. This system simply cannot accommodate the diversity of products supplied by individual small, polycultural farms without charging exorbitant prices for processing and distribution. Many smaller diversified operations are currently organizing and operating "food hubs," which allow farmers to pool or combine their production to provide the quantities needed to accommodate large-scale processing and distribution. However, collectives made up of many smaller operations are invariably less economically efficient than large specialized operations, leaving food hubs unable to compete economically. Food hubs have to find and connect with customers who share the values of farmers who choose to support small, polycultural farming operations for noneconomic reasons.

In the absence of major changes in farm policies, the future of small, polycultural farms ultimately depends on their ability to increase the economic efficiency with which they are able to connect with customers who share their ecological and social values, particularly in local communities. Changes in retailing, including food retailing, will create new opportunities for local, community-based food systems. For example, marketing via the Internet allows local food networks to bypass the current industrial system. Conventional food retailers, including mainstream supermarkets, are also exploring online marketing options. However, electronic aggregation and distribution, particularly for fresh, minimally processed foods, might be done more economically locally or bioregionally rather than nationally or globally. The most promising *current* government programs in advanced economies are those providing incentives and support for agroecologically sound, local community-based food systems.

Country Cases

United States: 10 Cents a Meal Program—Incentivizing Local Food Procurement

The robust farm-to-school movement in the United States is a ground source of new policies in support of polyfunctional agriculture, including smaller locally based family farms. The 2015 Farm to School Census found that 42 percent of U.S. schools participate in farm-to-school activities, from school gardens to local food purchasing (USDA Farm to School Census n.d.). Forty-six states had adopted supportive legislation. The farm-to-school movement builds on strong interest in having children learn where food comes from and appreciate the taste, variety, and nutrient density of foods grown closer to home. It also builds on public interest in keeping nearby farm families as neighbors, community-based businesses, and stewards of the land.

This case study describes Michigan's 10 Cents a Meal for School Kids & Farms program. 10 Cents is a state-funded pilot program providing schools with match incentive funding up to 10 cents per meal to purchase and serve Michigan-grown fruits, vegetables, and legumes. It is among the first state legislative efforts to back with dedicated funding, farm-to-school's primary objectives of improving children's health and farmers' livelihoods. Three other states (Oregon, New York, New Mexico) and Washington, D.C. had similar programs when Michigan's started in the 2016–2017 school year. 10 Cents has had significant farm-level impact, including development of new market infrastructure that accommodates and supports small polyfunctional farms.

The program targets tight school food budgets. Through federal child nutrition programs, U.S. schools have only about US$1 to US$1.20 per meal to spend, and, of that, only about 20 to 30 cents for fruits and vegetables. 10 Cents also works to ensure change at the farm level by specifying farm-gate or close to farm-gate products and by requiring procurement accounting. Specifically, 10 Cents is restricted to fresh and minimally processed Michigan fruits, vegetables, and dry beans. It also requires schools that receive 10 Cents matching grants to submit invoices that specify the name and location of Michigan suppliers.

In its third pilot year, 2018–2019, 10 Cents covered fifty-seven Michigan school districts, or roughly 10 percent of the total, reaching 135,000 school children in twenty-seven counties. Matching grant funding of US$493,500 in 2018–2019 effectively put a total of twice that, or nearly US$1 million, into local economies. The direct spending in the third year benefited 143 farms located in thirty-eight of Michigan's eighty-seven counties. It also supported twenty additional Michigan-based businesses that provide essential market infrastructure, such as food hubs, processors, and distributors. Food hubs are a new market intermediary, emerging in response to demand for greater trust and transparency in the supply chain (Colasanti et al. 2018). Food hubs provide aggregation and marketing services for source-identified products, particularly local and regional farm suppliers.

The Michigan state budget for 2021 provided $2 million for 10 Cents a Meal, up from $575,000 in 2019–2020. Schools all across the state, from Detroit to the Upper Peninsula, now are eligible to apply for the grant funds. Sponsors of early childhood education centers also can apply for the first time.

Annual reports, case studies, and news available on the program website document progress, perspectives, and outcomes (Groundwork Center for Resilient Communities n.d.). The program's effectiveness is demonstrated in stories that highlight shifts in eating habits and in local farm opportunity. Startling to many, for example, is the increase in school lunch participation and the reduction in cafeteria food waste that occurs when fresher, tastier local varieties are on offer. One district reported a 60 percent increase in high school students eating in the lunchroom. The following school food service director comment is common: "There is reduced food waste, with an increase in student consumption of fruits and vegetables during lunch. This is noticed not only by the lunchroom aides and cooks but by the custodial staff. They literally grab my arm, walk me to the trash, and show me how much food is not wasted anymore."

On the farm and infrastructure side, the story is about increased sales, market access, and security. Michigan Farm to Freezer, for example, purchases from local farms, small and large. It started with farm-to-school sales and has grown with the flexibility that 10 Cents provides school food service buyers. Schools are also turning to regional food hubs serving smaller farms for local products. As one food service director explains, "We are committing to buying apple slices from (the local food hub), and they are investing in a machine to do more sliced apples in bulk." Cooperatives are also forming, such as twelve growers in four counties now processing fresh vegetables largely for school markets. For smaller diversified growers, local wholesale orders help balance income streams from farmers' markets and community-supported agriculture box subscriptions. According to one 20-acre diversified vegetable operation, "The 10 Cents program has added reassurance to grow our business through loans for the building of a new barn and purchasing of more efficient equipment."

10 Cents is a food system–building policy, providing fresh and healthy local options and promoting the development of polyfunctional farms and the market infrastructure they need.

Sweden: "REKO-Ring"—Selling Food from Car Trunks

More and more Nordics are getting their food from the car trunk of a local farmer. *REKO* stands for *rejäl konsumtion*, or "fair consumption," and is a distribution model for direct sales of local food without intermediaries. REKO operates through closed Facebook groups and has become pivotal for Nordic polyfunctional farmers.

REKOs are co-created through the voluntarily work of food producers and consumers. Their success lies in administrative and logistical simplicity.

Initiators invite other interested parties to a first meeting where visions are defined and aligned, a Facebook page is set up, and page administrators are appointed. Additional producers and consumers are invited to join the Facebook group, a time and place is set for pickup, producers post their offerings on the group wall, and consumers make their orders in the comment field and pay up front, often using mobile payment systems. Parking lots are common pickup spots. Delivery takes place every week or every second week, depending on the size of the REKO.

REKOs started in Finland in 2013 and can now be found in Sweden, Denmark, Italy, South Africa, Canada, Ireland, and Iceland. The popular movement has gained public traction, and the governments of Sweden, Finland, and Norway have commissioned organizations to facilitate the establishment of REKOs. In 2017, the Swedish Rural Economy and Agricultural Societies were contracted to facilitate the establishment of REKOs by offering regulatory assistance and graphic material and to map the expansion of REKOs across the country (SREAS n.d.-b). Importantly, the societies do not administer REKOs. Indeed, the strength of the REKOs is that they emerge from local collaborations to meet local needs and conditions. The societies are currently producing a report to identify possible public support functions beyond the end of their commission in 2020. Similar public–private collaborations exist in Finland and Norway, where Finnish EKOnu and the Norwegian Farmers and Smallholders Union receive public funding to assist the growing REKO network (Norwegian Farmers and Smallholders Union 2018; EkOnu n.d.).

Another crucial form of public support given to Nordic REKOs is regulatory exceptions. In Sweden, the advance payment scheme means that, in a legal sense, REKOs do not exist, and therefore public vendor permits are not needed. The absence of requirement for a legal permit or permission to operate opens the way for broad, flexible participation. In addition, very small operations that sell on an occasional basis need not be registered with a municipal control authority and are exempt from paying the annual inspection fees, which can be large for a small operation. All REKO producers are responsible for the quality and safety of their products and for paying sales taxes; REKOs operate on collective trust. The open participation reduces the risk of misuse by producers and consumers alike.

There are currently more than 180 REKOs in Finland, 150 in Sweden, and 80 in Norway. The REKO in Trondheim, Norway is the largest in the world with more than 31,000 members. There are no official sale statistics, but some Swedish REKOs self-report sales of $US10,000 (SEK100,000) per pickup occasion. In Finland, yearly total revenues are estimated at $US30,000,000

(SEK300 million) (SREAS n.d.-a). The REKO distribution model is an important alternative market that allows established smallholders to make investments and new ones to enter into business.

Every REKO group has its own guiding principles and decides what can and cannot be sold. However, there is a common code of conduct across all REKOs: Only food from one's own production can be sold, no middlemen are allowed, all purchases are preordered and are business arrangements between one buyer and one seller, REKO memberships are free, and participants interact with honesty and respect. Similarly, what is to be considered local food is a question for the REKO members. Some REKOs define *local* as anything produced within the municipality's borders, and others apply the concept of food miles. Ultimately, the boundaries are determined by local demographic and geographic conditions: Densely populated Stockholm currently hosts ten REKOs, whereas in the sparsely populated Swedish North, one REKO often covers two or more municipalities. However, it is important to note that there is nothing inherently sustainable about local food; sustainable practices must be followed in order for REKO food to have a positive impact on food consumption. There are no official requirements that the products be produced by organic and diversified smallholders, but almost without exception, these are the characteristics of producers that participate in REKOs.

For producers, REKOs are a better economic alternative than farmers' markets, which are both time consuming and logistically challenging because sales are hard to predict. REKO markets also encourage capacity-building collaboration between producers. Neighboring farms often coordinate logistics, taking turns to collect and deliver goods to the delivery point. This saves time and money compared with conventional distribution options that often charge extra for smaller loads. REKOs also enable producers to build personal relationships with their consumers, necessary to communicate the additional social and ecological values of their products.

For consumers, REKOs offer products from multiple farms on a single online platform, making it more convenient than visiting individual farm shops. The food prices are largely comparable to supermarket prices; instances of higher REKO prices reflect the fact that smaller-scale production tends to have a higher cost of production per unit. The REKO offerings are determined by local supply and demand, retaining most wanted products and vetting out unwanted products. The supply varies with season, but meat, wild game, dairy, honey, vegetables, and baked goods are generally staples, along with eggs. The Swedish Rural and Agricultural Economy Societies note that if there are eggs for sale, the REKO is likely to be successful. On average, each REKO consists of thirty producers, of which half make product offerings on each pickup occasion.

Other benefits of Nordic car trunk food shopping include less packaging and less transportation. The preorder system also precludes impulse purchases, which encourages consumers to plan ahead and helps reduce food waste. Finally, many consumers testify that joining a REKO has introduced them to new and forgotten local specialties, expanding and enriching their culinary landscapes.

Conclusions

Diversified, polycultural farms have the capacity to restore and regenerate soil health and productivity by transforming agricultural wastes into productive inputs while using solar energy to sequester and store atmospheric carbon in biologically healthy soils. A global agriculture made up of small, polycultural farms would be capable of ensuring global food security in the face of inevitable climate change while moving toward carbon-neutral, or even carbon-negative, agricultural systems. In addition, a polyfunctional agri-food system would create new economic opportunities for small, individually owned and operated family farms and thus protect and restore social and economic integrity to rural communities.

The ecological and social integrity of small, polyfunctional farms depends on their adherence to the basic principles of agroecology. Agroecological integrity requires a meaningful sense of the interconnectedness of the well-being of farmers with the ecological health of *their* farm and the socioeconomic well-being of *their* community. The ecological integrity of communities likewise depends on the meaningful sense of being connected with their particular ecological places and the farmers who not only produce their food but also are caretakers of those places. Everything is interconnected, and the integrity of this connectedness depends on a personal sense of caring, sharing, and mutual responsibility.

The current prevalence of monofunctional farming systems is a consequence of applying industrial chemical and biological technologies to farming and decades of government programs that have absorbed the high agronomic and economic risks of large-scale, specialized farming operations. The future of small, polyfunctional farms depends on a fundamental shift in government policies from supporting large, monofunctional farms to incentivizing and supporting a transition to small, polyfunctional farming.

Urban, Vertical, Controlled-Environment Farming

Dickson Despommier and Charles Knirsch

> "The world isn't expanding, so we're going to go vertical simply because of that need."—*Steve Evans*

Over the next forty years farms will have to produce food for about two and a half billion more people, and the challenge of providing enough food for everyone in a sustainable, efficient, and cost-effective way is rising in significance. By minimizing the disrupting effects of climate change on seasonal weather patterns, overcoming transportation challenges, and significantly increasing yields, the emergent trend of vertical farming (VF) could herald the future of food production.

VF is defined as growing a wide variety of edible plants inside a multistory building (Despommier 2010).[1] This type of farming has many advantages. First, it optimizes space and reduces the carbon footprint and costs of transportation when compared with a conventional crop farm, because it can be located on a far smaller site and much closer to an established urban area. As the world population is urbanizing fast, this helps solve the problem of the lack of suitable soils in close proximity to rapidly expanding areas. Second, the process of crop production is insulated from seasonal weather patterns that are highly susceptible to disruption as a result of our changing climate. On a vertical farm, lighting, water, and temperature can all be optimized to remove climatic risks and increase production rates, allowing yields up to 100 times greater than standard yields of conventional agriculture.[2] Typically, soil is removed altogether, and crops are grown on membranes where they are sprayed with nutrient-rich solutions. Third, the use of a controlled environment eliminates the need for herbicides while reducing the losses from birds and insects that must be factored in on conventional farms.

Urgently Needed

The growth of the indoor urban farming industry, also dubbed controlled-environment agriculture (CEA), is being driven by science-based predictions from the National Aeronautics and Space Administration (NASA), the National Oceanic and Atmospheric Administration, the U.S. Environmental

Protection Agency, the USDA, and the World Health Organization, of the negative effects rapid climate change (RCC) over the next twenty-five years will have on outdoor agricultural industries. Outdoor crop failures due to drought, floods, and insect pests and increases in the frequency of outbreaks of foodborne illnesses have also contributed to the rise in interest in CEA at the commercial level as an alternative to traditional farming.

If RCC continues at its current rate, within the next twenty-five to fifty years outdoor agriculture will suffer catastrophic losses of essential crops and will be unable to supply enough food for the current population base of 7.8 billion people. Because our population will undoubtedly increase over that same time period, RCC has the potential to reduce the human population by starvation back to numbers well below 7 billion people. In other words, some 3 billion people may perish as the direct result of not having enough food to sustain their lives. Armed conflicts at the global level have arisen in the past over just such a situation and will predictably do so again if nothing is done to improve our failing food systems.

The challenges to make CEA common in all urban centers include political acceptance of the fact that urban agriculture is here to stay and needs the support of government that outdoor farming currently enjoys, acceptance by consumers of the nutritional benefits and safety aspects of crops grown indoors, and wider crop selection of field farming (e.g., root vegetables, vine vegetables, bush fruits). From a business point of view, challenges include the lack of technological certainty, because technology is evolving fast; the timing of returns, because vertical farming does not fit the traditional five-year holding period of private equity firms (although this period is lengthening); the significant upfront capital needs of vertical farms; and the size of the market, which, given the higher price of the product at present, is still in its infancy and does not always justify decisions to alter current purchasing programs by domestic supermarkets.[3]

Water- and Air-Based CEA Technologies

There are many technologies for growing food crops indoors, but the most popular ones use hydroponic and aeroponic technologies. Neither requires the use of soil, and both use far less water and nutrients (i.e., fertilizer) than outdoor traditional farming.

Hydroponics was first popularized by Dr. William Gericke at U.C.

Berkeley in the 1940s and has been increasing in popularity ever since. This method is carried out in two common configurations. The first is called nutrient film technology: The roots of the plants are covered with a thin layer of water that contains dissolved nutrients. The racks of plants are positioned on scaffolding that is slightly tilted, allowing gravity to feed the growing solution from rack to rack. Hydroponics uses much less water (70 percent or more) than traditional farming and has been used extensively in commercial vertical farms (e.g., see Green Sense Farms, Portage, Indiana).

In the 1980s, NASA commissioned studies carried out by Dr. Richard Stoner III and colleagues in Colorado, resulting in the invention of a second way of growing plants called aeroponics. Aeroponics uses specially constructed growing racks in which the plants' roots hang down in the air inside an airtight chamber. The nutrient solution is then sprayed inside the chamber, creating a mist. The roots remain well aerated while absorbing water and nutrients. Many crop species grown aeroponically mature faster than under hydroponic methods. Aeroponic systems use about 70–80 percent less water than hydroponic methods, making aeroponics the method of choice over the last several years in newly established vertical farms (e.g., see Aerofarms, Newark, New Jersey). Some newly designed aeroponic systems consist of tall, flat racks on the sides of which the plants grow (e.g., see Plenty, San Francisco, California). Another popular aeroponic system consists of tall plastic tubes (grow towers). The sides have ports cut out at regular intervals, allowing placement of plants. The roots hang inside the tube. A nutrient spray is injected into the tube, forming a mist that brings water and nutrients to the root systems of the plants (e.g., see Tower Gardens).

In both hydroponic and aeroponic facilities, the use of LED grow lights has assumed prominence over the last few years, as that technology has matured. LED lights are now cheap and long-lived, making them the ideal solution to continuous growing inside a multistory building. In many cases, the vertical farm has no windows.

Environmental Benefits of Vertical Farms

Thanks to a modern root-misting system, vertical farms use up to 95 percent less water than conventional field farms, which withdraw about three quarters of all available freshwater on the planet each year and have already contaminated with chemical and biological discharges 70 percent of all existing freshwater. Although saving water for farming is a global challenge, this new way of quasi-waterless farming is particularly helpful for countries with significant water shortages as part of their climate.[4]

Vertical farming also uses no soil and, if used at scale, can potentially reduce stress on the rural landscape, including less deforestation, and regenerate the third of Earth's soil that has been degraded through conventional agriculture. For example, establishing a widespread functional urban agricultural system includes the possibility of integrating vertical farming into all newly constructed buildings, regardless of their main function in the built environment (allowing the possibility of a city to feed all its inhabitants), rewilding large swathes of the rural landscape as outdoor farming becomes reduced in footprint, and reducing atmospheric carbon dioxide levels as forests replace abandoned farmland. In addition, vertical farming uses no pesticides and no herbicides, which makes their products naturally organic.

In addition, plants are grown in reusable cloth made from recycled plastic. And although this type of farming uses artificial lighting instead of sun, because the spectrum of light used to grow plants is reduced and LED lighting is used, the carbon footprint of artificial illumination is minimal. The sophisticated climate control system cuts the growing cycle of plants in half, so crops can be grown year-round but with a much smaller impact on the environment than conventional farming. Finally, vertical farming helps cut GHGs by reducing the distances over which food must be transported for final consumption.

Economic Benefits of Vertical Farms

The idea of vertical farming has finally taken root, and vertical farms have sprouted all over the world, from North America to Europe to Asia, promising increasing market share and profits. This reflects the fact that through vertical farming, farmers can meet most of the needs of today's consumer, which include competitively priced and locally grown produce that tastes fresh, is nutritious, and is available year-round at the same location where other shopping is currently done. And although the costs per pound of produce in vertical farms still exceed those of conventional farms, vertical farms are getting competitive (Tasgal 2019). Efficient deployment of additional technology and capital into each of these growing structures will allow the farms to get ever closer to fulfilling consumer demands.

The most recent economic surveys, especially those focused on the newly established vertical farming industry, predict that CEA will become a multi–billion-dollar enterprise within the next five to ten years, and Bloomberg has forecast that the vertical farming market will be worth US$16 billion globally by 2025. This means more jobs (including jobs not lost), new job descriptions, less concentration in the food market, a dramatic reduction in urban food deserts, and, potentially, a sharp reduction in teenage obesity due to the ready availability of highly nutritious, less fattening food choices, with all the ensuing economic gains described by Batini and Fontana in chapter 5 of this book.

Policies to Support Vertical Farming

Support of vertical farming can be achieved by repurposing existing support schemes for adaptive and sustainable farming.

In the United States, for example, a large portion of agriculture funding today goes to insurance policies protecting farmers from poor yields or adverse weather events that will increase as RCC makes previously fertile land marginally productive. A portion of these insurance funds could be productively invested in research on optimizing indoor growth in vertical farms and converting outdoor farmland to sustainably managed forests that will be needed to scale up the supply of the cross-laminated wood production industry. Other funds could be earmarked within existing funding programs dedicated to agricultural innovation. The USDA has established the Office of Urban Agriculture and Innovative Production, funded with US$5 million added to the 2018 Farm Bill. In addition, it also established the Urban, Indoor, and Other Emerging Agriculture Production Research, Education, and Extension Initiative, which will receive US$4 million per year until 2023. It authorizes competitive research and extension grants to support research, education, and extension activities for the purpose of facilitating the spread of urban, indoor, and other emerging agricultural production. The bill requires the Secretary of Agriculture to conduct a census of urban, indoor, and other emerging agricultural production.

Similarly, in the United Kingdom, a strategic policy for 2019–2020 funds focuses on integrated support of land management, the environment, and the interests of land managers and farmers. This also includes reallocation of a subsidy system based on total amount of land farmed to reward work toward integration activities in order to grow high-quality, sustainable food with environmental benefits. In a country with limited land availability and large urban population centers, this is a perfect opportunity to transition to a system of local food production based on vertical farming. And in Canada, US$134.4 million has been allocated in the national food policy to address a number of priority areas that a CEA plan would be able to address, including reducing food waste and providing sustainable food sources closer to the remote northern populations.[5] This focus on community-driven projects is in turn dependent on expertise in CEA to promote recognition that CEA can provide a solution at the local level. There is US$15 million in new funding in the Canadian bill for northern and isolated communities to buy equipment such as greenhouses and support training programs for indigenous local agriculture projects.

Funding to stimulate vertical farming as part of existing agriculture policies can go a long way. This funding should be accompanied by bold measures to initiate new educational programs aimed at creating a substantial pool of graduates knowledgeable in CEA (e.g., management, marketing, sales, and technical fields such as LED lighting, indoor growing methods, plant nutrition, and optimizing crop diversity in CEA facilities). Research and training are especially needed for work on higher-efficiency grow lights, closed-loop solar grid conversion to grow lights, efficiency of plant strain selection, pesticide-free strains, and plants adapted to decreased growing times, to increase indoor crops with more production cycles. Also, regulatory reform can go a long way in sustaining the growth of a market for vertically farmed products by, for example, ensuring proper labeling of products grown from CEA, and, on the training front, allowing the use of mixed-use buildings containing vertical farms for integrated culinary schools.

Country Cases

Japan

On March 11, 2011, a magnitude 9 earthquake changed forever the way Japan ensures that its citizens have enough to eat. The tsunami that rapidly followed that event trashed 5 percent of Japan's farmland, drowning the agricultural landscape of Sendai and contaminating the soil with saltwater. The next week, the nearby Daiichi nuclear reactor went critical, exploding and contaminating the surrounding area with radioactivity that forever eliminated the surrounding land as a potential source of food crops. The government rapidly enlisted numerous academic and industrial institutions in a crash program to establish a CEA-based food supply. Toshiba, Panasonic, Fujitsu, Mirai, Sony,

Mitsubishi, and Chiba University, to name a few of the more prominent players, responded to the emergency by quickly establishing numerous growing facilities (plant factories, or vertical farms) in various locations throughout Japan to produce mainly leafy green vegetables. As of 2019, there were an estimated 500 such facilities in operation. Not all of them succeeded, however, and the main reason for failure was the lack of experienced personnel at all levels. One of the most successful vertical farms is Spread. Its Techno Farm produces more than 30,000 heads of lettuce per day by using hydroponics and LED grow lights.

Singapore

The island country of Singapore is home to thirty-four commercial vertical farms. The government supports an expansion of the sector, especially after witnessing the challenges posed by the global food supply during the COVID-19 pandemic. Thus, the Singapore Food Agency (SFA) launched a 30x30 Express Grant in early 2020. The grant will sustain the country's agri-food industry and help speed up the increase in local production, with the goal of meeting 30 percent of Singapore's nutritional needs with food produced locally by 2030. Singapore aims to achieve food sovereignty within the next ten years.

United States

The vertical farm industry in the United States is in the middle of a strong growth phase, having started slowly some six to eight years ago. Existing vertical farm companies are currently in full production mode. Most of them grow leafy green vegetables of various kinds with LED grow lights. Several vertical farms (Aerofarms, Plenty, Green Sense Farms, Vertical Harvest) are profitable and are building new facilities in various cities in the United States. In contrast, several vertical farm companies have closed their doors, including FarmedHere in Bedford Park, Illinois, and Metropolitan Farms in Philadelphia.

Conclusions

As agrotechnology advances rapidly, consumers will no longer have their produce shipped months in advance and from thousands of miles away. Vertical farming uses a fraction of resources of conventional farming and allows farmers to grow locally and bring fresh produce to the mass market within days or even hours, reducing the carbon footprint associated with transporting food. Additionally, as climate change brings dramatic weather changes, CEA allows constant conditions regardless of weather patterns. VF thus promises dramatic environmental and economic gains, and policy should incentivize vertical farms to produce increasing shares of produce both domestically and across the world.

Regenerative Ocean Farming

Nicoletta Batini and Bren Smith

> "We must plant the sea and herd its animals using the sea as farmers instead of hunters. That is what civilization is all about—farming replacing hunting."—*Jacques-Yves Cousteau*

The sea has provided food to humans for thousands of years, and currently about 3 billion people around the world rely on seafood as their primary source of protein. However, overfishing with industrial methods has brought the planet's oceans to the brink of ecological collapse (see chapter 9). Estimates based on a multiyear study of prevailing fishing trends indicate that without changes, the world will run out of wild-caught seafood by 2048 (Worm et al. 2006).

At the same time, aquaculture—the practice of breeding fish at sea in fish farms, or aquafarms—has proven to be environmentally unsustainable because these farms tend to discharge waste, pesticides, and other chemicals directly into ecologically fragile coastal waters, destroying local ecosystems. Waste from the excessive number of fish can create huge blankets of green slime on the water's surface, depleting oxygen and killing much of the life in the water. These developments threaten seafood as a way to feed the world's growing population.

Stressed Oceans

Besides being a pillar of human nutrition, oceans are vital to Earth's climate because they sequester vast amounts of GHGs (see chapter 9). However, since the beginning of the Industrial Revolution, the level of carbon dioxide in the atmosphere, and hence in the ocean's surface waters, has increased by almost 30 percent. In response, those surface waters have become steadily more acidic, and structures made of calcium carbonate, such as shellfish and coral reefs, have begun to dissolve, gradually disrupting the functioning of the marine food supply chain.

The ocean has also become warmer as a result of decades of increasing anthropogenic GHG emissions. This warming means the oceans can absorb less CO_2 and are progressively less hospitable for many marine species, threatening the existence of all ocean life.

Healing the Oceans through Farming

Regenerative ocean farms (ROFs) can help address these challenges. ROFs grow shellfish, notably scallops, mussels, oysters, and clams, and seaweed through low-cost underwater gardens of a few acres each.[6] In this sense, ROFs replicate the concept of VF underwater but without the need for human-provided nutrients, because seaweeds and shellfish do not need to be fed; they grow with just sunlight and the nutrients and plankton already in seawater.

Environmental Benefits of Regenerative Ocean Farming

Like vertical farms on land, ROFs can solve the problem of resource scarcity and the high carbon footprint of conventional farming because they need no input and produce high yields in little space. In addition, ROFs have the ability to restore ecosystems in that they act as carbon and nitrogen sinks. Shellfish in these farms filter nitrogen and carbon out of the water column while providing vital habitats for hundreds of species. Similarly, seaweed is able to capture and store five times more carbon dioxide than trees, reducing acidification and boosting the ocean's GHG sequestration capacities. Farming seaweed for the purpose of climate mitigation, a natural geoengineering technique known as ocean macroalgal afforestation, shows tremendous promise. If less than 10 percent of the oceans were to be covered in seaweed farms, the farmed seaweed could produce enough biofuel to replace all of today's fossil fuel use while removing 53 billion tons of CO_2 per year from the atmosphere, restoring preindustrial levels (N'Yeurt et al. 2012).[7]

In terms of food production, ROFs need no inputs—no feeds, no fertilizers, no freshwater—making them the most sustainable form of food production on Earth. And like vertical farms on land, ROFs are much more productive than conventional farms. Farming less than 5 percent of U.S. seawaters—the equivalent of the size of Washington State—through a network of small underwater farms could feed the planet (Smith 2019).[8] When it comes to human diets and health, seaweeds, also known as sea vegetables, are a high-nutrient "superfood" rich in protein, iodine, and other minerals. Seaweed can also be beneficial if fed to animals; if used as ruminant forage, seaweed can reduce methane output from cattle by 50 to 99 percent depending on the type of seaweed (Kinley et al. 2016). If adopted globally, this could decrease yearly global GHG emissions by up to 15 percent.

Economic Benefits of Regenerative Ocean Farming

Ocean farming is a trade both old and new. Mussel cultivation can be traced to the thirteenth century, when an Irishman shipwrecked on the west coast of France tried to catch birds by tying nets to tall stakes and realized that the stakes were quickly covered with mussel seed. Centuries later, the U.S. coastlines are dotted with companies such as Bang's Island Mussels in Maine, Catalina Ranch in California, and American Mussel in Rhode Island, which keep the tradition alive through relentless innovation.

Today, the global market potential of ROFs is enormous because products from this type of sea polyculture can be sold as human food, as animal feed, as biofuels, and as fertilizers.

Globally, about 12 million tons of seaweed is grown and harvested annually, about three quarters of which comes from China. The current market value of the global crop is between US$5 and US$5.6 billion, of which US$5 billion comes from sale for human consumption. Production is expanding very rapidly, however.

Crucially, ROFs can create millions of blue-economy jobs. Climate change is an existential crisis for fishing communities. The ROF model is an opportunity for traditional ocean farmers (and fishers and others) to diversify their operations and income by using the entire water column to layer multiple, restorative species such as seaweed and shellfish on one farm. According to the World Bank, farming seaweed in 5 percent of U.S. waters, for example, has the potential to create 50 million jobs—the biggest job creator since World War II (World Bank Group 2016).

Policies to Support Regenerative Ocean Farming

Several economic policies and structural reforms can help promote eco-friendly ocean farming. The main ones, discussed by Smith et al. (2019) for the case of the United States, apply to other country cases as well, *mutatis mutandis*. Principal policies involve national support in the form of new subsidies or earmarking of existing environmental funds for the creation of a blue carbon fund. This fund would reward ocean farmers for carbon and nitrogen sequestration and include shellfish and seaweed, where possible, in public crop insurance schemes. Simplifying the permitting process for ROFs—often the main roadblock for seaweed and shellfish entrepreneurs—would also go a long way in unleashing the potential of this nascent but important industry.

Country Case: United States

Thimble Island Ocean Farm is one of the first ROFs in the United States—indeed, in the world. Located in Long Island Sound, Connecticut, this shellfish and seaweed farm was transformed into an incubator for sustainable food production, ocean conservation, and economic development. The farm's innovative vertical underwater gardening technique has made high yields on minimal acreage a reality while restoring ecosystems. It addition to food, fertilizer, and animal feed, the farm is creating bioplastics as an alternative to plastic straws. Thimble Island Farm now provides a blueprint for a new ocean economy. The NGO GreenWave replicates the Thimble Island Ocean Farming model by training and supporting regenerative ocean farmers throughout New England, California, New York, the Pacific Northwest, and Alaska.

Alternative Protein Farming

Bruce Friedrich and Stephen R. Kaufman

> "There's no way to produce enough meat for 9 billion people. Yet we can't ask everyone to become vegetarians."—*Bill Gates*

Widespread adoption of plant-based eating is an essential component of any effective strategy to address the growing climate crisis. Health experts and environmentalists have encouraged people to eat little or no meat, but their efforts have not broadly changed food choices. Because people in general want the convenience, feel, and taste of meat, there is a clear need for plant-based foods that retain the appeal of meat while avoiding the environmental (as well as animal welfare and human health) consequences of animal agriculture.

The Problem with Meat from Animals

As discussed by Batini and Pointereau in chapter 2, raising animals for food is one of the top contributors to the most severe environmental problems plaguing us, including water pollution, desertification, deforestation, biodiversity loss, and, perhaps most importantly, climate change (Bland 2012). A main reason is that most of the calories and protein fed to farmed animals is not converted to edible meat. Instead, they are used by the animals to live and to grow bones, blood, and other body parts that are not consumed.

It is difficult to substantially modify most of the leading contributors to GHG emissions, such as transportation, building materials, and climate control in homes and offices. However, it is easy for people to eat more plant foods and substantially reduce their individual carbon footprints.

Human and Animal Welfare Considerations

Animal advocates have documented the substantial suffering animals experience on concentrated animal feeding operations, also known as factory farms. Any moral code worthy of the term *moral* must condemn causing immense, unnecessary suffering and death to innocent individuals.

The human health costs of contemporary animal agriculture are also high, as documented in chapter 5. Finally, animal agriculture threatens food security. Worldwide, more than a third of all cultivated crops are fed to animals, driving up the cost of food, reducing access to food among poor people, and contributing to world hunger and malnutrition—a problem that is likely to worsen with population growth and projected dietary shifts (see chapter 2).

Alternative Protein Farming 1: Plant-Based Meat

Responding to consumer demands for safer, healthier, and more humane food, food manufacturers have designed a wide range of plant-based products to replicate the taste and texture of conventional meat, such as Tofurky deli slices,

Beyond Meat pork and beef, Field Roast Sausages, and the Impossible Burger (now sold at Burger King). These processed foods may not be quite as nutritious as whole-plant foods, although it is worth noting that their protein is more bioavailable than the protein in whole-plant foods. Also, they contain colon-friendly fiber that animal meat lacks and do not have any of the artery-clogging cholesterol found in animal meats. They also include complex carbohydrates, which animal meats lack, and they are generally lower in saturated fat. For example, Impossible Foods's plant-based sausage and pork have no cholesterol and, compared with the analogous animal meats, 50–70 percent more protein as a percentage of calories, less than half the total fat, and significantly less saturated fat. One of the most popular plant-based meats is the Beyond Meat "Beyond Burger," which many people have found cooks, feels, and tastes similar to a hamburger.

Alternative Protein Farming 2: Cultivated Meat

Another exciting technology is cultivated meat, a longstanding dream that is moving quickly toward reality. In 1931, Winston Churchill said, "We shall escape the absurdity of growing a whole chicken in order to eat the breast or wing, by growing these parts separately under a suitable medium" (Churchill 1931). Cardiologist Uma Valeti is bringing this vision to reality. In 2005, using stem cells to repair damaged heart tissue, Dr. Valenti wondered whether the same process could be used to grow meat in the laboratory (Bercovici 2017). In 2015, he launched Memphis Meats around the concept of growing meat directly from animal cells.

Cultivating meat from cells will diversify and bolster the protein supply by producing meat in a new way. Rather than raising and slaughtering animals, a new generation of "ranchers" will grow meat in a tank called a cultivator, which reproduces the biological process that happens inside an animal. It provides the basic elements needed to build muscle: water, proteins, carbohydrates, fats, vitamins, and minerals. The result is meat, identical to conventional meat at the cellular level, meaning it looks, tastes, and cooks the same. Missing are the potentially harmful hormones, antibiotics, and other additives used to make animals grow faster. Scientists can even design cultivated meat to be leaner and healthier, with less saturated fat and cholesterol.

Memphis Meats has been a leader in driving down the cost of producing cultivated meat. Bill Gates, Richard Branson, and venture capital guru Donald Fries are investors. And the meat industry also sees the future. Major meat conglomerates Cargill (the largest private company in the United States) and Tyson Foods have invested in Memphis Meats.

Environmental Benefits of Alternative Protein Farming

Replacing animal products with alternative protein products such as plant-based meat or cultivated meat promises enormous environmental benefits. Most plant-based meat is produced from soy and other legumes that have an extremely small carbon footprint relative to real meat (see chapter 2). Likewise, cultivated meat is a form of cellular agriculture that has been predicted to generate 74–87 percent less GHGs, to cause 94 percent less nutrient pollution, and to use 95 percent less land.[9]

Economic Benefits of Alternative Protein Farming

As discussed in Batini (2019, 25), "the potential for rapid scale up and cost reduction in the production of plant-based and cultivated meat, alongside the clear benefits from a prospective health, environmental, cultural, and economic impact's perspective, makes an attractive case for investment." This prediction is justified by what's actually happening: Impossible Foods has attracted US$770 million in investments since its founding in 2011, most recently US$300 million in May 2019. Beyond Meat follows with US$483 million in disclosed funding to date, including more than US$250 million through a 2019 initial public offering. On the cultivated meat side, Memphis Meats has raised roughly US$185 million across three rounds of funding, including a US$163-million Series B in early 2020. Investors have included massive meat conglomerates such as Tyson Foods and Cargill, as well as Singaporean sovereign wealth fund Temasek and Norwest, the venture capital company funded by Wells Fargo bank. Because of his concern for the climate, Bill Gates is an investor in Beyond Meat, Impossible Foods, and Memphis Meats. A recent study has found that three of the most populous countries in the world display high levels of acceptance of these products, with higher levels of acceptance in China (62 percent) and India (63 percent) than in the United States (33 percent) (Bryant et al. 2019).

Policies to Support Alternative Protein Farming

Plant-based and cultivated meat will be widely adopted only if they taste the same or better and cost the same or less. We now have plant-based hamburgers and sausage that taste similar to conventional animal meat, but they are still more expensive and consequently represent a small fraction of the "meat" market. With research and development, they can become tastier, more nutritious, and less costly.

Demonstrating the need for research support, Beyond Meat and Impossible Foods have been operational for only a few years, and together they have probably invested less than US$150 million into research and development.

On the cultivated meat side, although the cost of production has plummeted since the US$300,000 hamburger of August 2013, there is currently no infrastructure for the production of cultivated meat, and many basic scientific questions remain unanswered. Private investments in cultivated meat, which has been increasing quite rapidly, totaled US$73.3 million by the end of 2018 (Good Food Institute 2019).

There are good reasons for private investors to take interest. Dr. Liz Specht's analysis indicates that cultivated meat can eventually reach price parity with industrial animal meat (Specht 2020). However, because the threats of climate change and antibiotic resistance are imminent, we need government support for research and development to hasten the transformation to plant-based and cultivated meats. Even a small fraction of the U.S. government's support of agricultural research would almost certainly have tangible results. For plant-based meats, government grants could help develop protein-rich crop varieties, improve protein extraction methods, and optimize plant-based manufacturing methods.

For cultivated meat, federal grants could help scientists discover the best cell lines, optimize culture media, explore novel methods of tissue scaffolding, and improve cultivator (bioreactor) designs (Swartz 2019). If governments invested in plant-based meat and cultivated meat research centers at universities such as MIT and Stanford, it would be a game changer. Importantly, this information would be available to everyone, permitting smaller companies to enter the race to develop a wide range of plant-based and cultivated meats.

The barriers to widespread adoption of plant-based and cultivated meats are not only financial. Producers of animal-based meats, dairy, and eggs, with the assistance of their friends in state legislatures, have sought to prevent producers of plant-based alternatives from using the words *meat*, *milk*, and *eggs* (Selyukh 2019). The reason, they say, is that consumers mistakenly believe that the plant foods are actually animal-based. However, even a cursory look at the packaging of these plant-based products makes the source clear. Indeed, most consumers who choose these products do so because they want to avoid the animal-derived products for health, animal welfare, environmental, or other reasons.

To meet the environmental and human health challenges ahead, we need governments to be allies in the quest for plant-based and cultured meats. If governments play an appropriate role in research and development, as well as setting standards for food labeling, alternative meats can help protect our fragile environment and promote global health.

References

Altieri, M., C. I. Nicholls, A. Henao, and M. A. Lana. 2015. "Agroecology and the design of climate change-resilient farming systems." *Agroecology Knowledge Hub* 35 no. 3. http://www.fao.org/agroecology/database/detail/en/c/452669/

Anderson, L. S., and F. L. Sinclair. 1993. "Ecological interactions in agroforestry systems." *Agroforestry Abstracts* 6, no. 2: 57–91 and *Forestry Abstracts* 54, no. 6: 489–523. https://assets.publishing.service.gov.uk/media/57a08dcde5274a31e0001a3e/19930665034.pdf

Barrett, C., B. Bellemare, and J. Hou. 2010. "Reconsidering conventional explanations of the inverse productivity-size relationship." *World Development* 38, no. 1: 88–97.

Batini, N. 2019. "Transforming agri-food sectors to mitigate climate change: the role of green finance." *Quarterly Journal of Economic Research* 88, no. 3: 7–42.

Bercovici, J. 2017. "Why this cardiologist is betting that his lab-grown meat startup can solve the global food crisis." *Inc. Magazine*. https://www.inc.com/magazine/201711/jeff-bercovici/memphis-meats-lab-grown-meat-startup.html

Bland, A. 2012. "Is the livestock industry destroying the planet?" https://www.smithsonianmag.com/travel/is-the-livestock-industry-destroying-the-planet-11308007/

Bryant, C., K. Szejda, N. Parkh, V. Desphande, and B. Tse. 2019. "A survey of consumer perceptions of plant-based and clean meat in the USA, India, and China." *Frontiers of Sustainable Food Systems* 3. https://www.frontiersin.org/article/10.3389/fsufs.2019.00011

Cardinale, B. J., J. P. Wright, M. W. Cadotte, I. T. Carroll, A. Hector, D. S. Srivastava, M. Loreau, and J. Weis. 2007. "Impacts of plant diversity on biomass production increase through time because of species complementarity." *PNAS* 104: 18123–8.

Chase, C., K. Delate, M. Liebman, and K. Leibold. 2006. *Economic Analysis of Three Iowa Rotations*. Ames: Iowa State University.

Churchill, W. 1931. "Some election memories." *The Strand Magazine* 81, no. 484 (reprinted in *Popular Mechanics Magazine* [1932] 57, no. 3: 397).

Colasanti, K., J. Hardy, J. Farbman, R. Pirog, J. Fisk, and M. W. Hamm. 2018. *Findings of the 2017 National Food Hub Survey.* East Lansing: Michigan State University Center for Regional Food Systems and The Wallace Center at Winrock International.

De Shutter, O. 2016. As quoted in Andrea Germanos: "'Overwhelming' evidence shows path is clear: it's time to ditch industrial agriculture for good." Commondreams.org, June 2.

Despommier, D. 2010. *The Vertical Farm: Feeding the World in the 21st Century*. New York, N.Y.: Thomas Dunne Books.

EKOnu, n.d. *REKO.* https://www.ekonu.fi/reko-2

Environmental Defense Fund. 2018. *The Worlds Carbon Markets*. New York. https://www.edf.org/worlds-carbon-markets
Feldman, M., J. Ikerd, S. Watkins, C. Mitchell, J. Bowman, and C. R. Ostrander. 2020. *Regenerative Farming and the Green New Deal. Data for Progress.* https://www.dataforprogress.org/memos/regenerative-agriculture-and-the-green-new-deal
Francis, C. A. 1986. *Multiple Cropping Systems.* New York: Macmillan.
Gollin, D. 2018. "Farm size and productivity: lessons from recent literature." FAO, IFAD, ISPC/CGIAR and the World Bank Expert Consultation: Focusing Agricultural and Rural Development Research and Investment on Achieving SDGs 1 and 2. 11 January 2018.
Good Food Institute. 2019. *State of the Industry Report: Cell-Based Meat.* https://www.gfi.org/non-cms-pages/splash-sites/soi-reports/files/SOI-Report-Cell-Based.pdf
Groundwork Center for Resilient Communities. n.d. *Ten Cents a Meal for Michigan's Kids and Farms.* https://www.tencentsmichigan.org
High Level Panel of Experts on Food Security and Nutrition, Committee on Food Security. 2019. "Report on agroecological and other innovative approaches for sustainable agriculture and food systems that enhance food security and nutrition." Food and Agriculture Organization of the United Nations.
Ikerd, J. 2016. "Family farms of North America." Food and Agriculture Organization of the United Nations and the International Policy Centre for Inclusive Growth of the United Nations Development Programme Empowered Lives. Resilient Nations. Working paper no. 152.
Intergovernmental Panel on Climate Change (IPCC). 2019. "Climate change and land." World Meteorological Association and United Nations Environmental Program.
IPES-Food. 2016. "From uniformity to diversity: a paradigm shift from industrial agriculture to diversified agroecological systems." International Panel of Experts on Sustainable Food Systems, lead author E. Frison, lead editor, N. Jacobs. http://www.ipes-food.org/_img/upload/files/UniformityToDiversity_FULL.pdf
Kinley, R. D., R. de Nys, M. J. Vucko, L. Machado, and N. W. Tomkins. 2016. "The red macroalgae *Asparagopsis taxiformis* is a potent natural antimethanogenic that reduces methane production during in vitro fermentation with rumen fluid." *Animal Production Science* 56, no. 3: 282–9.
McIntyre, B. D., H. R. Herren, J. Wakhungu, and R. T. Watson, eds. 2009. *International Assessment of Agricultural Knowledge, Science and Technology for Development (IAASTD): Global Report.* Agriculture at a Crossroads. Washington, D.C.: Island Press.
Norwegian Farmers and Smallholders Union. 2018. *REKO network.* http://www.smabrukarlaget.no/norsk-bonde-og-smabrukarlag/matnyttig/lokalmatringer/reko-network
N'Yeurt, R. A., D. Chynoweth, M. Capron, J. Stewart, and M. Hasan, 2012. "Negative carbon via ocean afforestation." *Process Safety and Environmental Protection* 90: 467–74.
Prieto, I., C. Violle, P. Barre, J. L. Durand, M. Ghesquiere, and I. Litrico. 2015. "Complementary effects of species and genetic diversity on productivity and stability of sown grasslands." *Nature Plants* 2015, no. 1: 15033.
Quendler, E., J. Ikerd, and N. Driouech. 2020. Family farming between its past and potential future with the focus on multifunctionality and sustainability: a critical review. *CAB Reviews; Perspectives in Agriculture, Veterinary Science, Nutrition and Natural Resources* 15, no. 11: 1–17.

Ricciardi, V., N. Ramakutty, Z. Meharabi, L. Jarvis, and B. Chookiling. 2018. "How much of the world's food do smallholders produce?" *Global Food Security* 17: 64–72.

Selyukh, A. 2019. "What gets to be a 'burger'? States restrict labels on plant-based meat." National Public Radio, July 23.

Smith, B. 2019. *Eat Like a Fish*. New York: Knopf.

Smith, B., J. Bowman, and A. E. Johnson. 2019. *Memo: Blue Jobs and the Green New Deal.* https://www.dataforprogress.org/memos/blue-jobs

Song, L., and P. Moura. 2019. *An Even More Inconvenient Truth*. ProPublica.

Specht, L. 2020. "An analysis of culture medium costs and production volumes for cultivated meat." Washington, D.C.: The Good Food Institute.

Swartz, E. 2019. "Meeting the needs of the cell-based meat industry." https://www.gfi.org/images/uploads/2020/02/Cell-Based_Meat_CEP_Oct2019.pdf

Swedish Rural Economy and Agricultural Societies (SREAS). n.d.-a. *Det började I Finland.* https://hushallningssallskapet.se/forskning-utveckling-2/reko/starta-och-driva-reko-ring/det-borjade-i-finland/

———. n.d.-b. *REKO-ringar.* https://hushallningssallskapet.se/forskning-utveckling-2/reko/

Tasgal, P. 2019. "The economics of local vertical and greenhouse farming are getting competitive." *Agritech*, April.

U.S. Department of Agriculture, Farm to School Census. n.d. "Farm to school works!" https://farmtoschoolcensus.fns.usda.gov/

U.S. Department of Agriculture, Natural Resources Conservation Service. n.d. "Conservation Stewardship Program (CSP)." https://www.nrcs.usda.gov/wps/portal/nrcs/main/national/programs/financial/csp/

U.S. Department of Agriculture, Risk Management Agency. n.d. "Whole Farm Revenue Protection (WFRP)." https://www.rma.usda.gov/en/Policy-and-Procedure/Insurance-Plans/Whole-Farm-Revenue-Protection

World Bank Group. 2016. "Seaweed aquaculture for food security, income generation and environmental health in tropical developing countries." http://documents.worldbank.org/curated/en/947831469090666344/pdf/107147-WP-REVISED-Seaweed-Aquaculture-Web.pdf

Worm, B., E. B. Barbier, N. Beaumont, J. E. Duffy, C. Folke, B. S. Halpern, J. B. Jackson, H. K. Lotze, F. Micheli, S. R. Palumbi, E. Sala, K. A. Selkoe, J. J. Stachowicz, R. Watson, et al. 2006. "Impacts of biodiversity loss on ocean ecosystem services." *Science* 314, no. 5800: 787–90.

Wozniacka, G. 2019. "Can regenerative agriculture reverse climate change? Big Food is banking on it." NBC News, *Civil Eats*, October 29.

Endnotes

1. The term *vertical farming* was coined by Despommier. See https://www.newyorker.com/magazine/2017/01/09/the-vertical-farm and Despommier (2010). A single-story building used for the same purpose is called a greenhouse. Growing in a multistory edifice increases the number of plants that can be produced compared to rooftop farms and greenhouses, thereby making it commercially viable. The term *vertical farm* is often

misused, because many grow systems carried out in a single-story building are vertical in configuration. Growing plants vertically rather than horizontally does not qualify it as a vertical farm.

2. For example, in vertical farms such as MIRAI's facility near Tokyo—the world's largest city—are able to generate yields 50–100 times greater than what is possible in conventional crop farms.
3. Even if vertical farm–grown lettuce can be priced profitably at US$2–3 per unit at retail, conventionally grown lettuce can be priced below $1 (Tagsal 2019). Alternatively, conventionally grown lettuce can be priced at US$2 to US$3 per unit at retail and provide a much higher profit margin through the supply chain.
4. For example, Dubai imports most of its produce and has significant water shortages, and shortages are increasing as the planet is warming. Maraas, a lead investor in AeroFarm, the largest vertical farm in the world in terms of annual capacity, is a Dubai-based conglomerate with a goal of improving the city of Dubai.
5. https://ipolitics.ca/2019/03/19/budget-2019-canada-gets-a-national-food-policy/.
6. Bren Smith, GreenWave executive director and owner of Thimble Island Ocean Farm, pioneered the development of regenerative ocean farming.
7. Nine percent of the world's oceans is not a small area. It is equivalent to about four and a half times the area of Australia. But even at smaller scales, kelp farming has the potential to substantially lower atmospheric CO_2, and this realization has had an energizing impact on the research and commercial development of sustainable aquaculture. But kelp farming is not solely about reducing CO_2. In fact, it is being driven, from a commercial perspective, by sustainable production of high-quality protein.
8. A single acre of ocean can produce 25 tons of greens and 250,000 shellfish in five months.
9. https://www.gfi.org/files/sustainability_cultivated_meat.pdf.

PART II

GREENING FOOD DEMAND

CHAPTER 5

Greening Food Demand in Advanced Economies

Nicoletta Batini and Luigi Fontana

> "Healthy citizens are the greatest asset any country can have."—
> *Winston Churchill*

Our current food system is unable to deliver the right quantity or quality of food globally, leaving almost half of humanity chronically malnourished. For billions of people worldwide, food insecurity is an everyday challenge. According to *The State of Food Security and Nutrition in the World*, in 2018 about 820 million people went hungry and a third of all people did not get enough crucial vitamins and minerals, because they ate too little of the right foods. At the same time, 600 million people were classed as obese and 2 billion overweight, because they ate too much of the wrong foods (FAO, IFAD, UNICEF, WFP, and WHO 2019; figure 5-1).[1]

In advanced economies, food insecurity and malnutrition often go hand in hand because cheap processed foods tend to have more calories and fewer nutrients than healthier alternatives. This phenomenon of being "stuffed but starved" reflects a progressive transition to energy-dense but nutritionally poor food. The prevalent "Western diet" is characterized by high intakes of red and processed meat,[2] high-fat dairy, eggs, refined grains, potatoes, and a wide range of ultraprocessed food products (Tilman and Clark 2014).[3]

Because of these dietary changes, per capita caloric intake in advanced countries has soared to an average 3,400 per person in 2010–2015, up from 2,900 in 1964–1966, against an average recommended intake of 2,500 calories.[4] Animal-based protein intake now largely dominates overall protein

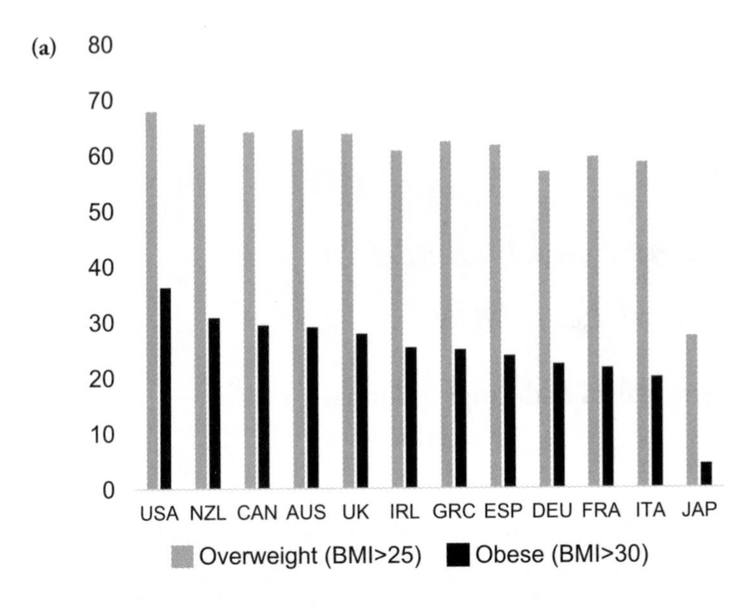

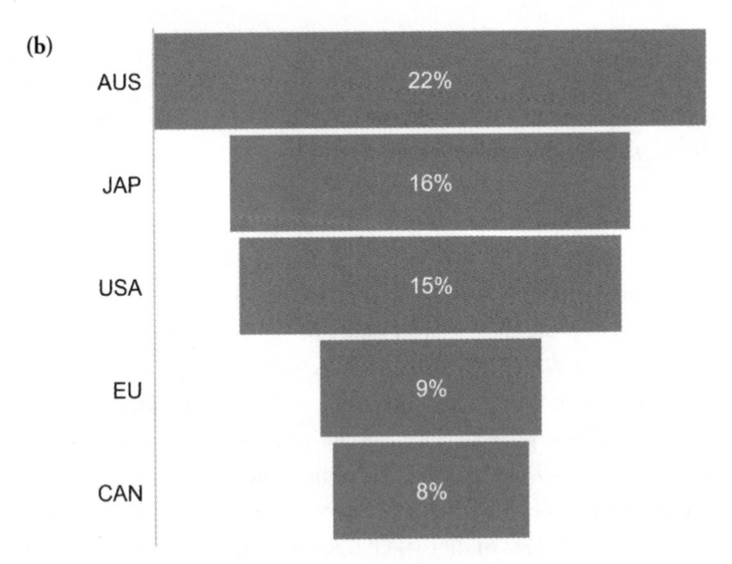

Figure 5-1. Prevalence of obesity and overweight among adults and total food insecurity, selected advanced economies. **(a)** Prevalence of overweight and obesity, both sexes, age-standardized estimates (as a percentage of population 18+ years old). **(b)** Food insecurity (as a percentage of total population). *Note: Overweight* refers to a body mass index (BMI) greater than 25; *obese* refers to a BMI greater than 30. *Source:* World Health Organization (2019), Pollard and Booth (2019).

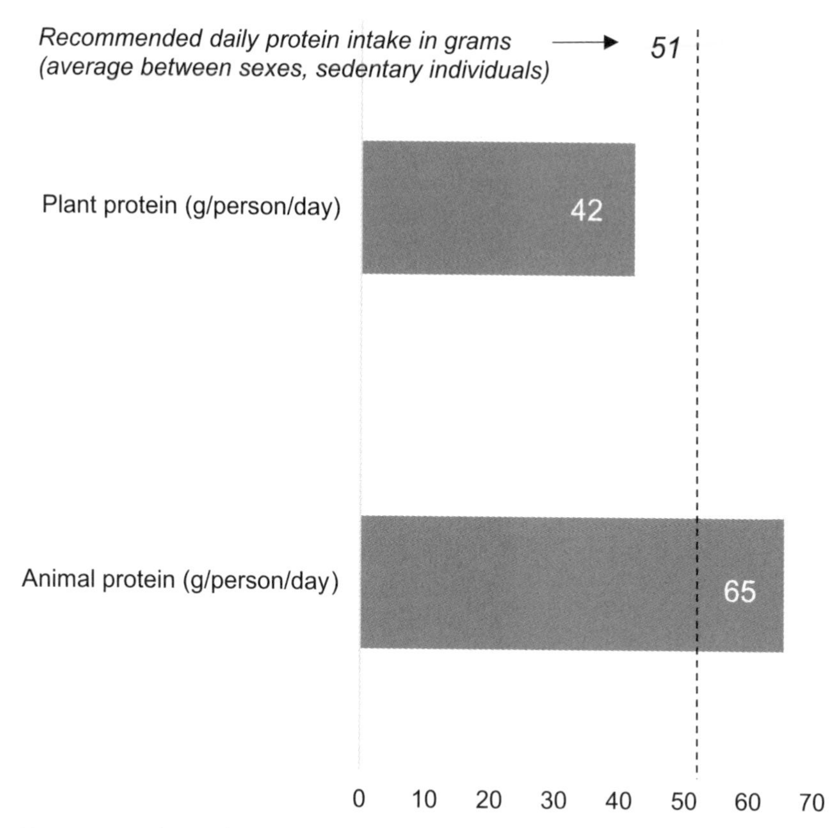

Figure 5-2. Advanced economies' animal- and plant-based protein intake versus recommended protein intake. *Source:* Food and Agriculture Organization et al. (2019).

intake in several countries (Roser and Ritchie 2020), although Millennials and Centennials have started to gradually reduce the share of animal protein they eat (Nielsen Homescan Panel Protein Survey 2017).[5] Against rising caloric trends, the source of calories has changed as well, with fat intake now being well above the maximum 30 percent recommended energy share in North America and Western Europe and saturated fats frequently above the 10 percent mark. Consumption of refined, processed foods and soft drinks has increased dramatically, while the intake of fruits and vegetables remains below the recommended 400 grams a day in most countries (figure 5-2).

As a result, the number of overweight and obese people has increased sharply over time: Taken together, a quarter of all people living in advanced economies are now obese and more than half overweight, relative to 10–15 percent and 30 percent in 1960, respectively.[6] Diet-related diseases affect children disproportionately: In 2016 the number of obese children five to nineteen years old was 124 million, more than eleven times the number of obese children in 1975 (NCD-RisC 2017). The number of obese or overweight children five years old and younger climbed from 32 million globally in 1990 to 41 million in 2016, according to World Health Organization (WHO) data, and about 149 million children under five years of age were stunted and 49 million wasted globally. If current trends continue, the number of overweight or obese children in that age group could increase to 70 million by 2025.

Dietary Risks to Health

The adoption of hypercaloric diets too high in animal protein, saturated fats, trans fats, sodium, and refined carbohydrates has been associated with an upward trend in noncommunicable diseases (NCDs), notably cardiovascular diseases, cancer, type 2 diabetes, nonalcoholic fatty liver disease, and cognitive impairment (WHO 2004; EC 2014). At the same time, evidence from experimental studies conducted on animals indicates that many of the most common chronic diseases can be prevented or greatly delayed by dietary manipulations that limit the accumulation of metabolic and molecular damage leading to tissue and organ dysfunction (Fontana et al. 2010). Independently of the type of food, preliminary evidence suggests that organic food may be safer because it is less likely to contain carcinogenic pesticide residues than conventional foods. A recent French epidemiological study has found that the most frequent consumers of organic food had 25 percent fewer cancers overall—with a particularly steep drop in the incidence of lymphomas and a significant reduction in postmenopausal breast cancers—than those who never ate organic (Baudry et al. 2018).

Today, seven out of ten deaths in the world are caused by NCDs, with higher percentages in advanced economies than in developing countries. For example, in 2018 nearly two thirds of all U.S. citizens suffered from at least one chronic disease, 40 percent had two or more chronic conditions (CDC 2020), and NCDs accounted for 88 percent of all deaths (WHO 2018). The European Union (EU) faces similar challenges, with 91 percent of deaths due to chronic diseases including cancer, cardiovascular disease, and diabetes and more people living longer with disabilities (GBD 2017). The incidence of these diseases is greater among sectors of the population with lower levels of income and education that tend to consume proportionately more of the cheapest highly processed and animal-based food (Campbell and Campbell 2006; Baraldi et al. 2018), a distribution pattern also observable in the less-advanced world. In practice, unhealthy Western diets mean that this year 11 million people will die earlier than they should and 255 million will be sick, much more than from drugs, alcohol, and tobacco combined (Afshin et al. 2019).

Absent intervention, these trends are expected to contribute to a dramatic escalation of government spending on healthcare as a percentage of gross domestic product (GDP) in many advanced economies and developing countries (Fontana 2018; figure 5-3). By 2050, if left unchecked, these dietary trends would also be a major contributor to an estimated 80 percent increase in greenhouse gas emissions from food production and land clearing.

"One Health"

Beyond the direct metabolic risks posed by poor diets, the current industrial food system poses additional, major threats to public health, because human well-being is closely linked to the health of animals and to environmental health. This is the principle underpinning "One Health," an approach that

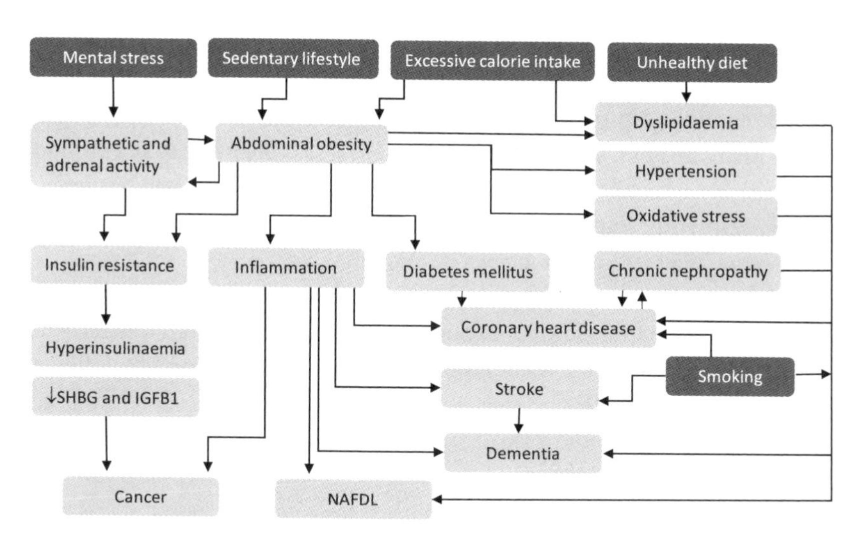

Figure 5-3. Unhealthy lifestyles and disease risk. *Note:* IGFBP1, insulin-like growth factor–binding protein 1; NAFLD, nonalcoholic fatty liver disease; SHBG, steroid hormone binding globulin. *Source:* Fontana (2018).

recognizes livestock agri-food systems as the crossroads of human, animal, and environmental health (FAO 2018).

One significant threat comes from antibiotic resistance. When antibiotics are overused, bacteria mutate and become resistant to the drugs created to kill them. Although the effectiveness of antibiotics and other antimicrobials depends on all major areas of use, including human and veterinary medicine, agricultural uses deserve special attention. Indeed, they account for 70–80 percent of the antibiotics and related drugs used in advanced and emerging market economies (O'Neill Report 2016; EFSA 2018).

Industrial animal agriculture—the prevalent form of animal farming worldwide—uses antibiotics primarily for nontherapeutic reasons. Notably, antibiotics are used to prevent infections in animals bred industrially that are typically confined in overcrowded and unsanitary operations; they are also included as growth promoters in feed to artificially increase the animal's weight gain. Although this lowers the price of meat, it also means antibiotics may no longer be effective when we really need them (Martin et al. 2015; WHO 2015).[7]

Antibiotic resistance threatens to return society to an earlier age when communicable illnesses were incurable, and people died as a result. Antimicrobial use in agriculture can also compromise other human therapies when bacteria develop cross-resistance—when their resistance to one drug also makes them resistant to other, related drugs.[8] A 2014 review led by Lord O'Neill for the U.K. government estimated that the potential impact of widespread antimicrobial resistance—as projected based on current trends—would lead to more deaths than cancer by 2050 (at 10 million per year compared with 8.2 million predicted from cancer) (O'Neill Report 2016). Globally, drug-resistant infections are currently implicated in 700,000 deaths each year and are thus the direct cause of a vast human and economic toll.

The second danger is the rise of global pandemics triggered by zoonotic diseases that jump from animals to humans. Intensive, industrial animal farming methods, rearing large numbers of animals in confined spaces, combined with breeding and feeding approaches designed to increase production, have dramatically increased the risk of certain diseases, such as those from the *Salmonella*, *Escherichia coli*, and *Campylobacter* bacteria (Jones et al. 2013). The consumption of wild animal food is another key source of zoonotic diseases. Intensive animal agriculture and trade for food of wild animals have led to periodic outbreaks of global pandemics such as the 1997 H5N1 highly pathogenic avian influenza, originated from a poultry outbreak in Hong Kong; the

2003 SARS coronavirus (SARS-CoV) outbreak, originated in China; and the recent 2020 outbreak of viral pneumonia in Wuhan, China, linked to a new type of coronavirus (SARS-CoV-2). Evidence shows that both SARS-CoV and SARS-CoV-2 developed in wet markets, which sell a huge variety of exotic live animals incubating these viruses and where close contact with humans gave the viruses an opportunity to mutate and make the leap to our species (Andersen et al. 2020).[9] All these pathogens, either bacterial or viral, are responsible for large numbers of foodborne human infections that can be fatal.[10]

Some aspects of current food systems aggravate these pathogeneses. Long-distance transport of animals increases the risk of infection for the aforementioned bacteria. Risk of exposure to foodborne pathogens also generally increases with consumption of fast-bred, lower-welfare animal products. It is not only what we eat that threatens us; influenza viruses that infect poultry and pigs can jump to humans, with devastating consequences (Jones et al. 2013) (figure 5-4). Crucially, this hazard is compounded by antimicrobial resistance; there is increasing concern about the emergence of *Salmonella*, *E. coli*, and other bacterial strains that are resistant to multiple antibiotics, potentially making the treatment of infections in animals and people more difficult.

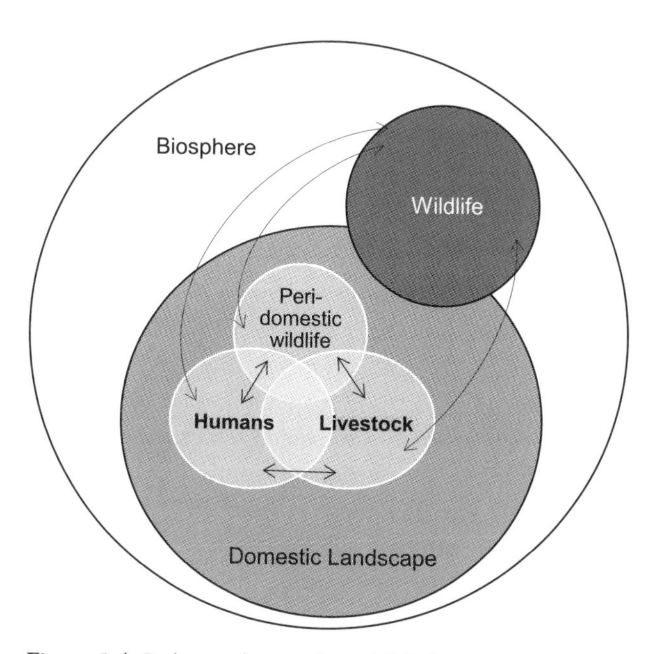

Figure 5-4. Pathogen flow at the wildlife–livestock–human interface. *Source:* Adapted from Jones et al. (2013).

Dietary 1.5°C Target

Science has identified diet patterns that are conducive to good health and longevity (Fontana and Partridge 2015) and are also compatible with international pledges to limit increases in global temperature to 1.5°C by 2050.

The EAT–Lancet Commission Report on Food, Planet, and Health by Willett et al. (2019) provides the most comprehensive review to date of what constitutes a healthy *and* sustainable diet. It starts by identifying four possible combinations of dietary patterns and food production approaches, namely "healthy and unsustainable" (win–lose), "unhealthy and sustainable" (lose–win), "unhealthy and unsustainable" (lose–lose), and "healthy and sustainable" (win–win).

According to this and other reports, a healthy and sustainable diet is both capable of optimizing health, defined as a state of complete well-being and not merely the absence of disease; and produced in sufficient amounts for the global current and future population while staying within planetary boundaries (Rockström et al. 2017; Willet et al. 2019). This includes maximum or minimum safe levels of climate change, ocean acidification, biogeochemical nitrogen and phosphorus cycles, global freshwater use, land system change, and the rate at which biological diversity is lost.

Table 5-1 summarizes guidelines for a planetary healthy diet, expressed as targets for specific food groups (e.g., 100 to 300 g per day of fruit) according to the EAT–Lancet's Report. In line with prior empirical nutritional findings, the EAT–Lancet planetary diet prescribes appropriate caloric intakes and consists largely of diverse plant-based foods and very low or no amounts of animal-sourced foods. It contains unsaturated rather than saturated fats and limited amounts of refined grains, highly processed foods, and added salt and sugars.[11]

This is fundamentally a flexitarian diet, which is largely plant based but can optionally include modest amounts of fish, meat, and dairy foods (Willett et al. 2019). Local interpretation and adaptation of the universally applicable planetary health diet is necessary and should reflect the culture, geography, and demography of the population and individuals.

A transformation to healthy diets as prescribed in table 5-1 on a global scale by 2050 will require substantial dietary shifts worldwide. These include, on average, a more than doubling in the consumption of plant-based foods (i.e., minimally processed grains, pulses, fruit and vegetables, and nuts and seeds), and a more than 50 percent reduction in global intake of less healthy foods (i.e., meat, dairy products, and added sugars) (Willett et al. 2019). An

Table 5-1. *Scientific Targets for a Planetary Healthy Diet, with Possible Ranges, for an Intake of 2,500 kcal/day*

	Macronutrient Intake (g per day, possible range)	**Caloric Intake (kcal per day)**
Whole grains *Rice, wheat, corn, and others*	232	811
Tubers or starchy vegetables *Potatoes and cassava*	50 (0–100)	39
Vegetables *All vegetables*	300 (200–600)	78
Fruits *All fruits*	200 (100–300)	126
Dairy foods *Whole milk or equivalent*	250 (0–500)	153
Protein sources		
Beef, lamb, and pork	14 (0–28)	30
Chicken and other poultry	29 (0–56)	62
Eggs	13 (0–25)	19
Fish	28 (0–100)	40
Legumes	75 (0–100)	254
Nuts	50 (0–75)	291
Added fats		
Unsaturated oils	40 (20–80)	354
Saturated oils	11.8 (0–11.8)	96
Added sugars		
All sugars	31 (0–31)	120

Source: Willett et al. (2019).

easy-to-remember rule for the average world citizen is "no animal products for breakfast or lunch" (Foer 2019). However, undernourished people who find it difficult to obtain adequate quantities of micronutrients from plant-source foods (e.g., in urban areas where it is difficult to buy affordable or good-quality fresh food[12]) or who depend on agropastoral livelihoods and animal protein from livestock could actually eat a little more meat and dairy.

Economic Benefits of Greening Food Demand in Advanced Economies

Shifting from the current Western diet toward one that is simultaneously healthy and sustainable promises vast socioeconomic and socioecological benefits. The five key gains from a globalized shift in diets are as follows:

- *Better health and lower healthcare costs.* The financial costs associated with treating chronic diseases are extremely high, and given that the average age of populations in advanced economies is increasing, chronic diseases will continue to place acute pressure on national budgets (Fontana et al. 2014). Besides, the costs of treating and caring for patients with multiple conditions tend to increase dramatically with the number and combination of comorbidities, although the pattern varies for certain diseases (Orueta et al. 2014). For example, cost-of-illness studies—including costs due to primary, inpatient and outpatient care, accident and emergency, and medications—put annual NCD-related spending in the United States at about US$2 trillion out of today's US$3.5 trillion total annual U.S. healthcare costs. This corresponds roughly to an annual tax rate of 11 percent on aggregate income and is widely expected to increase exponentially given projected changes in longevity and healthcare inflation (Chen et al. 2018).[13] At a global level, under current trends, NCDs are estimated to cause a cumulative global loss of output of US$47 trillion by 2030, that is, more than half of the 2018 global world product (Bloom et al. 2019). Research shows that more than 80 percent of cardiovascular diseases, 90 percent of type 2 diabetes and obesity, and at least 40 percent of cancers can be prevented through behavior, such as eating a healthy diet, exercising regularly, and avoiding smoking (WHO 2004; EC 2014). By reducing dietary risk factors, a healthy planetary diet could cut half of all private and public healthcare costs per advanced country, on average. This is equivalent to an economic gain of up to 6 percent of GDP annually, which could be used for productive investments in infrastructure, education, or research and development (e.g., see calculations for France in Batini 2019a). The economic gain would be higher in the United States given the higher share of healthcare spending in terms of GDP (Chen et al. 2018).
- *Higher productivity and growth.* Considering only the cost of NCD to

healthcare systems grossly underestimates their true cost. Production losses from illness and premature death and from the informal care of others contribute greatly to the overall financial burden. As a result of reduced labor supply and outputs, NCDs also lower tax revenues and returns on human capital investments. Estimates put these costs at US$0.8 trillion for the United States and US$0.2 trillion for the European Union (Luengo-Fernandez 2013; EHN 2017). These estimates are based on production losses due only to mortality and morbidity associated with cardiovascular disease (a fraction of the cost of all NCDs) and the total expenses of providing informal care for patients with cardiovascular disease. A reduced incidence of all NCDs, resulting from better diets, could thus boost productivity and potential growth by decreasing total population disability life years lost or years lost to premature death, proportionally.

- *Higher per capita income and saving.* Lower rates of NCD promise decreased disabilities and fewer premature deaths. This would result in more household income, reduced expenditures (including out-of-pocket payments for healthcare and reduced loss in saving and assets), and increased business opportunities. These gains are complex to estimate, but they are likely to be substantial in per capita terms.
- *Lower economic and financial risks from global pandemics.* A global progressive shift to a healthier planetary diet would curtail the consumption of meat (farmed or wild), eggs, and dairy, minimizing the likelihood of full-blown, global zoonotic pandemics. A significant universal reduction in demand for animal-based food would probably lead both to a global resizing of animal operations—reducing the emergence or reemergence of future zoonotic diseases linked to the agriculture–environment nexus—and a reduction in the exposure of the population to contaminated foods. The expected gain from a reduced likelihood of global pandemics is vast because the World Bank estimates US$3 trillion per severe pandemic (equivalent to a 5 percent of global world product loss), although the cost of certain pandemics, such as 2020's SARS-CoV-2 may be much larger than that, depending on ultimate mortality rates and duration of lockdowns.
- *Resilience of antibiotic treatments.* Halving the global consumption of meat and dairy could lead to uncrowded, nonintensive animal husbandry practices. This would allow a rapid discontinuation of the subtherapeutic use of antibiotics in animal agriculture. In turn, this

could halt the progressive development of resistant bacteria and help defuse the global drug resistance bomb. The economic gains of forgoing an antimicrobial resistance catastrophe in the future are colossal, because the cost of the alternative scenario of global antimicrobial resistance—as projected based on current trends—is estimated to be up to US$100 trillion. This is equivalent to 130 percent of the 2016 global world product (O'Neill Report 2016) with a reduction in population and an impact on ill health in the baseline scenario on world economic output of 2–3.5 percent per year by 2050. Additional economic losses of forgone medical treatments and procedures such as joint replacements, cesarean sections, chemotherapy, and transplant surgery that depend on antibiotics being available to prevent infections would double the costs under the baseline.[14]

Environmental Benefits of Greening Food Demand in Advanced Economies

In addition to providing health and economic benefits, a shift to well-designed, balanced plant-based diets can lessen environmental destruction (Baroni et al. 2007; Joyce et al. 2012; De Marco et al. 2014; Tilman and Clark 2014; Willet et al. 2019). A recent report by the Intergovernmental Panel on Climate Change (IPCC) on climate change and land use found that by 2050, a shift to plant-based foods could free up several million square kilometers of land and reduce global CO_2 emissions by up to 8 billion tons per year, relative to business as usual (IPCC 2019; figure 5-5). Accordingly, a global shift toward diets sourced 100 percent from plants could lead to a reduction in emissions equal to the sum of the current annual carbon emissions of the United States and India (i.e., a quarter of all global emissions). Expressed in fossil fuel emissions equivalent, this would correspond to replacing all fossil fuels energy plants with zero-carbon nuclear energy plants.

These results stem from estimates of the carbon cost of food, which generally find that producing and consuming plant-based food creates a fraction of the emissions from animal-based food. For example, greenhouse gas emissions from producing soya are one sixth of those from producing chicken, one fifteenth of those from producing milk, and one seventy-third of those necessary to produce beef, in equivalent proteins. Consuming meat from ruminants (i.e., cows and sheep) or their milk is by far the highest-impact factor in diets, with 1 kilo of beef protein roughly equal to driving a new car for a year or to

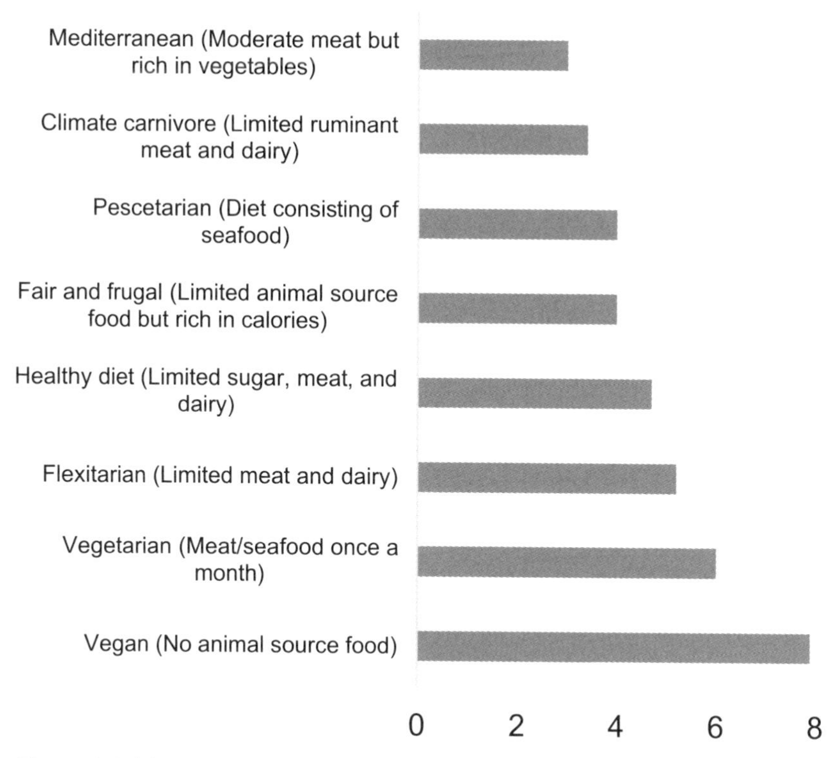

Figure 5-5. Mitigation potential of different diets. *Source:* IPCC (2019).

one passenger flying from London to New York and back (Searchinger et al. 2018). These are global average figures, calculated by beef production in places such as the Amazon Basin. However, even in areas with scant pristine forests, such as Europe, the carbon-equivalent costs of producing meat from cows are astonishing.[15]

Moreover, if global consumption of animal source food products decreased, leading to the adoption of a diet rich in plant-based foods, only 30–40 percent of the crops cultivated currently would be needed. This would markedly reduce water and land pollution from the intensive use of reactive nitrogen and phosphorus fertilizers (e.g., see Elser and Bennett 2011; Sutton et al. 2011), herbicides and pesticides, and the poor management of animal wastes (see Tilman et al. 2002; Hubbard et al. 2004). Topsoil impoverishment, overpumping of groundwater, and agriculture-related fuel consumption, as well as air pollution, would also be reduced. It has been estimated that in certain areas of the planet about 30 percent of particular matter (PM10 and PM2.5) is produced by livestock emissions and by the nitrogen fertilizers used for industrial agriculture (Pinder et al. 2007; Tsimpidi et al. 2007; Carnevale et al. 2010; Behera et al. 2013).

Policies to Green Food Demand in Advanced Economies

A variety of economic policies, structural reforms, and regulatory levers can be deployed to move food demand toward healthier and more sustainable options.

On the demand side, fiscal measures to shift the type, combination, and quantity of food people consume may include, as on the supply side, tax and subsidy adjustments.

Taxes on unhealthy foods. Just as carbon tax proposals aim to reduce the carbon footprint of the energy sector, taxes levied on "unsustainable" and "unhealthy" foods—notably meat, dairy, and ultraprocessed food—could discourage their overconsumption. Tax measures should focus on recalibrating indirect taxes on consumption and retailing based on the level of externalities these generate.

For example, a (Pigouvian)[16] tax on foods associated with high negative environmental and public health externalities could be introduced. This should be calibrated to the elasticity of each country-specific demand and the desired quantity equilibrium for these foods, along the lines proposed by Simon (2013) and Springmann et al. (2018) for the United States. The success of these taxes in shifting consumption is well known for tobacco smoking and alcohol, and recent evidence is emerging on their effectiveness in curbing the consumption of carbonated drinks, for example in Chile and Oman, where "sin" taxes to shift buying habits away from these goods were introduced in 2011 and 2017, respectively. Just as it has for cigarettes and alcohol, a tax on high-externality foods would pay a double dividend by simultaneously boosting revenues and lowering consumption (and related social and medical problems). Research shows that although they may not be immediately effective at curbing undesired consumption—as some "sin" tax experiments on fat and sugary food (e.g., in Denmark and Hungary) indicate—Pigouvian taxes on food may work well in the long run. Some findings indicate that a 10 percent increase in the price of foods consumed at home (excluding fruits and vegetables) lowers body fat by about 9 percent for men and by about 8 percent for women (Grossman et al. 2014).

Beyond the boost to fiscal revenues, this change could give consumers more accurate price signals about the true social and environmental cost of their food choices and potentially lead to a shift in consumption patterns. For the United States, for example, where the consumption of meat and dairy is much higher than in other advanced countries, Simon (2013) calculates that the combination of curtailing subsidies to industrial animal food production, introducing a 50 percent excise tax on meat and dairy, and excluding animal food from food support programs would reduce meat and dairy consumption by about half. The average U.S. retail price of a Big Mac, for example, is about $5.60. But with all the hidden expenses of meat production (including healthcare, subsidies, and environmental losses) the full burden on society is a hefty $12 per sandwich. This price, if actually charged, could more than halve the U.S. demand for burgers. Likewise, a gallon of milk would run $9 instead of $3.50, and a store-bought, 2-pound package of pork ribs would jump from $12 to $32.

More recent research on the United States calls for a federal excise tax on junk food (which would capture many of the common foods in the Western diet), defined through product category or combined category–nutrient approaches, because this appears to be legally and administratively feasible and has strong implications for nutrition policy (Pomeranz et al. 2018).[17] "The reason to use excise taxes is the expectation that [manufacturers] will pass on the increased costs by raising prices," Pomeranz says. "Consumers end up either avoiding the product or replacing it with something different. Or the manufacturers have the option to reformulate and come up with products that will not be taxed" (Weintraub 2018).

Tax credits or subsidies on healthy foods. Tax credits could be introduced in parallel, to offset the cost of higher taxes on unhealthy foods, as suggested by Simon (2013). This way, consumers' purchasing power will not be diminished, and they would better perceive the externality cost of different food products. The introduction of tax credits would also make healthier (more plant-based and organic food) diets more affordable, especially for lower-earning households, relative to less healthy food, chipping at health inequalities related to income disparities. (Curtailment and reorientation of subsidies on the production front would help lower prices of fresh food relative to processed food and animal-based food, reinforcing the price substitution effect.) Furthermore, though fiscally neutral, the spending-related stimulus would help offset the lower spending caused by other parts of the policy plan. Importantly, flanking the meat and dairy tax with a direct benefit to individuals would lessen the political economy challenge of a new tax, motivating voters and lawmakers to support the overall plan. The credit could be funneled via tax credits on specific foods to ensure proper targeting to consumers who have embarked in an actual demand shift toward sustainable products.

Health tax bonuses. Similarly to insurance companies around the world, governments can nudge patients with high dietary risk factors to adopt healthy lifestyles through fiscally neutral tax incentives.[18] In a similar vein to "eco-bonuses" for zero-carbon vehicles, "health tax bonuses" can be introduced to incentivize simple lifestyle changes, such as maintaining a healthy diet alongside being physically active, limiting alcohol use, and not smoking. One win–win approach consists of offering citizens of all ages an opt-in scheme, whereby participating subjects provide evidence of their key health markers (e.g., body mass index, blood cholesterol and glucose, and arterial blood pressure) at regular intervals, for example every three years. If the markers are within predetermined healthy ranges or are progressing toward those ranges between two consecutive measurements (at a rate that indicates a statistically significant behavioral modification toward healthy lifestyle), the person is awarded every successive year a discount on income taxes. This could be proportional to the healthcare savings that patient would generate for the public sector. Those adhering to the "health tax bonus" scheme would also have access to e-health, nutrition information, courses on healthy cooking and life skills, and regular preventive care support, including discounts or free access to certain services, such as public sport facilities. These additional services could be financed in part through the fiscal savings in healthcare spending generated by behavioral changes from the bonus schemes. If patient incentives for healthier eating are calibrated appropriately to account for country-specific and regional links between demographics, eating habits, and disease rates, health bonus schemes could rapidly help the public attain major health and environmental targets. They would also improve posttax and transfer income distribution and put public finances on a sustainable path. Finally, they would raise labor productivity and potential growth by virtue of the drop in disability-adjusted life years of different participating working-age cohorts.

Public–private partnerships to support nutrition research. Scientific research holds the key to increasing our understanding of the precise mechanisms of diet-related diseases. Thus, research can markedly influence global health and economies. Coordinated efforts of public and private partners can help support research in these areas through public investment in R&D or fiscal incentives. Specifically, six top nutrition research needs have been identified and are worthy of government support (Ohlhorst et al. 2013). These relate to the need to better understand the variability in individual responses to diet and foods (this includes research on omics, the microbiome, biological networks, and tissue specificity and temporality); the impact of nutrition on healthy growth, development, and reproduction (this includes research on epigenetics/imprinting, early nutrition, and nutrition and reproductive health); the role of nutrition in health maintenance (this includes research on optimal metabolic health and bodily functions and on energy balance); the role of nutrition in medical therapy and management (this includes research on disease development and progression and nutrition support for special subgroups); nutrition-related behaviors (this includes research on drivers of food choices, nutrition and brain functioning, and imprinting); and finally, the food supply and environment (which includes research on food environment and food choice, food composition, and novel foods and food ingredients). Progress in the fields of omics, bioinformatics, and biomarker discoveries that are responsive to dietary manipulations, together with the development and maintenance of up-to-date food and nutrient databases, and advancements in cost-effectiveness analysis to calculate and compare the costs and benefits of nutrition research interventions, would help speed discoveries in nutrition research and should therefore be publicly supported.

Beyond traditional fiscal measures, structural reforms to shift demand include the following:

Healthcare system reform. Modern medicine focuses on diagnosing and treating chronic diseases one at a time, mainly with drugs and surgery. Doctors are forced to treat many of the most common chronic diseases this way because they usually intervene after patients experience illness. Simple steps can be taken to gradually shift from the current "sick care" medical system to a preventive, health-promoting model. Four such steps include the following:

- *Medical education.* Modern medicine recognizes the importance of proper nutrition, but on average, medical schools dedicate only 1–2 percent of total lecture hours to nutrition education. Medical licensing exams test knowledge of nutritional deficiencies but not students' ability to advise patients about diet and lifestyle modifications. Training at the postgraduate level has followed suit: Typically, the word *nutrition* is not included in board examination requirements for internal medicine certification. Cardiology fellows around the advanced world do not need to complete a single requirement in nutrition counseling.

Reforming medical education, both didactic and experiential, to train future doctors in nutritional counseling can go a long way toward changing the profession's philosophy of care. This should be accompanied by administrative steps to develop explicit preventive and therapeutic health protocols. These protocols should emphasize the central role of nutrition and other lifestyle choices in the prevention of chronic diseases and the importance of "prevention units" within hospitals and other healthcare institutions.

- *Nutrition in electronic health records.* To provide proper nutritional counseling and care, doctors and other healthcare providers need better tools for electronic patient records. The documentation of nutrition care in a structured format (from screening and assessment to discharge) would allow health professionals to communicate patients' nutrition treatment plans and identify and treat nutrition problems or clinical conditions in each of these healthcare settings. To this end, healthcare organizations should work with their organization's information systems department to create tools for documentation of nutrition care in electronic health record. Comprehensive recommendations exist to help organizations choose and implement healthcare software (e.g., see Kight et al. 2020).
- *Reimbursement standards.* Nutrition-based treatment provided by a registered dietitian or nutritionist, also known as medical nutrition therapy, is a key component of managing specific NCDs, such as diabetes. To treat this condition, medical nutrition therapy includes a nutrition diagnosis as well as therapeutic and counseling services. These types of therapies should be considered when structuring healthcare coverage to ensure that patients can access them without financial disadvantage relative to other nonnutrition therapies.
- *Provider quality metrics.* Malnutrition can result in many poor health outcomes, including greater risks of sarcopenia, frailty, infections, and slower wound healing; increased office visits and readmissions; and decreased functionality. As a result, integrating nutrition (and physical exercise) care into healthcare providers' quality metrics can

improve patient outcomes and provider performance. Because poor nutrition can increase readmissions, complication rates, and mortality, there is a real opportunity to reduce healthcare costs when patients receive high-quality nutrition care.

Product market reform. Numerous measures can be considered to encourage consumers' demand of healthy and sustainable food products:

- *Limits on additives* (trans fat, salt, added sugars). Governments should dictate precise limits on food additives in line with directions from the Joint FAO/WHO Expert Committee on Food Additives, such as flavoring agents, preservatives, and coloring. Although some food additives, such as salt or sugar, have been in use for centuries for preservation, many new ones have been developed to meet the needs of industrial food manufacturing. National authorities should oversee food businesses, which carry the primary responsibility for ensuring that the use of a food additive is safe and complies with legislation.
- *Guidelines on marketing to children.* The food industry should develop and strictly adhere to advertising guidelines that minimize the risk of obesity in children, which is escalating worldwide. Absent adequate self-regulation, government can take action to enforce binding guidelines because children are uniquely vulnerable to the marketing of low-nutrition foods.[19]
- *Labeling.* Food labels can help consumers choose the products that best meet their health needs. (One of the best ways to increase nutrition, however, is consuming fresh foods—those typically without a package or food label.) Many manufacturers now place additional health information (e.g., nutrition scores called "traffic light labels") on the front of food packages (so-called front-of-pack food labeling). Similar labeling should be applied to restaurant menus.
- *Retailing and marketing regulation.* Grocery stores, supermarkets, and other large food retailers do not simply "store" food. In fact, they can play major roles in what consumers choose to eat and drink. This may not be breaking news to food marketers, but health advocates have been increasingly recognizing this role and have developed policies and interventions that target food retailers. Regulation can play a role by requiring or incentivizing grocery stores to establish practices and programs that promote health. Key practices include increasing their

stock of healthy foods; changing the placement of healthy foods in the store to attract consumers' attention; improving the ambiance around healthy products; donating healthy food samples, especially to children; providing postnutrition information; using on-site personnel to advise clients on how to choose and cook healthy food; offering special deals for healthy foods; and delivering educational material and programs. Analogous regulatory "nudges" can be deployed to shift meal and vending standards toward the promotion of healthier products.

- *Education reform.* It is critical to go beyond current government public awareness campaigns to help consumers more fully understand the public health and environmental impact of various foods. It is also essential to develop educational programs in primary, secondary, and tertiary schools. For example, university students should not only be taught career-specific information but also develop basic knowledge and practical skills necessary to promote human and environmental health. Learning a basic set of skills (e.g., how to choose healthy ingredients, cook nutritious meals, develop exercise plans, and meditate) can transform people's lives and the world we all live in.

Country Cases

Several countries have adopted policies to shift food demand toward healthier and more sustainable dietary choices. However, most of these efforts are country-specific, and no single nation has made the full range of fiscal and structural reforms previously described.

Fiscal Policies to Shift Food Demand

A growing number of countries have implemented or are considering applying food and drink taxes or subsidies to address the growing burden of obesity and dietary-related diseases. Specifically, states have been experimenting with taxing foods and drinks since the early 1980s (Mytton et al. 2012). In most nations, taxes have been applied to food and drink items that are clearly unhealthy or a luxury item, such as sugar-sweetened beverages and confectionery, with taxes often implemented as a sales tax (e.g., United States)[20] or an import duty (e.g., Fiji, Nauru, and French Polynesia). More recently, countries such as Chile, Denmark, Hungary, Oman, and Saudi Arabia and local governments around the world, such as Berkeley, California,[21] have enforced taxes on a wider range of foods and drinks, including products such as meat and dairy; taxes were based on the content of saturated fat, sugar, or salt. Mexico also introduced an 8 percent tax on nonessential energy-dense foods and a 10 percent tax on sugar-sweetened beverages in 2014. Among these, most have seen positive impacts from unhealthy food taxes. Evaluation of the Mexican tax reform found a 5 percent decrease in purchases of taxed foods in the first year, compared with no change in the purchase of untaxed products (Batis et al. 2017).

In Hungary, for example, local manufacturers of junk foods pay a "value-added tax" of 27 percent on top of the 25 percent tax that is normally imposed on most foods. Hungary's law levies the junk food tax based largely on sugar and salt content. Four years after Hungary's tax was initiated, more than 59 percent of consumers had lowered their consumption of the offending junk food products, according to a study conducted by the country's National Institute of Pharmacy and Nutrition and the WHO. Overweight or obese adults were twice as likely to change their eating habits as people of normal weight. When consumers were polled, they reported that they opted for less expensive products—but also that the taxes made them more mindful of the health risks of junk food. Hungary's food tax has been touted by the WHO as one of the most effective, because it has significantly reduced consumption of junk food products. Revenue from excise taxes can also be earmarked for places in the budget, such as health promotion. In its first four years in operation, the WHO reported, Hungary's tax brought in 61.3 billion forints (US$219 million) for public health spending. Another key finding from the Mexico and Hungary studies was that the junk food tax seemed to have the greatest effect among low-income groups and people who were big consumers of unhealthy foods before the tax implementation.

Another food pricing strategy is the adoption of food subsidy programs, which have been operating for many years in the United States and the United Kingdom. The Special Supplemental Nutrition Program for Women, Infants, and Children (WIC) in the United States commenced in 1972 to provide healthy foods, referrals to health and social services, and nutrition education to pregnant women and families with young children. The WIC program was developed to target common nutritional deficiencies in disadvantaged pregnant women and children and demonstrated significant improvements in pregnancy outcomes and children's nutritional status and early intellectual development. However, the rapid uptake of the program nationally made it difficult to conduct robust randomized trials, resulting in concerns about selection bias in existing evaluation studies.

Similarly, the longstanding U.K. Welfare Food Scheme program was expanded and renamed Healthy Start in 2006, with a renewed focus on improving the nutrition of low-income women and their children. Both WIC and Healthy Start have changed recently to provide more fruit and vegetables to address current nutritional challenges in target populations. Food subsidy programs remain topical in other countries; South Korea has trialed a program modeled on the WIC program, and the Food Miles program in Canada provides subsidies to wholesale distributors sending perishable foods by air to remote communities, which has reduced the family cost of healthy foods. A collation of existing evidence may contribute to future initiatives in this area.

A recent meta-analysis examining the joint impact of food subsidies and taxes across several countries (the United States, the Netherlands, France, New Zealand, and South Africa) indicated that subsidizing healthier foods tends to be effective in modifying dietary behavior. In the pooled analysis, each 10 percent decrease in the price of fruits and vegetables caused a 14 percent increase in their consumption, whereas each 10 percent reduction in the cost of other healthy foods increased their use by 16 percent. A change in price of fruits and vegetables was also associated with lower body mass index (BMI): for every 10 percent drop in cost, BMI declined by 0.04 kg/m^2. Conversely, each 10 percent price increase of sugar-sweetened beverages and unhealthy fast foods decreased their consumption by 7 percent and 3 percent, respectively. Every 10 percent price increase in unhealthy foods and drinks was associated with a trend toward lower BMI (for every 10 percent price increase, –0.06 kg/m^2), but this decrease did not achieve statistical significance. Even so, existing evidence is compromised by various study limitations: a small convenience sample of interventions limits the generalizability of study results, the absence of overall diet assessment limits the effectiveness in reducing total caloric intake, the short intervention and follow-up duration do not allow assessment of long-term impact, and the lack of cost-effectiveness analysis precludes comparison across competing policy scenarios.

Currently, there are limited country examples of health tax bonuses. In 2012, Ohio Senator Rob Portman proposed a Medicare "Better Health Rewards" program to reward seniors for not smoking and for achieving lower weight, blood pressure, glucose, and cholesterol. Today, several U.S. states policies are focusing on behavioral changes to improve health and control costs primarily among Medicaid populations. The State Children's Health Insurance Program (and other state-funded programs also apply the central concept of patient engagement, which is being promoted by the U.S. Department of Health and Human Services. The premise is that the motivating power of financial rewards for practicing healthy behaviors can have a significant impact on the efficiency and effectiveness of healthcare. Most incentive agendas focus on two major sources of morbidity and mortality: smoking and obesity. Several other countries have adopted financial incentives to encourage healthy lifestyles and primary prevention, but we could not find any program comparable to the proposal made here. Results from a meta-analysis revealed that the design of the particular financial incentive system may be a crucial element in its acceptability and traction (Tambor et al. 2016).

Other Policies to Green Food Demand

Internationally, progress on other policy levers to shift dietary patterns is fragmented:

- On nutrition training in medical schools, numerous efforts have been made over the past two decades to improve the knowledge and skills of medical students and physicians. However, with the move to a more integrated curriculum and problem-based learning at many medical schools, a substantial portion of the total nutrition instruction is occurring outside courses specifically dedicated to nutrition. As a result, nutrition education in medical school across the globe remains rudimentary, at best, and limited for the duration of graduate medical education for many specialties (Devries et al. 2019).
- The use of nutrition information in electronic health records remains sparse. In the United States and in Europe, despite progress on electronic health records (including cross-border), most files currently exclude nutrition information.[22]
- Globally, labeling of foods' nutritional content and healthiness continues to follow national guidelines. One of the most advanced labeling systems is Europe's Nutri-Score, developed by Santé Publique France (the French government's public health agency) and modeled on a nutrition profiling system derived from the U.K. Food Standards Agency. The Nutri-Score is a front-of-pack nutrition labelling scheme that uses a five-tier scale consisting of colored let-

ters ("dark green A," "light green B," "yellow C," "orange D," and "red E"). Foods are color-coded to provide consumers with an easily guide to the products' nutritional value, with "A" being a positive score and "E" being an adverse score. The calculation takes negative nutritional qualities such as sugar, saturated fat, and salt into account, as well as positive ones such as dietary fiber and protein. In 2019, Belgium launched the same Nutri-Score system as France, and other European member states such as Spain and Portugal are planning to follow.

In a similar vein, in 2016 Chile introduced a raft of regulations that included advertising restrictions on unhealthy foods, bold front-of-package warning labels, and a ban on junk food in schools to address the dramatic escalation in the country's rate of child and adult obesity. Three quarters of Chilean adults and more than half of children are overweight or obese; estimates by health officials indicate that the medical costs of obesity could consume 4 percent of the nation's healthcare spending by 2030, up from 2.4 percent in 2016. A recent evaluation of Chile's Law on Food Labeling and Advertising on sugar-sweetened beverage purchases from 2015 to 2017 indicates that the new labeling requirements have been very effective: Consumption of sugar-sweetened drinks dropped nearly 25 percent in the eighteen months after Chile adopted the new regulations (Taillie et al. 2020). Chile's experience is a very promising sign that mutually reinforcing policies can succeed in shifting dietary choices. Since then Peru, Uruguay, and Israel have adopted Chilean-style front-of-pack food labeling, Brazil and Mexico are expected to finalize similar labels in 2020, and another dozen countries are considering them as well.

- Countries are increasingly integrating nutrition education into their national curricula and school policies. However, more still needs to be done to reach the full potential of food and nutrition education in schools. FAO is currently working to understand how food and nutrition education is integrated into national education systems around the world and to examine the capacities and resources needed across the system.[23] Main findings from a 2017 FAO consultation, including a large sample of schools in low- and middle-income countries, showed that "nutrition education in general and particularly in schools has an extraordinarily low profile. Where it is part of the

> curriculum, we are not even sure how it is implemented because there is no monitoring, evaluation, evidence, or sharing of information. . . . We need to convince governments, donors and educators, and the entire education system of what nutrition education can do in schools, what is the long-term potential and why they should invest in effective models" (FAO 2017, 18).

Despite these mixed results, significant progress is being made in some developed economies. One of the most advanced is perhaps Japan, the country with the world's longest life expectancy at birth. In Japan, food and nutrition education is blended with lunch modalities at school cafeterias. Meals are prepared every morning with local seasonal products; nutritionists and other experts help children to learn about and enjoy healthy meals and to understand the concept of food sustainability. With the School Lunch Act of 1954 (launched initially to lift the population out of the suffering endured in the wake of World War II), school lunches became part of Japan's education system. Their goals were to enrich school life and promote cooperation by supporting healthy eating habits, propped up by important social rules. Children are responsible for setting and cleaning the tables, serving meals, learning good table manners, and developing a sense of gratitude for the food they are eating with their classmates. They can even take part in special lessons with school nutritionists to gain a greater understanding of the history and value of food. Other strict social rules also have to be obeyed, discouraging overfilling your plate or openly displaying dissatisfaction with food that has already been served. The details of the food programs can be changed to adapt to the specific requirements of each school, but the basic rules and composition of the menus have hardly changed in more than forty years, a testament to the brilliant Japanese notion of making school lunches a moment for education and growth.

Conclusions

Nutrition is vital, not only for the growth and development of healthy human beings but also in the prevention and treatment of many chronic diseases. Science has identified dietary patterns that are conducive to good health and longevity and are also compatible with international pledges to limit pollution and limit the rise in global temperature to 1.5°C by 2050. Meeting these goals requires reducing consumption of animal food products and decreasing protein and calorie intake to bring them in line with recommended nutritional values.

The economic and environmental gains of shifting diets are vast and potentially much larger than those promised by transition in other areas. The food we eat would be more nutritious, more varied, safer, more humanely raised, and more affordable. We would live longer, healthier, and more productive lives. Savings from lower health costs—one of the top expenditures for governments and households—could stabilize global finances. Labor productivity would rise with fewer work years lost because of ill health, disability, or early death. Critical progress would be made in eradicating world hunger, income inequality, and social immobility, averting mass migration due to climate change. Critically, a full transition toward diets that are predominantly plant based promises a reduction of up to a quarter of all global emissions.[24]

Taxes on unhealthy foods accompanied by subsidies on healthy ones, health tax bonuses, and a reform of medical systems to strengthen preventive care can go a long way in transitioning to healthy and sustainable diets. Structural reforms, notably labeling and regulation of unhealthy food and beverages, as well as education, can accelerate these shifts and ensure that they are durable.

References

Afshin, A., J. L. Peñalvo, L. Del Gobbo, J. Silva, M. Michaelson, M. O'Flaherty, S. Capewell, D. Spiegelman, G. Danaei, and D. Mozaffarian, 2019. "The prospective impact of food pricing on improving dietary consumption: a systematic review and meta-analysis." *PLoS One* 12, no. 3: e0172277.

Andersen, K. G., A. Rambaut, W. I. Lipkin, et al. 2020. "The proximal origin of SARS-CoV-2." *Nature Medicine* 26: 450–2.

Baraldi, L. G., E. Martinez Steele, D. S. Canella, and C. A. Monteiro. 2018. "Consumption of ultra-processed foods and associated sociodemographic factors in the USA between 2007 and 2012: evidence from a nationally representative cross-sectional study." *BMJ Open*, 8, no. 3: e020574.

Baroni, L., L. Cenci, M. Tettamanti, and M. Berati. 2007. "Evaluating the environmental impact of various dietary patterns combined with different food production systems." *European Journal of Clinical Nutrition* 61: 279–86.

Batini, N. 2019a. "Macroeconomic gains from agri-food reforms: the case of France." IMF working paper no. 19/41. Washington, D.C.: International Monetary Fund.

———. 2019b. "Transforming agri-food sectors to mitigate climate change: the role of green finance." *Quarterly Journal of Economic Research–Vierteljahrshefte zur Wirtschaftsforschung* 88, no. 3: 7–42.

Batis, C., J. A. Rivera, B. M. Popkin, and L. S. Taillie. 2017. "First-year evaluation of

Mexico's tax on nonessential energy-dense foods: an observational study." *PLoS Medicine* 13, no. 7: e1002057.

Baudry, J., K., E. Assmann, M. Touvier, B. Allès, L. Seconda, P. Latino-Martel, K. Ezzedine, P. Galan, S. Hercberg, D. Lairon, et al. 2018. "Association of frequency of organic food consumption with cancer risk:findings from the NutriNet-Santé prospective cohort study." *JAMA Internal Medicine* 178: 1597–606.

Behera, S. N., M. Sharma, V. P. Aneja, and R. Balasubramanian. 2013. "Ammonia in the atmosphere: a review on emission sources, atmospheric chemistry and deposition on terrestrial bodies." *Environmental Science and Pollution Research International* 20: 8092–131.

Bloom, D. E., M. Kuhn, and K. Prettner. 2019. Health and economic growth. In *Oxford Encyclopedia of Economics and Finance*. Oxford, UK: Oxford University Press.

Campbell, T. C., and T. M. Campbell. 2006. *The China Study: The Most Comprehensive Study of Nutrition Ever Conducted and the Startling Implications for Diet, Weight Loss and Long-Term Health.* Dallas, TX: BenBella Books.

Carnevale, C., E. Pisoni, and M. Volta. 2010. "A non-linear analysis to detect the origin of PM10 concentrations in northern Italy." *The Science of the Total Environment* 409: 182–91.

Centers for Disease and Control Prevention (CDC). 2020. "Chronic diseases in America." https://www.cdc.gov/chronicdisease/resources/press_room.htm

Chen, S., M. Kuhn, K. Prettner, and D. E. Bloom. 2018. "The macroeconomic burden of noncommunicable diseases in the United States: estimates and projections." *PLoS One* 13, no. 11: e0206702.

De Marco, A., M. Velardi, C. Camporeale, A. Screpanti, and V. Marcello. 2014. "The adherence of the diet to Mediterranean principle and its impacts on human and environmental health." *International Journal of Environmental Protection Policy* 2: 64–75.

Devries, S., W. Willett, and R. O. Bonow. 2019. "Nutrition education in medical school, residency training, and practice." *JAMA* 321, no. 14: 1351–2.

Elser, J., and E. Bennett. 2011. "Phosphorus cycle: a broken biogeochemical cycle." *Nature* 478, no. 7367: 29–31.

European Commission (EC). 2014. "Mapping dietary prevention of cancer in the EU28: European National Cancer Plans and their coverage of dietary prevention of cancer." S. Eisenwagen and S. Caldeira. A Science and Policy Report by the Joint Centre of the European Commission. https://ec.europa.eu/jrc/en/publication/eur-scientific-and-technical-research-reports/mapping-dietary-prevention-cancer-eu28-european-national-cancer-plans-and-their-coverage

European Food and Safety Authority (EFSA). 2018. "The European Union summary report on antimicrobial resistance in zoonotic and indicator bacteria from humans, animals and food in 2016." *EFSA Journal* 16, no. 2: 5182.

European Heart Network (EHN). 2017. *European Cardiovascular Disease Statistics, 2017 Edition*. Brussels, Belgium: European Heart Network AISBL.

EU, European Parliament Research Service (EPRS). 2017. *EU Action on Cancer*. London: EPRS.

Food and Agriculture Organization (FAO). 2017. "Stepping up school-based food and nutrition education." International Expert Consultation, Al Ain, United Arab Emirates, 28–30 November.

———. 2018. "One health: addressing transboundary plant, animal and fish pests and diseases: a case for regional cooperation." FAO Regional Conference for the Near East. Thirty-Fourth Session. Rome: FAO.

Food and Agriculture Organization of the United Nations (FAO), the International Fund for Agricultural Development (IFAD), the United Nations Children's Fund (UNICEF), the World Food Programme (WFP), and the World Health Organization (WHO) (SOFI). 2019. *The State of Food Security and Nutrition in the World 2019. Safeguarding Against Economic Slowdowns and Downturns.* Rome: FAO.

———. 2020. *The State of Food Security and Nutrition in the World 2020. Transforming Food Systems for Affordable Healthy Diets.* Rome: FAO.

Foer, J. S. 2019. *We Are the Weather: Saving the Planet Begins at Breakfast.* New York: Farrar, Strauss and Giroux.

Fontana, L. 2018. "Interventions to promote cardiometabolic health and slow cardiovascular ageing." *Nature Reviews Cardiology* 15: 566–77.

Fontana, L., B. K. Kennedy, V. D. Longo, D. Seals, and S. Melov. 2014. "Medical research: treat ageing." *Nature News* 511: 405.

Fontana, L., S. and Klein. 2007. "Aging, adiposity, and calorie restriction." *JAMA* 297: 986–94.

Fontana, L., and L. Partridge. 2015. "Promoting health and longevity through diet: from model organisms to humans." *Cell* 161, no. 1: 106–18.

Fontana, L., L. Partridge, and V. D. Longo. 2010. "Extending healthy life span—from yeast to humans." *Science* 328: 321–6.

Global Burden of Disease (GBD). 2017. "Findings from the Global Burden of Disease Study 2017." *Lancet* 392, no. 10159: 1683–2138, e14–e18.

Grossman, M., E. Tekin, and R. Wada. 2014. "Food prices and body fatness among youths." *Economics and Human Biology*, 12: 4–19.

Hubbard, R. K., G. L. Newton, and G. M. Hill. 2004. "Water quality and the grazing animal." *Journal of Animal Science* 82, E suppl: E255–63.

Ikeno, Y., G. B. Hubbard, S. Lee, S. M. Dube, L. C. Flores, M. G. Roman, and A. Bartke. 2013. "Do Ames dwarf and calorie-restricted mice share common effects on age-related pathology?" *Pathobiology of Aging & Age Related Diseases* 3. https://doi.org/10.3402/pba.v3i0.20833

Intergovernmental Panel on Climate Change (IPCC). 2019. *Climate Change and Land: An IPCC Special Report on Climate Change, Desertification, Land Degradation, Sustainable Land Management, Food Security, and Greenhouse Gas Fluxes in Terrestrial Ecosystems.* Geneva, Switzerland: IPCC.

Jones, B. A., D. Grace, R. Kock, S. Alonso, J. Rushton, M. Y. Said, and D. U. Pfeiffer. 2013. "Zoonosis emergence linked to agricultural intensification and environmental change." *Proceedings of the National Academy of Sciences of the United States of America* 110, no. 21: 8399–404.

Jones, K., N. Patel, M. Levy, et al. 2008. "Global trends in emerging infectious diseases." *Nature* 451: 990–3.

Joyce, A., S. Dixon, J. Comfort, and J. Hallett. 2012. "Reducing the environmental impact of dietary choice: perspectives from a behavioural and social change approach." *Journal of Environmental and Public Health* 2012: 978672.

Kight, C. E., J. M. Bouche, A. Curry, D. Frankenfield, K. Good, P. Guenter, B. Murphy,

C. Papoutsakis, E. Brown Richards, V. W. Vanek, et al. 2020. "Consensus recommendations for optimizing electronic health records for nutrition care." *Nutrition in Clinical Practice*, 35, no.1: 12–23.

Luengo-Fernandez, R., J. Leal, A. Gray, and R. Sullivan. 2013. "Economic burden of cancer across the European Union: a population-based cost analysis." *Lancet Oncology* 14, no. 12:1165–74.

Martin, M., S. E. Totthatil, and T. B. Newman. 2015. "Antibiotics overuse in animal agriculture: a call to action for health care providers." *American Journal of Public Health*, 105, no. 12: 2409–10.

Mattison, J. A., R. J. Colman, T. M. Beasley, et al. 2017. "Caloric restriction improves health and survival of rhesus monkeys." *Nature Communications* 8: 14063.

Most, J., V. Tosti, L. M. Redman, and L. Fontana. 2017. "Calorie restriction in humans: an update." *Ageing Research Reviews* 39: 36–45.

Mozzafarian, D. 2017. "Want to fix America's health care? First, focus on food." *The Conversation*. https://theconversation.com/want-to-fix-americas-health-care-first-focus-on-food-81307

Mytton, O. T., D. Clarke, and M. Rayner. 2012. "Taxing unhealthy food and drinks to improve health." *British Medical Journal* 344.

NCD Risk Factor Collaboration (NCD-RisC). 2017. "Worldwide trends in body-mass index, underweight, overweight, and obesity from 1975 to 2016: a pooled analysis of 2416 population-based measurement studies in 128·9 million children, adolescents, and adults." *Lancet* 390, no. 10113: 2627–42.

Nielsen Homescan Panel Protein Survey. 2017. http://nielsen.com

Nijdam, D., T. Rood, and H. Westhoek. 2012. "The price of protein: review of land use and carbon footprints from life cycle assessments of animal food products and their substitutes." *Food Policy* 37, no. 6: 760–70.

Ohlhorst, S. D., R. Russell, D. Bier, D. M. Klurfeld, Z. Li, J. R. Mein, J. Milner, A. C. Ross, P. Stover, and E. Konopka. 2013. "Nutrition research to affect food and a healthy life span." *Journal of Nutrition* 143, no. 8: 1349–54.

O'Neill Report. 2016. "The review on antimicrobial resistance (AMR): tackling drug-resistant infections globally: final report and recommendations." Chaired by Jim O'Neill, commissioned in 2014 by the UK Government and sponsored by the Wellcome Trust and the UK Department of Health. https://amr-review.org/

Orueta, J. F., A. Garcia-Alvarez, M. Garcia-Goni, F. Paolucci, and R. Nuno-Solinis. 2014. "Prevalence and costs of multimorbidity by deprivation levels in the Basque country: a population-based study using health administrative databases." *PLoS One* 9, no. 2: e89787.

Pinder, R. W., P. J. Adams, and S. N. Pandis. 2007. "Ammonia emission controls as a cost-effective strategy for reducing atmospheric particulate matter in the eastern United States." *Environmental Science & Technology* 41: 380–6.

Pollard, C. M., and S. Booth. 2019. "Addressing food and nutrition security in developed countries." *International Journal of Environmental Research and Public Health* 16, no. 13: 2370.

Pomeranz, J. L., P. Wilde, Y. Huang, R. Micha, and D. Mozaffarian. 2018. "Legal and administrative feasibility of a federal junk food and sugar-sweetened beverage tax to improve diet." *American Journal of Public Health* 108, no. 2: 203–9.

Ritchie, H., and M. Roser. 2017. "Meat and dairy production." OurWorldInData.org. https://ourworldindata.org/meat-production

Rockström, J., O. Gaffney, J. Rogelj, M. Meinshausen, N. Nakicenovic, and H. J. Schellnhuber. 2017. "A roadmap for rapid decarbonization." *Science* 355, no. 6331: 1269–71.

Roser, M., and H. Ritchie. 2020. "Food per person." OurWorldInData.org. https://ourworldindata.org/food-per-person

Searchinger, T. D., S. Wirsenius, T. Beringer, et al. 2018. "Assessing the efficiency of changes in land use for mitigating climate change." *Nature* 564: 249–53.

Simon, D. R. 2013. *Meatonomics*. Everyville, Calif.: Conari Press.

Springmann, M., D. Mason-D'Croz, S. Robinson, K. Wiebe, H. C. J. Godfray, M. Rayner, et al. 2018. "Health-motivated taxes on red and processed meat: a modelling study on optimal tax levels and associated health impacts." *PLoS One* 13, no. 11: e0204139.

Sutton, M. A., O. Oenema, and J. W. Erisman. 2011. "Too much of a good thing." *Nature* 472, no. 7342: 159–61.

Taillie, L. S., M. Reyes, M. A. Colchero, B. Popkin, and C. Corvalán. 2020. "An evaluation of Chile's Law of Food Labeling and Advertising on sugar-sweetened beverage purchases from 2015 to 2017: a before-and-after study." *PLoS Medicine* 17, no. 2: e1003015.

Tambor, M., M. Pavlova, S. Golinowska, J. Arsenijevic, and W. Groot. 2016. "Financial incentives for a healthy lifestyle and disease prevention among older people: a systematic literature review." *BMC Health Services Research* 16, suppl. 5: 426.

Tilman, D., K. G. Cassman, P. A. Matson, et al. 2002. "Agricultural sustainability and intensive production practices." *Nature* 418, no. 6898: 671–7.

Tilman, D., and M. Clark. 2014. "Global diets link environmental sustainability and human health." *Nature* 515, no. 7528: 518–22.

Tsimpidi, A. P., V. A. Karydis, and S. N. Pandis. 2007. "Response of inorganic fine particulate matter to emission changes of sulfur dioxide and ammonia: the eastern United States as a case study." *Journal of the Air & Waste Management Association* 57: 1489–98.

U.S. Department of Agriculture Economic Research Service. 2009. "Access to affordable and nutritious food: measuring and understanding food deserts and their consequences." Administrative publication no. AP-036. https://www.ers.usda.gov/publications/pub-details/?pubid=42729

Weintraub, A. 2018. "Should we tax junk foods to curb obesity?" *Forbes* June 10. https://www.forbes.com/sites/arleneweintraub/2018/01/10/should-we-tax-junk-foods-to-curb-obesity/#4f71340f7df6

Willett, W., J. Rockström, B. Loken, et al. 2019. "Food in the Anthropocene: the EAT–Lancet Commission on Healthy Diets from Sustainable Food Systems." *Lancet* 393, no. 10170: 447–92.

World Health Organization. 2004. *Global Strategy on Diet, Physical Activity and Health*. Geneva, Switzerland: WHO.

———. 2015. *Global Action Plan on Anti-Microbial Resistance*. Geneva, Switzerland: WHO. https://www.who.int/antimicrobial-resistance/publications/global-action-plan/en/

———. 2018. "United States of America." Noncommunicable Diseases (NCD) Country Profiles, 2018. https://www.who.int/nmh/countries/usa_en.pdf

———. 2019. "Noncommunicable Diseases: Risk Factors." The Global Health Observatory. World Health Data Platform. https://www.who.int/data/gho/data/themes/topics/topic-details/GHO/ncd-risk-factors

Endnotes

1. *The State of Food Security and Nutrition in the World* uses multiple indicators to monitor hunger and food insecurity in the world. Two of these indicators, the prevalence of undernourishment (PoU) and the prevalence of moderate or severe food insecurity in the population, based on the Food Insecurity Experience Scale (FIES), are being used to monitor the world's progress toward achieving Sustainable Development Goal 2. The PoU and the prevalence of food insecurity based on the FIES give different perspectives and use very different methods and sources of data. Revisions to data on food insecurity in China in 2019 led to a significant lowering of the estimates of world hunger for 2019, which in the 2020 *State of Food Security and Nutrition in the World* moved from 820 to 690 million. However, a preliminary assessment in the same report suggests that the COVID-19 pandemic may add 83 to 132 million people to the total number of undernourished in the world in 2020, depending on the economic growth scenario and the trend in food insecurity continues to point upward in coming years (FAO, IFAD, UNICEF, WFP, and WHO 2020).
2. As a global average, per capita meat consumption has increased approximately by 20 kilograms since 1961, with the global per capita average meat consumption reaching about 43 kilograms of meat in 2014 (Ritchie and Roser 2017). This increase in per capita meat trends implies that total meat production has been growing at a much faster than the rate of population growth. At a regional level, the average European and North American consumes nearly 80 kilograms and more than 120 kilograms, respectively. However, changes in consumption in high-income countries have been much slower, with most stagnating or even decreasing over the last fifty years. Consumption trends across Africa are varied: Some countries consume as little as 10 kilograms per person, about half of the continental average, and higher-income nations, such as South Africa, consume between 60 and 70 kilograms per person (see Batini 2019b).
3. The Western-versus-Eastern dichotomy has become less relevant because such a diet is no longer foreign to any global region (just as traditional East Asian cuisine is no longer "foreign" to the West), but the term is still a well understood shorthand in medical literature, regardless of where the diet is found.
4. https://www.who.int/nutrition/topics/3_foodconsumption/en/.
5. About a third of Millennials (Gen Y) and Centennials (Gen Z) eat meat alternatives every day, and 50 percent eat meat alternatives a few times a week (Nielsen Homescan Panel Protein Survey 2017).
6. https://www.cdc.gov/nchs/data/hestat/obesity_adult_07_08/obesity_adult_07_08.pdf.
7. The use of antibiotics in feed as growth promoters was banned in the EU in 2006, but it is still widely practiced elsewhere in the advanced world. See Regulation 1831/2003/EC on additives for use in animal nutrition, replacing Directive 70/524/EEC on additives in feeding-stuffs.
8. This has happened in Europe with vancomycin, one of the drugs of last resort for treat-

ing certain life-threatening infections. Data suggest that rising levels of vancomycin-resistant bacteria in hospitals may have resulted from use in agriculture of avoparcin, a drug chemically related to vancomycin. Because avoparcin and vancomycin are similar in structure, bacteria resistant to avoparcin are resistant to vancomycin as well.

9. Since the first human H5N1 outbreak occurred in 1997, there has been an increasing number of HPAI H5N1 bird-to-human transmissions, leading to clinically severe and fatal human infections.
10. More than 60 percent of the roughly 400 emerging infectious diseases that have been identified since 1940 are zoonotic (Jones et al. 2008).
11. Restricting calorie or protein intake in mice or introducing mutations in nutrient-sensing pathways can extend lifespans by as much as 50 percent. These "Methuselah mice" are more likely than controls to die without apparent disease (Ikeno et al. 2013). In Rhesus monkeys, reducing food intake with optimal nutrition also increases lifespan and protects against obesity, type 2 diabetes, cancer, cardiovascular disease, brain aging, and frailty (Mattison et al. 2017), and in humans it causes physiologic, metabolic, and molecular changes that protect against these pathologies (Fontana and Klein 2007; Most et al. 2017). Moreover, recent findings indicate that lowered intake of particular nutrients is also key in mediating the beneficial effects of a healthy diet, with protein, specific amino acids, and vegetable fiber playing prominent roles (Fontana and Partridge 2015). These findings are of particular importance because the recommended daily allowance for protein intake is 0.83 g/kg of body weight per day, yet at least 50 percent of men and women in many developed countries chronically consume twice as much of this amount.
12. In the United States, for example, it is estimated that about 23.5 million people live in food deserts. Nearly half of them are also low income. See U.S. Department of Agriculture Economic Research Service (2009).
13. See FightChronicDisease.org/pfcd-in-the-states.
14. Cesarean sections are estimated to currently contribute 2 percent to world GDP, joint replacements 0.65 percent, cancer drugs 0.75 percent, and organ transplants 0.1 percent. This would cost another $100 trillion by 2050.
15. A paper in the journal *Food Policy* estimates that 1 kilo of beef protein reared on a British hill farm whose soils are rich in carbon has a cost of 643 kg, and a kilo of lamb protein costs 749 kg (Nijdam et al. 2012).
16. A Pigouvian tax—from Arthur Pigou, a Cambridge University professor active in the first half of the twentieth century—adjusts the market for goods that cause externalities by raising the goods' costs and thereby reducing demand for them. Such a tax pays a double dividend by both generating revenue and reducing undesirable consumption. Ideally, the new revenue adds to—or replaces—general tax revenue and thus can be used to lower general taxes.
17. The literature identifies four methods of classifying foods for the purpose of taxation: by product category (such as soda or candy), broad nutrient criteria, specific nutrients or calories, or a combination. Some of the research also recommended a graduated taxation strategy, where the tax increases as the nutritional quality of the food decreases (e.g., as the sugar content increases, the tax increases). See Pomeranz et al. (2018).
18. Over the past decade, many private companies around the world have been rethinking their approach to employee health, providing a range of financial and other benefits

for healthier lifestyles. Life insurance has also realized the return on the investment, rewarding clients for healthier living with fitness tracking devices, lower premiums, and healthy food benefits, which pay back up to several hundred dollars each year for nutritious grocery purchases. It has been estimated that every dollar spent on wellness programs generates multiple dollars in savings from lower medical costs and absenteeism (Mozzafarian 2017). In 2012, Ohio Senator Rob Portman proposed a Medicare "Better Health Rewards" program to reward seniors for not smoking and for achieving lower weight, blood pressure, glucose, and cholesterol.

19. Children of different ages face diverse challenges to healthful eating and different vulnerabilities to food marketing. Young children do not understand the persuasive intent of advertising and marketing and are easily misled. Older children, who still do not have fully developed logical thinking, have spending money and opportunities to make food choices and purchases in the absence of parental guidance.
20. By 2009, thirty-three U.S. states had levied sales taxes on sugar-sweetened soft drinks, with an average tax rate of 5.2 percent.
21. Similar laws were passed in 2016 in San Francisco, Oakland, and Albany, California, as well as in Boulder, Colorado.
22. Since 2007, the European Nutrition for Health Alliance (ENHA) has worked with the European Parliament to include nutritional risk screening and good nutritional care in EU programs. Eighteen countries are currently involved in ENHA's Optimal Nutrition Care for All (ONCA) campaign: Belgium, Croatia, Czech Republic, Denmark, France, Germany, Israel, Italy, the Netherlands, Portugal, Republic of Ireland, Slovenia, Spain, Sweden, Austria, Poland, Turkey, and the U.K.
23. This work is part of the work agenda that FAO committed to during the Second International Conference on Nutrition and supports the Sustainable Development Goals.
24. In fossil fuel emission equivalent, this would correspond to replacing all fossil fuel energy plants with zero-carbon nuclear energy plants.

CHAPTER 6

Greening Food Demand in Less-Advanced Economies

Divya Mehra, Saskia de Pee, Jessica C. Fanzo, and Martin W. Bloem

"Food—there's no greater gift."—*Dikembe Mutombo*

Ensuring a diverse, healthy, and sustainable diet for our growing population is one of the greatest challenges of our times. Food has a direct impact not only on human health but on environmental sustainability (Willett et al. 2019). Growth of the global population, projected to exceed 9 billion by 2050, will be concentrated in a few countries, doubling in the least developed and stagnating in the developed world (Department of Economic and Social Affairs [DESA] 2019; Willett et al. 2019). Feeding this changing population with a healthy diet while reducing greenhouse gas (GHG) emissions, habitat loss, freshwater depletion, and pollution will require addressing components of the entire food system.

Diets and Health

Unhealthy diets accounted for the largest global burden of disease and 22 percent of all deaths among adults in 2017 (GBD Diet Collaborators 2019). The morbidity and mortality risks of unhealthy diets are greater than alcohol, drug, and tobacco use combined, contributing to obesity and noncommunicable diseases (NCDs) such as coronary heart disease, stroke, and diabetes. In fact, diet-related disease represents 16 percent of all disability-adjusted life years among adults globally. Healthcare costs associated with poor diets are equally alarming. For example, the economic impact of obesity, which is linked to all major NCDs, is estimated at US$2 trillion, or 2.8 percent of global gross domestic product (Dobbs et al. 2014). If low- and lower-middle income countries invested in the most cost-effective interventions for NCDs, by 2030 they would see a return of US$7 per person for every dollar invested (Food and Agriculture Organization of the United Nations [FAO] 2018b).

Although food production has consistently increased, reducing hunger and mortality, data from the recent Global Nutrition Report show that the world is generally eating poorly. This is a global problem, affecting every country and population group: 820 million people are still undernourished (not meeting energy needs), 149 million or almost 22 percent of all children are stunted (will suffer consequences of early-life undernutrition throughout life, including lower income earning potential and poor health), 49.5 million children are wasted (7.3 percent), 40.1 million children are overweight (5.9 percent), more than 2 billion people are micronutrient deficient, and 2.1 billion adults are overweight or obese (UNICEF 2019). Regardless of wealth, people from school age through adulthood are consuming diets dominated by refined grains and high-fat or high-sugar foods, unhealthy oils and drinks, and not enough nutritious foods such as fruits, vegetables, legumes, nuts, fish, dairy, eggs, and whole grains.

Although it is easy to propose a solution that focuses on diet diversity, this is often not an option in places where diets are dominated by staple foods because of lack of availability or affordability of healthier options. The focus needs to be on treating nutritional deficiencies, especially during critical periods in life, because of their immense impact on human capital. These deficiencies lead to stunting and other developmental problems, which can increase the risk of obesity and NCDs later in life. Subsequently, when options improve with economic growth and the food environment (e.g., access to food, healthy choices, retail or market setting, infrastructure, information about food) changes, a greater focus on healthy diets and limiting energy-dense, nutrient-poor foods is warranted, without losing sight of micronutrient deficiencies and vulnerabilities of specific groups.

A recent review of the economic effects of the double burden of malnutrition concluded that current models fall short of accurately evaluating that burden because evidence from low- and middle-income countries is often insufficient to support general conclusions. Double-duty interventions that address both forms of malnutrition might be more cost effective than separate interventions (Nugent et al. 2020).

Food Systems and the Environment

Food production has one of the largest influences of any sector on natural resources, GHG emissions, and therefore climate change. Forty percent of all land is used for agriculture; up to 30 percent of GHG emissions (carbon monoxide, methane, and nitrous oxide) and 70 percent of freshwater depletion can be attributed to food production (Woodward et al. 2014). Therefore, significant changes in agricultural production and consumption are necessary to reduce harm to the environment. This requires global and local analysis as well as action because countries are at different starting points with regard to health, food production, and consumption.

Just as agriculture drives climate change, climate change creates severe challenges for agriculture. The impact on the food system is tremendous, in terms of both quantity (e.g., reduction in yields, losses due to pests) and quality (e.g., lower nutritional content such as decreased zinc, iron, phosphorus, potassium, protein, and other nutrients in crops grown under elevated CO_2 conditions) (Myers et al. 2017). The threat to food security, brought about by extreme weather events and changing precipitation patterns, is already being observed in the drylands of Africa and high mountain regions of Asia and South America (Intergovernmental Panel on Climate Change [IPCC] 2019).

A related threat is the replacement of large agricultural landscapes with cultivated monocultures (Herrero et al. 2017). The loss of biodiversity in food and agriculture harms production systems and livelihoods, lessening resilience to shocks and stresses. Many countries have emphasized the importance of diversity in production, not only for food security and nutrition but also as a means of adapting to environmental challenges (FAO 2018a).

Economic and Environmental Benefits of Greening Food Demand in Less-Advanced Economies

Agriculture and the food system play a critical role in environmental health and human well-being. Investments in sustainable food systems can result in a cascade of positive outcomes, starting with green jobs and services. Innovation in this sector will also lead to better climate adaptation and mitigation.

Ultimately, the food system needs to be more productive, nutritious, climate smart, and resilient.

Economic Benefits

As of 2010, 78 percent of poor people lived in rural areas (WorldBankGroup 2015). Even accounting for urban migration, most poor people will still live in rural areas by 2030. Among poor working adults, agriculture accounts for about 65 percent of livelihoods (WorldBankGroup 2019a), and in 2014, about a third of global gross domestic product came from agriculture (WorldBankGroup 2019a). Consequently, addressing poverty by 2030 will require rural transformation and raising incomes of the rural poor. Growth in agriculture is two to four times more effective in reducing poverty than growth in other sectors (WorldBankGroup 2014) while not necessarily costing any more than investments made in other sectors (WorldBankGroup 2010).

Unfortunately, increased agricultural productivity does not necessarily lead to income gains for the smallholder farmer, and most food in developing countries is still produced on small family farms (FAO 2014). Instead, better livelihoods for small farmers require investment in access to markets, supply chains and other infrastructure, climate resilience, and agrobusinesses such as manufacturing, processing, and marketing (WorldBankGroup 2015). These investments not only increase productivity and efficiency but also lower food prices, which often make up a significant proportion of household expenditures, and this proportion goes down as incomes increase.

Environmental Benefits

Climate-smart agriculture has the potential to improve food and nutrition security while minimizing environmental damage to productive land, livestock, fisheries, and forests. It is operationalized through a three-pronged approach (WorldBankGroup 2019b): increased agricultural productivity and incomes of rural populations, greater resilience in the face of extreme weather events, and reduced emissions. To ensure that these approaches also meet nutritional needs, additional and more nuanced efforts are needed.

Resilience in the food system is essential from a macroeconomic perspective, given that extreme weather events can increase price volatility and availability, making it even more difficult for already vulnerable populations to access affordable food. Health problems from lack of nutritious food can in turn harm the local economy as productivity slows down (Rahman et al. 2019).

Recently the EAT–Lancet Commission brought together intersectoral experts from health, agriculture, and sustainability to develop targets for healthy diets and sustainable food production. These targets are in line with the Paris Agreement and meet the Sustainable Development Goals (SDGs) (Willett et al. 2019). The commission concluded that it is possible to provide healthy diets to a growing population by 2050 and beyond through the following five strategies: international and national commitments to healthy diets, reorienting agricultural priorities from quantity of food to quality, intensifying food production to increase high-quality output, strong and coordinated governance related to land and oceans, and halving food losses and waste in line with the SDGs.

Several nuances were missing in the EAT–Lancet study that need to be considered in a developing landscape. First, health was defined as the absence of NCDs among adults, leaving out nutrient needs during critical phases of life (e.g., addressing stunting), which is critical to reach the human capital development goals of lower middle-income countries. A related issue is the lack of consideration of affordability and availability of the right foods in less developed economies (Headey and Alderman 2019; Drewnowski 2020). Finally, the media messaging, news headlines, and soundbites that were picked up focused on reducing meat consumption, not accounting for the fact that many countries consume less than the EAT–Lancet planetary diet's average targets of animal-source foods. Recommendations on sustainable agricultural practices and food loss and waste were also missing from media coverage.

Policies to Green Food Demand in Less-Advanced Economies

The FAO and World Health Organization (WHO) aspirational definition of sustainable healthy diets is "dietary patterns that promote all dimensions of individuals' health and wellbeing; have low environmental pressure and impact; are accessible, affordable, safe and equitable; and are culturally acceptable" (WHO and FAO 2019). Yet the interplay between healthy diets, global food systems, and climate is complex: A diverse diet that minimizes environmental damage may or may not be healthy, depending on the nutritional content of the foods (Khoury et al. 2019). Similarly, a healthy diet may or may not have minimal environmental impact. Furthermore, we don't yet know whether all targets can be met at the same time. There is no one solution that can be applied to all contexts. Optimal diets differ at different phases of life and may take different forms in various countries. Depending on the starting point or baseline level of nutrition, individuals and communities may need to increase or decrease different foods or nutrients.

A recent analysis concluded that achieving healthy diets in many low- and middle-income countries would require an increase in GHG emissions and water use due to food production (Khoury et al. 2019). It is important to note that this conclusion was based on modifying an existing diet to ensure enough energy, protein, and servings of fruits and vegetables. This assumes that future fruit and vegetable supply could potentially meet a demand of at least 400 g per capita per day, which projections show may not be achievable everywhere, even if waste were close to zero (Mason-D'Croz et al. 2019). Other nutrient intakes were not taken into consideration.

To prevent undernutrition among pregnant and lactating women and young children in many parts of the world, a moderate intake of animal source foods or fortified foods and supplements is necessary. The level of necessary animal products depends on the level of undernutrition in low-income countries. Animal foods are a more concentrated source (and can be the only source) of some nutrients, so where dietary diversity is still low and staple food intake very high, animal foods can be very important to overall nutrition.

This implies a trade-off. Adequate diets in low-income countries may result in higher environmental costs, but they can be offset by an acceleration toward plant-based diets in high-income countries (Mason-D'Croz et al. 2019). In other words, a moderate intake of animal foods globally would mean a substantial decrease in many high-income countries but an increase up to a moderate level in lower middle-income countries. The right intake may not look too different across countries, but optimizing may mean a very different shift across different countries and spectrum of development.

Very few countries have implemented a comprehensive package of actions needed to significantly improve diets at the population level (Development Initiatives 2018). There is no dearth of existing policies; there are more than 1,000 national policies in 191 countries to support healthy diets (Development Initiatives 2018), such as taxes on sugar. However, in many developing countries a double burden of undernutrition and overnutrition is emerging. Forty-eight lower middle-income countries have a severe double burden[1] of malnutrition (Popkin et al. 2020). Governments, supported by the private sector and other partners, need to implement holistic plans to ensure healthy diets are affordable, accessible, and desirable for all (Popkin et al. 2020). To ensure access, links need to be drawn between social protection programs and food systems. Sustainable approaches can reduce undernutrition and poverty without resulting in obesity or failing to resolve micronutrient deficiencies.

Creating demand for healthy diets requires a comprehensive life-cycle approach, targeting different groups with tailored strategies from different actors and platforms (private sector, public sector, media, messaging in schools). Figure 6-1 provides a simple summary of engagement needed at different levels, from both demand and supply sides. Consumers, including the poorest, need to be empowered to demand and access nutritious foods. Facilitating this shift requires consideration of the sociocultural and community dynamics that influence consumption, in addition to the obvious driver, affordability. The private sector can provide insights on how to design behavior change communication and support national efforts to increase demand for healthy foods. In turn, increased demand should contribute to changing food systems and greater production of healthier foods.

Local institutional capacity and sensible regulation are equally important to change our food system. Policies that affect what is grown and its impact on the environment influence global food prices, which in turn affect processing, marketing, distribution, trade, and retailing of foods and ingredients (figure 6-1). Further downstream, diets should support consumers' health, which means that foods should be nutritious and safe. National dietary guidelines and policies (e.g., advertisements, procurement) support healthy diets and can be mainstreamed into wider social safety nets.

Country Case: Indonesia

As countries design strategies to achieve the SDGs for poverty reduction (SDG1), zero hunger and zero malnutrition (SDG2), health (SDG3), and climate (SDG13), their interconnectedness is paramount to consider and balance. For Indonesia, we assessed the extent to which the current food supply meets nutritional needs and what optimization of diets for nutritional content would mean for climate impact and vice versa, as well as what the cost of those diets would be and how that compares to what people currently spend on food.

More than one third of children under five years old are stunted, indicating a large problem of undernutrition; a quarter of adults are overweight or obese, and micronutrient deficiencies are widespread. Furthermore, more than half of today's adults suffered undernutrition in early childhood (e.g., in

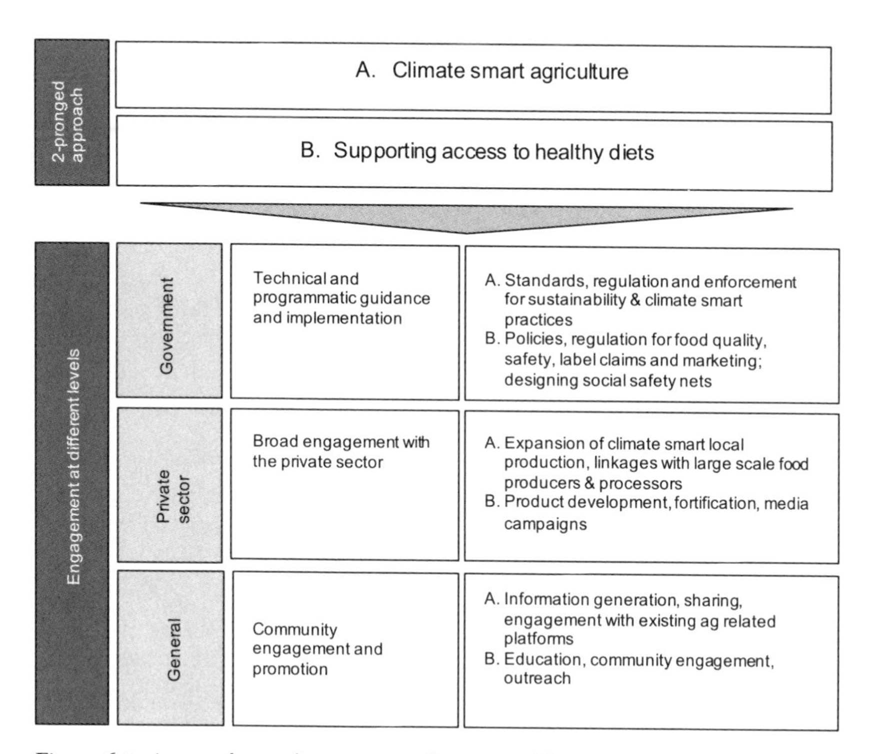

Figure 6-1. Approaches and engagement for sustainable, nutritious diets.

1995, 48 percent of children under five were stunted), increasing their risk of overweight or obesity and NCDs.

The diet in Indonesia is dominated by staple foods, mainly rice, that provide most of people's energy (70 percent), and calories are higher and protein intake lower than recommended. Because of a lack of diversity in their diets, many people do not get enough essential micronutrients such as iron, zinc, and vitamin A, which affects their short- and long-term health and development in many ways. Their intake of healthy foods is also too low to prevent NCDs. Excess calories, including from rice and foods high in fat and sugar, increase the prevalence of obesity, and micronutrient deficiencies persist. In Indonesia, affordability plays an important role in people's dietary choices (Baldi et al. 2013), in addition to culture, convenience, and the food environment.

We modeled different nutritious or climate-friendly diets (De Pee 2020, Kim et al. 2019) and compared them with current consumption with regard to cost and affordability, nutrient content, and climate impact (GHG emissions).[2] The current food supply provides approximately 2,607 kilocalories per capita per day and 56 grams of protein per capita per day. Reducing energy to an amount that is more in line with estimated needs (i.e. 2,300 kilocalories per capita per day) and ensuring that 12 percent of energy comes from protein would result in approximately 15 percent higher GHG emissions.

Increasingly plant-forward options, including the EAT–Lancet planetary health diet, were modeled so as to reduce the impact on the climate. They also complied with the WHO health advice to have no more than 10 percent of energy from sugar and at least five servings of fruits and vegetables a day. Figure 6-2 shows the GHG emissions for the different modeled diets in comparison to the current diet. The smaller the share of animal source foods (while maintaining a total intake of 69 grams of protein per capita per day), and particularly the lower the amount of red meat, dairy, and eggs, the lower the GHG emissions. Compared with GHG emissions from the current diet, the no-red-meat, pescatarian, low-food-chain, and vegan diets had lower GHG emissions, with only the latter two being below the target for sustainable food systems as proposed by the EAT–Lancet Commission (Willett et al. 2019).

The diet that was optimized to meet nutritional needs at the lowest possible cost had high GHG emissions, particularly on account of beef (figure 6-2 optimized). However, when the nutritional value of the other, more plant-based diets was examined, they did not meet the target for several nutrients (table 6-1), including vitamins A, D, B_1, B_2, folate, B_{12}, iron, calcium, zinc, and choline. Among the plant-forward diets, the EAT–Lancet, lacto-ovo vegetarian, and low-food-chain diets had fewer and smaller nutrient deficiencies.

This illustrates that in the case of Indonesia, meeting nutritional targets from the current food supply and in a cost-efficient manner would require an increase in consumption of foods that have a higher GHG footprint than the current diet. And some of the more plant-forward diets (EAT–Lancet and lacto-ovo) that had a better nutrient content also had higher GHG emissions than the baseline, in part because a greater amount of protein sources had to be included. The low-food-chain diet, which is largely plant food complemented by insects, snails, mollusks, and forage fishes, was an exception with low GHG emissions and better nutrient content, although it did not meet the nutrient targets.

All the diets, whether designed to meet nutrient requirements or be more climate friendly, were more costly than Indonesians' current diet. The increase ranged from 3 to 24 percent for vegan and lacto-ovo vegetarian diets, respectively. This was mainly because the higher amount of protein in the modeled diets, which adds diversity and meets nutritional guidelines, costs more.

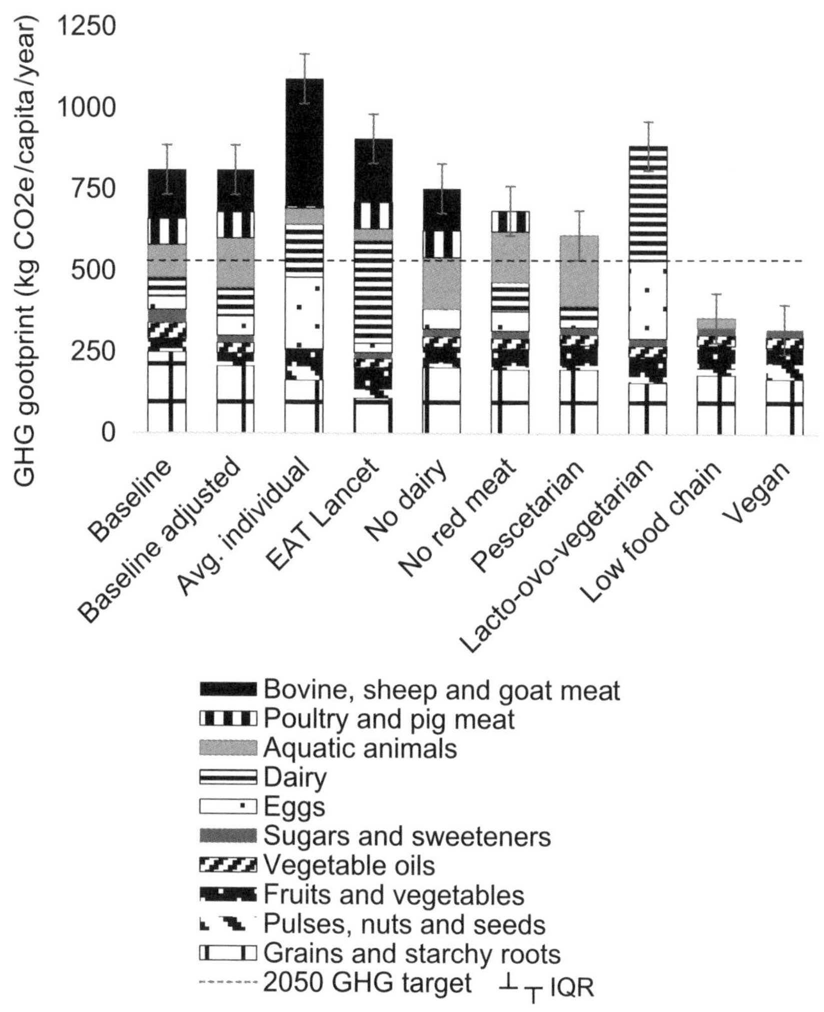

Figure 6-2. Greenhouse gas emissions for the modeled diets and per food group for Indonesia. *Note:* CO2e, carbon dioxide emissions; GHG, greenhouse gas.

Although we do not have data indicating whether people could spend more on food than they currently do, our data show that more than half the population would have to substantially increase their expenditure on food. An earlier analysis in Indonesia found that the proportion of the population that would be unable to afford a nutritious diet was much higher in poorer and more rural parts of the country, which was also where the prevalence of stunting was higher (Baldi et al. 2013).

TABLE 6-1. *Number of Nutrients for Which the Modeled Diets Provided at Least 100% or at Least 75% of the Targeted Nutritional Value*[a]

Modeled Diets[b]	**Number of Nutrients Met at 100% of Target (out of 18)**	**Number of Nutrients Met at 75% of Target (out of 18)**
Baseline	8	11
Adjusted baseline	9	11
Optimized (nutrients and cost)	16	17
EAT–Lancet	10	13
No dairy	9	11
No red meat	9	11
Pescatarian	9	11
Lacto-ovo vegetarian	10	14
Low food chain	9	12
Vegan	10	10

[a]Nutrients included in analysis: protein; essential amino acids (counted as one group); vitamins A, C, D, K, B_1, B_2, niacin, pantothenate, B_6, folic acid, B_{12}; iron; zinc; calcium; magnesium; choline. Vitamins D and K and choline were not included in the optimization model, so the optimized diet did not meet the target for vitamin D but almost met it for choline (97%). Targets were set at the level of the Nutrient Reference Values for the general population (Codex).

[b]For the last six diets, increasingly more plant-source protein was included, excluding certain animal sources of protein sources relative to the adjusted baseline diet while maintaining a protein content of 69 g, as follows: No dairy, protein supplied by red meat (not more than baseline), poultry, aquatic animals, eggs, pulses, soy; No red meat, protein supplied by dairy, poultry, aquatic animals, eggs, pulses, soy; Pescatarian, protein supplied by dairy, aquatic animals, eggs (not more than at baseline), pulses, soy; Lacto-ovo, protein supplied by dairy, legumes, nuts, seeds, and eggs; Low food chain, protein supplied by insects, forage fish, bivalve mollusks, pulses, soy; Vegan, protein supplied by pulses and soy.

Increasing dietary diversity also meant a substantial decrease of the amount of rice in the diet. Whereas the current intake provides approximately 70 percent of energy, all modeled diets decreased that, by 17 percent (to 1,523 kilocalories per capita per day) to as much as 33 percent (average individual) and 55 percent (EAT–Lancet planetary health diet). Reducing rice to that degree would entail major changes in dietary practices, not only in terms of what is consumed but also in terms of how it is prepared. Side dishes in Indonesia are very flavorful, which makes a nice complement to a large portion of rice, but they would need to be modified if less rice were eaten.

This example shows important avenues to explore diets that meet nutrient needs, reduce the risk of NCDs, limit climate impact, and are affordable, including the following:

- Lowering costs of nutritious foods through production and food value chain optimization, (e.g., reducing loss by keeping food fresh throughout transport and storage)
- Increasing nutritional value of foods through biofortification and postharvest fortification of foods for specific target groups (e.g., fortified infant cereal) and for the general population (fortified rice)
- Modifying methods of production and sourcing of foods to lower GHG emissions
- Exploring the potential of increasing consumption of nutrient-rich foods with a low climate footprint, such as low-food-chain animals such as forage fish and snails and high-quality protein-rich foods based on soy
- Finding ways to motivate consumers, and society at large, to change dietary patterns to include less rice and more nutritious foods
- Designing social protection instruments, such as social safety nets and school meals, to deliver better nutrition
- Modeling scenarios of the impact of economic growth on GHG emissions and meeting or not meeting nutrient needs with and without specific actions to increase the supply of affordable, nutritious foods

Simply put, Indonesians need to eat less rice and consume healthier and more nutrient-dense foods in order to prevent NCDs. This would require consumers to change their food choices but also for them to have enough purchasing power to do so. It would also mean that some foods, such as those indispensable for particular nutrients (e.g., vitamin B_{12}), would have a high GHG footprint. This case underscores the need for higher-income countries to reduce their consumption of high-GHG foods so that poorer countries can meet their nutritional needs without increasing emissions globally.

Conclusions

Countries will need to balance the trade-offs between meeting the nutritional needs of their populations, addressing issues of access and affordability, and developing food systems that are sustainable, all while ensuring socioeconomic development. There is no one solution that will work for all countries. Attaining optimal diets for different countries depends on their starting points and stages of development.

Achieving an adequate and healthy diet in most low- and middle-income countries will require a substantial increase in GHG emissions and water use due to food production (Kim et al. 2019). A certain amount of animal-based food will be needed in the regions of the developing world that struggle with nutrition deficiencies. Unfortunately, nutritious foods are not always available or affordable. Where needed, specialized nutritious foods can help close the gap to achieve good health, growth, and development. Local nutrient-rich foods and crops can be integrated in the diets.

The right balance for animal source products will depend on the level of undernutrition in countries. This may result in higher environmental costs in certain contexts, which would require a faster shift to more plant-forward diets in the United States, Europe, and advanced countries in Asia (Kim et al. 2019). Policy reforms need to accommodate these nuances, with careful attention to critical life phases to ensure gains in human capital.

References

Baldi, G., E. Martini, M. Catharina, S. Muslimatun, U. Fahmida, A. B. Jahari, Hardinsyah, R. Frega, P. Geniez, N. Grede, Minarto, M. W. Bloem, and S. de Pee. 2013. "Cost of the Diet (CoD) tool: first results from Indonesia and applications for policy discussion on food and nutrition security." *Food and Nutrition Bulletin* 34, 2 suppl.: S35–42. doi:10.1177/15648265130342S105

De Pee, S., J. F. Hardinsyah, B. F. Kim, R. D. Semba, A. Deptford, J. C. Fanzo, B. Ramsing, K. Nachman, S. McKenzie, and M. W. Bloem. 2020. "Balancing nutrition, health, affordability and climate goals: the case of Indonesia" [mimeo].

Department of Economic and Social Affairs (DESA), United Nations. 2019. "World population prospects." New York: UN Department of Economic and Social Affairs, Population Division.

Development Initiatives. 2018. "2018 global nutrition report: shining a light to spur action on nutrition." Bristol, UK: Development Initiatives.

Dobbs, R., C. Sawers, F. Thompson, J. Manyika, J. Woetzel, P. Child, S. McKenna, and A. Spatharou. 2014. "How the world could better fight obesity." Discussion paper, McKinsey Global Institute.

Drewnowski, A. 2020. "Analysing the affordability of the EAT–Lancet diet." *Lancet Global Health* 8, no. 1: e6–e7. doi:10.1016/S2214-109X(19)30502-9

Food and Agriculture Organization of the United Nations (FAO). 2014. "The state of food and agriculture: innovation in family farming." Rome: FAO.

———. 2017a. FAOSTAT Database for Food and Agriculture. Rome: FAO.

———. 2017b. FAOSTAT, "New Food Balances." Rome: FAO.

———. 2017c. Global Livestock Environmental Assessment Model, version 2.0, model description revision 3. Rome: FAO.

———. 2017d. Global Livestock Environmental Assessment Model, version 2.0, model description revision 4. Rome: FAO.

———. 2018a. "Food systems for healthy diets. Policy guidance note." Rome: FAO.

GBD Diet Collaborators. 2019. "Health effects of dietary risks in 195 countries, 1990–2017: a systematic analysis for the Global Burden of Disease Study 2017." *Lancet* 393, no. 10184: 1958–72. doi:10.1016/S0140-6736(19)30041-8

Headey, D. D., and H. H. Alderman. 2019. "The relative caloric prices of healthy and unhealthy foods differ systematically across income levels and continents." *Journal of Nutrition* 149, no. 11: 2020–33. doi:10.1093/jn/nxz158

Herrero, M., P. K. Thornton, B. Power, J. R. Bogard, R. Remans, S. Fritz, J. S. Gerber, G. Nelson, L. See, K. Waha, R. A. Watson, P. C. West, L. H. Samberg, J. van de Steeg, E. Stephenson, M. van Wijk, and P. Havlik. 2017. "Farming and the geography of nutrient production for human use: a transdisciplinary analysis." *Lancet Planetary Health* 1, no. 1: e33–42. doi:10.1016/S2542-5196(17)30007-4

Indonesia Bureau of Statistics (BPS). 2018. "Consumption expenditure of population of Indonesia 2018." https://www.ceicdata.com/en/indicator/indonesia/public-consumption-expenditure#:~:text=Indonesia's%20Public%20Consumption%20Expenditure%20data,USD%20bn%20in%20Sep%201998

Intergovernmental Panel on Climate Change (IPCC). 2019. "Climate change and land: an IPCC special report on climate change, desertification, land degradation, sustainable land management, food security, and greenhouse gas fluxes in terrestrial ecosystems." Geneva, Switzerland: IPCC.

Khoury, C. B., P. Oosterveer, L. Lamotte, I. D. Brouwer, S. de Haan, S. D. Prager, E. F. Talsma, and C. K. Khoury. 2019. "Development review: when food systems meet sustainability—current narratives and implications for actions." *World Development* 113: 116–30.

Kim, B. F., R. E. Santo, A. P. Scatterday, J. P. Fry, C. M. Synk, S. R. Cebron, M. M. Mekonnen, A. Y. Hoekstra, S. de Pee, M. W. Bloem, R. A. Neff, and K. E. Nachman. 2019. "Country-specific dietary shifts to mitigate climate and water crises." *Global Environmental Change* 62: 101926.

Mason-D'Croz, D., J. R. Bogard, T. B. Sulser, N. Cenacchi, S. Dunston, M. Herrero, and K. Wiebe. 2019. "Gaps between fruit and vegetable production, demand, and recommended consumption at global and national levels: an integrated modelling study." *Lancet Planetary Health* 3, no. 7: e318–29. doi:10.1016/S2542-5196(19)30095-6

Myers, S. S., M. R. Smith, S. Guth, C. D. Golden, B. Vaitla, N. D. Mueller, A. D. Dangour, and P. Huybers. 2017. "Climate change and global food systems: potential impacts on food security and undernutrition." *Annual Review of Public Health* 38: 259–77. doi:10.1146/annurev-publhealth-031816-044356

Nugent, R., C. Levin, J. Hale, and B. Hutchinson. 2020. "Economic effects of the double burden of malnutrition." *Lancet* 395, no. 10218: 156–64. doi:10.1016/S0140-6736(19)32473-0

Popkin, B. M., C. Corvalan, and L. M. Grummer-Strawn. 2020. "Dynamics of the double burden of malnutrition and the changing nutrition reality." *Lancet* 395, no. 10217: 65–74. doi:10.1016/S0140-6736(19)32497-3

Rahman, P. P., A. Aiyar, M. Abraham, and Andaleeb. 2019. "Managing climate change risks in food systems." In: *Transforming Food Systems for a Rising India. Palgrave Studies in Agricultural Economics and Food Policy*. London: Palgrave Macmillan.

Seimbang, Minister of Health of the Republic of Indonesia; Kementerian Kesehatan; Tabel Komposisi Pangan Indonesia; Menteri Kesehatan Republik; Pedoman Gizi. 2014, 2017, 2018. "Guidance on balanced diet."

UNICEF, WHO, World Bank Group. 2019. "Levels and trends in child malnutrition, UNICEF, WHO, World Bank Group joint child malnutrition estimates."

Willett, W., J. Rockstrom, B. Loken, M. Springmann, T. Lang, S. Vermeulen, T. Garnett, D. Tilman, F. DeClerck, A. Wood, et al. 2019. "Food in the Anthropocene: the EAT–Lancet Commission on healthy diets from sustainable food systems." *Lancet* 393, no. 10170: 447–92. doi:10.1016/S0140-6736(18)31788-4

Woodward, A., K. R. Smith, D. Campbell-Lendrum, D. D. Chadee, Y. Honda, Q. Liu, J. Olwoch, B. Revich, R. Sauerborn, Z. Chafe, U. Confalonieri, and A. Haines. 2014. "Climate change and health: on the latest IPCC report." *Lancet* 383, no. 9924: 1185–89. doi:10.1016/S0140-6736(14)60576-6

WorldBankGroup. 2014. "World Development Report 2008: agriculture for development." Washington, D.C.: World Bank. https://openknowledge.worldbank.org/handle/10986/5990

———. 2015. "Ending poverty and hunger by 2030: an agenda for the global food system." Washington, D.C.: World Bank. https://openknowledge.worldbank.org/handle/10986/21771

———. 2019a. "Agriculture and food overview." Washington, D.C.: World Bank. https://www.worldbank.org/en/topic/agriculture/overview

———. 2019b. "Climate smart agriculture overview." Washington, D.C.: World Bank. https://www.worldbank.org/en/topic/climate-smart-agriculture

WorldBankGroup, Independent Evaluation Group. 2010. "Cost–benefit analysis of World Bank projects." Washington, D.C.: World Bank. https://openknowledge.worldbank.org/handle/10986/2561

World Health Organization (WHO) and Food and Agriculture Organization of the United Nations (FAO). 2019. "Sustainable health diets: guiding principles." https://www.who.int/publications/i/item/9789241516648

Endnotes

1. Defined as a prevalence of wasting of greater than 15 percent, stunting of more than 30 percent, thinness in women of more than 20 percent, and an adult or child overweight prevalence greater than 20 percent.
2. Data come from the FAO (2017a, 2017b, 2017c, 2017d), a household expenditure survey (Indonesia 2018), food composition tables (Seimbang 2014, 2017, 2018), and a review of the life-cycle assessment literature (Kim et al. 2019).

PART III

GREENING FOOD WASTE

CHAPTER 7

Eliminating Food Waste

Geeta Sethi, Emilie Cassou, Lucia Patricia Avila Bedregal, Catherine "Simmy" Jain, Dipti Thapa, Xiaoyue Hou, and Luis Constantino

> "We are trashing our land to grow food that no one eats."
> —*Tristram Stuart*

A transformation of food systems is needed at a global scale to foster healthy people and a healthy planet. One of the greatest challenges humanity faces is that of feeding its growing population—projected to reach 9.7 billion people in 2050—under a changing climate while remaining within planetary boundaries and meeting the Sustainable Development Goals. Until now, food production has outpaced population growth but, as discussed in chapter 2, it has done so at great environmental cost (box 7-1). Moreover, environmental destabilization is making it ever harder for food systems to deliver and to do so sustainably. Climate change and resource degradation threaten to further slow already decelerating agricultural yield growth, beckoning farmers to resort to environmentally harsher practices. They are also increasing the vulnerability of the roughly 500 million family farms responsible for about half the world's food supply (Graeub et al. 2016). Meanwhile, despite food systems' impressive capacity to feed the world to date and a long-term decline in undernutrition, hunger has been rising since 2015, and more than 820 million people had insufficient food in 2018 (FAO, IFAD, UNICEF, WFP, and WHO [SOFI] 2019). Overall, at least 2 billion people were food insecure, many of them struck by the "hidden hunger" of micronutrient deficiencies (SOFI 2019; chapter 5). What's more, more than half the world's population may be experiencing various forms of diet-related disease, now the leading cause of death

BOX 7-1. FOOD SYSTEMS SUBSTANTIALLY CONTRIBUTE TO THE TRANSGRESSION OF SOME PLANETARY BOUNDARIES

Developed by a global community of scholars in 2009, the planetary boundaries concept is based on the idea of defining a "safe operating space for humanity" with respect to Earth's biophysical systems or processes (Röckstrom et al. 2009). That safe space is defined by nine planetary boundaries, and alarmingly, four have already been transgressed in the form of climate change, the loss of biosphere integrity, land system change, and altered biogeochemical cycles.

Food systems are not just at risk but also among the leading drivers of planetary excess. Food production is proving to be the largest user of water, nutrients, and land and one of the leading drivers of climate change, environmental degradation, and biodiversity loss (Willett et al. 2019). In fact, the contributions of food system activities to environmental destabilization can be underestimated when sustainability is assessed within too narrow a frame. To illustrate this idea, imagine a farm that uses inputs so efficiently that no nutrients leak into local groundwater and rivers. From a local perspective, that farm might be seen as being sustainable. Yet from a more systemic perspective, that farm may be part of a food system that generates considerable nutrient pollution. The nitrogen and phosphorus embedded in the food could be carried off the farm when the food is sold and consumed and, depending on their subsequent fate, never returned to the wider nutrient cycle (at least not benign versions of it). Depending on how they are managed, the nutrients present in food waste and excreta could be contributing to air and water pollution and climate destabilization.

globally (Afshin et al. 2019),[1] as a result of consuming low-quality diets that are unbalanced nutritionally, characterized by nutritional excesses as well as deficiencies. In light of these and other challenges, a wide range of scientists and policymakers are coalescing around the view that major shifts in global food systems are needed to make them more compatible with a changing climate and societal aspirations.

Food Loss and Waste: An Overlooked Candidate?

Among the host of immediate actions that could help make food systems more climate-friendly and sustainable, reducing the volumes of food that are lost or wasted is gaining attention as a significant yet largely overlooked candidate. *Food loss* typically refers to the discarding of food upstream in the food supply chain, from the farm to wholesale stages. Food waste typically refers to the discarding of food further downstream in the supply chain, at the retail and consumer levels. In either case, food is discarded for various reasons, ranging from spoilage—real or perceived—to real or suspected changes in food's quality, such as its appearance, flavor, texture, nutritional value, or safety.

The magnitude of food loss and waste (FLW) is undeniable. In 2015, the world lost or wasted an estimated 1.6 billion tons of food, nearly one third[2] of what it produced, and that amount was projected to reach 2.1 billion tons by 2030 (Food and Agriculture Organization of the United Nations [FAO] 2011; Hegnsholt et al. 2018). FLW is also a global phenomenon, occurring across countries of different income levels, albeit in different forms and at different rates. Overall, rates of waste have been lower, per capita, in low- and middle-income countries (LMICs), but that per capita gap is expected to narrow as their incomes rise and diets shift.

The concerns with FLW are multiple but can be grouped into two to three main buckets. They revolve around climate change and environmental sustainability on one hand and food and nutritional security on the other, and to some extent also on food sector competitiveness and livelihoods.

Climate Change and Environmental Sustainability

A first set of concerns with FLW has to do with the climate and environmental impacts of food production. The connection between FLW and climate change is drawn on the basis that the production and supply of discarded food accounts for about 7 percent[3] of global greenhouse gas emissions, excluding emissions from land use change (FAO 2013, 2019). As has often been pointed out, if FLW were a country, its carbon footprint would be the third largest in the world (FAO 2013). Noting that food production is among the leading drivers of climate change, the EAT–Lancet Commission estimated that by mid-century, halving FLW, as called for by the Sustainable Development Goals, could achieve a 5 percent reduction in agricultural greenhouse gas emissions (Willett et al. 2019). Though dwarfed by the levels of mitigation that could be achieved by changes in food production practices (10 percent) and especially a shift to plant-based diets (80 percent), the potential contributions of FLW reductions are still noteworthy. Moreover, the abatement potential associated with FLW may be larger because these estimates do not factor in the potential to cut emissions related to agriculture's expansion into forests and other natural landscapes. The cropland used to grow lost and wasted food, estimated at close to 200 million hectares per year, is an area roughly the size of Mexico, exceeding six decades of global cropland expansion (Kummu et al. 2012).

Meanwhile, the adverse environmental impacts of food production are not limited to climate forcing. Lost or wasted food accounts for nearly one quarter[4] of freshwater use and global fertilizer use, inefficient applications of which pollute water, soils, and air, contributing to biodiversity loss and to premature death and disability via a host of pathways (Kummu et al. 2012). Often considered and measured separately, these effects are seldom considered aggregately and are widely underappreciated (Cassou et al. 2018). From an environmental perspective, reducing FLW can be thought of as a means of increasing the productivity of all scarce natural resources, including that of land, freshwater, fisheries, and minerals for fertilizing. From a food security perspective, it may offer a means of increasing food output without farming additional land. One study estimated that halving FLW from 2010 to 2050 would reduce environmental pressure linked to agriculture by 6 to 16 percent depending on the environmental dimension considered (GHG emissions, cropland use, blue water use, and nitrogen and phosphorus application), pointing to its role in food system transformation (Springmann et al. 2018).

Food and Nutritional Security

FLW is also troubling in light of persistent food insecurity and the extent of malnutrition in all its forms. As noted, food insecurity remains an all too real challenge in today's world, yet about one quarter of available food calories are lost or wasted—that is, more than 600 kilocalories per person each day (Kummu et al. 2012). The share of calories lost or wasted is twice that if one factors in the reallocation of crops to feed, a part of the supply chain that conventional accounting methods overlook (box 7-2) (Ritchie et al. 2018). Food loss also represents a potential waste of essential nutrients. Some 60 percent of available micronutrients (not counting vitamin B_{12}) are lost to humans via FLW, based on FAO's 2011 estimates of FLW levels (Ritchie et al. 2018). This loss of nutrition is concentrated in the loss of nutrient-dense foods, many of which are particularly perishable and lost at higher rates than less nutritious foods (figure 7-1). Compared with cereals, roots, or tubers, fruits and vegetables are more likely to be lost completely to severe weather, pest and disease attacks, and less-than-ideal handling, particularly in countries with less sophisticated food marketing systems. In developing country contexts, FLW—particularly

(a)

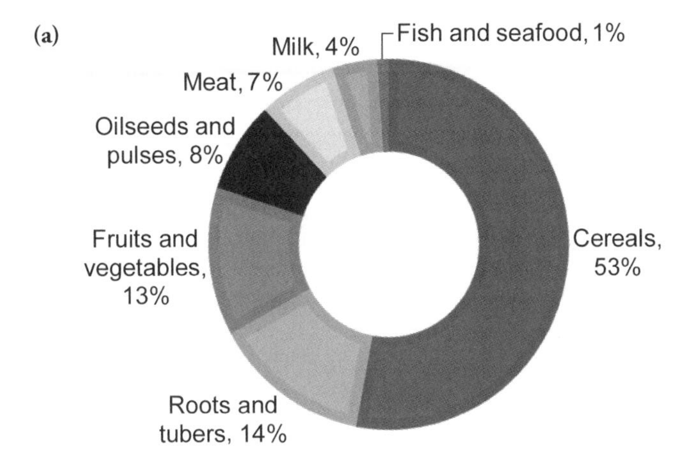

(b)

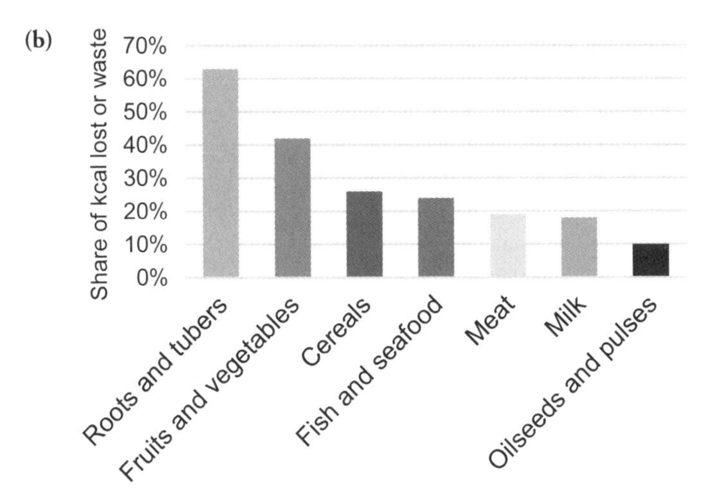

Figure 7-1. Levels and rates of caloric FLW by food category, 2009. **(a)** Shares of total caloric loss and waste. **(b)** Rates of caloric loss and waste. *Sources:* Lipinski et al. (2013), FAO (2011). *Notes:* WRI analysis based on FAO 2011 data. Total loss and waste is 1.5 quadrillion kilocalories, equivalent to 1.3 billion tons of food.

that of fruits and vegetables and other nutrient-dense foods—may be putting a ceiling on or at least slowing progress toward nutritional health.[5] By the same token, a shift over time to diets richer in highly perishable foods could increase rates of FLW even as it improves many people's health status.

Looking ahead, discarding less food would help close the impending food gap. Discarding less than the 30 percent of edible food wasted today could

BOX 7-2. FOOD LOSS AND WASTE IN ALL ITS FORMS: A NEW LOOK AT ANIMAL SOURCE FOODS

Animal source foods, including poultry products, red meats, dairy, and seafood, are not the food category most susceptible to losses. Their levels of waste are dwarfed by those of products more widely produced and consumed, such as cereals, roots, and tubers, and their rates of waste are topped by those of other perishable products such as fruits and vegetables. This difference in rates may be partly attributable to produce often having to travel farther than animal products, the latter often being slaughtered or collected near points of sale in many countries. However, lower losses among animal source foods may also be attributable in part to accounting. Loss estimates for animal source foods account for neither the energy and resources lost in the conversion of feed to food nor the consumption of unsafe food, both of which cast animal source foods in a more wasteful light.

Compared with plant-based foods, animal source foods are vastly more wasteful from an energy balance perspective. It takes about 99 calories of crops to produce 1 calorie of beef (Wirsenius et al. 2010), and even cattle's protein conversion efficiency hovers at only 4 percent. Even poultry and farmed fish products, though multiple times more energy efficient than ruminant livestock ones, waste nearly 90 percent of the calories used to grow them. By one estimate, about 43 percent of edible crop calories that are fed to farm animals are then returned to humans in the form of animal source foods (Kummu et al. 2012). This finding led the study in question to call the livestock sector a "net drain on food supply" (Kummu et al. 2012, 481). Yet crops diverted from the human food supply to serve as animal feed are not counted as FLW—at least not in the FAO's accounting system.

One study that factored in the allocation of crops to animal feed—and its return to the human food supply in the form of animal source foods—found that feeding farm animals accounted for the largest source of energy and digestable protein losses in the food system: 1,500 kilocalories and 70 grams of digestable protein per person per day. By factoring feed into the calculation, the study found that 2011 levels of total FLW (using FAO estimates) accounted for fully 54 percent of available calories (as opposed to one quarter of these) and 56 percent of digestible protein (Ritchie et al. 2018). The allocation of crops to animal feed also accounted for the largest supply chain losses of several micronutrients: folate, zinc, iron, vitamin A, and calcium.[a]

In addition, one study found that it generally takes more than three times more nitrogen to produce plant foods than aninal source ones because of the overall process of feeding and growing animals (Galloway and Cowling 2002). Per calorie, it takes about ten times more freshwater to produce beef, and three times more to produce chicken, than it takes to grow pulses (Mekonnen and Hoekstra 2012). One study of FLW found that 14 percent of irrigation water is used to grow animal feed (Kummu et al. 2012).

Separately, it bears noting that FLW does not account for the consumption of unsafe food (let alone the consumption food that is double-edged nutritionally[b]). Although this might be impractical from multiple points of view, it would also inflate the share of animal source foods in the loss and waste tally. Foodborne disease is heavily if not overwhelmingly attributable to animal source foods, including seafood. Bacterial pathogens are the biggest food safety problem in general, and the most important categories of these are zoonotic (Grace 2015). In fact, even food safety numbers only partially account for animal source food risk to the extent that a significant amount of foodborne disease affecting plant foods is attributable to cross-contamination. The latter occurs when plant-based foods are affected by animal-borne pathogens that become airborne or are communicated by contact with animals or humans, tainted water, or the use of inadequately treated manure-based soil amendments. Unsafe food in LMICs costs an estimated US$95 billion per year in lost productivity (Jaffee et al. 2018).

Notes

[a]However, the production of animal source foods is widely subsidized in the name of strengthening the dietary supply of these very nutrients.

[b]From a nutritional perspective, animal source foods are important sources of essential nutrients, including protein, iron, calcium, and vitamin B_{12}. However, animal source foods are not the only or even the optimal way of obtaining these or other nutrients from a health perspective, factoring in the unwanted substances and risks they also bring, or their co-liabilities. From a cost perspective, animal source foods may present advantages in some contexts under business-as-usual circumstances, shaped as they have been by vast public subsidies and investments in animal source food production (which evidently do not reflect current dietary health or environmental research). That cost advantage could be eroded with changes in agricultural landscapes, in their physical and policy incarnations.

help close the 50–60 percent food gap[6] anticipated by 2050 as the world gains another 2.7 billion[7] mouths to feed. Reasoning in calorie terms and on the basis of the FAO's 2011 FLW estimates, one study estimated that cutting losses from 24 to 12 percent of calories would close roughly one fifth of the calorie gap anticipated by 2050 (a gap of 6,000 trillion kilocalories per year) (Kummu et al. 2012). For the time being, however, food allocation is a bigger challenge than food scarcity, and current rates of FLW are not a reflection of global food scarcity. In fact, the quantities of calories and nutrients that are thrown out today would be more than enough to meet the nutritional needs of those who are malnourished (Berners-Lee et al. 2018; Ritchie et al. 2018). The world generates enough food to feed itself, and the challenge rests in getting that food to consumers who need it.

For some, geopolitical concerns about ensuring food security are another reason to deplore FLW at the country level. Domestic food loss is sometimes seen as increasing dependence on food trade and hence vulnerability to international price shocks and trade restrictions. Although food trade is generally a source of consumer welfare and resilience, national governments worry when they depend heavily on trading partners for national sustenance, and many aspire to partial self-sufficiency as a matter of national security.

Food System Competitiveness and Livelihoods

A third set of concerns with FLW comes from its economic value. In the face of persistent poverty and economic hardship, the value of lost and wasted food does not go unnoticed. Globally, FLW was estimated to be worth US$940 billion in 2011, based on the FAO's 2011 estimates and prevailing food prices (i.e., without consideration for its social costs) (FAO 2014). Though smaller in absolute terms, the loss of value is especially resonant in national contexts. In Nigeria, for example, lost and wasted food was worth about 9 percent of the country's gross domestic product (GDP) in 2017, based on prevailing food prices.[8]

The concern with FLW in this case is that it represents a form of inefficiency in itself or an indication that the food sector is underperforming. In either case, remedying FLW is seen as having the potential to drive economic benefits. Depending on how markets adjust, food suppliers might have more to sell and consumers more to spend. Lower losses might also reduce dependence on food imports, creating business for domestic suppliers, provided they are able to compete. One study that examined the potential economic gains from cutting FLW in the United States estimated that eleven discrete prevention, recovery, and recycling measures would potentially increase business profits by US$1.9 billion annually, with the lion's share of benefits going to the food service sector (ReFED 2016). A separate, global simulation found that reducing FLW by one quarter would have a small, positive effect on global GDP (Kuiper and Cui 2019). Whether or not the concerns just described are justified, calls to address FLW are gaining prominence for all of the aforementioned reasons.

Slow Mobilization in LMICs Despite Calls for Action

A growing number of international, government, and civil society organizations are embracing the view that cutting FLW can and must be part of the response to climate change and needed food system transformation. Over the past decade, a growing number of countries have started mobilizing around FLW as awareness of its stunning magnitude and ramifications has spread. It is now fueling a growing call to remedy what is viewed as a global problem as well as an opportunity to deliver dividends across multiple agendas. Reducing FLW, it is argued, will help combat hunger and malnutrition, cut pollution, free up freshwater resources, and stabilize the climate. For example, the 2018 World Resources Institute Report identifies reducing the loss and waste of food intended for human consumption as an important demand-side solution to achieving a sustainable food future. In 2019, the EAT–Lancet Commission report singled out reductions in FLW as crucial to achieving healthy diets and a sustainable food system. The same year, the FAO dedicated its annual State of Food and Agriculture (SOFA) report entirely to the topic of FLW. Meanwhile, its annual State of the Food Insecurity (SOFI) report highlighted the importance of preventing food losses in smallholder production, noting that in lower-income countries where food insecurity is often severe, access to food is closely associated with availability. Reductions in food loss, the report argues, would alleviate food shortages, increase farmers' incomes and access to food, and, if large enough to affect prices beyond the local area, also benefit the food insecure in cities.

Despite potentially having the most to gain, however—and early signs of this changing—few LMICs have embraced FLW mitigation as a priority. At the national level, most action has occurred in high-income countries. FLW is enshrined in the United Nations Sustainable Development Goal 12.3, calling to "halve per capita global food waste at the retail and consumer levels and reduce food losses along production" by 2030. Yet action to make this goal a reality is still limited. In Sub-Saharan Africa, Rwanda was the only country to have included an FLW target under its Paris Climate Agreement commitments. And even there, policy realities suggest that the FLW agenda has yet to be embraced in earnest. This situation raises the question of whether and how the now widely shared concerns about FLW can be treated as opportunities and turned into actions that advance burning policy priorities.

Policies to Eliminate Food Waste

Putting the FLW agenda into practice is less obvious than it seems. FLW is a plural problem, with its nature, its distribution, and drivers varying by commodity and geography. It is striking that the rate of discarded food lies in the 25–35 percent range across regions, considering how drastically its nature and origins vary from one region to another. The most salient difference between regions is the share of waste that occurs at the consumer level versus in the food marketing system. In low- and middle-income regions, the food handling, processing, and distribution portion of the supply chain is the leading source of FLW, followed by farming, whereas in high-income parts of the world the largest share of FLW occurs at the consumer level, again followed by farming (figure 7-2).

Somewhat less divergent rates of farm-level losses across regions belie significant differences in what drives them. Although farmers the world over contend with the vagaries of weather and outbreaks, farm-level losses in high-income countries are sometimes deliberate (driven by profit considerations), as when edible products are rejected for aesthetic and marketing reasons. This scenario is far less widespread in LMICs, where losses are overwhelmingly a manifestation of supply chain inefficiencies. In fact, FLW realities vary so significantly across regions that they might be thought of as completely separate phenomena, affecting different types of food for different reasons—and even with different consequences. Indeed, the reasons for deploring FLW, and hence the motives for taking remedial action, are also highly variable.

The plurality of food and loss situations points to different motives for addressing FLW and the need for different approaches. The loss of rice is not nutritionally equivalent to that of a tomato or a package of crisps, nor is it environmentally equivalent. Moreover, the later a commodity is lost in the supply chain, the larger its environmental footprint is, because resources are used to transport, transform, and store products. In addition, the significance of FLW varies in relation to not only its nature, but also its context. In a context of undernutrition or malnourishment, for example, discarding nutritious food is objectionable not so much from an environmental standpoint as from a nutritional and public health one. The problem, in this case, is not that the food was produced in the first place but that it was not eaten. Conversely, in

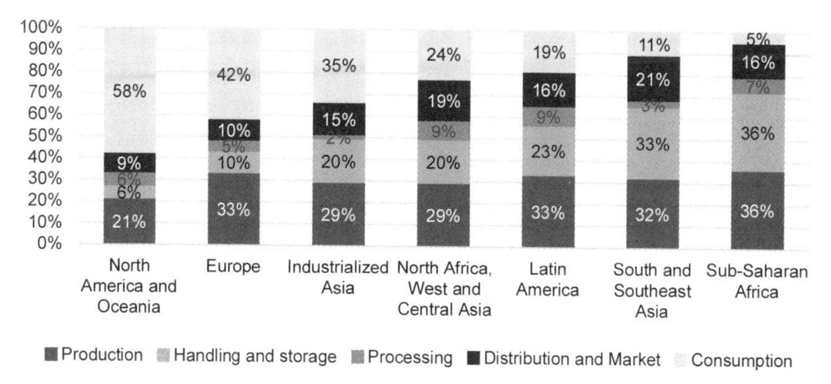

Figure 7-2. Distribution of FLW volumes across the supply chain by region, 2007. *Sources:* Based on Flanagan et al. (2019) and FAO (2011). *Notes:* WRI analysis based on FAO (2011).Values displayed are of FLW as a percentage of food supply, defined here as the sum of the "Food" and "Processing" columns of the FAO Food Balance Sheet, in tonnage terms. Not all numbers sum to 100 due to rounding.

contexts of food security, food waste can be a sign that food is being overproduced at needless cost to the environment. In this case, the problem is in fact that unneeded food was produced in the first place. Although they overly simplify reality, these scenarios illustrate how FLW can be problematic, from a societal perspective, for different reasons. They are also conceptually helpful for recognizing different problems with FLW in the world.

What can be achieved—and hence what policy objectives can be pursued—by cutting FLW also vary by circumstance. Not all FLW interventions are created equal; instead, their overall efficacy and distributional effects depend on points of intervention and market structure, that is, on where cuts are achieved in the supply chain and how buyers and sellers react. Reducing FLW does not automatically prevent food from being grown at the expense of the environment in the first place. Nor does it guarantee that more or better food will become accessible to consumers who need it or even that sellers will boost their sales revenue or profitability.

Simplified scenarios are again helpful to understand the potential for outcomes to vary. A reduction in FLW at a given stage in the supply chain generally increases the amount of food supplied at subsequent stages, and this increase in supply lowers its price. In turn, how this affects the disposable income of buyers and sellers depends on whether a lower price of food leads them to transact more or less (in volume terms). Lower prices may leave sellers (many of whom are also net food buyers) with less income to spend on food and other items, unless sales increase to the extent of offsetting lower prices and boosting their income. For their part, if food prices drop, buyers will see their purchasing power expand, allowing them to access more and better food or other items. However, it is possible that consumers in this position will waste food at higher rates, because they opt for more nutritious yet more perishable food items or simply become more profligate. The effects of reducing rates of waste at the consumer level are also ambiguous because they depend on whether consumers adjust by purchasing more or less food. How these scenarios play out depends on various market characteristics including supplier competitiveness and openness to trade, as well as consumer budgets, needs, and preferences.

The influence of such contextual variables is a source of complexity. Market characteristics are already numerous and varied, and to complicate matters, the markets with relevance include those for substitutes. Moreover, just as consumers can sometimes turn to food substitutes in reaction to market changes, sellers (and consumers) can sometimes turn to alternative use markets that use food as a feedstock for energy, feed, fiber, or fertilizer. Not only do these parallel markets influence responses to reductions in FLW, but they also affect overall environmental or nutritional outcomes given that substitutes (for both food and alternative uses of food) have different nutritional and environmental profiles.[9] Yet another source of complexity comes from differences in the cost of achieving a given decrease in FLW at different stages of supply chains for different commodities and in different places. The broad diversity of phenomena driving FLW points clearly to the need for a diverse toolbox of interventions (box 7-3). In some contexts, reducing losses of a given commodity may simply not be worthwhile, economically, if the cost of abatement outweighs its benefits, or even if it is more costly than other means of pursuing the policy goal of interest. Depending on what it entails, cutting FLW may or may not be the best means of addressing water overuse or boosting farmer incomes in a given context.

In sum, acting to prevent FLW is bound to have different returns on investment in different commodity sectors, stages of the value chain, market contexts, social and environmental circumstances, and of course geographies. Understanding the potential returns on investments in cutting FLW—as well as its distributional implications—calls for examining its effects empirically. So far, efforts to do just that underscore this point. Analyses that have attempted to sort out, even partially, the effects of intervening to curb FLW by using economic modeling have demonstrated that those effects can vary substantially (box 7-4).

BOX 7-3. THE DIVERSE DRIVERS OF FLW CALL FOR A DIVERSE TOOLBOX OF INTERVENTIONS

As noted, FLW can occur for different reasons even when it involves the same commodity and stage of the supply chain. An abundant literature hypothesizes about these reasons, suggesting limited commonality among high-income and lower-income countries. In relation to LMICs, information is viewed as a key constraint, particularly for smallholder farmers. More accurate weather information may reduce losses by helping farmers time their plantings better. A better command of quality standards and systems might help commercially oriented farmers reduce product rejections. In general, information about improved farming and storage practices could lead to less waste. The literature also highlights the role of technology and infrastructure constraints, and these go hand in hand with dysfunctional credit markets to the extent that they limit investments that would help prevent losses. Examples include investments in cooling systems, refrigeration, improved storage, and roads. In 2009, the International Institute of Refrigeration estimated that more than 200 million tons of food would be saved annually if developing countries acquired the cold chain capacities of wealthier countries. The literature also attributes losses to risk management strategies used by supply chain actors contending with the aforementioned constraints. Farmers may produce more and intermediaries transport more than they are contractually committed to sell because they know some could be lost. Food loss can be understood as the consequence of a risk management strategy that involves building up excessive inventories or reserves. Another, more general way to understand FLW is as a sign or consequence of incorrect food and resource pricing. FLW would be occurring at excessive levels because the resources used to produce them, or food prices themselves, do not reflect their true societal costs and benefits (including negative environmental externalities and positive nutritional ones). Excessive food waste would imply that food is underpriced.

Figure 7-3 (next page) presents an array of FLW prevention strategies that might correspond to its drivers at different stages of the supply chain.

More Investment in Evidence and Experimentation Is Needed

Today, although efforts to understand and tackle FLW are multiplying, there are still fewer answers than there are questions, at least as they relate to many LMICs. Although evidence is still limited on the volumes and rates of waste for major commodities at different stages of the supply chain in many LMICs, analytics are in even shorter supply to shed light on, for example:

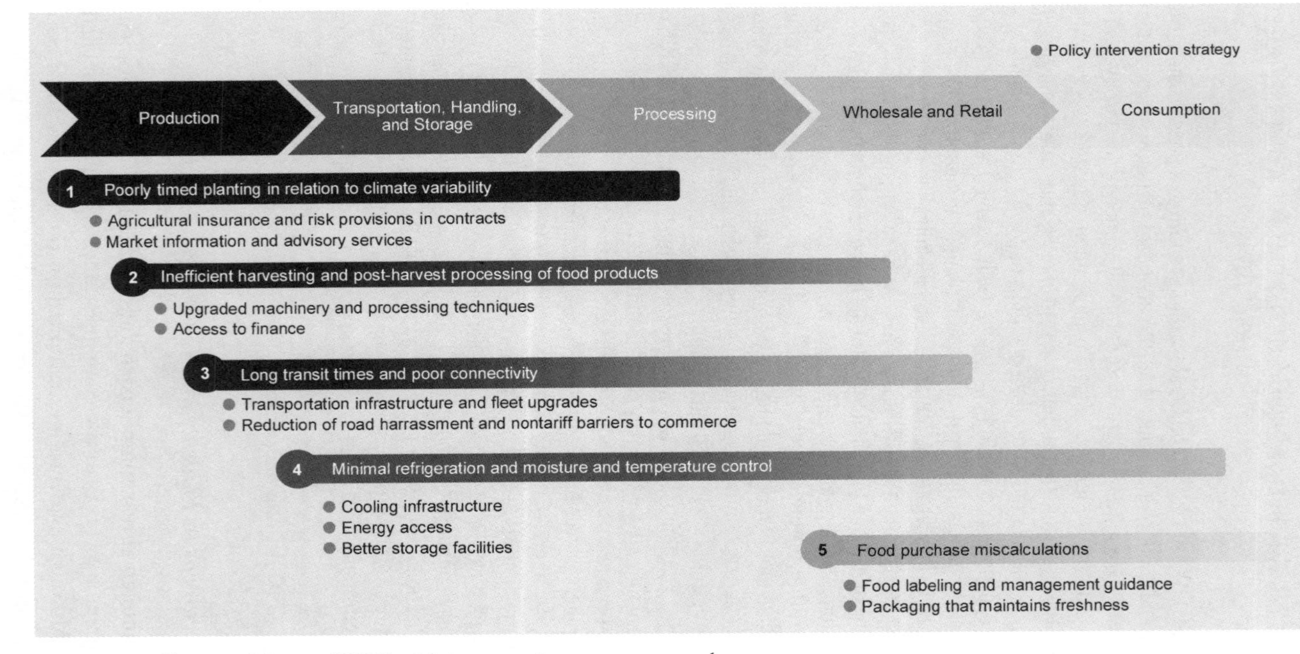

Figure 7-3. Aligning drivers of FLW with interventions: some examples.

BOX 7-4. EFFORTS TO MODEL THE IMPACTS OF FLW REDUCTIONS UNDERSCORE THE PROBLEM'S COMPLEXITY

One such effort led by a team at Wageningen University in 2019 simulated the effects of a 25 percent reduction in food losses on farms and in processing by using a global, economy-wide model.[a] Among its key findings were that cutting losses at these stages had negligible climate benefits, although it did result in substantial reductions in agricultural land use (a 0.7 percent decrease).[b] However, cutting upstream losses was found to have positive effects on food access. The model also showed that doing so–cutting losses in primary production–was more beneficial to consumer food access than cutting losses in processing–twenty times more in Sub-Saharan Africa and ten times more in Central and Southern Asia. However, the study warned that reducing losses at the processing stage could harm the food security status of vulnerable farming households by bringing about a fall in prices in the same two regions.

Sources: Based on Kuiper and Cui (2019), FAO (2019).

NOTES

[a]This reduction in losses can be represented as changes in productivity that increase global production by 4.3 percent, of which 2 percent is at the primary production stage and 2.3 percent at the processing stage (FAO 2019).

[b]The latter were not the results of domestic reductions in losses but ones achieved in trading partner countries. From a domestic perspective, reducing losses tended to improve the competitiveness of domestic food relative to imports and to stimulate domestic production and land use. Cutting losses upstream may also have resulted in more food traveling through the supply chain to consumers, and associated greenhouse gas emissions may have contributed to offsetting gains from decreased production. Other offsetting effects of resource allocation may also have been at play.

- The impacts of FLW on the environment, nutritional health, livelihoods, the balance of trade, and sector competitiveness
- The relative efficacy of different interventions—factoring in different possible instruments and points of entry into supply chains—for addressing outcomes of interest (e.g., emissions of various pollutants, food prices and households' access to nutritious foods, farmer incomes)
- The relative efficacy of interventions targeting FLW relative to other approaches to addressing issues of public import (e.g., ones relating to the environment, public health, farmer welfare)

- The distributional effects of such interventions, with consideration for the welfare of households of different levels of wealth and self-reliance, for farmers of different sizes and commercial orientation, for other supply chain stakeholders, and for producers of different (substitute and complementary) commodities, for example

More sophisticated decision support tools are needed to advance the FLW agenda. There is a particular need for analytic tools that can handle the complexity of the FLW challenge to help decision makers determine why and how to address it in ways that make sense domestically. Policymakers in LMICs face, with finite human, institutional, and financial capacity, tremendous pressure to address an ever-expanding set of issues being touted as tantamount to reaching national development objectives. As high-level evidence has emerged on the scale of FLW and its wide array of possible implications, FLW has become an additional issue to address in the pursuit of those objectives. As noted, high-level calls and commitments to act on the challenge are multiplying, including among LMICs, but in these contexts, the complexity of the issue has the potential to be paralyzing. FLW prevention may offer developing countries attractive means of pursuing some of their leading policy objectives, and better analytics are needed to show them how.

Country Cases: Rice in Nigeria and Vietnam

The contrasting cases of rice in Nigeria and Vietnam illustrate how the significance of FLW depends on the context. Rice is widely grown and consumed in both countries, playing a significant role with respect to food security and rural livelihoods. Both countries are among leading producers of the commodity in their respective regions. Both countries are also estimated to lose or waste on the order of 20 to 30 percent of the domestic rice supply and to do so heavily in transportation, handling, and storage. Rates of loss differ, however, in other parts of the supply chain, skewing further downstream in Vietnam than in Nigeria (figure 7-4).

However, contrasting national circumstances suggest that the loss of rice has a different significance for the two countries. Rice is arguably more important, nutritionally, in Vietnam than in Nigeria—at least in terms of its contributions to available calories. Per capita rice consumption has been rising in Nigeria, but it has been on the decline in Vietnam. And whereas Nigeria imports rice to meet demand, Vietnam has exported a surplus of rice since the

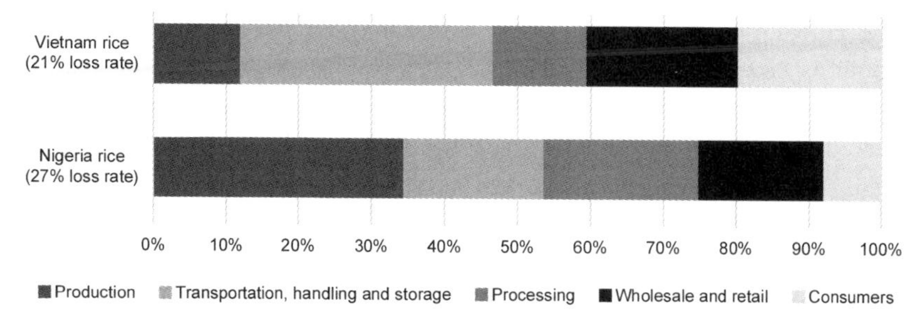

Figure 7-4. Distribution of loss and waste of rice in Vietnam and Nigeria. *Sources:* Authors' estimates using, for Vietnam, Vietnam Institute of Agricultural and Post-Harvest Technology 2016 data reported in Khoi (2017) and FAO (2011), and for Nigeria, Danbaba et al. (2019).

early 2010s—on the order of 6 million tons, or 14 percent of domestic production, worth about US$2.6 billion, in 2017. In fact, Vietnam has recently started shifting its focus to raising the quality, sustainability, and value of rice, and raising the national output of rice no longer enjoys the prominence it once did among national priorities. By contrast, Nigeria has been highly focused on raising the productivity of rice and displacing imports. In this respect, it has performed remarkably, cutting imports by 96 percent and import dependence from 30 to 1 percent between 2014 and 2017. This increase is due more to an expansion of rice planting than to increases in rice productivity. Meanwhile, Nigeria faces higher rates of undernutrition than Vietnam, where rates declined between 2004 and 2018 whereas those of Nigeria rose (SOFI 2019). Thus, for Nigeria reducing losses may be attractive to boost food availability and disposable income among food-insecure farming households, as well as to sustainably help domestic supply keep up with rising demand for rice. In Vietnam, where rice yields are high by global standards but rice production highly taxing on the environment, loss reductions may help lighten the environmental footprint of rice and improve the quality, branding, and pricing of its exports.

Conclusions

The magnitude of FLW is undeniable: The amount of food lost and wasted was about 1.3 billion tons in 2011 and is expected to grow to 2.1 billion tons by 2030. FLW is also a global phenomenon, occurring across countries of different income levels, albeit in different forms. In a context of a changing climate and growing ecosystem stress, it is notable that discarded food accounts for about 7 percent of global greenhouse gas emissions and a quarter of freshwater, fertilizer, and cropland use. In the face of persistent food insecurity, the amount of calories and nutrients that are thrown out today would be more than enough to meet the nutritional needs of those who are malnourished. And looking ahead, discarding less than the third of edible food that is wasted today would presumably help close the impending 50 to 60 percent food gap anticipated by 2050 as the world gains another 2.7 billion mouths to feed.

Recognizing the challenge and opportunity, a growing number of governments and civil society organizations are calling for cuts in FLW to be part of the response to the climate crisis and needed food system transformation. However, despite potentially having the most to gain, LMICs have yet to fully embrace FLW mitigation as an investment priority. On close examination, the FLW problem is complex and its pursuit more challenging than it may initially seem. Both the nature of the problem and the benefits to be reaped vary significantly by context and commodity. Evidence is limited on where and why losses occur, as well as on what works with respect to various and sometimes competing policy priorities—and with what impacts for whom. Today's momentum around the issue is a welcome development, but translating high-level commitments into effective national policies will require significant investments in experimentation and evidence generation.

References

Afshin, A., P. J. Sur, K. A. Fay, L. Cornaby, G. Ferrara, J. S. Salama, E. C. Mullany, et al. 2019. "Health effects of dietary risks in 195 countries, 1990–2017: a systematic analysis for the Global Burden of Disease Study 2017." *Lancet* 393, no. 10184: 1958–72. https://doi.org/10.1016/S0140-6736(19)30041-8

Berners-Lee, M., C. Kennelly, R. Watson, and C. N. Hewitt. 2018. "Current global food production is sufficient to meet human nutritional needs in 2050 provided there is radical societal adaptation." *Elementa: Science of the Anthropocene* 6, no. 1. http://doi.org/10.1525/elementa.310

Cassou, E., S. M. Jaffee, and J. Ru. 2018. *The Challenge of Agricultural Pollution: Evidence from China, Vietnam, and the Philippines.* Washington, D.C.: World Bank. https://doi.org/10.1596/978-1-4648-1201-9

Danbaba, N., P. Y. Idakwo, A. L. Kassum, C. Bristone, S. O. Bakare, U. Aliyu, I. N. Kolo, et al. 2019. "Rice postharvest technology in Nigeria: an overview of current status, constraints and potentials for sustainable development." *Open Access Library Journal* 6, no. 8: 1–23. https://doi.org/10.4236/oalib.1105509

Flanagan, K., K. Robertson, C. Hanson, and A. J. M. Timmermans. 2019. "Reducing food loss and waste: Setting a Global Action Agenda." Washington, D.C.: World

Resources Institute. https://www.wri.org/publication/reducing-food-loss-and-waste-setting-global-action-agendas

Food and Agriculture Organization of the United Nations (FAO). 2011. "Global food losses and food waste: extent, causes and prevention." Rome: FAO. http://www.fao.org/3/a-i2697e.pdf

———. 2013. "Food waste footprint: impacts on natural resources: summary report." Rome: FAO. http://www.fao.org/3/i3347e/i3347e.pdf

———. 2014. "Food wastage footprint: full-cost accounting, final report." Rome: FAO. http://www.fao.org/3/a-i3991e.pdf

———. 2019. "The state of food and agriculture 2019: moving forward on food loss and waste reduction." Rome: FAO. http://www.fao.org/3/ca6030en/ca6030en.pdf

Food and Agriculture Organization of the United Nations (FAO), the International Fund for Agricultural Development (IFAD), the United Nations Children's Fund (UNICEF), the World Food Programme (WFP), and the World Health Organization (WHO) (SOFI). 2019. *The State of Food Security and Nutrition in the World: Safeguarding against Economic Slowdowns and Downturns*. Rome: FAO. http://www.fao.org/3/ca5162en/ca5162en.pdf

Galloway, J. N., and E. B. Cowling. 2002. "Reactive nitrogen and the world: 200 years of change." *AMBIO* 30, no. 2: 64–71. https://www.researchgate.net/publication/11297112_Reactive_Nitrogen_and_The_World_200_Years_of_Change

Grace, D. 2015. "Food safety in low and middle income countries." *International Journal of Environmental Research and Public Health* 12, no. 9: 10490–507. https://doi.org/10.3390/ijerph120910490

Graeub, B. E., M. J. Chappell, H. Wittman, S. Ledermann, R. B. Kerr, and B. Gemmill-Herren. 2016. "The state of family farms in the world." *World Development* 87: 1–15. https://doi.org/10.1016/j.worlddev.2015.05.012

Hegnsholt, E., S. Unnikrishnan, M. Pollmann-Larsen, B. Askelsdottir, and M. Gerard. 2018. "Tackling the 1.6-billion-ton food loss and waste crisis." Boston, Mass.: The Boston Consulting Group. https://www.bcg.com/publications/2018/tackling-1.6-billion-ton-food-loss-and-waste-crisis.aspx

Jaffee, S., S. Henson, L. Unnevehr, D. Grace, and E. Cassou. 2018. *The Safe Food Imperative: Accelerating Progress in Low- and Middle-Income Countries*. Washington, D.C.: World Bank. https://doi.org/10.1596/978-1-4648-1345-0

Khoi, K. D. 2017. "Situation, policy and innovations on reducing postharvest loss in Vietnam." APEC Expert Consultation on Food Losses and Waste Reduction, June 12-13, 2017, Taipei City. http://apec-flows.ntu.edu.tw/upload/edit/file/2%20SR_2017_C_S4-01_Dr.%20Dang%20Kim%20Khoi.pdf

Kuiper, M., and H. D. Cui. 2019. "Using food loss reductions to reach nutritional and environmental objectives – a search for promising leverage points." Background paper for *The State of Food and Agriculture 2019: Moving Forward on Food Loss and Waste Reduction*. The Hague: Wageningen Economic Research.

Kummu, M., H. De Moel, M. Porkka, S. Siebert, O. Varis, and P. J. Ward. 2012. "Lost food, wasted resources: global food supply chain losses and their impacts on freshwater, cropland, and fertiliser use." *Science of the Total Environment* 438: 477–89. https://doi.org/10.1016/j.scitotenv.2012.08.092

Lipinski, B., et al. 2013. "Reducing food loss and waste." Working paper, installment 2 of *Creating a Sustainable Food Future*. Washington, D.C.: World Resources Institute. http://www.worldresourcesreport.org

Mekonnen, M. M., and A. Y. Hoekstra. 2012. "A global assessment of the water footprint of farm animal products." *Ecosystems* 15, no. 3: 401–15. https://doi.org/10.1007/s10021-011-9517-8

ReFED. 2016. "A roadmap to reduce US food waste by 20 percent." https://www.refed.com/downloads/ReFED_Report_2016.pdf

Ritchie, H., D. S. Reay, and P. Higgins. 2018. "Beyond calories: a holistic assessment of the global food system." *Frontiers in Sustainable Food Systems* 2: 57. https://doi.org/10.3389/fsufs.2018.00057

Rockström, J., W. Steffen, K. Noone, A. Persson, F. S. Chapin III, E. Lambin, T. M. Lenton, et al. 2009. "Planetary boundaries: exploring the safe operating space for humanity." *Ecology and Society* 14, no. 2. https://doi.org/10.5751/ES-03180-140232

Searchinger, T., R. Waite, C. Hanson, J. Ranganathan, P. Dumas, and E. Matthews. 2018. "World resources report: creating a sustainable food future. A menu of solutions to sustainably feed more than 9 billion people by 2050." Washington, D.C.: World Resources Institute. https://wriorg.s3.amazonaws.com/s3fs-public/creating-sustainable-food-future_2.pdf

Springmann, M., M. Clark, D. Mason-D'Croz, K. Wiebe, B. L. Bodirsky, L. Lassaletta, W. De Vries, et al. 2018. "Options for keeping the food system within environmental limits." Nature 562, no. 7728: 519–25. https://doi.org/10.1038/s41586-018-0594-0

United Nations Department of Economic and Social Affairs, Population Division (UNDESA). 2015. *World Population Prospects, the 2015 Revision*. New York: United Nations. http://esa.un.org/unpd/wpp/

Willett, W., J. Rockström, B. Loken, M. Springmann, T. Lang, S. Vermeulen, T. Garnett, et al. 2019. "Food in the Anthropocene: the EAT–Lancet Commission on healthy diets from sustainable food systems." *Lancet* 393, no. 10170: 447–92. http://dx.doi.org/10.1016/ S0140-6736(18)31788-4

Wirsenius, S., C. Azar, and G. Berndes. 2010. "How much land is needed for global food production under scenarios of dietary changes and livestock productivity increases in 2030?" *Agricultural Systems* 103, no. 9: 621–38. https://doi.org/10.1016/j.agsy.2010.07.005

Endnotes

1. Poor diets were responsible for 10.9 million deaths, or 22 percent of all adult deaths in 2017; they also resulted in 255 million disability-adjusted life years (DALYs). Cardiovascular disease was the leading cause, followed by cancers and diabetes.
2. In 2011, an FAO-commissioned report by the Swedish Institute for Food and Biotechnology estimated that roughly one-third of edible parts of food produced for human consumption globally was lost or wasted, corresponding to about 1.3 billion tons of food per year. Though debated, this study is the only one providing a global estimate covering all food production sectors and stages of the supply chain (FAO 2019). The 2015 estimate cited here is a Boston Consulting Group projection using the FAO estimate and other FAO data.

3. Still widely cited today, this figure is now dated, based on estimates for 2007. FLW was found to account for 3.3 gigatons of CO_2e emissions per year.
4. Estimates are again dated, based on data from 2005 to 2007.
5. From a nutritional health perspective, fruits and vegetables are underconsumed the world over, and in high-income countries, spoilage is not a major factor explaining its underconsumption. That said, to the extent that nonaffordability contributes to low consumption of fresh produce in high-income (as well as lower-income) countries, this scenario draws attention to the significance of the price tag associated with keeping spoilage—and losses—of healthy foods at bay.
6. Using the UN's population projections, the World Resources Institute estimated a need to produce 56 percent more food relative to a 2010 baseline (Searchinger et al. 2018), and the FAO estimated 50 percent more relative to 2012 (FAO 2017). The WRI scenario also foresees a 593-million-hectare land gap, equivalent to about one quarter of the area covered by tropical rainforests.
7. Compared with 2015 (UNDESA 2015).
8. This estimate was calculated by multiplying the share of GDP from the agriculture sector by the national food loss and waste estimate (40 percent) and taking that share of GDP compared with the national GDP, using data from World Bank Open Data and an estimate stated by Nigeria's Minister of Agriculture and Rural Development, Audu Ogbeh, in June 2017.
9. Uneaten food can be composted and used as fertilizer or turned into fuel and used for energy. Depending on alternative sources of these valuable products—or substitutes thereof—the conversion of food to fertilizer or energy can be more or less beneficial from environmental and political perspectives (though probably not optimal, to the extent that food crops are unlikely to be the most efficient feedstocks for these applications).

PART IV

CONSERVING LAND AND SEA TO SUPPORT FOOD SECURITY

CHAPTER 8

Conserving Land and Forests

Nicoletta Batini

> "A nation that destroys its soils destroys itself."
> —*Franklin D. Roosevelt*

Land and forests are at the heart of our food systems. They also play a unique role in the global carbon cycle. Therefore, their management and conservation are crucial for both the UN Sustainable Development Goals and the Paris Agreement's goal of limiting global warming to less than 2°C above preindustrial levels.

The major part of our food is directly or indirectly produced on soil (Food and Agriculture Organization of the United Nations [FAO] 2015). Soil also harbors three times as much carbon as Earth's atmosphere and four times the amount stored in all living plants and animals. Currently, soil removes about a quarter of the world's fossil fuel emissions each year because plants absorb carbon dioxide from the atmosphere and stabilize it in the soil. Most soil carbon is stored as permafrost and peat in Arctic areas and in moist regions such as the boreal ecosystems of northern Eurasia and North America. Soils in hot or dry areas store less carbon.

Likewise, trees provide soil and water conservation, facilitate carbon sequestration, improve biodiversity, and increase the number of pollinators and natural pest predators. Among forests, dense pristine tropical forests serve as special carbon sinks, removing carbon dioxide from the atmosphere as their carbon-hungry trees grow, locking carbon in their leaves, stems, seeds, and roots for as long as the trees live. And they serve an outsized role in sequestration: a recent study found that intact forests absorbed about a third of anthropogenic carbon emissions from all sources between 2007 and 2016, markedly reducing the rate of carbon dioxide accumulation in the atmosphere (Le Quéré et al. 2018). Tropical forests are also home to at least two thirds of the world's organisms, no fewer than 3 million species and possibly 10 times greater or more (see Juniper 2019; chapters 10 and 11).

Land and Forests Are Losing Carbon

Because almost half the land that can support plant life on Earth has been converted to croplands, pastures, and rangelands, soils have actually lost 50 to 70 percent of the carbon they once held (see chapter 2). Farming practices that disturb the soil—such as planting monocrops, tilling, lack of cover crops, excessive use of fertilizers and pesticides, and overgrazing—expose carbon in the soil to oxygen, allowing it to burn off into the atmosphere. Draining wetlands also causes soils to release carbon; for example, current plans to drain and drill a section of the peatland in Congo's Cuvette Centrale could release as much carbon as the total annual emissions of Japan, because wetlands absorb five times as much carbon per acre as rainforests (Sun and Carson 2020). Together, these activities that disturb the soil have contributed about a quarter of all the anthropogenic greenhouse gas emissions that are warming the planet. And as the planet gets warmer, soils will release more carbon than previously believed: 4°C of warming as envisaged under current business as usual. IPCC (2019) scenarios could result in soils releasing as much as 37 percent more carbon dioxide than normal (Hicks Pries et al. 2017).[1]

Similarly, tree cover loss in the tropics has risen steadily over the past two decades, with intact tropical forests now disappearing at the rate of forty football fields every minute (figure 8-1). Natural disasters such as fires and tropical storms play a growing role, especially as climate change makes them more frequent and severe. But forest clearing for agriculture and other uses continues to drive large-scale deforestation. For example, 17 percent of the Amazon has been cleared at one time or another. Another 20 percent has been degraded. In 2019, the deforestation rate shot up 30 percent from the year before. Eighty percent of deforested Amazon land ends up as cattle pasture for meat that is either consumed domestically or exported by large, globally operating meat corporations (Global Forest Atlas 2019). The combination of climate change and deforestation could lead to an Amazon forest collapse, with huge releases of carbon and effects on climate systems. Changes in wind speeds, rainfall

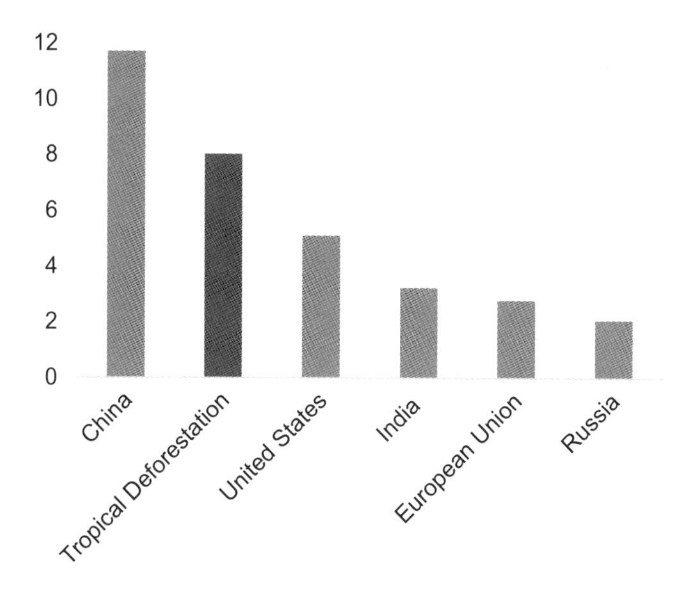

Figure 8-1. CO_2 emissions from tropical deforestation in country terms. *Source:* Data reported in Seymour and Busch (2016).

patterns, and atmospheric chemistry would be felt across the globe, starting with a rapid desertification of the American Midwest and the Rio de la Plata region, the granaries of the Western Hemisphere (Juniper 2019).

Over the past few years, the largest tropical forest losses were reported in Brazil, the Democratic Republic of Congo, and Indonesia (figure 8-2). Losses were particularly devastating in Brazil and Colombia, where national policies promote industrial agriculture. These policies have been associated with a rapid increase in the rate of illegal clearing for not only cattle ranching, logging, and road and dam building but also coca farming and mining (Climate Action Tracker 2019). By contrast, unlike most tropical forests, Indonesia experienced a drop in tree cover loss in 2017, including a 60 percent decline in primary forest loss. However, pristine forest loss continued in Sumatra (Global Forest Watch 2020; Supriatna et al. 2020).

Widespread forest degradation and deforestation reduce forest resilience to fires and drought because more solar radiation hits the forest floor. Plants dry out, the entire forest becomes more flammable, and carbon losses increase. The breakneck speed of human-made deforestation is also a key cause of defaunation and the prime cause of the planet's mass extinction. Extinction in turn accelerates forest loss, because forests are in a symbiotic relationship with many

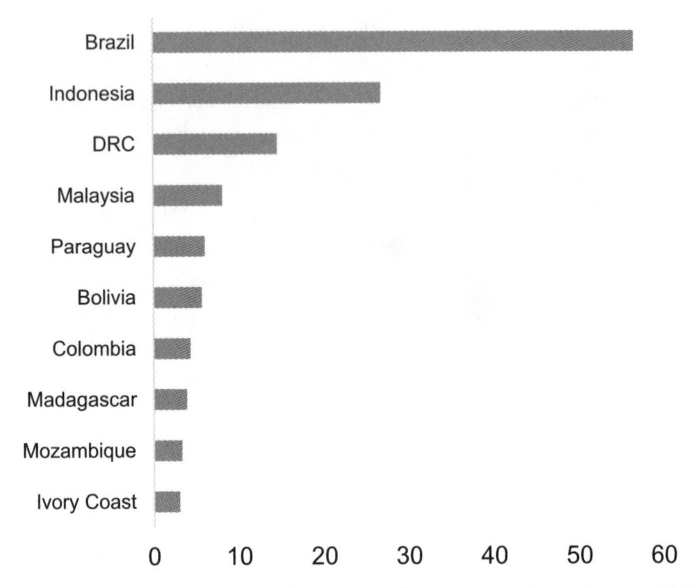

Figure 8-2. Top ten tropical countries for tree cover loss. *Source:* Global Forest Watch, 2020.

animal species and depend for survival on a complex web of services that these species provide (Kolbert 2014). Against this background, forests could soon serve no longer as a carbon sink but rather as a source, adding to global greenhouse gas emissions. Tropical forest loss accounted for 8 percent of the world's annual CO_2 emissions in 2018, significantly higher than the EU's contribution to global warming in the same year (Global Forest Watch 2020).[2] A recent study estimated that the Amazon forest's carbon sink capacity, which is the amount of carbon absorbed through photosynthesis that outweighs the amount of carbon emitted by tree loss, will reach zero by 2035. Carbon sink capacity of African forests will also decline 14 percent by 2030 (Hubau et al. 2020).

Conserve 30 Percent of the Earth's Land by 2030 to Stay Within 1.5°C

"Conserving ecosystems" is an explicit commitment by about two thirds of Paris Agreement signatories because natural ecosystems are key to maintaining human prosperity in a warming world (Seddon et al. 2019). The importance of forests for human sustenance and survival is also enshrined in the United Nations Sustainable Development Goals; SDG15 aims to sustainably manage forests together by protecting, restoring, and promoting sustainable use of terrestrial ecosystems, combating desertification, halting and reversing land degradation, and halting biodiversity loss. It acknowledges that forests are deeply intertwined with healthy living, because they are key to human prosperity and well-being all over the world (UN 2015).

Research since the Paris Agreement suggests that the simplest way to stabilize the climate is to maintain and restore at least *half* of Earth's land area as intact natural ecosystems by 2050, in combination with energy transition measures (Tallis et al. 2018; Teske 2019). A 30 percent conservation target for the terrestrial realm by 2030 is considered a reasonable milestone toward the larger end goal of half of the planet protected by 2050 (Baillie and Zhang 2018). This goal matches the 30 percent target proposed by the International Union for the Conservation of Nature (IUCN) as a critical step for marine conservation (see chapter 9). Because these measures will take time to be enacted, they will probably require additional restoration efforts to create negative emissions and offset the clearing and release of greenhouse gases (Dinerstein et al. 2019). The Global Deal for Nature divides the terrestrial realm in 846 ecoregions including terrestrial, freshwater, and marine areas, to serve as a conservation template that can help guide and monitor conservation efforts by providing increased representation of critical habitats and biomes (Dinerstein et al. 2019).

Within general conservation, forest conservation, especially the conservation of intact forests,[3] is a critical way to combat global warming. Peatlands, tundra, mangroves, and ancient grasslands are also significant carbon storehouses. They conserve distinct mixes of plants and animals and should be preserved alongside intact forests. Ancient grasslands store approximately as much carbon globally as forests and are extremely biodiverse. Because the majority of grassland carbon is stored deep under the ground, grasslands are a reliable carbon sink, especially in the face of climate-sensitive disturbances such as fires (Dinerstein et al. 2019).

Environmental Benefits of Conserving Land and Forests

Achieving the Paris Agreement's goals will probably involve removing carbon dioxide from the atmosphere, according to the Intergovernmental Panel on Climate Change (IPCC 2018). However, if used on a scale large enough to be effective, strategies such as capturing and storing carbon emissions from biofuel-burning power plants or planting new forests to absorb carbon can either put more pressure on natural resources or be too expensive. On the other hand, sequestering carbon in soil is safe and economical. Better land management and agricultural practices could increase the ability of soils to store carbon, combating global warming. And given the amount of soil organic carbon in our biomass and the atmosphere combined, even minor changes in that pool will have huge effects for the atmosphere.

The rate at which soil can store organic carbon depends on soil texture and structure, rainfall, temperature, farming systems, and soil management. Strategies to increase the carbon storage rate include soil restoration and woodland regeneration, no-till farming, cover crops, nutrient management, manuring and sludge application, improved grazing, water conservation and harvesting, efficient irrigation, agroforestry practices, and growing energy crops on spare lands. If combinations of these techniques are used, global croplands have the potential to store an additional 1.85 gigatons of CO_2 each year—as much as the global transportation sector emits annually. Moreover, soils could continue to sequester carbon for twenty to forty years before they become saturated (Lal 2004; Zomer et al., 2017). Increasing the carbon content of the planet's soils by just 2 percent could offset 100 percent of all greenhouse gas emissions currently going into the atmosphere (Lal 2019). Project Drawdown (an organization that analyzes and shares information on climate solutions) considers conservation agriculture one of the "greatest opportunities to address human and climate health, along with the financial well-being of farmers" (Project Drawdown 2019).[4] In addition to mitigating climate change by maintaining or increasing carbon content, healthy soils supply the essential nutrients, water, oxygen, and root support that our food-producing plants need to grow and flourish. They are the basis for healthy food production (FAO 2015a). However, it is unclear how long it may take for soil to absorb large amounts of carbon from the atmosphere, and some postulate that it could take at least a hundred if not a thousand years (He et al. 2016).

Protecting forests offers an equally safe and effective way to achieve meaningful carbon dioxide removal and neutralize emissions while sheltering ecosystems more generally. Today, forest landscapes (mosaics of forests, naturally treeless ecosystems, and deforested areas), usually referred to as the forest zone, extend over 5.8 billion hectares, or 44 percent of Earth's ice-free land area. (For comparison, Brazil has a land area of 0.84 billion hectares. Earth has a total ice-free land area of about 13 billion hectares.) Within these exist intact forest landscapes (IFLs). IFLs are "a seamless mosaic of forests and associated natural treeless ecosystems that exhibit no remotely detected signs of human activity or habitat fragmentation and are large enough to maintain all native biological diversity, including viable populations of wide-ranging species" (Potapov et al. 2017, 1). In 2013, they totaled less than 1.2 billion hectares, or a fifth of the total forest zone area. Half are in tropical areas, namely in the Amazon and Congo River basins, the islands of Borneo and New Guinea, and the Southeast Asian highlands. Another third are the boreal forests of North America and Eurasia (Potapov et al. 2017).[5] IFLs are particularly important because they are large continuous areas, and forests' ability to perform ecosystem functions and withstand natural disturbance and climate change are functions of their size.

Forest conservation is crucial for stabilizing global temperatures, but its climate mitigation value will soon decline if deforestation continues at the current pace (Maxwell et al. 2019). For example, had we protected the portion of intact tropical forests that has been cleared, logged, or otherwise disrupted between 2000 and 2013, a surface area of approximately 28 million hectares (about 5 percent of remaining intact forests), those forests could have sequestered almost 4 gigatons of CO_2 by 2050. That is equivalent to about 11 percent of current global emissions.

Forests and trees also prevent soil erosion and water contamination, protect land and soil fertility, and avert landslides and floods. Tree roots serve as natural nets spreading far into the ground to hold soil in place. When trees prevent soil runoff, the soil retains essential nutrients and remains fertile. Trees also add manure to the soil from falling leaves and dried branches. Importantly, forests maintain an area's water cycle by absorbing moisture through leaves and roots. They are a natural storage system for rainwater and slow down the atmosphere's aridity. Trees prevent freshwater lakes from losing moisture and drying up. And because about two thirds of all species on Earth live in these intact forests, their conservation is key to averting mass extinction (Kolbert 2014).

Economic Benefits of Conserving Land and Forests

Healthy soils are more productive and resilient to climate change, as demonstrated in parallel studies comparing organically and conventionally farmed land (chapter 2). Soil health is defined as "the capacity of soil to function as a living system" (FAO 2015a, 1). Healthy soils support a community of soil organisms that protect plants from diseases and pests, help plant roots retain water and nutrients, and ultimately improve crop production. These communities boost agricultural productivity. Project Drawdown estimates that shifting from conventional to regenerative farming could provide a lifetime operational cost saving of US$2.3–3.5 trillion and lifetime net profit gain of US$135–206 billion on an investment of US$79–116 billion (Project Drawdown 2019). Wetlands, areas consisting of marshes and swamps with carbon-rich soil that offer a natural buffer in the face of tropical cyclones, have an estimated worth of US$1.8 million per square kilometer because of their ability to shelter property from coastal damage (Sun and Carton 2020).

Forests, especially large intact forests, affect local, regional, and global climate, governing the water cycles that nourish rain-fed crops (almost 80 percent of agricultural land worldwide relies on rain-fed production systems, and these systems provide 62 percent of the world's food). Thus, preserving forests allows fertile regions of the world to avoid desertification. Aside from their strong impact on climate systems, forests have always been a great source of economic goods. The paper factory depends on wood pulp supplied from trees. Lumbering is the main occupation of people in the coniferous forest region. When a forest is properly managed and saplings planted regularly, forests become a sustainable source of timber: The World Bank estimates that the timber sector is worth about US$600 billion and gives work to about 50 million people globally, including 13 million formal jobs (World Bank Group 2016). Forests also provide employment to local people who gather forest products to turn into handicrafts and are home to a kaleidoscope of indigenous communities. The Paris Agreement gives attention to indigenous peoples, reflecting a growing acknowledgment of their knowledge, rights, and crucial roles in protecting some of the world's most important and biodiverse places. In fact, forested areas managed by local communities consistently see less deforestation than protected forests (Porter Bolland et al. 2012).

Last but not least, limiting human activity to areas removed from intact, pristine ecosystems is key to avoiding close contact between human populations and wildlife, one of the prime causes of viral pandemics. Coronaviruses, Ebola, and HIV pathogens, for example, have all emerged from wildlife reservoirs and crossed to the human species because of close contact with or consumption of wildlife from forested areas (Bloomfield et al. 2020). Their enormous human and economic toll could have been avoided if forests were conserved properly through better land and forest management policies.

Policies to Conserve Land and Forests

Across all Nationally Determined Contributions under the Paris Agreement, forests represent a quarter of all planned emission reductions by 2030. But most national governments do not prioritize the conservation of intact tropical forests as a way to meet their commitments under the Paris Agreement. For example, reduced emissions from land use and land cover change account for a quarter of all planned emission reductions (Grassi et al. 2017), but intact forest retention is seldom a part of these planned reductions (Watson et al. 2018). Also, little is planned globally to retain or improve carbon sequestration in soil, and progress on this front is further complicated by the fact that only recently have we been able to estimate carbon emissions associated with intact forest loss (Maxwell et al. 2019).

However, a vast literature is exploring the economic policies that can foster land and forest conservation. Batini and Pointereau examine policies for land conservation and the reconversion of conventionally farmed soils into organically farmed soils in chapter 2. For forest conservation, many policy tools exist. Countries such as Costa Rica and Brazil have managed to conserve forests in the past without limiting economic growth (FAO 2015b). In many other countries, however, forest conservation policies clash with growth because there are few economic alternatives to agriculture and ranching, which drive deforestation (Barbier 2004). Conservation is also difficult to enforce, reflecting institutional weaknesses (Barbier et al. 2005). Food insecurity can complicate conservation further (Ericksen et al. 2011). In such countries, efforts to reduce deforestation tend to be more successful if coupled with policies that preserve agricultural output and keep food prices stable.

Fiscal Policy

- *Taxes.* Environmental taxes can support sustainable forest management by making landowners pay for the consequences of deforestation (Kalkuhl and Edenhofer 2017; Heine et al. 2020). Environmental taxes on farmed and forested land should be set in a way that the net incentives from cutting down forests to create clear land are negative. This is done by setting taxes lower on forested land than on cleared land and by ensuring that the production of commodities that drive deforestation is not subsidized.[6] These fiscal incentives can be supported by subsidies that encourage landowners to keep their land forested or to rewild previously cleared forest areas (Heine and Hayde 2020).
- *Feebates (or tax rebates).* Feebates are a combination of an excise tax with tax discounts. The tax component discourages environmentally

damaging activities, and the rebate promotes the same activities if they are certified to be environmentally nonimpacting. This way, feebates create an incentive for cattle, agriculture, and timber companies to choose sustainable forest activities and avoid deforestation (Parry 2020).

- *Direct cash or noncash transfers, and ecological fiscal transfers.* Similar to fiscal tools used in the energy sector to spur a green transition, these measures are incentives for conservation because they either reward environmental efforts or they compensate landowners for any income lost from not clearing land or from reforesting or rewilding land for carbon sequestration. Sometimes these transfers are administered by apportioning central revenues to regional or municipal governments based on select environmental indicators, such as the ecological status of a certain protected area or the provision of ecological services (e.g., in Brazil, France, India, and Portugal) (Droste et al. 2017; Heine and Hayde 2020).
- *Export tariffs.* Taxes on exported timber and other forest products, levied by customs authorities, are effective in countries with multiple forest operators, a large share of informal operators, or weak government capacity with complex tax enforcement. The taxes are effective when products from forests exit the country through specific points such as shipping ports or border crossings. When combined with fiscal rebates for third-party certification, export tariffs can foster sustainable production (Heine and Hayde 2020).

Structural Reforms Including Land and Forest Reform

A number of regulatory and forest management measures can be enacted in combination with fiscal policies to ensure preservation of forest wildlands. These include the following:

- *Mapping.* Governments should create a standardized and robust mapping and monitoring system that can be implemented at national to global scales. Although a number of global ecosystem wilderness and intactness maps have been created over the past thirty years, national data collection methods have never been standardized. Without robust statistics, it becomes much more difficult to understand the biodiversity loss and reduced carbon sequestration capacity caused by deforestation. The need to accurately monitor forest cover and quality is crucial to understanding the costs of deforestation. For example, using an approach that combines ground-based surveys with satellite imagery, a recent study estimated that there are more than 3 trillion trees on Earth, half in tropical and subtropical forests and the rest evenly distributed between boreal and temperate regions (Crowther et al. 2015). The study estimated that more than 15 billion trees are cut down each year. Continuous satellite monitoring of land use change and tree density coupled with ground-based monitoring[7] are necessary to guide efforts to halt deforestation and forest degradation.

- *Natural capital accounting.* National governments must better and more broadly account for the full carbon impact of intact forest retention and land use change. For example, emission baselines should consider selective logging and other more hidden degradation processes as well as traditional forest clearance, which is more readily observed but concentrated at forest margins. Recent advances in modeling capacity and the understanding of trends in forest degradation and general land use change will improve emission baseline estimates (Searchinger et al. 2018).
- *Land reforms that empower indigenous people.* Research shows that indigenous people and local communities, especially when women are involved, are better conservation stewards because they have adapted to live sustainably within ecosystems (Cook et al. 2019). But in many countries with intact forests, rampant land speculation, cattle ranching to serve the increasing international demand for meat, and illegal forest activities mean that land is increasingly removed from local communities' supervision, creating an adverse impact on deforestation. In the Brazilian Amazon, for example, a marked reduction in deforestation would require the government to quickly adopt policies resembling those used between 2005 and 2014. In these policies, indigenous environmental leaders were empowered and authorities aggressively targeted environmental crime by putting criminals in jail and destroying their mining and logging equipment, including chainsaws and earthmovers. These policies have been reversed, and the region has become lawless, spurring deforestation.
- *Conventions to ban the demand of products derived from deforestation.* Advanced economies are major importers and consumers of many commodities, including embodied deforestation. Because they are

responsible for deforestation, they could provide solutions by adopting coherent approaches, including shifts in consumption. For example, Europe's imports of agricultural products—ranging from beef and soybeans from Latin America, to palm oil from Southeast Asia, to cocoa from Africa—are responsible for more than a third of deforestation (European Commission 2013). Advanced economies should develop national strategies to fight deforestation, eliminate it from agricultural commodity chains, and move to a fully sustainable commodity supply, as advocated by a coalition of European partners including Denmark, Germany, Italy, the Netherlands, Norway, and the United Kingdom (Batini 2020). These plans should promise key regulatory changes, from origin certification to consumer sensitization. To be effective, they need to be flanked with measures changing agricultural production systems. Effective changes include reducing animal herds that feed on imported soy, operating a shift in diets toward plant-based foods, and developing domestic agroforestry, as advocated in chapter 2.

Public International Finance

- *International funding schemes.* A number of funding schemes are designed to avoid land use and land cover change emissions in developing nations. Notably, the UN Reducing Emissions from Deforestation and Forest Degradation (REDD) Programme, born in 2008 from a collaboration between the UN Development Programme (UNDP), United Nations Environment Programme, and FAO, incentivizes developing countries to either reduce greenhouse gas emissions or facilitate carbon dioxide removal from the atmosphere by increasing forestland. The scheme offers technical and financial support for developing countries to reduce emissions from forestry. It is managed by the Forest Carbon Partnership Facility through two funds, which are publicly and privately financed by a group of donors. Currently, there are REDD+ initiatives in fifty-seven countries.[8] However, REDD+ projects have not always worked well for environment and people: Early projects led to rights violations, particularly violations of communities' land ownership and forest use rights. Other REDD+ projects have been accused of gaining financial reward for only limited additional forest protection. Other forest conservation funding initiatives such as the Central Africa Forest Initiative share similar issues, as seen in the case of the planned drilling of Congo's Cuvette Centrale (Cannon 2019). National laws should provide for inclusive stakeholder participation so that all stakeholders are able to input their views and meaningfully contribute to decision making on REDD+ projects and other forest conservation initiatives and law and policy reform (ClientEarth 2020).

- *Forest conservation targets and green carbon funds*. National governments should complement existing initiatives by establishing a global target for conservation and financing national "green carbon funds" aimed at conserving critical terrestrial biomes, similar to the "Blue carbon fund" that has been proposed for ocean conservation (see chapter 9). Financing could be made conditional on third-party certification, the provision of technical assistance, and preferential credit schemes (Heine and Hayde 2020). Countries protecting intact forests could use these as natural capital collateral to tap green finance, including funds from international financial organizations, to fund energy and land use transition policies and projects (see Batini 2019). On a global basis, 0.8–1 percent of global gross domestic product or US$598–824 billion is needed per year over the next ten years to finance the gap between current funding for nature conservation and what is needed. The 2018 total global conservation investment was between US$124–143 billion (Paulston Institute, 2020). To put it into context, the United States spends US$70 billion every year on pet food (Euromoney 2019).

Country Cases

Costa Rica

With a land area of only 51,000 square kilometers, equivalent to 0.03 percent of the planet's surface, Costa Rica has a vast range of ecological conditions, from steamy, humid coasts, to hot, dry lowlands up to cool, mountainous cloud forest. It is a uniquely diverse place and home to almost 5 percent of global biodiversity.

In large part, this conservation success reflects the country's environmental protection systems, considered to be the most advanced in the world. After the National Forestry Law in 1969, Costa Rica created a system of national parks and biological reserves. It now protects 27 percent of its land in national parks, wildlife refuges, and more than 100 private reserves, all administered under the National System of Conservation Areas, which is part of the Ministry for Environment and Energy. Costa Rica is the first tropical country to radically reverse the process of deforestation, with forest cover increasing from just 21 percent in 1990 to 52 percent in 2005. After a difficult start,[9] conservation policies were buttressed in the early 1980s and are now paid for in part by a 3.5 percent carbon tax levied on hydrocarbons set up in 1997 and destined to launch a system of payments for environmental services. Conservation efforts were linked to the development of a strong ecotourism industry—a concept largely pioneered in Costa Rica—which now attracts more than 3 million visitors, generates almost US$4 billion for the economy annually (2018 data), and is a top source of income and foreign exchange. Park fees are in large part retained to purchase land, extend areas under protection, and maintain existing forests.

Bhutan

Like Costa Rica, Bhutan is one of the tiniest countries in the world. But its success in conservation is larger than most. Environmental conservation is one of the four pillars of Bhutan's Gross National Happiness philosophy, and Bhutan's constitution mandates the permanent preservation of two thirds of the country's land under forest cover. Bhutan's location in the eastern Himalayas, with its mix of alpine terrain and subtropical plains, receives more rainfall than its west-neighboring countries, and this fosters forest growth. The forests contain numerous deciduous and evergreen species, ranging from oak and pine forests to tropical hardwood. More than half of the country is protected, creating a continuous area of intact forests interwoven with free-flowing rivers— the biggest percentage of any Asian country.

Knowing the economic and environmental value of making its forestry sustainable, Bhutan grew progressively more conscientious about forestry management in the 1970s. In 1977, supported by the World Wildlife Fund (WWF), Bhutan buttressed its forest management through training programs, forest boundary demarcation, and the construction of guard posts and a patrol road that would eventually become the Royal Manas National Park. In 1986, Bhutan declined aid from the World Bank aimed at building a hydroelectric project on the Manas Chhu that would have flooded this major conservation area on the southern Bhutan–India border. By the late 1980s, nine additional forest and wildlife preserves had been created, primarily along the southern border with India. In 1991 the government, with assistance from UNDP and the World Wildlife Fund, established a trust fund aimed at producing up to US$1 million per year for training in forestry.

In 2018, the Bhutan government, donors, and partners from around the world created Bhutan for Life, a US$43 million fund that will be combined with US$75 million from the Bhutan government. The fund will permanently protect Bhutan's network of protected areas for fourteen years, after which Bhutan will be able to fund its conservation autonomously. It imitates similar conservation initiatives launched by the WWF (and other partners) to protect the Brazilian Amazon and forests in Colombia and Peru. Like those, it is based on a novel approach to funding called Project Finance for Permanence, which rests on two specific financing features. The first feature is a single closing, a financial structure whereby donors commit a certain amount but do not pay unless a certain collective amount is reached. The second is a transition fund, whereby once the deal is closed, the monies donated are paid out over time based on whether certain conservation conditions have been reached. The project provides a long-term funding commitment by the government as part of the single closing arrangements to promote ownership. The aim of this type of project is to get around challenges to conservation posed by earlier patchy, short-term and insufficient funding programs for managing protected areas. As in Costa Rica, sustainable economic development, such as ecotourism and organic farming, is to be allowed in the protected areas. This initiative is a true example of how the Bhutanese seek balance.

United Kingdom's Eastern Coast Wetlands

Wallasea Island on England's eastern coast hosts the largest restored coastal wetland in Europe, a successful example of land rewilding. Ecologists say coastal wetlands like these are capable of trapping carbon up to forty times faster per hectare than tropical rainforests. But over the past 400 years, farmland cultivation, coastal development, and rising sea levels have combined to destroy 91 percent of wetland habitats on the Essex coast. Worldwide, 35 percent of global wetlands were destroyed from 1975 to 2015, according to the United Nations. In Europe, home to some of the most densely populated land in the world, and where true wilderness has become almost nonexistent, several publicly and privately funded rewilding projects have emerged. Rewilding initiatives such as Wallasea are multiplying, peatland bogs in Germany are being returned to their pristine state, and forests are being replanted in the

Scottish Highlands. These projects not only sequester carbon but also boost biological diversity and help land adapt to the changing climate by preventing floods and wildfires.

Conclusions

When grasslands are converted or soil is tilled, forests are slashed, burned, and cut down, and wetlands are drained or burned, the greenhouse gases originally stored in these ecosystems escape back into the atmosphere and heat the planet. At least half of the carbon in Earth's soils has been released into the atmosphere over the past centuries, and just a fifth of Earth's original forests remains in large, natural ecosystems, half of which is considered under threat.

The value of healthy soil and intact forests becomes clearer as we approach the long-term 2050 milestone when humanity should be transitioned from net emissions to net sequestration. If we do not keep our soil healthy and our remaining forests intact, it will be impossible to implement the climate goals outlined in the Paris Agreement. But soil cannot continue to sequester carbon if it continues to be disturbed, and intact forests cannot sequester carbon if they are increasingly felled. Failing to account for forgone carbon removals can distort priorities for mitigation action within and beyond the forest sector. Rooting carbon back into the ground through regenerative agriculture is one of the greatest opportunities to address human and climate health. Likewise, intact tropical forests are a safe and effective way to achieve meaningful carbon dioxide removal and neutralize emissions from other sources.

Fiscal policies and structural reforms at both the national and international levels are well suited to ensure conservation of land and forests, and successful examples exist of places that have accomplished these goals with benefits for the economy and the environment. Mapping land and accounting for natural capital are essential ingredients for successful conservation efforts, and innovative techniques are now available to do this accurately and globally.

References

Baillie, J., and Y. P. Zhang, 2018. "Space for nature." *Science* 361: 1051.

Barbier, E. B. 2004. "Explaining agricultural land expansion and deforestation in developing countries." *American Journal of Agricultural Economics* 86, no. 5: 1347–53.

Barbier, E. B., R. Damania, and D. Leonard. 2005. "Corruption, trade and resource conversion." *Journal of Environmental Economics and Management* 50, no. 2: 276–99.

Batini, N. 2019. "Reaping what we sow." *Finance and Development*, The Climate Issue. Washington D.C.: International Monetary Fund.

———. 2020. "The role of global demand on deforestation: the case of France." In *Designing Fiscal Instruments for Sustainable Forests*, ed. D. Heine and E. Hayde. Washington, D.C.: World Bank.

Bloomfield, L. S. P., T. L. McIntosh, and E. F. Lambin. 2020. "Habitat fragmentation, livelihood behaviors, and contact between people and nonhuman primates in Africa." *Landscape Ecology* 35: 985–1000.

Cannon, J. C. 2019. "$65 million deal to protect Congo's forests raises concerns." *Mongabay*. https://news.mongabay.com/2019/10/65-million-deal-to-protect-congos-forests-raises-concerns/

ClientEarth. 2020. *Practical Guide on Law Reforms in the Forest Sector. With Lessons from Côte d'Ivoire, Ghana, Liberia and the Republic of Congo*, ed. N. Faure, T. Venisnik, and B. Ichou. London: ClientEarth.

Climate Action Tracker. 2019. "Country summary: Brazil." https://climateactiontracker.org/countries/brazil/

Cook, N. J., T. Grillos, and K. P. Andersson. 2019. "Gender quotas increase the equality and effectiveness of climate policy interventions." *Nature Climate Change* 9: 330–4.

Crowther, T., H. Glick, K. R. Covey, C. Bettigole, D. S. Maynard, S. M. Thomas, J. R. Smith, G. Hintler, M. C. Duguid, G. Amatulli, et al. 2015. "Mapping tree density at a global scale." *Nature* 525: 201–5.

Dinerstein, E., C. Vynne, E. Sala, A. R. Joshi, S. Fernando, T. E. Lovejoy, J. Mayorga, D. Olson, G. P. Asner, J. E. M. Baillie, et al. 2019. "A Global Deal For Nature: guiding principles, milestones, and targets." *Science Advances* 5, no. 4: eaaw2869.

Droste, N., C. Becker, I. Ring, and R. Santos. 2017. "Decentralization effects in ecological fiscal transfers: the case of Portugal." UFZ Discussion Papers Department of Economics no. 3/2017. Leipzig, Germany: Helmholtz-Zentrum für Umweltforschung GmbH-UFZ.

Ericksen, P., P. Thornton, A. Notenbaert, L. Cramer, P. Jones, and M. Herrero. 2011. "Mapping hotspots of climate change and food insecurity in the global tropics." *CCAFS Report* 5: 1–56.

Euromoney. 2019. "Conservation finance: Costa Rica costs its success." https://www.euromoney.com/article/b1hhymxdycwtkz/conservation-finance-costa-rica-costs-its-success?copyrightInfo=true

European Commission. 2013. "The impact of EU consumption on deforestation: comprehensive analysis of the impact of EU consumption on deforestation." Technical report no. 2013-063. Brussels: European Commission.

Food and Agriculture Organization of the United Nations (FAO). 2015a. "Healthy soils are the basis for healthy food production." FAO Factsheet. http://www.fao.org/3/a-i4405e.pdf

———. 2015b. *Global Forest Resources Assessment 2015*. Rome: FAO. http://www.fao.org/3/a-i4808e.pdf

Global Forest Atlas. 2019. "Cattle ranching in the Amazon region." https://globalforestatlas.yale.edu/amazon/land-use/cattle-ranching

Global Forest Watch. 2020. "We lost a football pitch of primary rainforest every 6 seconds in 2019." https://blog.globalforestwatch.org/data-and-research/global-tree-cover-loss-data-2019

Grassi, G., J. House, F. Dentener, S. Federici, M. den Elzen, and J. Penman. 2017. "The key role of forests in meeting climate targets requires science for credible mitigation." *Nature Climate Change* 7: 220–6.

He, Y., S. E. Trumbore, M. S. Torn, J. W. Harden, L. J. S. Vaughn, S. D. Allison, and J. T. Randerson. 2016. "Radiocarbon constraints imply reduced carbon uptake by soils during the 21st century." *Science* 353, no. 6306: 1419–24.

Heine, D., and E. Hayde. 2020. "Environmental taxation and sustainable forest management." In *Designing Fiscal Instruments for Sustainable Forests*, ed. D. Heine and E. Hayde. Washington, D.C.: World Bank.

Heine, D., E. Hayde, and S. Speck. 2020. "Environmental taxation and sustainable forest management." In *Designing Fiscal Instruments for Sustainable Forests*, ed. D. Heine and E. Hayde. Washington, D.C.: World Bank.

Hicks Pries, C. E., C. Castanha, R. C. Porras, and M. S. Torn. 2017. "The whole-soil carbon flux in response to warming." *Science* 355, no. 6332: 1420–3.

Hubau, W., S. L. Lewis, O. L. Phillips, K. Affum-Baffoe, H. Beeckman, A. Cuní-Sanchez, A. K. Daniels, C. E. N. Ewango, S. Fauset, J. M. Mukinzi, et al. 2020. "Asynchronous carbon sink saturation in African and Amazonian tropical forests." *Nature* 579: 80–7.

Intergovernmental Panel on Climate Change (IPCC). 2018. *Special Report: Global Warming of 1.5°C*. Geneva, Switzerland: IPCC.

———. 2019. "Climate change and land: an IPCC special report on climate change, desertification, land degradation, sustainable land management, food security, and greenhouse gas fluxes in terrestrial ecosystems." Geneva, Switzerland: IPCC.

Juniper, T. 2019. *Rainforest: Dispatches from Earth's Most Vital Frontlines*. Washington, D.C.: Island Press.

Kalkuhl, M., and O. Edenhofer. 2017. "Ramsey meets Thunen: the impact of land taxes on economic development and land conservation." *International Tax and Public Finance* 24, no. 2: 350–80.

Kolbert, E. 2014. *The Sixth Extinction: An Unnatural History*. New York: Henry Holt & Co.

Lal, R. 2004. "Soil carbon sequestration impacts on global climate change and food security." *Science* 304.

———. 2019. "What is regenerative agriculture?" *Green America Magazine*. https://greenamerica.org/food-climate/restore-it/what-regenerative-agriculture

Le Quéré, C., R. M. Andrew, P. Friedlingstein, S. Sitch, J. Pongratz, A. C. Manning, et al. 2018. "Global carbon budget 2017." *Earth System Science Data* 10: 405–48.

Maxwell, S. L., T. Evans, J. E. M. Watson, A. Morel, H. Grantham, A. Duncan, N. Harris, P. Potapov, R. K. Runting, O. Venter, et al. 2019. "Degradation and forgone removals increase the carbon impact of intact forest loss by 626%." *Science Advances* 5, no. 10: 2546.

McFarland, W., S. Whitley, and G. Kissinger. 2015. *Subsidies to Key Commodities Driving Forest Loss. Implications for Private Climate Finance*. London: Overseas Development Institute.

Parry, I. 2020. "Rationale for, and design of, a feebate for forest carbon sequestration." In *Designing Fiscal Instruments for Sustainable Forests*, ed. D. Heine and E. Hayde. Washington D.C.: World Bank.

Paulson Institute, 2020. "Financing Nature: Closing the Global Biodiversity Financing Gap." A partnership between the Paulson Institute, the *Nature Conservancy*, and Cornell Atkinson Center for Sustainability. Washington D.C., Paulson Institute.

Porter-Bolland, L., E. A. Ellis, M. R. Guariguata, I. Ruiz-Mallén, S. Negrete-Yankelevich, and V. Reyes-García. 2012. "Community managed forests and forest protected areas: an assessment of their conservation effectiveness across the tropics." *Forest Ecology and Management* 268: 6–17.

Potapov, P. M., C. Hansen, L. Laestadius, S. Turubanova, A. Yaroshenko, C. Thies, W. Smith, I. Zhuravleva, A. Komarova, S. Minnemeyer, and E. Esipova. 2017. "The last frontiers of wilderness: tracking loss of intact forest landscapes from 2000 to 2013." *Science Advances* 3, no. 1: e1600821.

Project Drawdown. 2019. "Regenerative annual cropping." https://www.drawdown.org/solutions/regenerative-annual-cropping

Searchinger, T. D., S. Wirsenius, T. Beringer, and P. Dumas, 2018. "Assessing the efficiency of changes in land use for mitigating climate change." *Nature* 564: 249–53.

Seddon, N., B. Turner, P. Berry, A. Chausson, and C. A. J. Giradin. 2019. "Grounding nature-based climates solutions in sound biodiversity science." *Nature Climate Change* 9: 84–7.

Seymour, F., and J. Busch. 2016. *Why Forests? Why Now? The Science, Economics and Politics of Tropical Forests and Climate Change*. Washington, D.C.: Center for Global Development.

Sun, F., and R. T. Carston. 2020. "Coastal wetlands reduce property damage during tropical cyclones." *PNAS*. https://doi.org/10.1073/pnas.1915169117

Supriatna, J., M. Shekelle, H. A. Fuad, N. L. Winarni, A. A. Dwiyahreni, M. Farid, . . . Z. Zakaria. 2020. "Deforestation on the Indonesian island of Sulawesi and the loss of primate habitat." *Global Ecology and Conservation* 24: e01205.

Tallis, H. M., P. L. Hawthorne, S. Polasky, J. Reid, M. W. Beck, K. Brauman, J. M. Bielicki, S. Binder, M. G. Burgess, E. Cassidy, et al. 2018. "An attainable global vision for conservation and human well-being." *Frontiers in Ecological Environment* 16: 563–70.

Teske, S. 2019. *Achieving the Paris Climate Agreement*. Berlin: Springer.

United Nations. 2015. "Transforming our world: the 2030 Agenda for Sustainable Development Resolution adopted by the General Assembly on 25 September 2015." A/RES/70/1. https://www.un.org/ga/search/view_doc.asp?symbol=A/RES/70/1&Lang=E

Watson, J. E. M., T. Evans, O. Venter, B. Williams, A. Tulloch, C. Stewart, I. Thompson, J. C. Ray, K. Murray, A. Salazar, et al. 2018. "The exceptional value of intact forest ecosystems." *Nature Ecology and Evolution* 2: 599–610.

World Bank Group. 2016. "Forests generate jobs and incomes." https://www.worldbank.org/en/topic/forests/brief/forests-generate-jobs-and-incomes

Zomer, R. J., D. A. Bossio, R. Sommer, et al. 2017. "Global sequestration potential of increased organic carbon in cropland soils." *Scientific Reports* 7: 15554.

Endnotes

1. Syria and Libya are examples of what excessive soil disturbance can lead to. Roman tax records show that those areas grew ample amounts of wheat, but as farmers continued to

plow their fields, they exposed valuable microbes, and topsoil eroded. Today those areas barely have any soil to grow crops.

2. Tree cover loss is not the same as deforestation. *Tree cover* can refer to trees in plantations as well as natural forests, and tree cover loss is the removal of tree canopy due to human or natural causes, including fire.
3. Tropical forests cover only 7 percent of Earth's land area.
4. Project Drawdown estimates that if 221–322 million hectares were converted from conventional to conservation or regenerative farming by 2050 from the currently estimated 11.84 million hectares, CO_2 emissions could be reduced by 14.5–22.3 gigatons, from both sequestration and reduced emissions.
5. The 1.8 billion hectares of remaining world forests includes smaller fragments that no longer provide a safe environment for native flora and fauna.
6. In 2015, for example, both Brazil and Indonesia subsidized four key deforestation-driving commodities 100 times more than the amount they received internationally to protect their forests though the REDD+ funding scheme (McFarland et al. 2015).
7. Ground-based monitoring allows measurement of data such as tree height, diameter at base height, and stem density, which cannot be captured by satellite imaging. Ground-based monitoring is particularly important to REDD+ monitoring, reporting, and verification of tree carbon stocks.
8. REDD+ refers to conservation of forest carbon stocks, sustainable management of forests, and enhancement of forest carbon stocks.
9. Deforestation rates did not decrease immediately, however. Between 1970 and 1980, in fact, another 29 percent of forest cover was lost, mainly because of the World Bank and the International Monetary Fund's insistence on increased agricultural export production for debt-servicing purposes.

CHAPTER 9

Conserving the Oceans

Nicoletta Batini and Rodolfo Werner

> "How inappropriate to call this planet Earth when it is clearly Ocean." —*Arthur C. Clarke*

Water is essential for life, and Earth is the only planet that is known to have large, stable bodies of liquid water on its surface.[1] Earth's water is contained predominantly in five great oceans and 113 seas that together cover approximately 72 percent of the planet's surface.[2]

Oceans generate most of the oxygen we breathe and drive the water cycle that dominates weather on land and in the atmosphere, regulating Earth's climate. They also absorb about 30 percent of carbon dioxide produced by humans, buffering the impact of global warming. Crucially, oceans clean the water we drink and host three quarters of all life on Earth.[3] Such variety of marine life is vital not only for the planet's biological diversity but also for human nutrition. Approximately 3 billion people rely on wild-caught and farmed seafood as their primary source of protein, and oceans also offer a multitude of medicines.[4]

Beyond keeping our planet habitable, oceans contribute to the world economy and socioeconomic development, which is why to "conserve and sustainably use the oceans, seas and marine resources for sustainable development" is one of the seventeen UN Sustainable Development Goals (SDG14: "Life Below Water"). At a global level, the market value of marine and coastal resources and industries is about 5 percent of global GDP (UN 2015). Marine fisheries directly or indirectly employ more than 200 million people, and more than 3 billion people depend on marine and coastal biodiversity for their livelihoods. Throughout history, oceans have served as vital conduits for trade and transportation. So even now, long after the continents have been mapped and their interiors made accessible by road, river, and air, most of the world's people live no more than 200 miles from the sea.

Oceans Are Dying

We are using the sea at a great rate, polluting it, and developing its coastal borders. As a result, today the oceans of the world are under serious threat. Three major sets of threats can be identified:

- *Ocean acidification and climate change.* Ocean acidification, which scientists call the evil twin of global warming, is caused when CO_2 emitted by human activity dissolves into seawater. Since the end of the preindustrial era, oceans have absorbed about 29 percent of global CO_2 emissions. Carbon pollution changes the ocean's chemistry, making it more acidic and less able to capture CO_2 and act as an immense carbon sink for human emissions.[5] Acidification, global warming, and other ongoing environmental phenomena such as deoxygenation, melting ice, and coastal erosion cause great damage to marine ecosystems and pose real threats to the survival of many marine species. Ocean acidification affects migratory routes and distribution, causing imbalances in marine food chains. It also destroys most forms of life at the bottom of the food chain because it is particularly harmful to species that build their skeletons and shells from calcium carbonate, such as clams, mussels, crabs, phytoplankton, and corals. For example, half of the world's corals have disappeared in the last thirty years, and they may disappear entirely by midcentury if global average temperatures rise 2°C or more above preindustrial levels (IPCC 2019). This is particularly important because healthy coral reefs work as "nurseries" and shelter areas for a variety of species that provide food for humans, especially many fishing communities.

Because of its devastating effects on marine life, ocean acidification affects people's livelihoods and the well-being of communities and local economies. In the United States of America alone, if CO_2 emissions continue unabated, by the end of the century annual supplies of clams could decrease by 35 percent, oysters by 50 percent, and scallops 55 percent, leading to cumulative consumer losses of about US$230 million. Under this same scenario, ocean acidification paired with warming could cost US$140 billion in recreational benefits lost from activities in coral reefs. The U.S. coral reef recreation industry could decline in value by more than 90 percent by 2100. Warming waters are already having devastating effects on fisheries in the U.S. Northwest and causing multi–million-dollar losses to local economies. Some of the highest-revenue fisheries in the world, such as shellfish fisheries in Oregon and Washington State, are already witnessing a severe drop in crab populations, probably because of ocean acidification. In response, the Pacific Coast Federation of Fishermen's Associations filed a lawsuit against thirty fossil fuel companies in 2018. Warming ocean temperatures have also caused a rapid increase of toxic algal blooms in the East Pacific, which produce neurotoxins that endanger human health. As a result, many U.S. West Coast fisheries have been forced to shut down in recent years.

- *Overexploitation and destruction of marine habitats.* Fishing is one of the most significant drivers of ocean wildlife population decline and marine habitat destruction. Catching fish is not inherently bad for the ocean, except when there is overfishing. However, since the end of World War II, many navy vessels and technologies have been repurposed to make commercial fishing more productive, resulting in overfishing. High-tech systems such as sonar, originally developed for military purposes, and vessels such as supertrawlers with mechanized nets have allowed humans to exploit deeper waters at farther-flung locations, capturing fish faster than the fish can reproduce. The number of overfished stocks globally has tripled in half a century, and today one third of the world's assessed fisheries are pushed beyond their biological limits, with 90 percent of global fish stocks overexploited or fully exploited. The annual growth rate of fish available for human consumption has now surpassed that of meat from all terrestrial animals combined (FAO 2018). Overfishing is also closely tied to bycatch, the unwanted sea life that is caught along with the target species. Bycatch is a serious marine threat and causes the needless loss of billions of fish and hundreds of thousands of sea turtles, seabirds, and marine mammals, including cetaceans. Overfishing of species with long life cycles and at the top of food chains cause irreversible damage to the harmony of marine life. For example, 70–100 million sharks are killed per year for luxury cooking and alternative medicine, especially in China. Both overfishing and bycatch reflect a serious lack of global and national fishery management and nonenforcement of existing rules.[6] In addition to fishing, marine engineering and oil drilling cause permanent damage to oceans' health. All changes in the marine environment caused by development and construction, deep hole drilling, and other human-related interventions acutely change the marine habitat, generating disturbances and producing pollutants. All these factors contribute to the destruction of natural ecosystems and compromise the survival of marine species.

- *Ocean pollution.* About 8 million tons of garbage are dumped into the ocean every day. Eighty percent of marine pollution comes from land, mostly litter left on beaches or thrown into inland waterways, such as rivers and streams, that ends up in the ocean. Coastal waters are deteriorating because of pollution and eutrophication. If no action is taken, eutrophication—the process by which waters get overfilled with nutrients, leading to plant overgrowth and, eventually, a depletion of dissolved oxygen and a destruction of aquatic life—could increase in a fifth of all large marine ecosystems by midcentury. The pollution situation is more serious when it comes to nonbiodegradable waste such as plastics, which range from large pieces of fishing gear that entrap marine animals to microplastics and nanoplastics resulting from the breakdown or photodegradation of plastic waste in surface waters. The ocean is increasingly becoming a "plastic soup" that is killing hundreds of marine animals each day as they get trapped in plastic debris or confuse it for food.

Discarded fishing gear and other large plastic objects, a fifth of which are believed to be debris from the 2011 Japanese tsunami, together with microplastics, have created a huge, swirling pile of trash in the Pacific Ocean. That pile is now three times the size of France. Known as the Great Pacific Garbage Patch, it is about 1.6 million square kilometers in size, up to sixteen times bigger than previous estimates (Lebreton et al. 2018). In addition to garbage from land, agricultural fertilizers and pesticides end up in the ocean, creating dead zones and causing irreversible and fatal changes to the species, such as reproductive damage. In addition to agriculture, coastal aquaculture increases pollutants in marine waters. Like industrial animal farming (see chapters 2 and 5), the production of fish and bivalves involves antibiotics and other toxic chemical use, a phenomenon clearly evident in Asian waters from the intensive production of Vietnamese clams. Moreover, mercury and fat-soluble pollutants dissolved in the water severely affect fish and shellfish because mercury concentrates in their bodies, often in the form of a highly toxic compound. This is why predatory fish such as swordfish and sharks, or predatory birds such as osprey and eagles, have higher concentrations of mercury in their bodies than accounted for by direct exposure alone. Species can reach concentrations of mercury in their bodies up to ten times higher than the species they consume. This process is called biomagnification. For example, herrings contain mercury levels at about 0.1 parts per million, whereas predators such as sharks contain mercury levels greater than 1 part per million. Bioaccumulation in seafood carries over into human populations, where it can result in mercury poisoning. The presence of mercury in fish can raise health concerns, particularly for women who are or may become pregnant, nursing mothers, and young children.

Although these threats are well documented, studying the ocean is an expensive and exclusive undertaking, and much of it, especially the remote and deeper zones, remains underinvestigated. Only about 5 percent of the ocean has been thoroughly studied, and there are still vast unknowns and uncertainties about emerging challenges related to ocean acidification, melting polar ice, and the impact of microplastics.

We Can Save the Oceans by Protecting 30 Percent of Them

According to the UN's World Database on Protected Areas, which records information submitted by countries on marine protected areas (MPAs), only about 7 percent of the ocean, an area the size of North America, is protected by implemented and actively managed MPAs. Approximately half of that is highly protected in true no-take, no-mining marine reserves (Marine Conservation Institute 2019).

To spare oceans from further destruction and ensure that ecosystems stay healthy enough to adapt to climate change, 30 percent of all oceans must become protected soon (International Union for Conservation of Nature [IUCN] 2016). This recommendation also pertains to the high seas, areas beyond national jurisdictions. According to the IUCN, this requires expanding existing MPAs and establishing new MPAs. In IUCN terms, these MPAs are clearly defined geographic spaces that are recognized, dedicated, and managed through legal or other effective means to achieve the long-term conservation of nature. Similar calls have been made in the Global Deal for Nature Report

(Dinerstein et al. 2019) and the 30x30: A Blueprint for Ocean Protection (O'Leary et al. 2019).

Aside from protecting biodiversity, creating a global network of marine protected areas should be of global interest. Underwater ecosystems play an important role in mitigating the impacts of climate change, with krill, fish, cetaceans, and squid in the sea helping to regulate carbon in the atmosphere. These animals feed on the phytoplankton that draws carbon out of the atmosphere, and then they process it into solid feces that sink to the bottom of the sea, where the carbon remains. Thus, marine reserves can also act as climate reserves. Protecting 30 percent of the ocean will increase the climate resiliency of local communities.

Clearly, protected areas only shelter marine species from certain regulated human activities but do not address acidification, plastic pollution, agricultural waste, or overfishing. Yet by creating these protected spaces where fishing and deep seabed mining are forbidden, oceans are given a chance to adapt and recover from other threats posed by human activities such as climate change and marine pollution. Chapter 2 in this book proposes measures to drastically reduce global emissions and chemical discharges from agriculture into the sea.

Economic Benefits of Conserving the Oceans

Healthy oceans and marine ecosystem services underpin the ocean economy and provide critical support functions for human health and well-being. Protecting coastal and marine habitats could help, for example, in climate mitigation and food provisioning. More than two thirds of the ocean's annual economic value depends on healthy ocean assets (World Economic Forum 2020). By cultivating sustainable fisheries and tourism, island and coastal communities can secure essential revenues while restoring ocean health and protecting healthy ecosystems. Restoring fisheries beyond protected areas can also lead to greater ecosystem resilience. Thus, halting the rapid decline in marine habitat health can help stop draining one of the world's natural economic engines. Every dollar invested in marine protected areas is expected to return at least three dollars' worth of benefits, including livelihoods, fisheries, and coastal protection.

Crucially, healthy oceans are a vital source of employment globally. They already result in hundreds of millions of blue economy jobs, 50 percent of which are occupied by women.

Environmental Benefits of Conserving the Oceans

Defending at least 30 percent of the ocean from overfishing, habitat destruction, and exploitation by establishing MPAs is essential for meeting a broad range of environmental goals. Marine reserves—the strongest form of MPA, in which all extractions are prohibited—can restore ocean health by protecting biodiversity, enhancing ecosystem resilience, supporting fishery productivity, and safeguarding unique cultural traditions historically tied to the seas. Protected areas yield many benefits, including some that reach far beyond the MPA boundaries. For example, MPAs can connect important feeding, mating, and calving grounds for vulnerable species (Lester et al. 2009; Sala and Giakoumi 2018). They can build ocean resilience to climate-related disturbances such as ocean acidification, increased storm intensity, shifts in species distribution, decreased productivity, and reduced oxygen availability.[5]

Policies to Conserve the Oceans

No Man's Sea

The oceans had long been subject to the "freedom of the seas" doctrine—a principle put forth in the seventeenth century that limited national jurisdiction over the oceans to a narrow sea belt surrounding a nation's coastline. The rest of the seas were declared free for all and belonged to no one. This situation lasted into the twentieth century, but by midcentury there was an impetus to extend national claims over offshore resources. There was a growing concern over the toll on coastal fish stocks taken by long-distance fishing fleets, as well as pollution and wastes from vessels carrying noxious cargoes across the globe. The navies of maritime power nations were competing for a worldwide presence in surface waters and even under the sea.

The 1982 United Nations Convention on the Law of the Sea

To this end, in 1982 the United Nations adopted the UN Convention on the Law of the Sea (UNCLOS), which extended international law to the vast, shared water resources of our planet. The UNCLOS resolved several important issues related to ocean usage and sovereignty, as it established freedom-of-navigation rights, set territorial sea boundaries 12 miles offshore, set exclusive economic zones up to 200 miles offshore, set rules for extending continental shelf rights up to 350 miles offshore, created the International Seabed Authority, and created other conflict resolution mechanisms (e.g., the UN Commission on the Limits of the Continental Shelf). The United Nations Environment Programme (UNEP), particularly through its Regional Seas Programme, acts to protect oceans and seas and promote the sustainable use of marine resources. The Regional Seas Conventions and Action Plans are the world's only legal framework for protecting the oceans and seas at the regional level. UNEP also created the Global Programme of Action for the Protection of the Marine Environment from Land-based Activities. It is the only global intergovernmental mechanism directly addressing the link between terrestrial, freshwater, coastal, and marine ecosystems.[7]

The 2020 Aichi Biodiversity Target

Although the UNCLOS provided solutions to some key questions on ocean sovereignty and usage, it failed to address the rapid degradation of marine habitats and resources, especially in the high seas. But for decades, scientists had been calling for marine protected areas to cover at least 20 percent of the ocean. The world met them halfway in with the Aichi Biodiversity Targets, a set of twenty global targets under the Strategic Plan for Biodiversity 2011–2020. Target 11 stipulated achieving 10 percent protection of coastal and marine areas by 2012, especially areas of particular importance for biodiversity and ecosystem services, under the UN Convention on Biological Diversity (CBD).[8] The deadline was later extended to 2020 after it was clear the world would miss its original goal. In 2018, members of the IUCN called for protecting at least 30 percent of the ocean by 2030 through a network of MPAs and other effective conservation measures. This recommendation also pertained to the high seas—areas beyond the jurisdiction of any country—and was nonbinding, but it garnered widespread support from the governments and global organizations at the 2016 IUCN World Conservation Congress in Honolulu. That same year, the FAO Port State Measures Agreement entered into force as a binding international treaty aimed at denying illegal fishers access to ports and markets. And advances in science and technology allow real-time tracking and monitoring of vessels. However, even as eighty-seven parties to the CBD have achieved their terrestrial protection goals as of 2017, less than 4 percent of oceans currently fall within an MPA, even with the U.S.

expansion in 2017 of the Papahānaumokuākea Marine National Monument in the northern Hawaiian Islands.

At the fifteenth meeting of the Conference of the Parties to the CBD in 2021, parties are expected to adopt a new ten-year global biodiversity framework with goals and targets for ocean protection.

The Role of Economic Policy and Structural Reforms

Although human impacts on our oceans are severe, solutions exist. Policymakers have a number of legal, regulatory, and economic means at their disposal to achieve both the SDG14, which is to conserve and sustainably use our ocean and marine resources, and the relevant 2011–2020 Aichi Biodiversity Targets. Relevant policy instruments include regulatory, economic, management, and voluntary approaches. However, the pace of policy action is not keeping up with the increasing pressures on the ocean. Key structural reforms include the following:

- *Expansion of MPA targets to arrive at 30 percent of all seas.* There is compelling evidence that ecosystems can recover if appropriate action is taken.[9] At home, countries should adopt ambitious ecosystem management. They should set aside zones, equivalent to 30 percent of their national waters, that are completely off-limits to any human activity. Other zones should be opened to certain uses, such as recreation, research, and well-managed fishing activities. For marine areas in the high seas, it would be important to support and adhere to the UN proposal for a High Seas Conservation Treaty that should have been formalized in 2020 but is currently on hold during the COVID-19 pandemic crisis. The new treaty aims to place 30 percent of the high seas off limits to unregulated exploitation, according to the maps prepared by the 30x30 Blueprint for Ocean Conservation.
- *Establishment of catch shares fishery management.* Under this scheme, commercial fishers have a stake in maintaining healthy fish populations because they are granted a percentage of the total allowable catch. As more fish are available, the fishers get a larger share.

Additional structural reforms could be implemented globally based on policy recommendations made by Smith et al. (2019) to expand the U.S.

Green New Deal to the blue economy. These recommendations are meant to accelerate the recovery process of protected areas, increase their economic value, and enhance carbon sequestration. They include the following:

- *Ocean habitat restoration.* Governments should support state and national restoration programs, including replanting of seagrasses, wetlands, mangroves, shellfish, and seaweeds. Funding for these programs could come from a "blue carbon fund." Restoration programs could also involve job creation for unemployed or underemployed locals in the programs' construction and maintenance, including restoration, replanting, conservation of coastal ecosystems, and development of climate adaptation infrastructure.
- *Blue carbon fund.* Establish a domestic blue carbon fund for ocean-based emission reductions, including seaweed, seagrass, and other ocean and estuary restoration programs. The fund would earmark either new or existing funds under national budgets dedicated to climate change mitigation and adaptation processes. Innovative financing based on valuations of natural marine capital (both fauna and flora), as discussed in Chami et al. (2020), could be used to finance the blue carbon fund. More generally, natural capital valuations can provide market value benchmarks that allow the creation of fauna-and-flora bonds for investors interested in conservation, biodiversity offset markets, and insurance markets for accidental kill (e.g., vessel strikes of cetaceans). Such valuations are also key for the pricing of debt-for-nature swaps, which are becoming fashionable again as well as more promising amid the post-COVID climate/biodiversity and debt crisis.
- *Blue carbon zones.* New zones dedicated to ocean carbon sequestration should be established in national waters. These zones would be included in the 30 percent share of national waters protected by new MPAs.
- *Community-based fisheries.* Provide loans, tax breaks, and other subsidies to rebuild depleted fishing stocks (where appropriate), improve domestic seafood processing infrastructure and working waterfronts, and expand community-based fishery programs and access.
- *Restorative ocean farming.* Support climate-smart aquaculture, specifically restorative ocean farming, by cultivating seaweeds and shellfish. This can simultaneously sequester millions of tons of carbon, create

millions of new jobs, and reduce food insecurity (see chapter 4). When used in nonfood products such as fertilizers, animal feeds, and bioplastics, seaweeds and shellfish can mitigate the climate impact of numerous industries. For example, it can reduce cattle methane output by up to 58 percent (Mernit 2018).

- *Reducing sea pollution at sea.* Although sea pollution and plastic garbage often originate from human activities on land, activities at sea are polluting too. Governments can help mitigate ocean acidification by reducing the global shipping industry's CO_2 emissions. For example, in 2018 the UN's International Maritime Organization approved the world's first broad agreement to cut greenhouse gas emissions from worldwide ocean shipping. The agreement called on shipping companies to reduce emissions by the year 2050 to 50 percent of their 2008 level, with emission growth peaking as soon as possible. Because ships are often registered independently from their owners' nationality or the ports they visit, this can be done only by a global agreement. Currently, ships run almost entirely on fossil fuels. Generally, the dirtiest grades of oil and emissions from shipping have been projected to rise 250 percent by 2050 without controls. Meeting the new goals would require that ships significantly increase fuel efficiency and make a transition to low- and zero-carbon fuels such as biofuels or perhaps hydrogen, while new propulsion technologies are adopted, some of which are still untested.
- *Mainstreaming conservation.* It is crucial that governments prioritize and start mainstreaming marine conservation and the sustainable use of marine resources across all sectors of the ocean economy. Marine ecosystem considerations must be embedded into key policies and plans, including national development strategies, marine spatial planning, and ecosystem-based fishery management plans. Scaling up policy instruments for ocean conservation and sustainable use is crucial in order to achieve SDG14 and related goals. In addition, because there have been few rigorous impact evaluation studies on marine conservation and sustainable use policies, further effort is needed to evaluate the effectiveness of existing policies and identify how they can be improved.
- *Strategic planning.* It is imperative to develop both a strategy for scaling up impact evaluation studies and policies relevant to ocean conservation and the sustainable use of marine resources. Plans should

include an examination of how to ensure a good balance between different types of national and international policy instruments and prioritizing larger programs and initiatives where ocean conservation is a priority.

Discussions on ocean sustainability tend to focus on legal and regulatory tools such as ecosystem management policies on fishing activities or regulations on fishing gear and total allowable catches. But one of the most important and overlooked tools that policymakers should consider is the implementation of fiscal policies. Fiscal policies are a way governments can use fiscal instruments to influence the behavior of natural resource users and promote specific political, economic, social, and environmental outcomes. In the fishery sector, fiscal instruments are often used to regulate activities, generate revenue, provide social support to vulnerable groups, and promote environmentally friendly technologies. Fiscal instruments can be designed to provide incentives for achieving SDG14 and the goal of leaving no one behind. Fiscal instruments for sustainable fishery management include taxes, subsidies, and conditional transfers:

- *Tax reform.* Taxation can regulate behavior by imposing additional operating costs. In the fishery sector, taxes are used to regulate fishing input (e.g., through the introduction of licensing fees) and output (e.g., through taxes on total catch landed). Input and output taxes are often combined with regulatory controls on fishing vessel numbers, size, and gear. Although taxation can help promote sustainable fishery management, in practice results are mixed. On one hand, taxation can provide valuable revenue to be reinvested in the fishery sector, improving marine resource management. On the other hand, tax policies often prioritize short-term budgetary needs and lead to unintended consequences. There are many examples of a tax regime leading to the underdeclaring of catches and increased sales in unregulated markets. To counter this, governments should repurpose taxation to prioritize sustainability efforts in tandem with other regulatory regimes. Tax levels should be set to reflect the social value of the marine stock, the marginal productivity of each fleet, and the fishing activity's impact on the health of fishing stocks.
- *Subsidy reform.* Subsidies for fishing are promoting the swift depletion of several fish stocks and species. They are also blocking efforts

to save and regenerate global fisheries and related jobs. As a result, ocean fisheries generate US$50 billion less per year than what they could otherwise (UN 2015). Subsidies may include direct payments, the provision of goods or services, price support, or the waiving of revenue otherwise due. Global fishing subsidies are estimated at US$35 billion annually. They are classified into three types: capacity-enhancing subsidies, beneficial subsidies, and ambiguous subsidies. Capacity-enhancing subsidies make fishing activities artificially profitable by reducing costs or increasing revenues and thereby incentivize fishing beyond economically or environmentally sustainable levels. They include support for fuel, boat construction and repair, vessel modernization, fishing gear, and port construction. About US$20 billion—or 57 percent—of global fishery subsidies are capacity-enhancing (Steinbach et al. 2017). Beneficial subsidies support fishery management, research, and development. They help increase fish stocks, improve fishery habitats, sustain monitoring of stock levels, and facilitate the establishment and management of MPAs. They also improve planning for resource extraction that balances social, economic, and environmental outcomes. Beneficial subsidies are estimated at US$11 billion annually. Finally, ambiguous subsidies in the fishery sector can lead to either resource management or resource exploitation. They include fisher assistance programs, community development programs, and vessel buyback schemes. These subsidies often aim to achieve social and economic outcomes for vulnerable groups, even at the expense of increasing fishery production. Ambiguous subsidies amount to US$4 billion each year.

- *Conditional transfers.* These transfers provide benefits to recipients, provided that they comply with specific requirements. They are often used to alter behavior for a specific objective. In development policy, conditional cash transfers have been widely used to reduce poverty and improve social outcomes such as school enrolment or to encourage local participation in restoring degraded ecosystems. In environmental policy, another form of conditional transfer known as payment for ecosystem services incentivizes environmentally focused management of activities so that ecosystems continue to deliver services such as flood protection. Another form of transfers, ecological fiscal transfers, also reward local jurisdictions for investing in ecosystem services. In the fishery sector, for example, ecological fiscal trans-

> fers could be used to compensate fishers whose livelihoods are affected by the imposition of no-take zones or MPAs.

Fiscal policy in the fishery sector should be enshrined in clearly designed regulations with defined access and user rights. Also, better stakeholder engagement can ensure that the framework is transparent and decision makers are held accountable. Capacity building and institutional strengthening can support these efforts in countries that struggle to meet requirements. Incentive alignment helps fiscal policy play a proactive role in achieving SDG14 and the "leave no one behind" agenda. Incentive structures must be brought into line to achieve a balance between economic, social, and environmental outcomes.

Globally, this balance has not been met. On the contrary, the dominant logic behind fiscal policy on fisheries has been to use capacity-enhancing fiscal incentives to promote economic or social outcomes. These incentives have ended up greatly damaging the environment (including depleting fish stocks) and distorting the way benefits for the fishing industry have been distributed, both between and within countries. Consequently, in many cases benefits have gone primarily to owners of industrialized fleets and away from artisanal, poor fishers. Thus, subsidies need to be reformed to ensure a fair distribution of benefits.

The ideal balance will be country- and context-specific. For instance, in poor countries where most peoples' livelihoods rely on oceans, policymakers may pursue policies that maximize short-term social or economic outcomes by offering fuel subsidies or lowering taxes on landed catch, even if these may lead momentarily to increased fishing activities. Alternatively, they may follow the example of Kiribati by introducing large MPAs like the Phoenix Islands Protected Area, where fines are imposed on illegal fishing activity in order to preserve stocks for the long term.

Country Case: Antarctica

Antarctica and the Southern Ocean are governed by the Antarctic Treaty System (ATS), a complex of arrangements made for the purpose of regulating relations between states in the Antarctic. At its heart is the Antarctic Treaty itself. The original signatories of the treaty were the twelve nations active in the Antarctic during 1957–1958, namely Argentina, Australia, Belgium, Chile, France, Japan, New Zealand, Norway, South Africa, Soviet Union, United Kingdom, and the United States. The treaty was signed in Washington, D.C.

at the end of 1959 and entered into force in mid-1961. The Consultative Parties (currently twenty-nine) include the original parties and other states that accede to the treaty and demonstrate their interest in Antarctica by carrying out substantial scientific activity there.

The treaty's primary aim is to ensure the peaceful use of Antarctica in the interest of all humankind. To this end, the treaty holds all territorial claims in abeyance; promotes scientific research and the exchange of data; forbids military activity in the region, except in support of science; and prohibits nuclear explosions and the disposal of nuclear waste. The treaty applies to the area south of 60° south latitude, including all ice shelves and islands. There is no other political system like the ATS that requires international collaboration in research and conservation.[10]

The treaty is augmented by recommendations adopted at Consultative Meetings, by the Protocol on Environmental Protection to the Antarctic Treaty (Madrid, 1991), and by two separate conventions, the Convention for the Conservation of Antarctic Seals (London, 1972) and the Convention for the Conservation of Antarctic Marine Living Resources (CCAMLR; Canberra, 1980). The adoption of Southern Ocean MPAs at CCAMLR strengthened the ATS by creating areas that will be the responsibility of and managed by all members. The adoption of MPAs reinforces the internationality of the areas involved by moving away from any geopolitical claims and providing political stability to the region.

The Krill Convention

The Southern Ocean is one of the least altered marine ecosystems on Earth. Encompassing 10 percent of the world's ocean, it is home to thousands of unique species including millions of penguins that depend on large swarms of krill, a tiny shrimplike crustacean, and other forage species that form the base of a delicate food web. Scientists believe this ecosystem is changing because of temperatures that are warming faster than anywhere else on Earth. However, the ATS protects primarily the terrestrial part of Antarctica because when the treaty was signed, fishing operations in the region were largely outside the scope of commercial fisheries, except for whale and seal hunting.

In the decades after the ATS ratification, active fishing began: Antarctic rock cod and ice fish became heavily sought after, and their overfishing eventually led to the overexploitation of stocks. Fishing fleets, initially from the Soviet Union, started touring the region in search for Antarctic krill (*Euphausia superba*).[11] Krill is used mainly for meal and oil used to feed farm-raised salmon and for humans as a dietary supplement of omega 3 fatty acids.

In recent years, krill fishing has become a lucrative business, and commercial fishers from several other countries entered the business. This resulted in a sharp increase in catches from about 100,000 to 380,000 tons between 2005 and the last fishing season in 2019. The use of new technologies to catch and process krill is changing the economics of the fishery and represents new management and conservation challenges.

Given krill's key role in the Antarctic marine ecosystem, the increase in krill fishing activities generated concern, resulting in the CCAMLR, also known as the "Krill Convention," in 1982. CCAMLR applies to all Antarctic populations of fish, mollusks, crustaceans, and seabirds that are south of the Antarctic Convergence.[12] The Antarctic Convergence represents the transition zone between the warm and saline waters of the north and the coldest and lowest-salinity waters of the south.

The CCAMLR Commission manages krill fisheries in the Antarctic in a way that minimizes ecosystem impacts, in accordance with CCAMLR conservation principles. CCAMLR has been the first international agreement to incorporate ecosystem and precautionary approaches as basic principles for the management of marine living resources (Gonzalez and Kinkelin 2009). CCAMLR (Article II.2; https://www.ccamlr.org/en/organisation/camlr-convention-text#II) defines conservation to allow for "rational use." The original documents that formed the CCAMLR's foundation described rational use as "wise use," "keeping for future use," or management that would "result in an equitable distribution of benefits between present and future users of the resource" (Holt and Talbot 1978). Within CCAMLR, rational use allows for scientific and commercial harvesting of living resources as long as activities do not cause changes in the exploited and dependent populations or significant adverse effects on their ecosystems that are not reversible in twenty to thirty years (Article II).

Although catch limits now exist for krill in the Antarctic Peninsula/Scotia Sea region, where the fishery currently operates, these limits are set for large areas of the ocean and do not take into account the smaller-scale interactions between the fishery, krill, and krill predators. Nearly all krill catch is concentrated within 100 kilometers of known breeding colonies of land-based krill predators. It is very difficult to quantify the feeding needs of krill-dependent predators in areas of overlap between the fishery and the krill predators. The combined impact of climate change and krill fishing poses an additional challenge for ecosystem-based management of the krill fishery. Antarctic krill is one of the largest biomasses on the planet and is a keystone species for the Antarctic marine ecosystem as well as the main prey for most top predators in Antarctica.

Until 2007, the Antarctic krill fishery was poorly regulated (Gonzalez and Kinkelin 2009). Significant progress was made when CCAMLR subdivided Area 48 and placed fishing catch limits for each subarea (figure 9-1). This was an interim step until CCAMLR was able to agree on a feedback management approach to the fishery. In June 2019, an international and multi-stakeholder workshop was conducted on krill fishery management (Trathan et al. 2019). The workshop's aim was to explore how management strategies for the krill fishery can be harmonized with the development of marine protected areas. One important outcome of the meeting was the agreement on an "overall vision" and that vision's incorporation of krill fishery management. The agreed overall vision is unprecedented and read as follows: "A healthy Antarctic marine ecosystem in the context of climate change and fisheries for Antarctic krill, maintained by application of best practices in science and management informed by common goals, enhanced communication, collaboration, understanding, and commitments by all stakeholders" (CCAMLR 2019).

CCAMLR's MPAs

At the 2002 World Summit on Sustainable Development, world leaders made a commitment to establish a series of MPAs based on science and international legislation by 2012. Recognizing the value of MPAs to sustain the health of the marine ecosystem, CCAMLR became the first international organization to commit to creating a network of MPAs. The establishment of MPAs in the CAMLR Convention Area[13] is one of the most significant issues discussed within the ATS governing bodies in recent years.

The first CCAMLR MPA workshop was convened in 2005 to develop advice on MPA designation and discuss how MPAs could contribute to CCAMLR objectives. A second workshop was organized in 2017 where a broad-scale bioregionalization of the Southern Ocean was conducted. In 2009, CCAMLR designated its first MPA, covering 94,000 square kilometers in the South Atlantic, and further committed to work toward a representative system of MPAs in the Convention Area by 2012 (CCAMLR, XXVIII, para 7.19). A third MPA workshop was convened in 2011, followed by a 2012 technical workshop to analyze gaps in MPA planning.

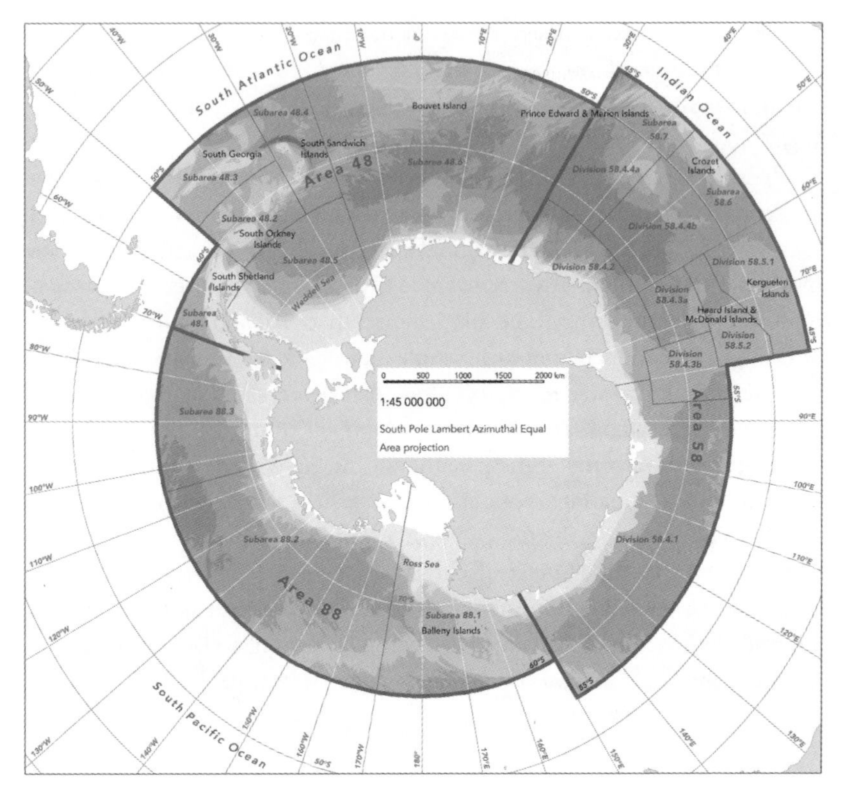

Figure 9-1. Map of the CCAMLR area. *Source:* https://www.ccamlr.org/en/document/organisation/map-ccamlr-convention-area.

At the 2011 meeting, the adoption of Conservation Measure (CM 91-04; https://www.ccamlr.org/en/measure-91-04-2011) was a key step in consolidating the MPA process because it provided an explicit general framework for the establishment of CCAMLR MPAs. This measure ensures that the process is carried out in an orderly manner and follows guidelines that were agreed upon by the members of the commission. That year, CCAMLR also identified nine planning domains within the Convention Area to systematically run the process at the geographic level.

The Ross Sea Region Marine Protected Area

In 2016, CCAMLR established the world's largest MPA in the Ross Sea Region (Domain 8), an area that covers 2.06 million square kilometers (CM

91-05; https://www.ccamlr.org/en/measure-91-05-2016). The Ross Sea is one of the most biologically productive and diverse areas of the Southern Ocean.

By creating the Ross Sea Region MPA (RSRMPA), CCAMLR members[14] agreed to ban commercial fishing in an area of more than 2 million square kilometers. This MPA, which is three times the size of France, set a precedent for protection at sea because it was the first time that a large-scale MPA was created as a result of international cooperation (Dolan et al. 2017). The tension between fishing interests and protection interests of Antarctic water reflects the tension within CCAMLR about its purpose and mandate. Article II of the CCAMLR states that the commission's objective is "the conservation of Antarctic marine living resources," where conservation includes "rational use." Rational use allows commercial fishing but requires a strict precautionary and ecosystem-based approach. Some fishing countries, particularly during the MPA negotiations, have started to reinterpret the agreements of the CCAMLR by referring to rational use as a right to fish and not as a conservation responsibility.

The RSRMPA is designed to encourage international research among all CCAMLR members interested in operating in this region. The results of research and monitoring carried out by the different members must be reported to the Scientific Committee.

Current MPA Proposals in the CCAMLR

As of 2019, there are three additional proposals for the creation of MPAs in the Southern Ocean being considered at CCAMLR. The proposals are at different levels of progress.

Eastern Antarctica

In the case of the waters of East Antarctica, Domain 7 (the Antarctic area south of the Australian continent), the proposal was first presented in 2012. Although it was endorsed by the Scientific Committee and passed on to the commission in 2013, it has not been adopted yet.

This proposal was prepared by Australia, France, and the European Union. The MPA proposal covers part of East Antarctica and was designed taking into account the uncertainty about current availability of scientific information in this particular area. The proposal originally included a mosaic of seven areas and was modified to the point that only three of the seven proposed areas remained. These changes reflect in part what has been called the "erosion by negotiation" of conservation values and of the MPA's original purpose. It is worth mentioning that this proposal currently has the explicit support of all CCAMLR members except China and Russia.

Weddell Sea MPA

The Weddell Sea region, Domains 3 and 4, includes a large, deep bay off the eastern Antarctic Peninsula and is one of the most intact ecosystems in the world. The region is highly productive, with a high concentration of sea ice that provides the ideal habitat for Antarctic krill. At present, however, the Weddell Sea is under threat from climate change.

Although the presence of sea ice has historically hindered fishing in the Weddell Sea region, there is a growing interest in fishing in this area. Because of the threat posed by climate change and the potential increase in fishing pressure in this area, protecting the Weddell Sea through an MPA that includes ecologically intact, diverse, and extraordinary areas is imperative.

In 2016, the European Union presented the proposal for the Weddell Sea MPA to the CCAMLR Scientific Committee. Despite a good-quality proposal, no real progress has been made in recent years, and countries such as China and Russia continue to discuss the validity of the information used to prepare this proposal. This is concerning because this proposal includes the best available science, as recognized by the CCAMLR Scientific Committee in 2016.

During the last CCAMLR meeting (November 2019), the European Union and its member states proposed, together with Norway, that CCAMLR adopt an MPA across the Weddell Sea region in two phases. The addition of Norway as a proponent of this MPA proposal showed the European Union's willingness to openly and transparently work with other CCAMLR countries to advance the commission's important conservation work. Unfortunately, no progress was made at the last CCAMLR meeting, where China and Russia continued to block consensus on the adoption of this MPA.

The Antarctic Peninsula and the Scotia Sea (Domain 1)

The protected waters and deep channels that run through the Antarctic Peninsula and the South Shetland Islands (located in Domain 1) give rise to important marine currents that allow a rich circulation of nutrients. This phenomenon leads to incredible productivity, contributing to the region's high concentration of Antarctic krill (*Euphausia superba*), supporting the reproduction and feeding of a wide variety of species of penguins, flying seabirds, seals, and whales.

This region is one of the areas of Antarctica with the greatest human activity, potentially influencing the marine ecosystem. It is the most popular tourist attraction in Antarctica and experiences the most scientific research programs.

The western part of the Antarctic Peninsula is one of the planet's fastest-warming regions because of climate change. The marine fauna in this region has suffered from intense extractive activities. It has been the scene of the overexploitation of seals, whales, and two species of commercially valuable fish, the Antarctic rock cod and ice fish. Seal and whale populations have largely recovered in this area, but the rock cod and ice fish have not, so fishing for both species is banned.

The highest level of krill fishing was reached in the early 1980s with more than half a million tons. After the dissolution of the Soviet Union in the early 1990s, fishing fell dramatically. The current level of Antarctic krill fishing is the highest in the last two decades, at a total of 380,000 tons in the last fishing season.

Historically, fishing has taken place during the summer, during the penguin breeding season when parents cannot travel great distances from the colonies in search of food. Loss of sea ice results in an overlap between fishing operations (usually coastal) and penguin feeding areas. Not only is fishing conducted year-round, but also fishing vessels can enter new areas near the coast that are now free of ice. Fishing's potential impact has become even more worrying in the last ten years, as fishing activities have concentrated in certain places such as the Bransfield Strait, an important penguin feeding ground during the breeding season.

Starting in 2012, Argentina and Chile have been leading the process to create an MPA in Domain 1. As a result, more than 180 layers of scientific information have been analyzed through an international collaboration of CCAMLR members. It is important to highlight that the process carried out by Argentina and Chile has received the sustained support of all CCAMLR members.

The proposal was officially presented to the CCAMLR Scientific Committee at the annual meeting in October 2018 and received broad support by a majority of members. MPA proponents engaged in a collaborative, transparent, and science-based process that exemplified best practices for actionable science and co-production.

The proposal was revised in 2019 to incorporate feedback from CCAMLR members. Also, Argentina and Chile established a multinational Expert Group to engage all interested members in the discussion and to develop a research and monitoring plan. Nevertheless, the MPA proposal was not adopted, largely because of political barriers, as it was again blocked by China and Russia. Clearly, scientific best practices are not sufficient to drive consensus on CCAMLR MPAs. The adoption of any MPA relies on political will to fulfill the promise made in 2009 to create a representative network of MPAs in the Southern Ocean.

Benefits of Antarctic MPAs to Conservation and to Political Stability

In recent years, a vast number of publications have stressed the importance and benefits of MPAs not only to conserve marine ecosystems but also to safeguard fishing resources. MPAs that are large, isolated, well enforced, long lasting, and prohibiting of any fish or resource extraction are successful and beneficial. These MPAs create a spillover effect, where adult fish from the MPA area spill over into adjacent fishing grounds and improve marine health in waters outside the protected regions. To achieve effective conservation results and help rebuild depleted fish stocks, at least 30 percent of the global ocean should be set aside in MPAs.

MPAs in Antarctica can contribute to marine ecosystem resilience in the face of climate change by eliminating additional pressures such as fishing activity. Some of the most pronounced effects of climate change on Earth, such as warming and acidifying seas and changes in sea ice concentration and duration, are found in Antarctica. In addition to offering resilience in the light of a warming Antarctica, MPAs also function as a natural laboratory to study how marine ecosystems react to ocean warming and acidification.

MPAs in Antarctica contribute also to carbon sinks. Phytoplankton absorbs CO_2 through photosynthesis from the atmosphere near the surface of the water and stores it as carbon. Antarctic krill feed on this microscopic phytoplankton (algae) near the ocean surface and move to much deeper waters, injecting carbon dioxide into the deep water as they excrete waste. Around 23 million tons of carbon are locked in this way every year, equivalent to the carbon from 35 million cars. Thus, the protection of some areas would allow Antarctic krill to continue providing this important ecological service.

The establishment of CCAMLR MPAs will be another important step to allow the commission to implement Principle 2 of the CCAMLR. The coexistence of closed areas and fishing grounds has been contemplated and included in all MPA proposals. The conservation of Antarctic marine living resources (the prime objective of CCAMLR) allows the rational use of those resources, and thus fishing can continue in CCAMLR waters, as long as the area's conservation needs are met.

The MPAs being proposed (or adopted, as in the case of the RSRMPA) are very balanced. They provide for both conservation objectives and also current and future fishing activities. For example, because concentrated krill fishing along the Antarctic Peninsula is concerning, the current proposal will displace only some of the fishing effort in that area. Consequently, current important fishing areas in the Antarctic Peninsula will not be affected by the MPA.

Although it varies between areas, the existing scientific information is sufficient to make informed decisions when proposing MPA establishment in the Southern Ocean. The preparation of individual MPA proposals provides a great opportunity to synthesize existing baseline information, identifying gaps or needs to include in the research and monitoring plans once the MPA is established.

Especially in this era of environmental change, MPAs in the Southern Ocean provide reference areas to study the effects of climate change. Of course, the time framework for ecological processes includes at least several decades, especially considering natural environmental changes and the impact of climate change. Therefore, MPA proposals should be permanent and not time limited.

In the context of CCAMLR, MPAs were defined when members agreed unanimously to adopt CM 91-04, which provides a framework for the establishment of CCAMLR MPAs. The framework and elements included in CM 91-04 represent the clear definition of a CCAMLR MPA. CM 91-04 also specifies the general information needed to prepare any further conservation measures that would establish individual MPAs in the Convention Area.

CM 91-04 mentions the need to present an MPA's specific objectives, provide its spatial boundaries, and indicate what activities will be restricted, prohibited, or managed in the MPA. Also, the CM 91-04 requests that the elements of an MPA's research and monitoring plan be formulated, indicating that all members may undertake research and monitoring activities in accordance with this plan.

Collaboration between members on research activities should be a pillar of MPA establishment and monitoring. Thus, MPAs should be used purposefully to enhance science and governance, as well as marine conservation in the Southern Ocean.

Once the Scientific Committee agrees on the proposal, the commission's adoption of the proposal becomes a purely political matter. Adoption of the RSRMPA was a good practical indication of CCAMLR's legal capacity to establish MPAs.

Despite the geopolitical concerns expressed by some members in the past, establishment of MPAs in the Southern Ocean will strengthen the international nature of those areas. Areas will become CCAMLR MPAs, and their governance, management, and monitoring will fall under the responsibility and scrutiny of all commission members. All this will help to strengthen the governance of the CCAMLR waters, providing an extra layer in the region's political stability.

CCAMLR is a leader in international ocean management and must carry forward its commitment to achieve a meaningful system of MPAs in the Southern Ocean. But CCAMLR needs to maintain this momentum to complete its work within a reasonable time frame. This includes adopting the well-developed MPA proposals currently under discussion, completing work on other proposals, and filling the gaps that exist in various domains.

CCAMLR is the only governing body in the world that has successfully created MPAs in international waters that have been agreed upon unanimously by 24 countries and the European Union. The international ocean community looks to CCAMLR as a model for protecting other areas in the high seas, and this incredible cooperation between world powers, even in times of war, has a broader impact that cannot be overstated.

Conclusions

All life on Earth depends directly on the health of the oceans, and seafood is the number one source of animal protein in the world. However, oceans are under enormous threat. Overfishing, deep-sea mining, and pollution and acidification from climate change are disrupting marine life and oceans' ability to mitigate climate change by absorbing carbon dioxide. Seas beyond national jurisdiction languish in a totally unprotected, lawless state, exposing our greatest natural common to unchecked exploitation. By unleashing the potential of our waters, we can curb climate change, secure one of Earth's primary food sources, and at the same time create new jobs.

Saving the oceans before exploitation of fish stocks hits the point of no return requires rapidly establishing conservation targets for at least a third of the ocean. Economic policies such as taxes and appropriate subsidies can create the right incentives for fishers and other industries such as shipping and tourism. Blue carbon funds can reward ocean activities that foster carbon sequestration and conservation. Promoting sustainable community fisheries and restorative seaweeds and seafood farming can contribute to conservation while providing large economic benefits. Strategic planning and mainstreaming ocean conservation in policy can go a long way in achieving these goals.

References

Chami, R., C. Fullenkamp, F. Berzaghi, S. Español-Jiménez, M. Marcondes, and J. Palazzo. 2020. "On valuing nature-based solutions to climate change: a framework with application to elephants and whales." Economic Research Initiatives at Duke (ERID) working paper no. 297. Durham, NC: Duke University.

Committee for the Conservation of Antarctic Marine Living Resources (CCAMLR). 2019. "Report of the Thirty-Eighth Meeting of the Scientific Committee," 21–25 October 2019. Hobart, Australia: CCAMLR.

Dinerstein, E., C. Vynne, E. Sala, A. R. Joshi, S. Fernando, T. E. Lovejoy, J. Mayorga, D. Olson, G. P. Asner, J. E. M. Baillie, et al. 2019. "A global deal for nature: guiding principles, milestones, and targets." *Science Advances* 5, no. 4: eaaw2869.

Dolan, R., C. Brooks, and R. Werner. 2017. "The world's largest protected area in the Ross Sea, Antarctica." *Antarctic Affairs* IV: 13–18.

Food and Agriculture Organization of the United Nations (FAO). 2018. *The State of the World Fisheries and Aquaculture.* http://www.fao.org/state-of-fisheries-aquaculture

Gonzalez, V. G., and R. Werner Kinkelin. 2009. "Preserving the Antarctic marine food web: achievements and challenges in Antarctic krill fisheries management." In *Ocean Yearbook*, Vol. 23. Leiden, the Netherlands: Martinus Nijhoff.

Holt, S. J., and T. M. Lee. 1978. "New principles for the conservation of wild living resources." *Wildlife Monographs* 59: 3–33.

Intergovernmental Panel on Climate Change (IPCC). 2019. *Special Report: Global Warming of 1.5°C.* Geneva, Switzerland: IPCC.

International Union for Conservation of Nature and World Commission on Protected Areas (IUCN). 2016. *An Introduction to the IUCN Red List of Ecosystems: The Categories and Criteria for Assessing Risks to Ecosystems.* Gland, Switzerland: IUCN.

Lebreton, L., B. Slat, F. Ferrari, et al. 2018. "Evidence that the Great Pacific Garbage Patch is rapidly accumulating plastic." *Scientific Reports* 8, no. 4666.

Lester, S. E., B. S. Halpern, K. Grorud-Colvert, J. Lubchenco, et al. 2009. "Biological effects within no-take marine reserves: a global synthesis." *Marine Ecology Progress Series* 384: 33–46.

Marine Conservation Institute. 2019. *Marine Protection Atlas.* https://marine-conservation.org/mpatlas/

Mernit, J. L. 2018. "How eating seaweed can help cows belch less methane." *Yale Environment* 360. https://e360.yale.edu/features/how-eating-seaweed-can-help-cows-to-belchless-methane

O'Leary, B. C., H. L. Allen, K. L. Yates, R. W. Page, A. W. Tudhope, C. McClean, A. D.

Rogers, J. P. Hawkins, and C. M. Roberts. 2019. *30x30: A Blueprint for Ocean Protection*, University of Oxford, University of York, Greenpeace.

Sala, E., and S. Giakoumi. 2018. "No-take marine reserves are the most effective protected areas in the ocean." *ICES Journal of Marine Science* 75, no. 3: 1166–8.

Smith, B., J. Bowman, and A. E. Johnson. 2019. "Memo: blue jobs and the Green New Deal." https://www.dataforprogress.org/memos/blue-jobs

Steinbach, D., M. Essam, and P. Steele. 2017. "A sustainable future for fisheries: how fiscal policy can be used to achieve SDG 14." IIED briefing paper. London: International Institute of Environment and Development.

Trathan, P. N., G. Watters, N. Bransome, S. Davie, P. E. Skogrand, R. Werner, A. Kavanagh, C. Johnson, and J. Arata. 2019. "SC-CAMLR-38/BG/18: report from the Workshop on Krill-Fishery Management for Subareas 48.1 and 48.2." Meeting documents for the Thirty-eighth Meeting of the Scientific Committee of the Commission for the Conservation of Antarctic Marine Living Resources. https://www.ccamlr.org/en/sc-camlr-38

United Nations. 2015. *Sustainable Development Goals*. https://www.un.org/sustainabledevelopment/oceans/

World Economic Forum (WEF). 2020. "World ocean agenda." https://www.weforum.org/projects/a-new-vision-for-the-ocean

Endnotes

1. Water on other worlds exists in diverse forms on moons, dwarf planets, and even comets. Billions of years ago, Venus may have been our solar system's first ocean world. Venus lacks a strong global magnetic field, which on Earth helps to protect our atmosphere. A runaway greenhouse effect raised temperatures enough to boil off the water, which escaped into space because of the solar wind.
2. Earth's oceans contain about 96.5 percent of all the planet's 326 million trillion gallons of water. Less than 3 percent of all water on Earth is freshwater (usable for drinking), more than two thirds of Earth's freshwater is locked up in ice caps and glaciers, and of that (equal to about 1 percent of all Earth's unlocked freshwater) four fifths is used in agriculture.
3. Oceans contain nearly 200,000 identified species, but actual numbers may lie in the millions.
4. Creatures and substances found in the deep sea are being investigated for treating cancer, cystic fibrosis, and Alzheimer's disease and could even provide a solution to the global crisis of antibiotic resistance.
5. There are significant differences in the way these phenomena affect the oceans across gradients of temperature, latitude, and depth because the rate at which water absorbs CO_2 decreases as water temperature increases.
6. The absence of a definition of the size of the animals or the time of capture, which allows the capture of juveniles or females with eggs, are some of the recurring problems.
7. The United Nations Educational, Scientific and Cultural Organization, through its Intergovernmental Oceanographic Commission, coordinates programs in marine research, observation systems, hazard mitigation, and ocean and coastal area management.The

International Maritime Organization is the key United Nations institution for the development of international maritime law.

8. The CBD is a legally binding international treaty that seeks to ensure conservation of the world's biological diversity and promote sustainable use and equitable sharing of the benefits of that biodiversity.
9. For example, a five-year, US$50-million Global Environment Facility–funded program called the Common Oceans ABJN Program, launched by the FAO and partners, has made important progress in protecting international waters' biodiversity by rendering fishing in these waters less harmful to several marine species, including sea turtles and tuna. See http://www.fao.org/news/story/en/item/1258859/icode/.
10. An Antarctic Treaty Consultative Meeting is held annually to discuss matters of mutual party interest on the region. During each meeting, there is also a meeting of the Committee for Environmental Protection.
11. Soviet krill fishing was economically viable only with huge economic subsidies, and when the Soviet Union split the catch, levels fell drastically until the beginning of 2000, when the fishery was resumed.
12. Currently, two main commercial fisheries operate in the Convention Area, a very lucrative fishery that targets Antarctic (*Dissostichus mawsonii*) and Patagonian toothfish (*Dissostichus eleginoides*) (usually marketed as one species) and another that targets Antarctic krill (*Euphausia superba*).
13. This document refers to the Convention for the Conservation of Antarctic Marine Living Resources as "CAMLR Convention" or "Convention" and to the Commission for the Conservation of Antarctic Marine Living Resources as "CCAMLR" or "Commission."
14. CCAMLR now has twenty-six members (twenty-five countries and the European Union) since The Netherlands joined the CAMLR Commission in November at the 2019 meeting.

CHAPTER 10

Conserving Mammals

Ivon Cuadros-Casanova and Carlo Rondinini

> "In pushing other species to extinction, humanity is busy sawing the limb on which it perches." —*Paul Ehlrich*

There are 5,850 known species of living mammals across the world (IUCN 2020a). Their diversity in size and form, from tiny bats to deep-diving whales, has enabled them to conquer all ecosystems on Earth. Alongside birds, reptiles, insects, and worms, mammals play a key role in food webs, featuring as both top predators and abundant prey. They act as ecosystem engineers, creating suitable habitats for other species, dispersing seeds, and ensuring the smooth working of global matter and energy cycles (Lacher et al. 2019). These functions add to their well-recognized contributions to the food system, such as pest control and pollination, and their direct supply of protein from game.

Regions with greatest mammal biodiversity include mountainous regions and low-latitude areas in the Andes mountain range, Atlantic forests in South America, and regions in Sub-Saharan Africa and Southeast Asia—all areas severely threatened by dramatic habitat loss (Grenyer et al. 2006; Pouzols et al. 2014; figure 10-1). With most mammal species living in forests, increased rates of deforestation due to agricultural expansion, and to a lesser extent logging and wood harvesting, are among the main threats to mammals.

Beyond agriculture, overexploitation, including hunting of wildlife for food, poses an additional key threat to mammals and is contributing to their global extinction (Ripple et al. 2016).[1] The so-called bushmeat crisis, a term

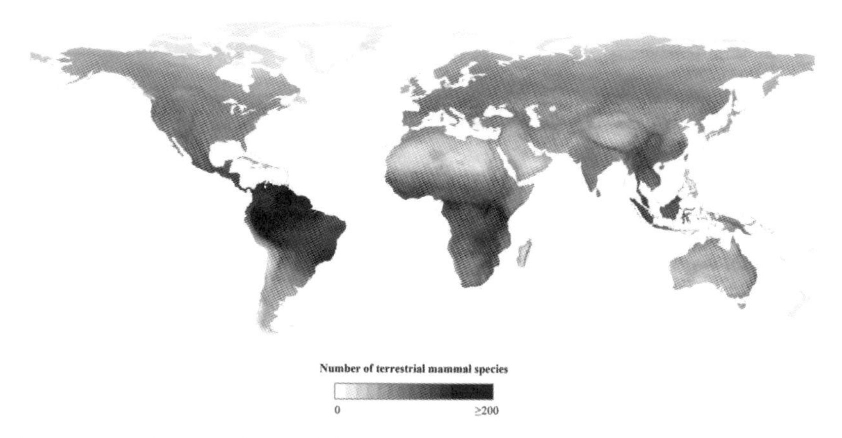

Figure 10-1. Species richness of global terrestrial mammals (~1 kilometer spatial resolution). *Source:* Modified from IUCN and CIESIN (2015).

used to describe the overharvesting of wildlife, has long been identified as an extraordinary threat to food security and to public health through emergent zoonotic diseases (Nasi et al. 2008). A recent global study showed that regions with high environmental degradation and human encroachment in previously biodiverse areas face major emerging zoonose risks (Allen et al. 2017), highlighting the link between ecosystem health, biodiversity conservation, and human health.

Mammals at Risk

To track the evolution of mammal species and help guide efforts to protect their diversity, the International Union for the Conservation of Nature (IUCN) has developed and maintains the Red List, the most widely used system for categorizing the extinction risk of species. According to the IUCN Red List, at least 21 percent of all mammal species are threatened with extinction, with estimates climbing up to 36 percent because of partial data deficiency (figure 10-2), that is, a lack of information sufficient to determine the extinction risk of some species (IUCN 2020a).

About four fifths of the species for which data are deficient live in the tropics, regions home to some of the most diverse world habitats but also characterized by rapid land use transformation and habitat degradation. This implies that the largest knowledge gaps in terms of species extinction risks are concentrated in areas in high need of conservation. Similarly, most newly

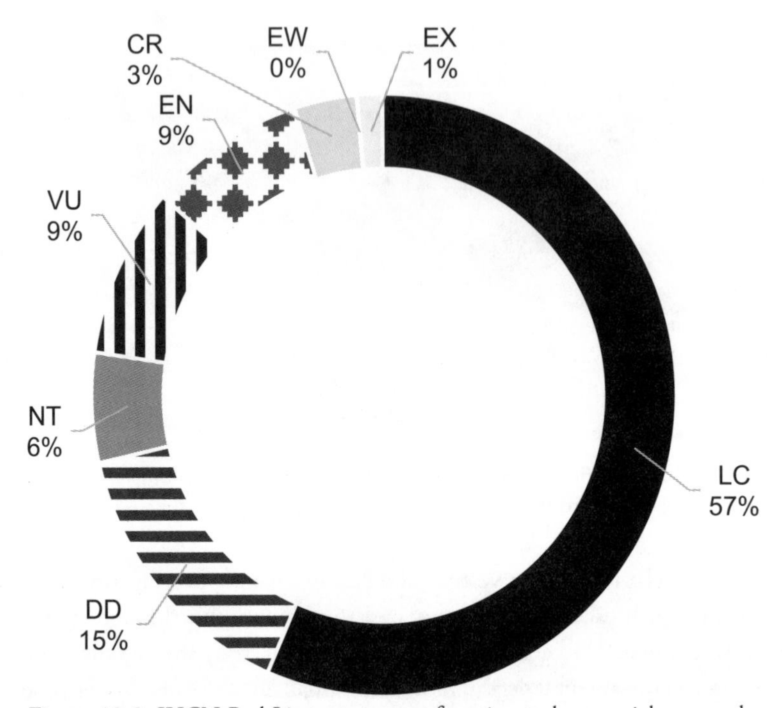

Figure 10-2. IUCN Red List assessment of marine and terrestrial mammals, including 5,850 species assessed. Source IUCN (2020a). *Notes:* Categories: EX, Extinct, EW, Extinct in the Wild, CR, Critically Endangered, EN, Endangered, VU, Vulnerable, NT, Near Threatened, DD, Data Deficient, LC, Least Concern.

described species live in areas of high endemism but also rampant development (Reeder et al. 2007).

Agriculture, the First Cause of Mammal Declines

The high level of globalization of our food supply implies that food is often consumed far from where is produced and where environmental damages take place; indeed, most agriculture expansion and intensification in intact tropical forests reflect production of commodities destined for export. Specifically, by far the leading cause of deforestation is cattle ranching, as intact forests are cleared for pasture. Other causes of deforestation, in order of importance, are crop agriculture of soy and palm trees for the production of palm oil, followed by mining and logging (see chapter 8). Eighty to 99 percent of the biodiversity impact of food crop consumption in industrialized countries occurs abroad (Green et al. 2019).

Expansion of palm oil, a strictly tropical crop, has put the major producing countries on an extinction highway. From 1990 to 2005, 57 percent of palm oil expansion occurred at the expense of primary forests in Malaysia and Indonesia, which are on track to lose 75 percent of their total forest area and up to 42 percent of all their regional species by 2100. At least half of these species are found nowhere else in the world (Brook et al. 2006; Koh and Wilcove 2008). Some of these forests' most majestic and iconic mammal species are already on the verge of extinction, such as the Sumatran rhino (*Dicerorhinus sumatrensis*), recently declared extinct in Malaysia, with only a tiny population surviving in Indonesia (Gokkon 2019), or the three remaining species of orangutan, all listed as critically endangered (Ancrenaz et al. 2016; Nowak et al. 2017; Singleton et al. 2017). Forest loss due to palm oil plantations is also disrupting the ecological and water balance that sustain other productive activities in nearby areas. Similarly, the fast encroachment on large areas of Colombian forests, the first palm oil producer in Latin America to export more than 50 percent of its production, has locally displaced characteristic fauna of the Chocó biogeographic region, one of the most biodiverse regions of the country and the world (Myers et al. 2000). In addition, intensive pesticide use involved in growing palm trees has polluted water sources, making economically unviable many other crops in the region, including palm oil itself, the production of which suffered a steep decline a few years after being introduced (Lizcano 2018).

Overexploitation

Alongside agriculture-driven deforestation, overexploitation for food is one of the most important threats to mammals and many other animals. Nearly all countries and territories of the world (89 percent) have bird species that are threatened by overexploitation (BirdLife 2012), and for some species such as tortoises and turtles in Asia, hunting is a particularly serious threat. Yet hunters usually kill more mammals than birds, and more birds than reptiles. Thus, mammals appear to be more affected by overexploitation, with larger species, especially primates (126 species) and ungulates (65 species), particularly targeted. Notably, all the 301 mammals that are threatened by hunting are found in developing countries, and only 8 of these species are also found in developed countries (Ripple et al. 2016).

Defaunation, or the depletion of wildlife populations (Dirzo et al. 2014), is driven mainly by subsistence hunting and commercial hunting (Redford 1992), both legal and illegal. Subsistence hunting by low-density populations living in tropical forest and rural areas is a vital protein source, generally more important to indigenous people who have exercised this practice for centuries than to new settlers whose income allows them to access the domesticated animal market. Between 5 and 8 million people in South America, mostly indigenous and semirural communities, regularly rely on wild meat or bushmeat as an important component of household food security (Rushton et al. 2005), not necessarily in terms of quantity but as a key element in diet (Van Vliet et al. 2015). In the Amazonian trinational frontier, nutrients obtained through hunting activities and fishing play a key role in diversifying and enriching modern diets in semiurban areas. Bushmeat represents approximately 32 percent of the caloric intake, 72 percent of consumed protein, and 77 percent of iron in the diet of families who still consume it, and they obtain significantly higher amounts of vitamin C, iron, and zinc than families who do not eat bushmeat (Sarti et al. 2015). The number of households consuming bushmeat in the Amazon region could be considered low (14.3 percent) if compared with other tropical regions and reflects a change in food habits, because people living in transition zones between rural and urban areas experience an abrupt decrease in bushmeat consumption, replaced by an increasing intake of frozen chicken and beef (Nardoto et al. 2011).

In rural households of Central Africa, bushmeat represents up to 88 percent of the overall protein intake and nearly 100 percent of animal proteins (Koppert et al. 1996), suggesting that the meat supply from hunting is higher than the nonwild meat supply locally generated or imported (Fa et al. 2003). In a remote area of the eastern rainforest in Madagascar, wildlife consumption was associated with significantly higher concentrations of hemoglobin, an oxygen-carrying protein in red blood cells whose deficiency can lead to anemia. The removal of bushmeat would translate into a 29 percent increase in the number of children suffering from anemia, and three times the number of cases for children in the poorest households. The relation between micronutrient deficiencies such as iron anemia and the likelihood of developing other diseases, with negative health consequences for brain metabolism, neurotransmitter function, motor development, and emotional regulation, demonstrates the significant and far-reaching effects of losing wildlife species in the absence of other meat alternatives (Golden et al. 2011).

Although bushmeat contributes substantially to the diets of indigenous and semiurban communities (Koppert et al. 1996; Fanzo et al. 2013; Cawthorn and Hoffman 2015), human dependence on bushmeat results in unsustainable demand. This phenomenon is further aggravated by resource extraction from primary forests and higher failure rates in rain-fed crop production due to climate instability (Fa et al. 2005). Overexploitation as a byproduct of forest encroachment is exemplified in Maiko National Park, an emblematic protected area embedded in the West African rainforest of the Democratic Republic of Congo, hosting unique biodiversity and wilderness preserved in more than 10,000 square kilometers of intact primary habitats. The park is home to endemic species such as Grauer's gorilla and the okapi, as well as forest elephants, leopards, chimpanzees, and giant pangolins. This natural richness has also attracted a big bushmeat trade that is exacerbated by illegal mining of a mineral called coltan, an essential component of phones, computers, and solar panels (Ridder et al. 2013). Since the early 2000s, demand for bushmeat from Maiko has increased dramatically as thousands of people have settled near the mines, and animals in a radius of 5 to 10 square kilometers around mining camps have become a target. The bushmeat trade enabled by these mines is considered the single biggest threat to wildlife in the park (Redmond 2001; Hayes and Burge 2003; Fritts 2019). For instance, the Grauer's gorilla population has dropped by 77 percent over a twenty-year period, and it is now listed as critically endangered on the IUCN Red List (Plumptre 2016).

Extraction industries propel forest encroachment and exacerbate fauna overexploitation. In Central Africa, for example, industrial logging has become the most extensive land use, with more than 600,000 square kilometers under concession, occupying 30 percent of a forest considered among the most pristine on Earth (Laporte et al. 2007). The illusion of a job opportunity in the logging industries attracts locals along with a large migration of hunters, traders, and their families, facilitating the establishment of villages with a fragile emerging subeconomy in remote areas (Cawthorn and Hoffman 2015). The human influx and increased forest access rapidly generate a huge demand for bushmeat as a response to the difficulty of accessing other meat options. The initial informal demand for bushmeat transforms into an in situ market with potential links to more developed external economies (Poulsen et al. 2009). Bushmeat consequently becomes a valuable commodity, transforming a subsistence activity into a commercial one, where profit is the main objective (Cawthorn and Hoffman 2015). Overexploitation of wildlife amid extraction activities in Central Africa exemplifies a worldwide trend that has put 285 mammal species on the threatened list of extinction due exclusively to human consumption (Ripple et al. 2016).

Consumption rates of bushmeat vary substantially worldwide depending on land productivity for other uses, abundance of wildlife, price and accessibility of meat alternatives, and wealth and preferences of consumers (Coad et al. 2019). A consistent relationship between wealth and wildlife consumption emerged across African countries, indicating that bushmeat is consumed in greater proportions (relative to other meats) depending on location by households with different income levels, namely wealthier households in urban areas and poorer households in rural areas (Brashares et al. 2011). In the Congo Basin, for example, urban consumption is widespread and correlated with income (Mbete et al. 2011), and although individual urban intake appears lower than that for rural people, aggregate consumption is higher in urban areas as a result of a larger population (Nasi et al. 2011). In Asian urban markets, the massive demand for wildlife products reflects status as such products are seen as a luxury good rather than a necessary protein source. In poorer countries, such as Laos, by contrast, game may constitute a significant supplement to urban diets, although diets have turned progressively to protein from farmed animals after the depletion of wildlife (Bennett and Rao 2002). In South America, urban bushmeat consumption was previously considered negligible (Rushton et al. 2005), but recent evidence shows that wildlife trade is increasing in response to external demand. In Peru, for example, current levels of the trade in primate species have been compared to numbers before the 1973 ban on international trade (Shanee et al. 2017). Increasing urban demand worldwide suggests that the consumption of bushmeat is no longer driven by subsistence needs but rather is increasingly spurred by a global and dynamic market thriving on the often illegal trade in "food delicacies" (Barnett 2000).

Commercial hunting includes the consumption of body parts as medicine (affecting sixty-seven species of mammals globally), the capture of live animals for the pet trade (forty-six species), and ornamental uses such as trophies (thirty-six species) (Ripple et al. 2016). Live trade and ornamental use affect wild mammals living primarily in Southeast Asia and secondarily in Africa and Latin America (Baillie et al. 2004), with an exorbitant demand for various wildlife products originating in China, Southeast Asian countries, the United States, and the European Union. More than 260 tons of wild meat per year were estimated to be smuggled in personal baggage into just one European airport (Paris Roissy-Charles de Gaulle) in 2008 (Chaber et al. 2010). Pangolins, the most traded wild mammal, and jaguar body parts are quoted in the Asian market at prices as high as cocaine (Navia 2018). According to a local newspaper, in one day about 4 tons of smuggled frozen pangolins were seized in Zhuhai, China, one of the largest cases of smuggling a protected animal (Liu and Weng 2014). Pangolins are imported mostly from Africa but also from Malaysia (EIA 2020), and jaguars are taken from throughout their geographic range in South America. Both species are prized because of nonscientific claims of medicinal use, consumed as "wildlife delicacies," and, in the case of jaguar fangs, seen as a symbol of status, strength, and power. Demand for wild meat by growing numbers of urban and foreign consumers as a symbol of wealth rather than an alternative to rural poverty has fueled a globalized market with unsustainable levels of hunting, originating mostly in tropical regions and targeting population centers all over the world. The illegal wildlife trade market has been estimated at between $7 and $23 billion a year (Wilkie and Carpenter, 1999; Nellemann et al. 2016).

The bushmeat crisis caused by commercial and subsistence hunting is catastrophic not only for wildlife but also for the livelihoods of people who rely on it as a major source of protein. Exploitation rates for countries in the Congo Basin indicate that if current extraction levels continue, there will be a severe protein deficit by 2050 and insufficient non-bushmeat protein produced to replace the amounts supplied by wild meat (Fa et al. 2002). Most countries in the region, where 60 percent of all mammal species hunted are exploited unsustainably, will have to find different sources of protein from the agricultural sector (Fa et al. 2003). Conversely, if harvesting is reduced to sustainable levels, proteins from sources other than bushmeat will not be able to meet the dietary needs because of the low agricultural production, a limited livestock sector, and a rapidly increasing population (Barnett 2000). A severe loss of bushmeat protein will exacerbate malnutrition and poverty, putting the livelihoods of millions of people at risk unless alternatives are promptly developed (De Merode et al. 2004; Cawthorn and Hoffman 2015).

Beyond the devastating impacts on human food security and biological diversity, the economic and consequences of wild animal trade cannot be overstated. For example, pangolins are a prime suspect among possible animal sources of the COVID-19 pandemic that originated in Wuhan, China, because dozens of people infected early in the outbreak worked in a live-animal market where pangolins were traded, although tests of coronavirus samples found at the market have yet to determine the precise animal source of the pathogen. The SARS epidemic in 2002 also originated in China and is believed to have jumped to humans from civets also in a market illegally trading wildlife (Cyranoski 2020).

Invasive Alien Species

Invasive species are a product of human activities that deliberately or accidentally transport and introduce large numbers of species to areas beyond their natural distribution. They have a range of well documented impacts in their new environments, including direct competition for resources or the introduction of pathogens that sicken or kill native species, and they are often cited as one of the most common causes of recent and ongoing extinctions (Doherty et al. 2016). Alien species were listed as the single cause of extinction for 47 percent of all extinct mammal species in the IUCN Red List (Bellard et al. 2016). Introduced species, including mammals, at times responding to specific agricultural aims, have extinguished native species in many parts of the world. For example, Pacific rats reached New Zealand with the first human immigrants. Now evidence of predation on invertebrates and vertebrates shows that Pacific rats are responsible for local and global extinctions of species including beetles, grasshoppers, land snails, frogs, lizards, small seabirds, and land birds (Atkinson 1996).

Not only biodiversity is threatened by alien species. Feral pigs, native to Eurasia and North Africa and introduced in the United States and Australia, are estimated to cause about $0.8 billion in damages to the agricultural sector in the United States and at least $80 million per year in Australia. Soil erosion, damage to agricultural crops including vegetables, fruits, orchards, and vineyards, and the spread of diseases to livestock including tuberculosis, brucellosis, and rabies are among the negative consequences. Introduced rodents are also among the species causing serious damage to farms, industries, and homes all over the world, demonstrating our limited ability to control exotic species once introduced. On farms, rats and mice are particularly abundant and destructive, causing $19 billion in damages per year in the United States and about $25 billion per year in India (Pimentel et al. 2001).

Climate Change

Climate change is expected to alter species distribution, abundance, phenology (the timing of events such as migration or breeding), morphology (size and shape), and genetic composition (Baillie et al. 2004). Although few mammal species have been recorded to be affected by climate change, a recent analysis of observed impacts has shown that the proportion of mammals already experiencing negative effects may be ten times higher than previously thought (Pacifici et al. 2017). Under a business-as-usual scenario with increasing greenhouse gas emissions, 16 percent of species are predicted to become extinct as their geographic ranges become unsuitable due to climate-related effects (Urban 2015; Costa et al. 2018).

Some species are already experiencing the effects of climate change on their survival (Jones and Rebelo 2013). For instance, in 2018 in Portugal some bat colonies completely avoided winter hibernation, a synchronized natural strategy to avoid the lack of food resources in winter that should normally happen between December and February, and for the first time recorded, some individuals gave birth earlier. The effects of a changing climate are potentially catastrophic for bats, especially in temperate areas, because the absence of hibernation can start pregnancies sooner, putting the offspring at risk of malnutrition and mortality (Briggs 2018).

Temperature variations are also influencing the progression and severity of emerging pathogens (Verant et al. 2012). White-nose syndrome is a recently discovered fungal pathogen in bats that seems to be exacerbated by increased energetic stress and is causing the most precipitous decline in bat populations ever reported. By 2012, the pathogen had killed more than 5 million individuals belonging to seven different species in the United States (Wibbelt et al. 2010; Reeder et al. 2012), including the little brown bat (*Myotis lucifugus*), once a common species whose population declined by 1 million individuals, almost causing its regional extinction (Frick et al. 2010). Extrapolations based on the 4–8 grams of insects that each little brown bat can eat per night averaged about 1,000 metric tons of insects that are no longer being consumed each year (Sherwin et al. 2013). The extraordinary capacity of bats to eat huge numbers of insects, including agricultural pests, exemplifies their contribution to the regulation of population cycles and potential outbreaks (Whitaker 1995). Emerging diseases in mammal species providing key ecosystem functions such as pest control could prove economically disastrous for the agricultural sector (Boyles et al. 2011).

Conservation Goals and Targets

Recognizing the importance of biodiversity (of genes, species, and ecosystems) underpinning Earth systems on which human economic and social systems rely, and acknowledging that biodiversity is under threat due to human activities, international treaties and conventions have been set to guide countries on conservation priorities with a broad range of objectives. The Convention on International Trade in Endangered Species of Wild Fauna and Flora, for example, is an international agreement between governments that entered into force in 1975 and aims to ensure that international trade in wild animals and plants does not threaten their survival.

The UN Environment Programme also recognized the need for an international convention on the protection of biodiversity. A process that started in 1988 took the form of a global commitment to sustainable development, recognized as the Convention on Biological Diversity and entered into force with 168 countries in December 1993. Since then, several decisions, conferences, reports, strategic plans, protocols, and assessments have been developed to create a framework where countries can follow the state and trends of diversity but are also informed of further relevant steps to implement actions at the national, cross-sectoral, and policy level that would lead to the overall goal of protecting global biodiversity. As part of the Convention on Biological Diversity actions, the Aichi Targets have been established as a strategic plan to be implemented between 2010 and 2020. Aichi Target 12 in particular requires that by 2020 the extinction of known threatened species has been prevented and their conservation status, particularly of those most in decline, has been improved and sustained (see also chapters 8, 9, and 11 in this book). However, biodiversity continues to decline steeply, and recent projections suggest that it is unlikely that most of the Aichi targets will be achieved.

More recently developed, the Sustainable Development Goals have been promoted by the United Nations as another attempt to call for political action to stop worldwide biodiversity decline. In particular, Goal 15 establishes that "urgent and significant action [should be taken] to reduce the degradation of natural habitats, halt the loss of biodiversity and, protect and prevent the extinction of threatened species" by 2030. In an attempt to describe which actions would be necessary to achieve these goals, Visconti et al. (2016) estimated how a set of different economic scenarios could affect conservation objectives. Under a business-as-usual scenario, where patterns of consumption and production remain the same as in the recent past and human population follows current trends, land use and climate change are predicted to outpace the ability of many mammal species to adapt, causing a steady decline in species richness and abundance. In contrast, under a "consumption change" alternative scenario, driven by measures to reduce deforestation and logging and set aside areas for biodiversity protection, the percentage of large mammals at risk of extinction is reduced from the current 34 percent to 18 percent.

Reducing meat consumption is a key element of proposed scenarios in which both biodiversity and zero hunger targets are achieved. A major misuse of natural resources derives from livestock production, with only 10 to 30 percent of animal feed ultimately converted into edible products. Additionally, based on dietary recommendations, a major reduction in meat intake could take place in every region of the world except for Africa and some areas in Asia. Food waste reduction is an important complement because one third of global food production is lost, with most of it occurring at the retail and consumption stage in North America, Oceania, and Europe. Improved access and distribution of food and a substantial reduction in consumption of meat and dairy products are projected to significantly lower the amount of agricultural land needed to maintain a stable and sufficient food supply in the long term, and they will increase the likelihood of meeting biodiversity objectives (Van Vuuren et al. 2012 and chapter 5).

Interestingly, a report issued in January 2020 that was intended to describe the consequences of environmental degradation in terms of gross domestic product (GDP) highlights converging points between biodiversity conservation scenarios and better economic performance. For instance, up to 2050, a business-as-usual scenario would result in GDP losses of about 0.7 percent per year due to the loss of ecosystem services, whereas a "global conservation" scenario, with targeted environmental changes, would be the only one yielding global GDP gains (Johnson et al. 2020).

The Intergovernmental Science-Policy Platform on Biodiversity and Ecosystem Services (IPBES) has documented that by maintaining the current unsustainable patterns of food production and consumption, most countries will miss the agreed biodiversity goals for 2030 and 2050, with negative impacts on the contributions of nature to human well-being. However, it also demonstrates that scenarios that take substantive and immediate action to halt environmental degradation and avoid species extinction are still a possible pathway to achieve the goals (Díaz et al. 2019). If Sustainable Development Goals and future biodiversity and environmental targets are to be achieved, each country must take responsibility and define how to act to stop and reverse the declining biodiversity trend (Mace et al. 2018). Institutional capacity and funding availability highly influence the achievement of suggested targets; therefore, governments play a central role defining and enforcing national and regional actions to achieve the global targets. Broader recognition of the role of business and finance sectors has also shed light on a dramatic change in efforts to be led by them, because their global reach through international trade and globalized value chains gives them the capacity to drive biodiversity protection (Díaz et al. 2019).

Economic and Environmental Benefits of Conserving Mammals

Our global food supply depends on well-functioning ecosystems, and biodiversity is the backbone of those systems (Díaz et al. 2019). Natural areas, from the boreal forests to the tropics, need healthy fauna to support human populations (Redford 1992). Some examples of how mammals participate in ecosystem functions and provide benefits to people are shown in table 10-1. One way mammals contribute is by increasing biomass production and carbon capture in soil, which is important to both crop production and climate change mitigation (Sobral et al. 2017). When carcasses, food scraps, and animal feces decompose, microbes break them down into a nutrient-rich soil that stores carbon or releases it for plants to grow and store it. Organic carbon is the basis of soil fertility, an essential element of crop productivity (Herrick and Wander 2018). Additionally, soil's ability to sequester carbon is increasingly recognized as essential to limiting climate change (chapter 8).

Increasing studies report the potential mammals have as an effective, economical, and simple way to capture carbon from the atmosphere. For instance, whales have a great capacity to sequester carbon to the deep sea. When they die, they sink to the bottom of the ocean, taking an average of 33 tons of CO_2 out of the atmosphere. Whales also act as multipliers of phytoplankton, some of the smallest creatures on Earth and the base of aquatic food webs in the ocean (Lavery et al. 2014; Roman et al. 2016). In balanced ecosystems the importance of phytoplankton also lies in their role as a key mediator of the biological carbon pump, responsible for the net transfer of CO_2 from the atmosphere to the oceans and then to the sediments, subsequently maintaining atmospheric CO_2 at significantly lower levels than would otherwise be the case (Riebesell et al. 2007; Basu and Mackey 2018). More whales equal more phytoplankton, more fish in the ocean, and less CO_2 in the atmosphere. On top of their intrinsic value as living creatures, carbon sequestration, fishery enhancement, and tourism make whales' contribution to healthy ecosystems worth billions of dollars, adding to the increasing reasons to protect them (Roman et al. 2014; Chami et al. 2019).

TABLE 10-1. *Examples of Mammal Species' Role and Their Contribution in the Ecosystem*

Role or Contribution	Mammal Species	Common Name	Effects in the Ecosystem
Top predators	*Canis lupus* *Gulo gulo* *Puma concolor* *Panthera onca* *Ursus americanos* *Ursus arctos* *Ursus maritimus*	Gray wolf Wolverine Puma, cougar Jaguar Black bear Grizzly bear Polar bear	Absence of apex or top predators, generally large carnivores, reduces control over mesopredators, which can reduce populations of birds, including pollinators and pest regulators (Crooks and Soulé 1999; Prugh et al. 2009).
Pollinators	For a comprehensive list of flying pollinator mammal species, see Regan et al. (2015).		Bats are the principal pollinators among mammals, pollinating a large number of economically and ecologically important plants known to provide valuable products to humans, including numerous fruits and important commodities for the industry (Regan et al. 2015; Bumrungsri et al. 2009).
Terrestrial seed dispersers	*Sciurus granatensis* *Macaca nemestrina* *Muntiacus muntjak* *Loxodonta africana* *Sus scrofa* *Tapirus indicus* *Helarctos malayanus* *Antechinus stuartii* *Petaurus breviceps* *Ateles paniscus*	Red-tailed squirrel Pig-tailed macaque Red muntjac African forest elephant Eurasian wild pig Malayan tapir Sun bears Brown antechinus Sugar glider Red-faced spider monkey	Play a key role in the maintenance and natural regeneration of forest areas, especially in the tropics (McConkey 2000). Their presence ensures forest functionality and more productive agroforestry systems (Paolucci et al. 2019). As forest cover influences interactions between land surface and the lower atmosphere, forests have the capacity to affect regional climate (Lawrence and Vandecar 2015; McAlpine et al. 2018). For instance, in Borneo, historical climate analyses showed that deforestation is associated with increased daily temperatures and reduced precipitation, which in turn affects the agricultural production of important crops such as palm oil (Oettli et al. 2018).

Note. List of species given is not comprehensive.

Lower livestock productivity rates, stagnant crops, and the projected scarcity of limiting resources such as water exemplify the increasing threat that climate change poses to agricultural production. Between 2003 and 2013, the agricultural sector in developing countries in Africa, Asia, and Latin America absorbed one quarter of the total economic losses caused by climate-related extremes. Frequent, intense, unpredictable climatic disasters such as droughts, floods, and storms caused an estimated $70 billion lost in production for the livestock and crops subsector (FAO 2015). In Europe, the heat catastrophe of 2003 produced livestock and crop losses of approximately $12.3 billion, and countries such as Portugal faced the worst forest fire season in decades, with wildfire deaths and 400,000 acres of timber loss (Epstein and Mills 2005). Other significant threats to livestock include the higher risk of contagion of new diseases, nutritional deficiencies, and heat stress, resulting in an overall reduction in production. Lower supplies of milk and meat and the disruption of reproductive processes have been demonstrated to cause decline and instability in prices and loss in net values of animal stocks (Kuczynski et al. 2011; Escarcha et al. 2018).

Here again, natural ecosystems offer solutions, because biodiversity is increasingly relevant for the possibilities that genes and gene combination offer to adapt to extreme weather conditions, diseases, and parasites (Lande and Shannon 1996). Genetic manipulation to produce new breeds and crop varieties has increased in recent decades. Enhancement of animal adaptations to extreme environmental conditions and increased tree productivity in forestry systems are only a couple of the many success stories of the use of genetic diversity (Maxwell 1994; Diaz et al. 2019). The sustainability of animal production systems thus depends on the continuing availability of a wide diversity of animal genetic resources and raw materials, many of which are uniquely contained in the forests and natural habitats of the world (Kantanen et al. 2015).

Mammal Conservation in Agricultural Landscapes

Policies to preserve mammals are essential to ecosystem function and food production systems. Most of these policies can be put into practice on a regional or local basis and support integrated management of agricultural and biodiversity areas, as detailed below.

1. Restriction of agricultural expansion in areas of special importance for biodiversity to maintain critical habitat.

- Prioritize the conservation of areas holding special values for biodiversity (endemic species, high species richness, endangered species) to prevent the conversion of forest or natural habitats to agricultural production. Restrict the future expansion of agriculture, including industrial-scale logging, to preexisting cropland or degraded habitats.
- Avoid protected area downgrading, downsizing, and degazettement (Mascia et al. 2014).
- Develop landscape-scale planning programs that integrate the sustainable use of natural resources and make use of diverse conservation strategies (Garnett et al. 2018; IUCN WCPA 2019).

2. Promote long-term sustainable and productive use of current agricultural land.
    - Payments for biodiversity to farms that provide evidence of good ecological performance, including allocating a minimum permanent percentage of agricultural land as biodiversity promotion areas. Increased benefits if allocated within a connectivity matrix that favors the migration of apex species (Jason et al. 2016; and chapter 2).
    - Payments for good practices to farms able to demonstrate the implementation of management measures, for example through the adoption of physical barriers that prevent human–wildlife conflicts (Payán et al. 2013; Valderrama et al. 2016).
    - Compensation for production losses (livestock, fruits, vegetables) due to human–wildlife conflicts while implementing landscape-level, long-term institutional strategies to prevent further conflicts.
    - Taxes to limit the excessive use of synthetic inputs. Restrictions based on scientific recommendations of what is biologically sustainable in the local context. This will also reduce greenhouse gas emissions, with positive effects on both biodiversity and climate change mitigation.
    - Penalties for water contamination and tradable water right permits to limit water consumption above established thresholds according to farm size, crop type, and other local users.
    - Eliminate subsidies that contribute to unsustainable use of resources and reduce biodiversity (e.g., overuse of synthetic inputs such as fertilizers and pesticides).
    - Develop and implement policies to promote good agricultural practices that increase local conservation of biodiversity, for example, by retaining natural habitats in farmlands (Dicks et al. 2014).

- Promote well-conserved habitats for species connectivity within the agricultural matrix (Crick et al. 2020).
- Promote mixed farming practices and crop heterogeneity at the landscape level, which are particularly beneficial for farmland wildlife.
- Restrict the use of alien species unless absolutely necessary, and only then under tight introduction measures.

3. Ensure funding for research and implementation of conservation strategies that favor both biodiversity and agricultural production.
   - Redirect funds collected from environmental taxes (e.g., carbon tax), fees, and penalties to biodiversity conservation and sustainable agricultural development, for example by providing farmers with incentives for innovation in good environmental practices.
   - Allocate resources to benefit farmers who adhere to ecological certification programs. Provide payments for production costs, especially when farmers are transitioning to better practices and probably facing higher costs (Blackman and Naranjo 2010).
   - Fund joint strategies by environmental and agricultural agencies and external independent monitors, to promote good production standards at the individual farm level.
   - Secure sufficient, stable, and long-term financial resources that attract producers to implement sustainable production strategies.
   - Encourage conversion to ecological intensification strategies (Garibaldi et al. 2019) by offering clear economic benefits for demonstrating good practices.

4. Increase collaboration between public and private sectors at the local, regional, and international levels.
   - Ensure that producers and suppliers have access to information and technology that enable them to benefit from organic production, certification programs, and fair or direct trade markets.
   - Increase collaboration between various government agencies (environment, agriculture) to identify agricultural production areas where it is possible to conserve biodiversity through connecting corridors of natural habitat (Parmesan 2006; Aguiar et al. 2016).
   - Develop joint strategies with farmers to achieve stable or high crop productivity and resilience in the long term by protecting ecosystem services such as natural pest control and pollination.

- Facilitate data exchange between research institutions, universities, and private and government entities that promote sound agricultural practices.
- Promote education and research that increase public and government awareness of consumption, production, and trade patterns and their effects on human well-being and biodiversity.

5. Cooperation between agricultural, environment, and interior ministries to develop policies that support sustainable agriculture and biodiversity.
   - Ensure institutional capacity and transparency for the enforcement of international treaties and conventions.
   - Enforce international commitments and national regulations across all actors in the supply chain, including producers, suppliers, and final consumers.

Country Cases

Beaver Comeback

Beavers once lived throughout Eurasia, but by 1920 the species had reached a historical low, with fewer than 1,200 individuals surviving in five fragmented populations. Agricultural expansion and overexploitation for beavers' fur and supposed medicinal benefits put this large rodent at the edge of extinction. Hunting restrictions and long-term conservation efforts to recover their natural habitats have allowed a remarkable recovery over the past forty years (Deinet et al. 2013). Completely extirpated from Latvia and Sweden in the nineteenth century, those two countries currently represent almost 50 percent of the total European population, an extraordinary recovery because there are more than 100,000 individuals in Latvia.

Beavers are recognized as ecosystem engineers; the river canals, dams, and ponds they build create microhabitats for other species, including insects, amphibians, fishes, and birds (Deinet et al. 2013). In the United States, beaver constructions along rivers improve habitat quality and the quantity of steelhead trout and salmon, both important species for the fishing industry (Malison et al. 2015; Bouwes et al. 2018). Ponds also raise groundwater elevation, increasing river flows throughout the summer as water is slowly released. This increases habitat for fish during hot, dry summers. Raising the groundwater level also increases the number of birds and invertebrate biomass, which benefits agricultural production and biodiversity (Oomes et al. 1996).

Another important service provided by beavers is carbon storage. Differences in total organic carbon between abandoned and active beaver meadows suggest that carbon storage declines substantially as beavers disappear and meadows dry out (Wohl 2013). Maintaining beaver populations in the wild results in ponds standing as substantial sinks for watershed nitrogen, reducing eutrophication and habitat degradation and improving water quality (Lazar et al. 2015).

Beaver reintroduction programs provide nature-based solutions to water shortages in agricultural landscapes (Puttock et al. 2017), which are proven to be more cost-effective than human intervention. Although beavers were almost extinguished because of their great capacity to modify landscapes, sometimes causing flooding in lowland areas, the current consensus is that their benefits outweigh the disadvantages. Nonetheless, ecologically sound management is needed in areas where they share their habitat with people and agricultural landscapes.

Poison-Free Pest Control

The remarkable usefulness of bats has long amazed farmers (Olson and Maher 2018). Today, bats are increasingly recognized for their effective pollination of fruits and their capacity to control pests (Riccucci and Lanza 2014; Aziz et al. 2017).

Bats eat up to 100 percent of their body mass in insects on a nightly basis, benefiting farmers in countries around the globe, including Brazil, Indonesia, Spain, and the United States. This natural pest control is an effective alternative to excessive pesticide use, which threatens human health and the environment. In Spain, for example, the soprano pipistrelle bat controls infestations of a moth species known as the rice borer; the economic value is at least €21 per hectare, equivalent to the avoided pesticide expenditure alone (Puig-Montserrat et al. 2015).

Biodiversity of bats in their natural ecosystems is essential to prevent pest outbreaks. In a tropical lowland forest in Panama, the diversity of bats and birds reduces insects on plants, thus reducing herbivory and the risk of pest outbreaks. Experiments show that bat-exclosed plants suffered 209 percent more herbivory than control areas where bats were present, demonstrating a dramatic ecological effect previously overlooked (Goldingay et al. 1991; Kalka et al. 2008). Understanding the mechanisms that link ecological systems to human well-being is fundamental in a changing world. Because of the complexity of natural processes, it is sometimes difficult to recognize nature's benefits to humans. Despite their ecological importance and contribution to human food security (Wanger et al. 2014), 192 out of 1,280 species (15 percent) are currently categorized as endangered (IUCN 2020b).

Conclusions

The global pattern of mammal diversity is similar to that of birds and amphibians, with the greatest numbers of species residing in regions such as Sub-Saharan Africa, Southeast Asia, and the Andes mountain range and the Amazonas in South America. Because the majority of mammal species prefer forests as their main habitat, deforestation and forest degradation are among the main reasons for mammal population decline. The encroachment of the agricultural frontier into natural habitats, intensive pesticide use in large extensions of heavily industrialized crops, invasive species, and overexploitation of hundreds of species have put at the verge of extinction approximately 22 percent of all mammal species. As people have begun to recognize this decline in biodiversity and its threat to human well-being and food security, many have called for international treaties and conventions to reverse this trend. Unfortunately, we are far from achieving these targets, as biodiversity continues a steep decline.

The positive feedback between biodiversity and well-functioning ecosystems underpins human well-being and the entire global food system. Healthy populations of diverse mammal species have the potential to control crop pests, create microhabitats for other beneficial organisms, increase ecosystems' capacity to absorb carbon, and offer genetic opportunities for adaptation of domesticated animals. Mammals are outstanding allies in a changing world where events that jeopardize our ability to produce food, such as severe droughts, pest outbreaks, and climate instability, have become the new normal. Actionable policies are essential to protect mammals' diversity and their contributions to sustainable agricultural practices.

References

Aguiar, L. M. S., E. Bernard, V. Ribeiro, R. B. Machado, and G. Jones. 2016. "Should I stay or should I go? Climate change effects on the future of Neotropical savannah bats." *Global Ecology and Conservation* 5: 22–33.

Allen, T., K. A. Murray, C. Zambrana-Torrelio, S. S. Morse, C. Rondinini, M. Di Marco, N. Breit, K. J. Olival, and P. Daszak. 2017. "Global hotspots and correlates of emerging zoonotic diseases." *Nature Communications* 8, no. 1: 1–10.

Ancrenaz, M., M. Gumal, A. J. Marshall, E. Meijaard, S. A. Wich, and S. Husson. 2016. "*Pongo pygmaeus* (errata version published in 2018)." *The IUCN Red List of Threatened Species* 2016: e. T17975A123809220.

Atkinson, I. 1996. "Introductions of wildlife as a cause of species extinctions." *Wildlife Biology* 2, no. 1: 135–41. https://doi.org/10.2981/wlb.1996.011

Aziz, S., G. Clements, K. McConkey, T. Sritongchuay, S. Pathil, M. Nur Hafizi Abu Yazid, A. Campos-Arceiz, P.-M. Forget, and S. Bumrungsri. 2017. "Pollination by the locally endangered island flying fox (*Pteropus hypomelanus*) enhances fruit production of the economically important durian (*Durio zibethinus*)." *Ecology and Evolution* 7, no. 21: 8670–84. https://doi.org/10.1002/ece3.3213

Baillie, J., C. Hilton-Taylor, and S. Stuart. 2004. "A global species assessment." Gland, Switzerland: IUCN.

Barnett, R. 2000. *Food for Thought: The Utilization of Wild Meat in Eastern and Southern Africa.* Cambridge, UK: TRAFFIC East/Southern Africa.

Barry, J., M. Elbroch, M. Aiello-Lammens, R. Sarno, L. Seelye, A. Kusler, H. Quigley, and M. Grigione. 2019. "Pumas as ecosystem engineers: ungulate carcasses support beetle assemblages in the Greater Yellowstone Ecosystem." *Oecologia* 189, no. 3: 577–86. https://doi.org/10.1007/s00442-018-4315-z

Basu, S., and K. R. M. Mackey. 2018. "Phytoplankton as key mediators of the biological carbon pump: their responses to a changing climate." *Sustainability* 10, no. 3: 869.

Bellard, C., P. Cassey, and T. Blackburn. 2016. "Alien species as a driver of recent extinctions." *Biology Letters* 12, no. 4. https://doi.org/10.1098/rsbl.2015.0623

Bennett, E. L., and M. Rao. 2002. "Wild meat consumption in Asian tropical forest countries is this a glimpse of the future for Africa." Pages 39–44 in *Links between Biodiversity, Conservation, Livelihoods and Food Security: The Sustainable Use of Wild Species for Meat*, ed. S. Mainka and M. Trivedi. Gland, Switzerland and Cambridge, UK: IUCN.

BirdLife International. 2010. "Unsustainable exploitation of birds is most prevalent in Asia." http://datazone.birdlife.org/sowb/casestudy/163

Blackman, A., and M. Naranjo. 2003. "Does eco-certification have environmental benefits? Organic coffee in Costa Rica." *Ecological Economics* 83: 58–66.

Bouwes, N., N. Weber, C. Jordan, C. Saunders, I. Tattam, C. Volk, J. Wheaton, and M. Pollock. 2018. "Corrigendum: ecosystem experiment reveals benefits of natural and simulated beaver dams to a threatened population of steelhead (*Oncorhynchus mykiss*)." *Scientific Reports* 8: 46995. https://doi.org/10.1038/srep28581

Boyles, J., P. Cryan, G. McCracken, and T. Kunz. 2011. "Economic importance of bats in agriculture." *Science* 332, no. 6025: 41–2. https://doi.org/10.1126/science.1201366

Brashares, J. S., C. D. Golden, K. Z. Weinbaum, C. B. Barrett, and G. V. Okello. 2011. "Economic and geographic drivers of wildlife consumption in rural Africa." *Proceedings of the National Academy of Sciences* 108: 13931–6.

Briggs, H. 2018. "Extreme weather potentially catastrophic for bats." BBC News. https://www.bbc.com/news/science-environment-43812484

Brook, B., C. Bradshaw, L. Pin Koh, and N. Sodhi. 2006. "Momentum drives the crash: mass extinction in the tropics." *Biotropica: The Journal of Biology and Conservation* 38, no. 3: 302–5. https://doi.org/10.1111/j.1744-7429.2006.00141.x

Bumrungsri, S., E. Sripaoraya, T. Chongsiri, K. Sridith, and P. A. Racey. 2009. "The pollination ecology of durian (*Durio zibethinus*, Bombacaceae) in southern Thailand." *Journal of Tropical Ecology* 25, no. 1: 85–92. https://doi.org/10.1017/S0266467408005531

Caveljer, J., D. Lizcano, E. Yerena, and C. Downer. 2011. "17. The mountain tapir (*Tapirus pinchaque*) and Andean bear (*Tremarctos ornatus*): two charismatic, large mammals in South American tropical montane." *Tropical Montane Cloud Forests: Science for Conservation and Management* 172.

Cawthorn, D.-M., and L. C. Hoffman. 2015. "The bushmeat and food security nexus: a global account of the contributions, conundrums and ethical collisions." *Food Research International* 76: 906–25.

Chaber, A. L., S. Allebone-Webb, Y. Lignereux, A. A. Cunningham, and M. Rowcliffe. 2010. "The scale of illegal meat importation from Africa to Europe via Paris." *Conservation Letters* 3, no. 5: 317–21. https://doi.org/10.1111/j.1755-263X.2010.00121.x

Chami, R., T. Cosimano, C. Fullenkamp, and S. Oztosun. 2019. "Nature's solution to climate change. A strategy to protect whales can limit greenhouse gases and global warming." *International Monetary Fund: Finance & Development* 56, no. 4: 34–8.

Coad, L., J. E. Fa, K. Abernethy, N. Van Vliet, C. Santamaria, D. Wilkie, H. R. El Bizri, D. J. Ingram, D.-M. Cawthorn, and R. Nasi. 2019. *Towards a Sustainable, Participatory and Inclusive Wild Meat Sector*. Bogor, Indonesia: Center for International Forestry Research (CIFOR).

Costa, W. F., M. Ribeiro, A. M. Saraiva, V. L. Imperatriz-Fonseca, and T. Cristina Giannini. 2018. "Bat diversity in Carajás National Forest (eastern Amazon) and potential impacts on ecosystem services under climate change." *Biological Conservation* 218: 200–10.

Crick, H., I. Crosher, C. Mainstone, S. Taylor, A. Wharton, P. Langford, J. Larwood, J. Lusardi, D. Appleton, P. Brotherton, S. Duffield, and N. Macgregor. 2020. *Nature Networks Evidence Handbook*. Natural England research report NERR081. York: Natural England.

Crooks, K., and M. Soulé. 1999. "Mesopredator release and avifaunal extinctions in a fragmented system." *Nature* 400, no. 6744: 563–6. https://doi.org/10.1038/23028

Cyranoski, D. 2020. "Mystery deepens over animal source of coronavirus." *Nature* 579, no. 7797: 18–9.

De Merode, E., K. Homewood, and G. Cowlishaw. 2004. "The value of bushmeat and other wild foods to rural households living in extreme poverty in Democratic Republic of Congo." *Biological Conservation* 118, no. 5: 573–81.

Deinet, S., C. Ieronymidou, L. McRae, I. Burfield, R. Foppen, B. Collen, M. Böhm, and BirdLife ZSL. 2013. "Wildlife comeback in Europe: the recovery of selected mammal and bird species." Final report to Rewilding Europe by ZSL, BirdLife International and the European Bird Census Council. London: ZSL.

Díaz, S., J. Settele, E. Brondízio, H. Ngo, M. Guèze, J. Agard, A. Arneth, P. Balvanera, K. Brauman, S. Butchart, et al. 2019. "Summary for policymakers of the global assessment report on biodiversity and ecosystem services of the Intergovernmental Science-Policy Platform on Biodiversity and Ecosystem Services." Bonn, Germany: IPBES.

Dicks, L. V., J. E. Ashpole, J. Dänhardt, K. James, A. M. Jönsson, N. Randall, and D. A. Showler. 2014. *Farmland Conservation: Evidence for the Effects of Interventions in Northern and Western Europe*. Vol. 3. Exeter, UK: Pelagic Publishing Ltd.

Dirzo, R., H. Young, M. Galetti, G. Ceballos, N. Isaac, and B. Collen. 2014. "Defaunation in the Anthropocene." *Science* 345, no. 6195: 401–6. https://doi.org/10.1126/science.1251817

Doherty, T. S., A. S. Glen, D. G. Nimmo, E. G. Ritchie, and C. R. Dickman. 2016. "Invasive predators and global biodiversity loss." *Proceedings of the National Academy of Sciences* 113, no. 40: 11261–5.

Downer, C. C. 2001. "Observations on the diet and habitat of the mountain tapir (*Tapirus pinchaque*)." *Journal of Zoology* 254, no. 3: 279–91. https://doi.org/10.1017/S0952836901000796

Elbroch, M., M. Peziol, and H. B. Quigley. 2017. "Vertebrate diversity benefiting from carrion provided by pumas and other subordinate, apex felids." *Biological Conservation* 215: 123–31. https://doi.org/10.1016/j.biocon.2017.08.026

Environmental Investigation Agency (EIA). 2020. "Illegal trade seizures: pangolin." https://eia-international.org/wildlife/wildlife-trade-maps/illegal-trade-seizures-pangolins/

Epstein, P. R., and E. Mills. 2005. *Climate Change Futures: Health, Ecological and Economic Dimensions.* Cambridge, Mass.: Center for Health and the Global Environment, Harvard Medical School.

Escarcha, J., J. Lassa, and K. Zander. 2018. "Livestock under climate change: a systematic review of impacts and adaptation." *Climate* 6, no. 3: 54. https://doi.org/10.3390/cli6030054

Fa, J. E., D. Currie, and J. Meeuwig. 2003. "Bushmeat and food security in the Congo Basin: linkages between wildlife and people's future." *Environmental Conservation* 30, no. 1: 71–8.

Fa, J. E., C. A. Peres, and J. Meeuwig. 2002. "Bushmeat exploitation in tropical forests: an intercontinental comparison." *Conservation Biology* 16, no. 1: 232–7.

Fa, J., S. Ryan, and D. Bell. 2005. "Hunting vulnerability, ecological characteristics and harvest rates of bushmeat species in Afrotropical forests." *Biological Conservation* 121, no. 2: 167–76. https://doi.org/10.1016/j.biocon.2004.04.016

Fanzo, J., D. Hunter, T. Borelli, and F. Mattei. 2013. *Diversifying Food and Diets: Using Agricultural Biodiversity to Improve Nutrition and Health.* Abingdon, UK: Routledge.

Food and Agriculture Organization of the United Nations (FAO). 2015. *The Impact of Natural Hazards and Disasters on Agriculture and Food Security and Nutrition: A Call for Action to Build Resilient Livelihoods.* Rome: FAO.

Frick, W. F., J. F. Pollock, A. C. Hicks, K. E. Langwig, D. S. Reynolds, G. G. Turner, C. M. Butchkoski, and T. H. Kunz. 2010. "An emerging disease causes regional population collapse of a common North American bat species." *Science* 329, no. 5992: 679–82.

Fritts, R. 2019. "Agriculture, mining, hunting push critically endangered gorillas to the brink." *Mongabay Environmental News.* https://news.mongabay.com/2019/07/agriculture-mining-hunting-push-critically-endangered-gorillas-to-the-brink/

Garibaldi, L., N. Pérez-Méndez, M. P. Garratt, B. Gemmill-Herren, F. Miguez, and L. Dicks. 2019. "Policies for ecological intensification of crop production." In *Trends in Ecology and Evolution.* Amsterdam: Elsevier Ltd. https://doi.org/10.1016/j.tree.2019.01.003

Garnett, S., N. Burgess, J. Fa, A. Fernández-Llamazares, Z. Molnár, C. Robinson, J. Watson, et al. 2018. "A spatial overview of the global importance of indigenous lands for conservation." *Nature Sustainability* 1, no. 7: 369–74. https://doi.org/10.1038/s41893-018-0100-6

Gokkon, B. 2019. "Malaysia's last Sumatran rhino dies, leaving Indonesia as the final refuge." *Mongabay Environmental News.* https://news.mongabay.com/2019/11/malaysias-last-sumatran-rhino-dies-leaving-indonesia-as-the-final-refuge/

Golden, C. D., L. C. H. Fernald, J. S. Brashares, B. J. R. Rasolofoniaina, and C. Kremen.

2011. "Benefits of wildlife consumption to child nutrition in a biodiversity hotspot." *Proceedings of the National Academy of Sciences* 108, no. 49: 19653–6.
Goldingay, R. L., S. M. Carthew, and R. J. Whelan. 1991. "The importance of non-flying mammals in pollination." *Oikos* 61, no. 1: 79. https://doi.org/10.2307/3545409
Green, J., S. Croft, A. Durán, A. Balmford, N. Burgess, S. Fick, T. Gardner, J. Godar, C. Suavet, and M. Virah-Sawmy. 2019. "Linking global drivers of agricultural trade to on-the-ground impacts on biodiversity." *Proceedings of the National Academy of Sciences* 116, no. 46: 23202–8. https://doi.org/10.1073/pnas.1905618116
Grenyer, R., D. Orme, S. Jackson, G. Thomas, R. Davies, J. Davies, K. Jones, V. Olson, R. Ridgely, and P. Rasmussen. 2006. "Global distribution and conservation of rare and threatened vertebrates." *Nature* 444, no. 7115: 93–6. https://doi.org/10.1038/nature05237
Hayes, K., and R. Burge. 2003. "Coltan mining in the Democratic Republic of Congo: how tantalum-using industries can commit to the reconstruction of the DRC." Cambridge, UK: Fauna & Flora International Cambridge.
Herrick, J., and M. Wander. 2018. "Relationships between soil organic carbon and soil quality in cropped and rangeland soils: the importance of distribution, composition, and soil biological activity." In *Soil Processes and the Carbon Cycle*. Boca Raton, FL: CRC Press, 405–25.
International Union for Conservation of Nature (IUCN), World Commission on Protected Areas (WCPA). 2019. "Recognising and reporting other effective area-based conservation measures." Gland, Switzerland: IUCN. https://doi.org/10.2305/IUCN.CH.2019.PATRS.3.en
International Union for Conservation of Nature and Natural Resources (IUCN). 2020a. *The IUCN Red List of Threatened Species*, Version 2019-3. https://www.iucnredlist.org
———. 2020b. "Chiroptera." In *The IUCN Red List of Threatened Species*, Version 2019-3. Accessed January 20, 2020. https://www.iucnredlist.org
International Union for Conservation of Nature (IUCN) and Center for International Earth Science Information Network (CIESIN). 2015. "Gridded species distribution: global mammal richness grids, 2015 release." NASA Socioeconomic Data and Applications Center (SEDAC). https://doi.org/10.7927/H4N014G5
Jason, P., V. Voora, M. Lynch, and A. Mammadova. 2016. "Voluntary sustainability standards and biodiversity: understanding the potential of agricultural standards for biodiversity protection." Winnipeg, Canada: International Institute for Sustainable Development.
Johnson, J., U. Baldos, T. Hertel, C. Nootenboom, S. Polasky, and T. Roxburgh. 2020. "Global futures: modelling the global economic impacts of environmental change to support policy-making." Technical report. https://www.wwf.org.uk/globalfutures
Jones, G., and H. Rebelo. 2013. "Responses of bats to climate change: learning from the past and predicting the future." Pages 457–78 in *Bat Evolution, Ecology, and Conservation*. New York: Springer.
Kalka, M., A. Smith, and E. Kalko. 2008. "Bats limit arthropods and herbivory in a tropical forest." *Science* 320, no. 5872: 71. https://doi.org/10.1126/science.1153352
Kantanen, J., P. Løvendahl, E. Strandberg, E. Eythorsdottir, M. H. Li, A. Kettunen-Praebel, P. Berg, and T. Meuwissen. 2015. "Utilization of farm animal genetic resources in a changing agroecological environment in the Nordic countries." *Frontiers in Genetics* 6: 52. https://doi.org/10.3389/fgene.2015.00052

Koh, L. P., and D. Wilcove. 2008. "Is oil palm agriculture really destroying tropical biodiversity?" *Conservation Letters* 1, no. 2: 60–4. https://doi.org/10.1111/j.1755-263x.2008.00011.x

Koppert, G. J. A., E. Dounias, A. Froment, and P. Pasquet. 1996. "Consommation alimentaire dans trois populations forestières de la région côtière du Cameroun: Yassa, Mvae et Bakola." *L'Alimentation en Forêt Tropicale, Interactions Bioculturelles et Perspectives de Développement* 1: 477–96.

Kuczynski, T., V. Blanes-Vidal, B. Li, R. S. Gates, I. de Alencar Naas, D. J. Moura, D. Berckmans, and T. M. Banhazi. 2011. "Impact of global climate change on the health, welfare and productivity of intensively housed livestock." *International Journal of Agricultural and Biological Engineering* 4, no. 2: 1–22.

Lacher, T. E. Jr., A. D. Davidson, T. H. Fleming, E. P. Gómez-Ruiz, G. F. McCracken, N. Owen-Smith, C. A. Peres, and S. B. Vander Wall. 2019. "The functional roles of mammals in ecosystems." *Journal of Mammalogy* 100, no. 3: 942–64.

Lande, R., and S. Shannon. 1996. "The role of genetic variation in adaptation and population persistence in a changing environment." *Evolution* 50, no. 1: 434. https://doi.org/10.2307/2410812

Laporte, N. T., J. A. Stabach, R. Grosch, T. S. Lin, and S. J. Goetz. 2007. "Expansion of industrial logging in Central Africa." *Science* 316, no. 5830: 1451.

Lavery, T. J., B. Roudnew, J. Seymour, J. G. Mitchell, V. Smetacek, and S. Nicol. 2014. "Whales sustain fisheries: blue whales stimulate primary production in the Southern Ocean." *Marine Mammal Science* 30, no. 3: 888–904.

Lawrence, D., and K. Vandecar. 2015. "Effects of tropical deforestation on climate and agriculture." *Nature Climate Change* 5, no. 1: 27–36. https://doi.org/10.1038/nclimate2430

Lazar, J., K. Addy, A. Gold, P. Groffman, R. McKinney, and D. Kellogg. 2015. "Beaver ponds: resurgent nitrogen sinks for rural watersheds in the northeastern United States." *Journal of Environmental Quality* 44, no. 5: 1684–93. https://doi.org/10.2134/jeq2014.12.0540

Liu, Y., and Q. Weng. 2014. "Fauna in decline: plight of the pangolin." *Science* 345, no. 6199: 884. https://doi.org/10.1126/science.345.6199.884-a

Lizcano, M. 2018. "Colombia: la palma de aceite pone en jaque la flora y la fauna del pacífico." *Mongabay Environmental News*. https://es.mongabay.com/2018/11/colombia-palma-de-aceite-pacifico/

Mace, G., M. Barrett, N. Burgess, S. Cornell, R. Freeman, M. Grooten, and A. Purvis. 2018. "Aiming higher to bend the curve of biodiversity loss." *Nature Sustainability* 1, no. 9: 448–51. https://doi.org/10.1038/s41893-018-0130-0

Maine, J., and J. Boyles. 2015. "Bats initiate vital agroecological interactions in corn." *Proceedings of the National Academy of Sciences of the United States of America* 112, no. 40: 12438–43. https://doi.org/10.1073/pnas.1505413112

Malison, R., L. Eby, and J. Stanford. 2015. "Juvenile salmonid growth, survival, and production in a large river floodplain modified by beavers (*Castor canadensis*)." *Canadian Journal of Fisheries and Aquatic Sciences* 72, no. 11: 1639–51. https://doi.org/10.1139/cjfas-2015-0147

Mascia, M., S. Pailler, R. Krithivasan, V. Roshchanka, D. Burns, M. J. Mlotha, D. R. Murray, and N. Peng. 2014. "Protected area downgrading, downsizing, and degazette-

ment (PADDD) in Africa, Asia, and Latin America and the Caribbean, 1900–2010." *Biological Conservation* 169: 355–61. https://doi.org/10.1016/j.biocon.2013.11.021
Maxwell, G. 1994. "Pharmaceuticals from plants: great potential, few funds. Editorial." *Lancet* 343: 1513–5.
Mbete, R. A., H. Banga-Mboko, P. Racey, A. Mfoukou-Ntsakala, I. Nganga, C. Vermeulen, J.-L. Doucet, J.-L. Hornick, and P. Leroy. 2011. "Household bushmeat consumption in Brazzaville, the Republic of the Congo." *Tropical Conservation Science* 4, no. 2: 187–202.
McAlpine, C., A. Johnson, A. Salazar, J. Syktus, K. Wilson, E. Meijaard, L. Seabrook, P. Dargusch, H. Nordin, and D. Sheil. 2018. "Forest loss and Borneo's climate." *Environmental Research Letters* 13, no. 4: 44009. https://doi.org/10.1088/1748-9326/aaa4ff
McConkey, K. 2000. "Primary seed shadow generated by gibbons in the rain forests of Barito Ulu, central Borneo." *American Journal of Primatology* 52, no. 1: 13–29. https://doi.org/10.1002/1098-2345(200009)52:1<13::AID-AJP2>3.0.CO;2-Y
Myers, N., R. Mittermeler, C. Mittermeler, G. Da Fonseca, and J. Kent. 2000. "Biodiversity hotspots for conservation priorities." *Nature* 403, no. 6772: 853–58. https://doi.org/10.1038/35002501
Nardoto, G. B., R. S. S. Murrieta, L. E. G. Prates, C. Adams, M. E. P. E. Garavello, T. Schor, and A. De Moraes. 2011. "Frozen chicken for wild fish: nutritional transition in the Brazilian Amazon region determined by carbon and nitrogen stable isotope ratios in fingernails." *American Journal of Human Biology* 23, no. 5: 642–50.
Nasi, R., D. Brown, D. Wilkie, E. Bennett, C. Tutin, G. Van Tol, and T. Christophersen. 2008. "Conservation and use of wildlife-based resources: the bushmeat crisis." Technical series no. 33. Bogor, Indonesia: Secretariat of the Convention on Biological Diversity, Montreal, and Center for International Forestry Research.
Nasi, R., A. Taber, and N. Van Vliet. 2011. "Empty forests, empty stomachs? Bushmeat and livelihoods in the Congo and Amazon Basins." *International Forestry Review* 13, no. 3: 355–68.
Navia, R. 2018. "Bolivia: Mafia le arranca los colmillos al jaguar, el gran felino de América." *Mongabay Environmental News*. https://es.mongabay.com/2018/01/bolivia-jaguar-colmillos-mafia/
Nellemann, C., R. Henriksen, A. Kreilhuber, D. Stewart, M. Kotsovou, P. Raxter, E. Mrema, and S. Barrat. 2016. "The rise of environmental crime: a growing threat to natural resources, peace, development and security." Nairobi: UNEP.
Nowak, M. G., P. Rianti, S. Wich, A. Meijide, and G. Fredriksson. 2017. "Pongo tapanuliensis." *The IUCN Red List of Threatened Species* 2017: e.T120588639A120588662. https://dx.doi.org/10.2305/IUCN.UK.2017-3.RLTS.T120588639A120588662.en
Oettli, P., S. Behera, and T. Yamagata. 2018. "Climate based predictability of oil palm tree yield in Malaysia." *Scientific Reports* 8, no. 1: 1–13. https://doi.org/10.1038/s41598-018-20298-0
Olson, S., and J. L. Maher. 2018. "Bat week: the superpowers of bats (photos)." *Mongabay Environmental News*. https://news.mongabay.com/2018/10/bat-week-the-superpowers-of-bats-photos/
Oomes, M., H. Olff, and H. J. Altena. 1996. "Effects of vegetation management and raising the water table on nutrient dynamics and vegetation change in a wet grassland." *Journal of Applied Ecology* 33, no. 3: 576. https://doi.org/10.2307/2404986
Pacifici, M., P. Visconti, S. Butchart, J. Watson, F. Cassola, and C. Rondinini. 2017. "Spe-

cies' traits influenced their response to recent climate change." *Nature Climate Change* 7, no. 3: 205–8. https://doi.org/10.1038/nclimate3223

Paolucci, L., R. Pereira, L. Rattis, D. Silvério, N. Marques, M. Macedo, and P. Brando. 2019. "Lowland tapirs facilitate seed dispersal in degraded Amazonian forests." *Biotropica* 51, no. 2: 245–52. https://doi.org/doi:10.1111/btp.12627

Parmesan, C. 2006. "Ecological and evolutionary responses to recent climate change." *Annual Review of Ecology, Evolution, and Systematics* 37, no. 1: 637–69. https://doi.org/10.1146/annurev.ecolsys.37.091305.110100

Payán, E., C. Carbone, K. Homewood, E. Paemelaere, H. Quigley, and S. Durant. 2013. "Where will jaguars roam? The importance of survival in unprotected lands." Pages 603–27 in *Molecular Population Genetics, Evolutionary Biology and Biological Conservation of Neotropical Carnivores*, ed. M. Ruiz-Garcia and J. Shostell. Hauppauge, N.Y.: Nova Science Publishers.

Payán, E., O. Moreno, A. Mejía, M. Fonseca, and C. Valderrama. 2015. "Plan de manejo para la conservación del jaguar (*Panthera onca*) en el Valle del Cauca, Colombia." https://www.cvc.gov.co/sites/default/files/Planes_y_Programas/Plan-de-manejo-para-la-conservacion-del-jaguar_Panthera.pdf

Pimentel, D., S. McNair, J. Janecka, J. Wightman, C. Simmonds, C. O'Connell, and E. Wong. 2011. "Economic and environmental threats of alien plant, animal, and microbe invasions." *Agriculture, Ecosystems & Environment* 84, no. 1: 1–20.

Plumptre, A., S. Nixon, R. Critchlow, G. Vieilledent, R. Nishuli, A. Kirkby, E. Williamson, J. Hall, and D. Kujirakwinja. 2016. "Status of Grauer's gorilla and chimpanzees in eastern Democratic Republic of Congo: historical and current distribution and abundance." Unpublished report to Arcus Foundation, USAID and US Fish and Wildlife Service.

Poulsen, J. R., C. J. Clark, G. Mavah, and P. W. Elkan. 2009. "Bushmeat supply and consumption in a tropical logging concession in northern Congo." *Conservation Biology* 23, no. 6: 1597–608.

Pouzols, F. M., T. Toivonen, E. Di Minin, A. Kukkala, P. Kullberg, J. Kuustera, J. Lehtomaki, H. Tenkanen, P. Verburg, and A. Moilanen. 2014. "Global protected area expansion is compromised by projected land-use and parochialism." *Nature* 516, no. 7531: 383–6. https://doi.org/10.1038/nature14032

Prugh, L., C. Stoner, C. Epps, W. Bean, W. Ripple, A. Laliberte, and J. Brashares. 2009. "The rise of the mesopredator." *BioScience* 59, no. 9: 779–91. https://doi.org/10.1525/bio.2009.59.9.9

Puig-Montserrat, X., I. Torre, A. López-Baucells, E. Guerrieri, M. M. Monti, R. Ràfols-García, X. Ferrer, D. Gisbert, and C. Flaquer. 2015. "Pest control service provided by bats in Mediterranean rice paddies: linking agroecosystems structure to ecological functions." *Mammalian Biology* 80, no. 3: 237–45. https://doi.org/10.1016/j.mambio.2015.03.008

Puttock, A., H. A. Graham, A. M. Cunliffe, M. Elliott, and R. E. Brazier. 2017. "Eurasian beaver activity increases water storage, attenuates flow and mitigates diffuse pollution from intensively-managed grasslands." *Science of the Total Environment* 576: 430–43. https://doi.org/10.1016/j.scitotenv.2016.10.122

Redford, K. 1992. "The empty forest." *BioScience* 42, no. 6: 412–22. https://doi.org/10.2307/1311860

Redmond, I. 2001. "Coltan boom, gorilla bust." Report for the Dian Fossey Gorilla Fund (Europe) and Born Free. http://bornfree.codeomega.co.uk/wp-content/uploads/2016/12/coltan.pdf

Reeder, D. M., C. L. Frank, G. G. Turner, C. U. Meteyer, A. Kurta, E. R. Britzke, and M. E. Vodzak. 2012. "Frequent arousal from hibernation linked to severity of infection and mortality in bats with white-nose syndrome." *PLoS One* 7 (6).

Reeder, D., K. Helgen, and D. Wilson. 2007. "Global trends and biases in new mammal species discoveries." Occasional Papers, Museum of Texas Tech University. https://doi.org/10.5962/bhl.title.156951

Regan, E., L. Santini, L. Ingwall-King, M. Hoffmann, C. Rondinini, A. Symes, J. Taylor, and S. Butchart. 2015. "Global trends in the status of bird and mammal pollinators." *Conservation Letters* 8, no. 6: 397–403. https://doi.org/10.1111/conl.12162

Riccucci, M., and B. Lanza. 2014. "Bats and insect pest control: a review." *Vespertilio* 17: 161–9.

Ridder, M. de, M. Ericsson, A. Usanov, W. Auping, S. Lingemann, L. T. Espinoza, M. Farooki, H. Sievers, and M. Liedtke. 2013. "Coltan, Congo and conflict: Polinares case study." The Hague Centre for Strategic Studies.

Riebesell, U., K. G. Schulz, R. G. J. Bellerby, M. Botros, P. Fritsche, M. Meyerhöfer, C. Neill, et al. 2007. "Enhanced biological carbon consumption in a high CO_2 ocean." *Nature* 450, no. 7169: 545–8.

Ripple, W., K. Abernethy, M. Betts, G. Chapron, R. Dirzo, M. Galetti, T. Levi, P. Lindsey, D. Macdonald, and B. Machovina. 2016. "Bushmeat hunting and extinction risk to the world's mammals." *Royal Society Open Science* 3, no. 10: 160498. https://doi.org/10.1098/rsos.160498

Roman, J., J. A. Estes, L. Morissette, C. Smith, D. Costa, J. McCarthy, J. B. Nation, S. Nicol, A. Pershing, and V. Smetacek. 2014. "Whales as marine ecosystem engineers." *Frontiers in Ecology and the Environment* 12, no. 7: 377–85.

Roman, J., J. Nevins, M. Altabet, H. Koopman, and J. McCarthy. 2016. "Endangered right whales enhance primary productivity in the Bay of Fundy." *PloS One* 11, no. 6.

Rushton, J., R. Viscarra, C. Viscarra, F. Basset, R. Baptista, and D. Brown. 2005. "How important is bushmeat consumption in South America: now and in the future." Wildlife policy briefing no. 11. London: Overseas Development Institute.

Sarti, F. M., C. Adams, C. Morsello, N. Van Vliet, T. Schor, B. Yagüe, L. Tellez, M. Paula Quiceno-Mesa, and D. Cruz. 2015. "Beyond protein intake: bushmeat as source of micronutrients in the Amazon." *Ecology and Society* 20, 4.

Shanee, N., A. P. Mendoza, and S. Shanee. 2017. "Diagnostic overview of the illegal trade in primates and law enforcement in Peru." *American Journal of Primatology* 79, 11: e22516.

Sherwin, H. A., W. I. Montgomery, and M. G. Lundy. 2013. "The impact and implications of climate change for bats." *Mammal Review* 43, no. 3: 171–82.

Singleton, I., S. A. Wich, M. Nowak, and G. Usher. 2017. "*Pongo abelii* (errata version published in 2018)." *The IUCN Red List of Threatened Species* 2017: e.T121097935A123797627. https://dx.doi.org/10.2305/IUCN.UK.2017-3.RLTS.T121097935A115575085.en

Sobral, M., K. Silvius, H. Overman, L. Oliveira, T. Raab, and J. Fragoso. 2017. "Mammal diversity influences the carbon cycle through trophic interactions in the Amazon."

Nature Ecology and Evolution 1, no. 11: 1670–6. https://doi.org/10.1038/s41559-017-0334-0

Urban, M. 2015. "Accelerating extinction risk from climate change." *Science* 348, no. 6234: 571–3. https://doi.org/10.1126/science.aaa4984

Valderrama, C., R. Hoogesteijn, and E. Payán. 2016. *GRECO: Manual de campo para el manejo del conflicto entre humanos y felinos.* Panthera y USFWS. Cali, Colombia: Fernando Peña Editores.

Van Vliet, N., M. P. Quiceno, D. Cruz, L. J. Neves de Aquino, B. Yagüe, T. Schor, S. Hernandez, and R. Nasi. 2015. "Bushmeat networks link the forest to urban areas in the trifrontier region between Brazil, Colombia, and Peru." *Ecology and Society* 20, no. 3.

Van Vuuren, D. P., M. Kok, S. van der Esch, J. C. M. van Meijl, and A. A. Tabeau. 2012. *Roads from Rio+ 20: pathways to achieve global sustainability goals by 2050.* PBL.

Verant, M. L., J. G. Boyles, W. Waldrep Jr., G. Wibbelt, and D. S. Blehert. 2012. "Temperature-dependent growth of *Geomyces destructans,* the fungus that causes bat white-nose syndrome." *PloS One* 7, no. 9.

Visconti, P., M. Bakkenes, D. Baisero, T. Brooks, S. Butchart, L. Joppa, R. Alkemade, M. Di Marco, L. Santini, and M. Hoffmann. 2016. "Projecting global biodiversity indicators under future development scenarios." *Conservation Letters* 9, no. 1: 5–13. https://doi.org/10.1111/conl.12159

Wanger, T. C., K. Darras, S. Bumrungsri, T. Tscharntke, and A. M. Klein. 2014. "Bat pest control contributes to food security in Thailand." *Biological Conservation* 171: 220–3. https://doi.org/10.1016/j.biocon.2014.01.030

Whitaker, J. 1995. "Food of the big brown bat *Eptesicus fuscus* from maternity colonies in Indiana and Illinois." *American Midland Naturalist* 346–60.

Wibbelt, G., M. S. Moore, T. Schountz, and C. C. Voigt. 2010. "Emerging diseases in Chiroptera: why bats?" *Biology Letters* 6: 438–40. http://doi.org/10.1098/rsbl.2010.0267

Wilkie, D. S., and J. F. Carpenter. 1999. "Bushmeat hunting in the Congo Basin: an assessment of impacts and options for mitigation." *Biodiversity & Conservation* 8, no. 7: 927–55.

Wohl, E. 2013. "Landscape-scale carbon storage associated with beaver dams." *Geophysical Research Letters* 40, no. 14: 3631–6. https://doi.org/10.1002/grl.50710

Wright, J., C. Jones, and A. Flecker. 2002. "An ecosystem engineer, the beaver, increases species richness at the landscape scale." *Oecologia* 132, no. 1: 96–101. https://doi.org/10.1007/s00442-002-0929-1

Endnote

1. Like mammals, birds and amphibians also suffer tremendously from habitat loss and overexploitation to different degrees, and their endangerment is strictly related to the threats to mammal population from agriculture and other human activities, leading, in turn, to pollution, climate change, and species invasion (Grenyer et al. 2006).

Chapter 11

Conserving Insects

Michael J. Samways, Pedro Cardoso, and Charl Deacon

> "The beauty of a crisis is that it holds within its image inherent change." —*Yatri*

More than 1 million insects have been scientifically described, with an estimated five times that number probably still to be discovered. With this diversity of species, it comes as no surprise that various insect groups play significant roles in human food production. Aboveground, many help crop production through pollination, decomposition, and multiple other ecosystem services. Conversely, a small but important number are pests, reducing production both before and after harvest. Belowground, insects of many kinds, along with fellow invertebrates such as mites, millipedes, and certain crustaceans, help maintain a healthy soil. A few others are pests of plant roots. Both above and below ground, some insects do harm by transmitting plant diseases, as do others to livestock. The key to safe and sustainable future food production is to encourage the insect species that maintain natural ecosystem processes while controlling pests largely by ensuring balanced crop systems and without damaging the environment or human health.

A Multitude of Little Workers

Insects live in, on, or among a vast array of living and dead plant, animal, and fungal tissue. About a quarter feed on each other as parasites or predators.

Insects often also live in partnerships with many other organisms. Mutually beneficial bacteria and other single-celled organisms living within insects' bodies enable them to digest cellulose, making them significant herbivores globally. Critically, their partnership with flowering plants, including many crop species, has enabled both pollinators and plants to largely shape the green world as we know it.

Although plants make up the bulk of the world's structural diversity, it is insects and other invertebrates that underpin that diversity. These tiny animals break down living and dead organic matter, making smaller fragments available to other organisms, such as bacteria and fungi. This activity leads to healthy soil formation and, importantly, the release of nutrients then available for new plant growth.

It is the abundance, as well as the diversity, of insects that is so important for sustaining the world's terrestrial ecosystems, both natural and agricultural. Large numbers, coupled with mobility (often through flight), enable insects to distribute nutrients across landscapes and even regions. High above us, there are trillions of individual insects on the move, making use of atmospheric airflows. By moving around and playing out roles as predators, prey, competitors, and vectors of nutrients, energy and pathogens, these insects greatly influence our global ecosystem (Hu et al. 2016).

Insects as Service Providers

Insects play a major role in the ecosystem goods and services on which humans depend. For a sustainable future, we need to maintain the circular strategy of conserving intact ecosystems to conserve insects, which, in turn, keep ecosystems healthy and resilient. Simply put, we benefit when insects benefit from effective conservation action.

Ecosystem goods and services include production of goods (e.g., food, new chemicals), regulation services (e.g., water filtration, biological control of pests), supporting services (e.g., soil formation, nutrient cycling, pollination), and cultural services (e.g., spiritual, aesthetic, recreational) (Millennium Ecosystem Assessment 2005). Although most insects play a role, directly or indirectly, in all of these, some insects, such as pests and parasites, harm human well-being. Yet the good news is that the insect pests have natural control agents, including parasitic wasps and predatory insects such as ladybugs and lacewings.

All Is Not Well for Insects

The International Union for Conservation of Nature (IUCN) Species Survival Commission's Red List (www.iucnredlist.org) to date has been able to assess only a few of the vast number of insect species. Nevertheless, the threats facing those that have been Red-Listed also affect insects in general. Those threats include habitat loss from logging, habitat loss from agriculture, infrastructure development such as urbanization, habitat loss and fragmentation from transportation and service corridors, invasive alien species, changes in fire regimes, pollution, climate change and severe weather, and mining (Gerlach et al. 2012). For freshwater insects, the most severe threats include pollution, dam construction, and poor water management, which together pose a greater threat than all other categories (Darwall et al. 2012). These pressures and subsequent threats to humankind are now of great concern globally (Cardoso et al. 2020).

Alarmingly, any one threat is often made worse when two or more threats operate together, such as habitat loss combined with insecticide drift, leading to lack of functional activity. These adverse combinations on the ground are all further influenced by climate change, which becomes ever more critical when insect population densities become lower. It is then a downward spiral toward impoverished ecosystems and increased risk to long-term food production.

Climate change is about more than a rise in temperature. It also includes more intense, widespread and longer-lasting weather-induced events, including increased severity and frequency of droughts, fire, storms, and floods. Indirectly, increased Earth crust activity leads to higher volcanic activity, with risk not just of large pyroclastic outpourings but also widespread dust events (Thornton 1996). All these factors affect insect numbers and their activity.

Other threats, local in effect, have an impact across the world simply because they have become common. Such threats include the widespread application of many types of pesticides that enter soil and freshwater systems. The spread of invasive alien species is also a major problem. These invasive species range from terrestrial, bankside, and aquatic plants to new insect and mite pests on plants, rats and mice consuming the local insect fauna, and crayfish and mussels changing the character of freshwater communities.

In addition to global threats, insects are subject to various types and proportions of threats at different locations, depending on the human activity taking place. Threats facing tropical forests include great destruction of trees and loss of a host of local species of significant ecological value. This not only changes natural ecosystem processes but also reduces opportunities for sustainable food production. In Europe in particular, increased atmospheric and agricultural nitrification of grasslands and rivers have great impacts on ecosystem stability and functioning. Meanwhile, certain towns and cities are facing more extreme floods, often resulting from tree removal in the upper reaches of rivers or the draining of natural flood barriers such as marshes. All these physical and chemical changes have major impacts on local insect species (figure 11-1).

Additional human-induced threats to insects include increased light, noise, and electromagnetic pollution. In addition, one harmful change can lead to another. Loss of wilderness is associated with roads penetrating intact ecosystems, fragmenting them, and leading to establishment of other human infrastructures, followed by establishment of villages with food gardens and the application of harmful pesticides. Villages then become towns, bringing other changes, such as direct killing by moving traffic, greatly increased light pollution that disorients night-flying insects, and water pollution that kills aquatic insects.

Many impacts are not immediately obvious and are known as enigmatic ecological impacts (Raiter et al. 2014). These include cumulative effects (individual impacts accumulate over space or time, and then only become significant in their totality, e.g., long-lasting insecticide residues, a gradual increase in abundance and number of invasive alien species), offsite impacts (difficult to account for at one site but impactful elsewhere, such as excessive nutrient input, or light or water pollution farther away, removal of marshland leading to great changes in river dynamics), cryptic impacts (might not be immediately obvious, including effects on insect movement, communication, or reproduction, and even interactions with other insect species, as well as sublethal doses of insecticides that do not necessarily kill insects but have subtle effects on behavior and reproduction, in turn leading to population decline), and secondary impacts (not considered the prime focus but have a harmful impact, such as a road being cut for access to a site of interest or a new dam or area of forest being logged). Enigmatic ecological impacts are not mutually exclusive and often operate synergistically, with far-reaching effects on ecological stability.

The urgency of addressing current impacts is brought home when we bear in mind that an estimated 10^9 hectares of natural ecosystems will be converted to agriculture by the year 2050, with a 2.4- to 2.7-fold increase in nitrogen- and phosphorus-driven eutrophication of terrestrial, freshwater,

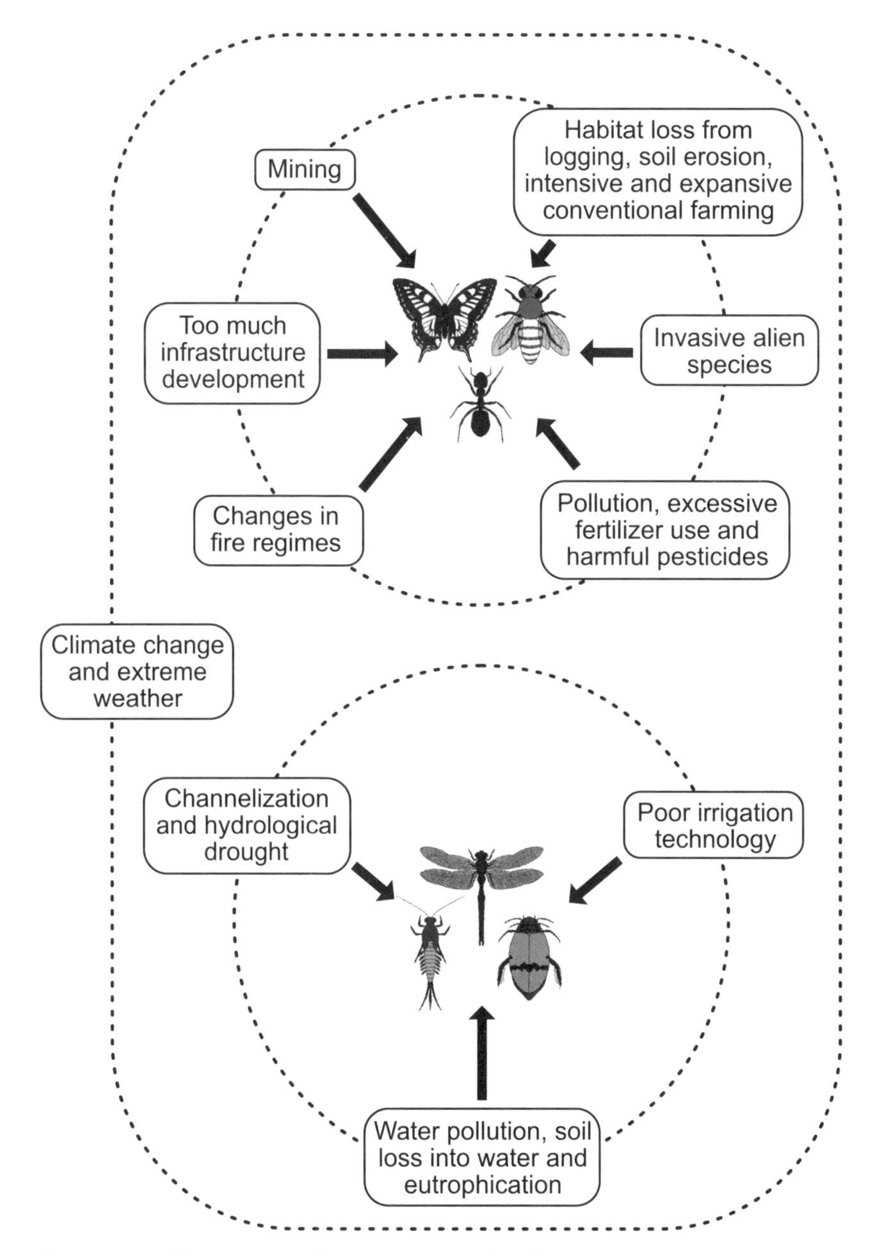

Figure 11-1. The important threats to terrestrial and aquatic insects.

and near-shore marine ecosystems (Tilman et al. 2001). Ways of getting off this treadmill are being explored, but still much more conservation action is urgently needed. In terms of insects, there have been some worrying signs, which have shaken the general perception that we need not bother ourselves with insects when perceived "bigger issues" such as political upheaval are at stake. Among the recent shocks is the massive loss of pollinators in many parts of the world. It is tangible and real, and it affects us directly by reducing our food supplies (Vanbergen et al. 2013). Populations of some bumble bees in the United States have declined by as much as 96 percent in abundance, and geographic ranges have decreased from 23–87 percent in just twenty years (Cameron et al. 2011). Similar losses may occur among soil organisms. These stealth events (recognized only after having seriously taken hold) mean that insect conservation is a vital and urgent challenge, with plenty of solutions available (Samways 2020; Samways et al. 2020).

Valuing Insects

To conserve insects, we need to better communicate their value from societal, political, and scientific perspectives. Valuation is the foundation for what we do in practice, as it sets standards and directions. Yet valuing insects in purely economic terms is not always beneficial for biodiversity conservation as a whole. As with many other aspects of conservation, sound economic ethics should be integrated with a broad understanding of how ecosystems affect our well-being (Chan et al. 2016). This requires a focus on functional diversity, summed up as how, when, and where insects interact with each other and with other organisms. In short, insects are more than just items with individual value; instead, they maintain the warp and weft of terrestrial and aquatic life.

Ecosystem function can be evaluated on different spatial scales, from the smallest, such as microhabitat or local patch, to farm-sized patches of land, to the interactive relationship between farms and with surrounding natural areas, and finally to whole regions and the planet. We cannot, and certainly do not, understand all the interactions in which insects are involved, especially when we consider that a very small ecosystem of just a thousand species translates into a potential of half a million interactions. But a sensible shortcut is to conserve healthy functioning ecosystems, with natural and high levels of species richness and composition (Dainese et al. 2019). This is a benchmark against which we compare farming systems for their ability to remain intact after harvesting. Healthy farming systems must be resilient, especially in the face of climate change (Papanikolaou et al. 2017).

The challenge is that ecosystem function and resilience, just like insect conservation, are often perceived as unseen, abstract, and nebulous issues. Because most insects are not iconic or even particularly visible, their conservation can be difficult to justify. The justification becomes more apparent, however, when we focus on the landscape level. Even without a detailed understanding of ecology, people can appreciate the importance of a visibly healthy landscape. Strategic conservation of landscapes means that we can simultaneously conserve many species and their interactions. Furthermore, by taking this approach, insect conservationists can help guide sustainable food production (Gennari and Navarro 2019). The landscape approach is quite literally the larger picture, and individual insects are the brush strokes in that picture.

The insect crises unfolding in many quarters of the world are now causing an awakening in the collective human psyche (Simaika and Samways 2018). People around the globe are beginning to realize that the unprecedented, colossal loss of insects must absolutely be reckoned with, alongside climate change.

Insect Populations Are Naturally Dynamic

Insect populations are highly dynamic over time. Individuals shift around the landscape as they respond to environmental conditions such as seasonal changes in temperature and rainfall. Insects are constantly in search of optimal conditions to feed, breed, and rest, leading to the continual reshaping of biological communities. In turn, plant-dependent insects drive the population dynamics of parasitic and predatory insects, which also respond to prey and the changing conditions around them (figure 11-2).

Many traditional farmers recognize these dynamics because they are intimately connected with the land, quite literally on a minute-by-minute basis. They appreciate that sustainability, especially in hard climatic times, takes priority over maximizing food production per unit area, the essential principle of mechanized conventional agriculture.

Traditional food production involves covering the soil by establishing living, often usable cover crops or by spreading plant remains as mulch to encourage a living rather than a dead soil base. Nurse trees are used to protect the young crop plants, and crop types are often intermixed (known as polycropping) to encourage a range of natural enemies and reduce pest outbreaks and disease spread. Pest caterpillars that have died naturally are pounded into

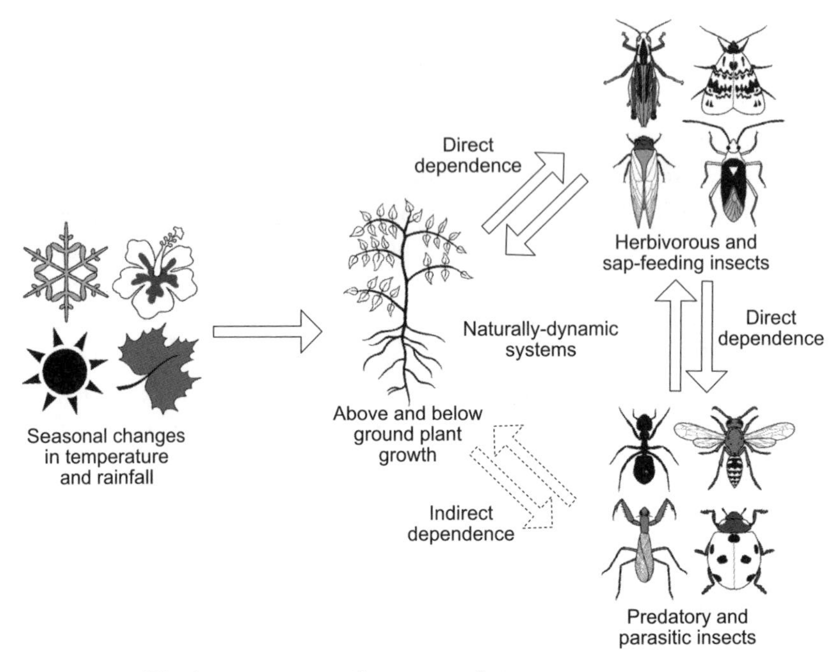

Figure 11-2. The dynamic nature of insect populations.

water, and the organic solution is then applied to the crop to control further caterpillar outbreaks, subjecting the pest to specific viral pathogens that do not put human health at risk.

We have a lot to learn from these traditional systems. They were honed through survival within the farming community over millennia. Bringing in products, whether new plant varieties, pesticides, or fertilizers, could be done only by horse and cart. Food production was (and still is in some parts of the world) based on self-reliance, unlike the hugely negentropic, internationalized system of modern conventional agriculture, where pesticides, fertilizers, and other inputs are often internationally sourced. These inputs require huge economic outlays for manufacturing and transport, which inevitably means that production must be maximized to cover basic costs while making a profit.

The modern focus on high yields has clear downsides. Globally, an average of 35 percent of crop yields are lost to preharvest pests, and in some developing countries these losses can reach 70 percent (Popp and Hantos 2011). Problems do not end there, with postharvest losses to pests and deterioration sometimes being total (Boxall 2001). Meanwhile, almost 36 billion tons of soil erode from arable lands per year (Borrelli et al. 2013). This is of great concern because soil structure can take decades to recover, if at all, once the living soil layer, the 30 centimeters between life and death of the planet, is lost. Restoring forests can take decades, if not centuries. The full complement of insects can also take this long (and sometimes longer) to recover.

But let us not be naive either. There is no paradise in farming traditionalism. Pests, diseases, droughts, frosts, excessive clouding from volcanism, and political pressures and upheavals, have all contributed to food production disasters in the past, leading to famine. The human response was to move away to new areas or somehow pull through, surviving on scavenged resources.

The path to more resilient, more reliable food production is to take the best of traditionalism (working with nature not against it) while avoiding the risks by using the best modern knowledge and technology. We have a long way to go, because ecological illiteracy is common among the nearly 2.5 billion smallholders who cultivate the world's arable land. The concept of the value of ecosystem services such as biological pest control is unknown to almost 70 percent of them, deepening their dependency on chemically synthesized pesticides. Much more must be done to educate these farmers on agroecological approaches if there is to be a sustainable future for the land (Wyckhuys et al. 2019). This is underscored by the fact that there are about 200,000 acute poisoning deaths from pesticides each year, 99 percent of which occur in developing countries (United Nations 2017).

Economic and Environmental Benefits of Conserving Insects

All ecological services can be translated into monetary value. Costanza et al. (1997) estimated a global value of ecosystem services at US$33 trillion annually. In turn, in just the United States, ecosystem services provided by insects have been estimated at US$57 billion per year, and services provided by dung beetles to the cattle industry reach US$380 million (Losey and Vaughan 2006), and in the United Kingdom, dung beetle services have an annual value of £367 million (Beynon et al. 2015). Insect pollination has a global economic value in the region of US$235–577 billion per year (IPBES 2016). This means that preserving ecosystem services provided by insects is not only good for the species but economically sensible and the only way forward. As an example, the economic benefit of switching from conventional to organic-based pollination in the case of oilseed rape in Ireland is US$4.38 million, with pollinator exclusion leading to a 27 percent decrease in number of seeds produced and a 30 percent decrease in seed weight per pod (Stanley et al. 2013).

It is important to be careful when considering monetary value alongside insect conservation value. Cost-effective strategies that promote crop pollination by wild bees use a different set of species from threatened bees of conservation significance (Kleijn et al. 2015). Another note of caution is that many of the current estimates of service value focus on easily visible species such as decomposition and dung beetles, pollination and bees, and energy flow and aquatic insects. In reality, it is the vast hoard of tiny insects, both adult and young, that play a major role in maintaining soil quality or keeping pests at bay. It is critical to expand our vision to lesser known and more cryptic groups and activities that we suspect are playing a major role in underpinning food production.

Policies for Insect Conservation

Engaging Ecological Principles

Better stewardship of agroecosystems is critically needed to optimize the value of natural processes. A transformation to ecologically sound methods of farming would be a win–win, where agriculture conserves insects while becoming more sustainable overall. The aim is to preserve a mosaic of natural areas across the agricultural landscape so that habitats are available for a wide range of insect species at various life stages.

This is done by planting or allowing establishment of natural vegetation both within fields (intercrops) and around the fields (Winter et al. 2018). Although there are globally accepted principles for accomplishing this, each farming area tailors its precise methods to the local environmental and socioeconomic conditions. This approach considers insect abundance and diversity.

Consideration of spatial scale relative to function is also important. For example, wasps used to control pests vary in their ability to disperse and locate the pests. In short, agricultural landscapes should function as do local natural ecosystems, with adequate species to sustain key services, such as pollination, decomposition of organic matter, and biological control of pests.

Positive Strategies

Agroenvironment schemes are effective when based on sound ecological, management, and social practices. However, biodiversity-friendly farming does not automatically ensure that every ecosystem service is provided. Instead, each farm has to be managed with the desired service (e.g., pollination vs. biological control) in mind.

Uncultivated areas, such as hedgerows and flowery roadsides, can greatly increase the diversity of insects, such as pollinators and natural predators of pest species. This means increasing the proportion of natural land relative to planted areas. Further improvements come from establishing pesticide-free field borders and introducing conservation headlands (the outer margins of crop fields with reduced pesticide input). These improvements all support insect survival in the face of climate change while maintaining crop production. They tend to be most effective on farms that have preserved some natural areas, whereas highly degraded systems must be rehabilitated over time.

One of the most effective strategies for conserving insects is transitioning from conventional to organic production. Farmers can begin the process in individual fields, expanding over time to other fields nearby. A first premise is to cultivate great vegetation variety, in terms of both plant structure and range of plant resources, especially flowers (Holzschuh et al. 2007). Organic and diversified fields with high-quality habitats have higher bee species richness than seen in monocultures, for example. Even remnant prairie wetlands provide high-quality habitat for many native pollinators while also benefiting production (Vickruck et al. 2019).

When compared with conventional farming, organic farming leads to an average increase of 30 percent in species richness, with benefits greatest on fairly intensive farms (Tuck et al. 2014). These benefits assume that local insect species are present nearby, which may not always be the case when extensive and intensive farms make the transition from monocultures to organic and diversified fields. Again, spatial scale is important, with most improvement in species diversity at the field level (10.5 percent improvement), followed by the farm level (4.6 percent) and then the region (3.1 percent) (Schneider et al. 2014). However, some caution and knowledge of natural insect residents is needed, because gains vary between crops and insect groups. Although some highly productive cereal fields make gains in insect diversity, they experience a reduction in yield. Although insect conservation is more effective in low-productivity systems or on nonagricultural land, in the case of cereals, grouping organic farms into one area is the best practice so that neither yield nor insect diversity is harmed (Gabriel et al. 2013). Set-aside conservation areas and organic fields can function as source habitats for conventionally managed fields, suggesting countryside-wide benefits to insect diversity from organic farming (Rundlöf et al. 2008) (figure 11-3).

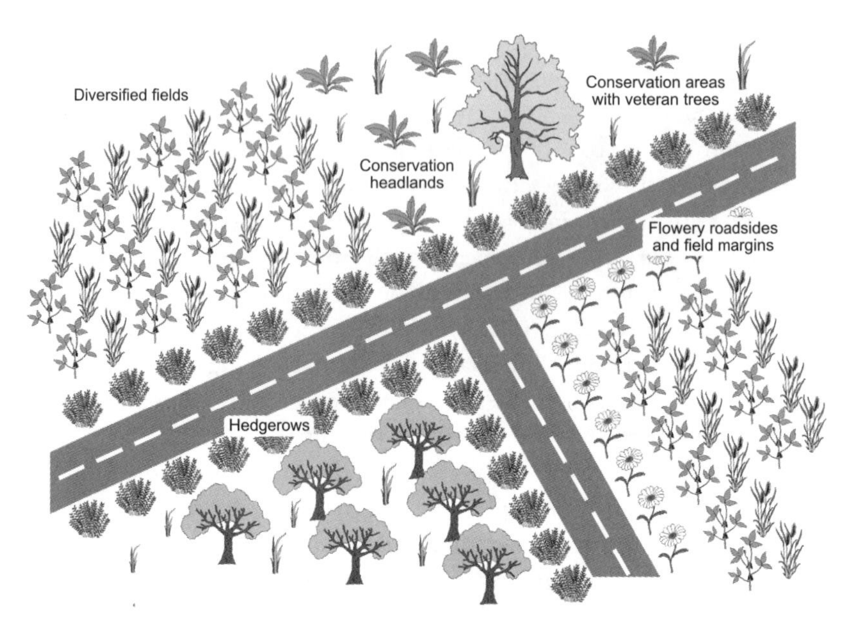

Figure 11-3. Positive strategies for better use and conservation of insects in food production.

Country Cases: Eating Insects

Humans, especially in warm climates, have eaten insects for millennia, with 2 million people today making insects a part of their everyday diet. Insects are nutritious, high in protein, dietary minerals (including calcium, copper, iron, selenium, and zinc), and healthy fatty acids, all of which are particularly important for children's health (figure 11-4). Insects eaten include beetles (31 percent of all insect species eaten globally), moth larvae (18 percent), bees, wasps, and ants (14 percent), sucking insects such as cicadas and true bugs (13 percent), termites (3 percent), dragonflies (3 percent), flies (2 percent), and other insects (5 percent), illustrating the variety of insects and the types available for human consumption according to local ecosystems and human cultures (van Huis 2013).

Although some cultures have always eaten insects, the idea is spreading even in societies where this has not traditionally been common. The practice is being driven by an urgent need to produce more protein for both humans and livestock. Domestic red meat production requires huge resources, including three times the energy per unit weight as insects.

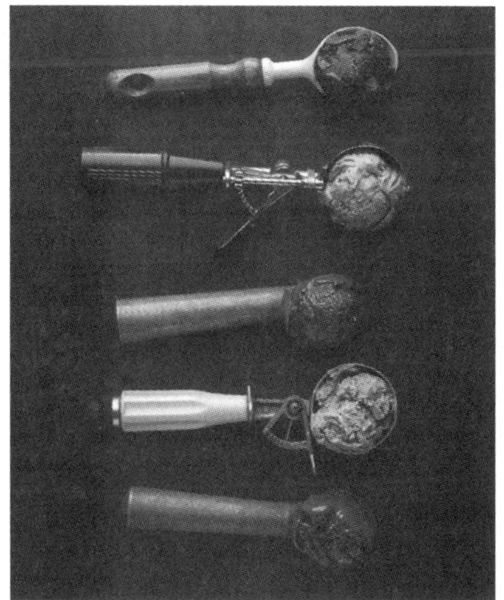

Figure 11-4. Versatility of insects as human food. *Photos:* Gourmet Grubb, Cape Town. *Notes:* EntoMilk, dairy alternative made entirely from black soldier fly larvae (top left). Gourmet gelatos, styled ice cream made from EntoMilk, honey, and natural flavoring ingredients (top right). Dumpling made with EntoMilk filling, served at The Insect Experience, Cape Town, 2019 (left). A canape served at The Insect Experience, a tartlet filled with EntoMilk paneer and wild mushrooms topped with toasted black soldier fly larvae and microgreens (below).

However, collecting or rearing insects for consumption has challenges. One problem is that insects, at least in modern Westernized societies, are often considered dirty and even disgusting. This perception challenge is being overcome by developing food products that are more visually appealing, such as creative cubes made of insects. Soups also work well; the larvae of the European cockchafer beetle are a traditional component of soup in Central Europe.

Insects traditionally have been harvested from the wild, mostly for personal consumption or for sale at local markets, where pound for pound, insects can attain a better price than beef. Although wild harvesting of insects in rainforests can risk overexploitation of the target species, it can indirectly protect forests and the insect species that are not being eaten. For instance, using trees for wild harvesting of insects means they are protected, and along with them, specialist insect species in threatened primary forest. In contrast, edible insects can also cause crop damage, and so the more they are harvested, the better.

More recently, attention has turned to developing insect farms. They focus on particular species and are considered an environmentally sustainable food system. Insects are classed as mini-livestock, requiring far less space than other livestock, and they provide good and quick financial returns. But rearing insects on a large scale is new, not easy, and still very much in the experimental stage. Besides technical challenges, there is also a risk with transporting and rearing insects for consumption outside their native ranges. This may be a gateway to the spread of invasive alien species, significantly damaging ecosystems. Consequently, the blossoming entomophagy industry may benefit from more research on the insects that can be reared within their native ranges, in order to reduce the risk of accidental invasions.

Some edible insects can be semicultivated by manipulating their habitat, including certain termites and various moth larvae in Africa, eggs of bugs in Mexico, and palm weevils in tropical Asia and South America. The highly predaceous Asian weaver ant (*Oecophylla smaragdina*) has been used to protect crops such as citrus from pests for more than 2,000 years. Its larvae and pupae are also popular as food items. The worker ants are tangy and used to garnish fish soup.

Managing Insect Pests for Safer Food

Reducing pest populations to minimize yield losses is one of the central challenges of farming. Losses can be high, especially in developing areas, where a third of the crop may be eaten by pests. Although synthetic pesticides have greatly reduced crop loss, many carry risks for both human health and biodiversity. Because of their short lifespans and quick reproduction, many pests have become genetically resistant to many insecticides, reducing their effectiveness. This can result in farmers applying yet more insecticides and getting on a never-ending treadmill of pesticide resistance.

A safer and more effective approach is integrated pest management (IPM). IPM uses natural approaches, such as using natural predators and parasites as biological control agents against insects and other pests. These controls are combined with ecologically sound growing methods such as intercropping. Conservation headlands are also put into place, where no pesticides or herbicides are applied, such as with potato and wheat cultivation. This encourages the growth of broad-leaved plants, which not only increase insect species richness but also invite the natural enemies of pests.

Even restricting the numbers of types and applications of pesticides benefits many insects. In France, pesticide use can be reduced by 42 percent without any negative effects on productivity and profitability on high-intensity farms (Lechenet et al. 2017). Insect pests can also be precision-controlled by applying insecticides only where they are especially bad (i.e., in pest hotspots). Other spatially explicit approaches include application of benign insecticides to the tops of citrus trees to reduce extremely high levels of the red scale (*Aonidiella aurantii*) pest in that part of the tree. Meanwhile, lower down in the trees, natural enemies are used, including the ladybug (*Chilocorus nigritus*), which reduces the fully adult stages, and parasitic wasps (*Aphytis* spp.) against the younger stages.

The biological control component of IPM has worked particularly well in woody crops. On Indonesian cacao farms, ants eat herbivorous pests on the crop, and a 30–40 percent shade tree cover maintains the effectiveness of this natural control. European hedgerows improve connectivity across agricultural areas, which improves biological control and pollinator activity. Mature hedgerows are especially valuable for slow-dispersing predatory ground beetles, and high spatial and temporal variation of wild plant growth in and around fields also promotes ground beetle activity.

The use of natural biological control is further enhanced when farms switch from conventional to organic methods. When farms cooperate on IPM at large scales, a coordinated approach known as area-wide pest management, they not only improve the strategy's effectiveness but also promote conservation of insects in general, especially when conservancies (areas of set-aside land) are also involved.

IPM involves a thorough understanding of the biology of individual pests and their predators. The full pest complex of a particular crop in a local area also needs to be understood in order to reduce pesticide use. Pesticides are then only used at specific times and very strategically. However, concentrations must never be reduced, because doing so would increase chemical resistance, especially as the climate warms.

Generalist natural predators with many prey–pest hosts, as well as introduced biological control agents, respond better to complex landscapes than simplified conventional systems. This contrasts with the activity of specialist natural enemies, which respond more positively at the small spatial scale of a field or small farm. Natural enemies and pollinators have similar responses to landscape complexity, indicating that both will benefit from well-designed and well-managed agroecosystems. Overall, pest control can be up to 46 percent less effective in simple, homogeneous agricultural systems than in complex systems with varied vegetation within and around crop fields (Rusch et al. 2016).

This means that conserving and restoring natural or seminatural habitats is an essential first step in ensuring that pests can be controlled through natural enemies. There can also be highly targeted improvements, such as providing more nectar for hoverflies, the larvae of which are important predators of aphids. Overall, better and more sensitive IPM is essential for the resilience of agroecosystems, especially in the face of climate change (figure 11-5).

Insect Conservation and Food Production in South Africa

South Africa is not only a dry country but also subject to El Niño–Southern Oscillations. Water availability is therefore a crucial issue, making food production challenging and unpredictable. Not surprisingly, reservoirs, both large and small, are a common sight across the region and on farms. Maintaining these water reserves emanating from runoff and percolation is critical. Using them efficiently is essential not only for food production but also for ensuring that ecosystem processes continue into the future.

Inevitably, there is some tension between food production and biodiversity conservation vying for water resources. This ostensible competition is magnified in dry South Africa, where most soils are not highly fertile, yet it is home to three global biodiversity hotspots with very high levels of local endemism. Maintaining the balance between food production and biodiversity conservation is challenging, but in reality, mutually acceptable approaches to water use have been widely adopted. One of the reasons for this is that both

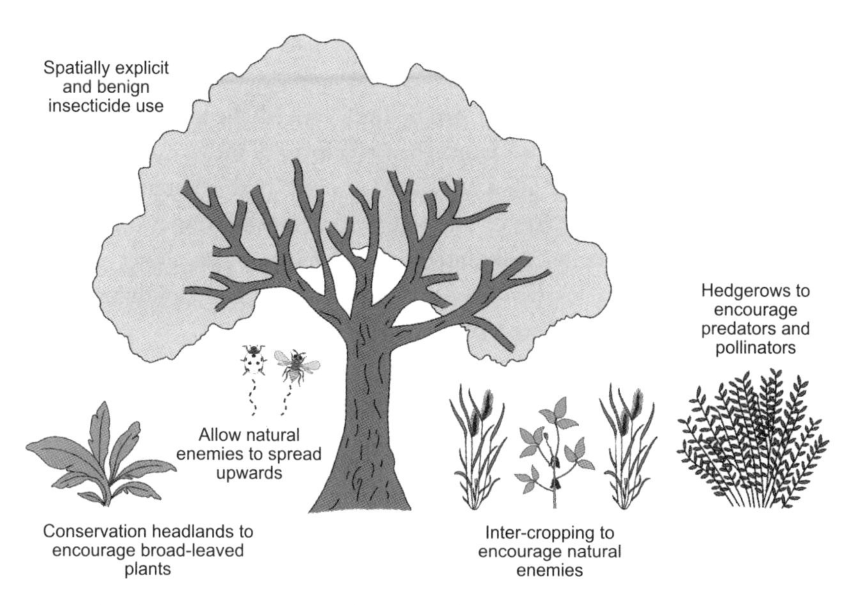

Figure 11-5. Important aspects of integrated pest management for insect pest suppression.

face a common threat: invasive alien plants (IAPs) (mostly eucalypts, mesquites, and pine trees).

Among the IAPs, alien trees are particularly threatening to both sectors. In former years, IAPs had severely invaded water courses and placed substantial pressure on groundwater resources. Consequently, IAPs placed a huge burden on water delivery to both natural and agricultural systems, especially because these alien trees are so thirsty. In response, a national Working for Water Programme was instigated not only to recharge catchments and alleviate the pressure on groundwater resources but also to supply jobs in a country where more than a quarter of the population is unemployed. Biodiversity conservation was not initially on the agenda. But it soon became clear that after tree removal, both aquatic and terrestrial biodiversity can recover quickly. This was a pleasant surprise, but it also raised alarm bells that irreplaceable biodiversity was gradually being lost to a far greater extent than was realized. After an extensive survey of dragonflies, three species that were considered possibly extinct were found only where alien trees had been removed. Other narrow-range endemic dragonflies were at extremely low levels and surviving in a few uninvaded remnants. Other aquatic insects were in the same position. In short, the nationwide Working for Water Programme not only alleviated poverty but also was welcomed by the agricultural and conservation sectors. It is still an ongoing process to prevent alien recovery.

Terrestrial systems are also affected by IAPs. Indeed, the harmful footprint of IAPs is much greater on soil fauna than any form of intensive agriculture. But the good news is that when IAPs are removed, both natural vegetation and the soil fauna recover remarkably well. Although some aspects of species composition may be temporarily lost, they can return when source habitats are nearby. Important ecosystem services, such as healthy soil, pollination, and natural enemy presence, return in abundance.

Two central methods of protecting indigenous biodiversity, including insects, are land sparing and land sharing. Land sparing is practiced by establishing large-scale networks of interconnected conservation corridors. These ecological networks were pioneered in the forestry industry but are now being expanded to the agricultural sector (figure 11-6, above). Land sharing focuses on intercropping, where vegetation is established between cropping rows (figure 11-6, below). These sparing and sharing approaches are complementary and increasingly embraced by the farming community. Farmers are establishing conservancies, moving from conventional to organic agriculture, and developing a general willingness to work with, rather than against, nature. Together, these approaches are a win–win for food production and biodiversity conservation, both of which need reliable water sources.

Additionally, nationwide networks of protected areas and biosphere reserves are moving the country toward more security for both human food and local biodiversity. These advances are driven by increasingly effective cooperation between the agriculture and conservation sectors, which have become united in the face of the dual threats of water scarcity or unreliability and invasive plants.

Conclusions

The futures of humans and insects are entwined. They depend on healthy soil, water, air, and all biotic *interactions*. Earth is fragile but resilient. It has seen many changes and even great upheavals during its lifetime. Today it is richer in biodiversity than ever before. Maintaining the rich fabric of biodiversity gives both Earth and humans options for survival. Yet Earth will survive no matter what, albeit in a different biotic guise. We may not do as well. Our future now depends on ensuring that our actions focus on maintaining all biodiversity for planetary resilience. Maintaining the lives of insects is a major part of

Figure 11-6. Land uses techniques to foster biodiversity. *Notes:* Land sparing using corridors of remnant natural grassland between plantation blocks is good for indigenous biodiversity but also can be used for low-level herding (above). Land sharing using vegetated intercrops between vine rows enables many types of insects to ebb and flow across the landscape (below). *Photos:* M. J. Samways.

the resilience challenge. We desperately need to change our relationship with nature to provide us with food into the future. We have much of the basic science and technology for doing this. Now, especially in response to the ravages of the COVID-19 pandemic, is an opportunity to change our outlook and ways of working with nature and not against it. It is a time to reflect on all of life, including the great milieu of insects hidden in plain view, so essential to our survival, to seize the opportunity to strategize and act rapidly for a healthy planet for all life.

References

Beynon, S. A., W. A. Wainwright, and M. Christie. 2015. "The application of an ecosystem services framework to estimate the economic value of dung beetles to the U.K. cattle industry." *Ecological Entomology* 40: 124–35.

Borrelli, P., D. A. Robinson, L. R. Fleischer, E. Lugato, C. Ballabio, C. Alewell, S. Meusburger, B. Schütt, V. Ferro, V. Bagarello, K. Van Oost, L. Montanarella, and P. Panagos. 2013. "An assessment of the global impact of 21st century land use change on soil erosion." *Nature Communications* 8.

Boxall, R. A. 2001. "Post-harvest losses to insects: a world overview." *International Biodeterioration & Biodegradation* 48: 137–52.

Cameron, S. A., J. D. Lozier, J. P. Strange, J. B. Koch, N. Cordes, L. F. Solter, and T. L. Griswold. 2011. "Patterns of widespread decline in North American bumble bees." *Proceedings of the National Academy of Sciences of the USA* 108: 662–7.

Cardoso, P., P. S. Barton, K. Birkhofer, F. Chichorro, C. Deacon, T. Fartmann, M. J. Samways. 2020. "Scientists' warning to humanity on insect extinctions." *Biological Conservation* 242: 108426.

Chan, K. M. A., P. Balvanera, K. Benessaiah, M. Chapman, S. Díaz, E. Gómez-Baggethun, R. Gould, N. Hannahs, K. Jax, S. Klain, et al. 2016. "Opinion: Why protect nature? Rethinking values and the environment." *Proceedings of the National Academy of Sciences of the USA* 113: 1462–5.

Costanza, R., R. d'Arge, R. de Groot, S. Farber, M. Grasso, B. Hannon, et al. 1997. "The value of the world's ecosystem services and natural capital." *Nature* 387: 253–60.

Daniese, M., E. A. Martin, M. A. Aizen, M. Albrecht, I. Bartomeus, R. Bommarco, . . . I. Steffen-Dewenter. 2019. "A global synthesis reveals biodiversity-mediated benefits for crop production." *Science Advances* 5: eaax121.

Darwall, W., M. Seddon, V. Clausnitzer, and N. Cumberlidge. 2012. "Freshwater invertebrate life." Pages 26–32 in *Spineless: Status and Trends of the World's Invertebrates*, ed. B. Collen, M. Böhm, R. Kemp, and J. E. M. Baillie. London: Zoological Society of London.

Gabriel, D., S. M. Sait, W. E. Kunin, and T. G. Benton. 2013. "Food production vs. biodiversity: comparing organic and conventional agriculture." *Journal of Applied Ecology* 50: 355–64.

Gennari, P., and D. K. Navarro. 2019. "The challenge of measuring agricultural sustainability in all its dimensions." *Journal of Sustainability Research* 1: e190013.

Gerlach, J., S. Hoffman Black, A. Hochkirch, S. Jepsen, M. Seddon, S. Spector, and P. Williams. 2012. "Terrestrial invertebrate life." Pages 46–7 in *Spineless: Status and Trends of the World's Invertebrates*, ed. B. Collen, M. Böhm, R. Kemp, and J. E. M. Baillie. London: Zoological Society of London.

Holzschuh, A., I. Steffan-Dewenter, D. Kleijn, and T. Tscharntke. 2007. "Diversity of flower-visiting bees in cereal fields: effects of farming system, landscape composition and regional context." *Journal of Applied Ecology* 44: 41–9.

Hu, G., K. S. Lim, N. Horvitz, S. J. Clark, D. R. Reynolds, N. Sapir, and J. W. Chapman. 2016. "Mass seasonal bioflows of high-flying insect migrants." *Science* 354: 1584–7.

IPBES. 2016. "The assessment report of the Intergovernmental Science-Policy Platform on Biodiversity and Ecosystem Services on pollinators, pollination and food production." S. G. Potts, V. L. Imperatriz-Fonseca, and H. T. Ngo, eds. Bonn, Germany: Secretariat of the Intergovernmental Science-Policy Platform on Biodiversity and Ecosystem Services.

Kleijn, D., R. Winfree, I. Bartomeus, L. G. Carvalheiro, M. Henry, R. Isaacs, A.-M. Klein, C. Kremen, L. K. M'Gonigle, R. Rader, et al. 2015. "Delivery of crop pollination services is an insufficient argument for wild pollinator conservation." *Nature Communications* 6: 7414.

Lechenet, M., F. Dessaint, G. Py, D. Makowski, and N. Munier-Jolain. 2017. "Reducing pesticide use while preserving crop productivity and profitability on arable farms." *Nature Plants* 3: 17008. doi:10.1038/nplants.2017.8

Losey, J. E. and M. Vaughan. 2006. "The economic value of ecological services provided by insects." *BioScience* 56: 311–23.

Millennium Ecosystem Assessment. 2005. *Ecosystems and Human Well-Being: Synthesis.* Washington, D.C.: Island Press.

Papanikolaou, A. D., I. Kühn, M. Frenzel, and O. Schweiger. 2017. "Semi-natural habitats mitigate the effects of temperature rise on wild bees." *Journal of Applied Ecology* 54: 527–36.

Popp, J., and K. Hantos. 2011. "The impact of crop protection on agricultural production." *Studies in Agricultural Economics N.* 113: 47–66.

Raiter, K. G., H. P. Possingham, S. M. Prober, and R. J. Hobbs. 2014. "Under the radar: mitigating enigmatic ecological impacts." *Trends in Ecology and Evolution* 29: 635–44.

Rundlöf, M., J. Bengtsson, and H. G. Smith. 2008. "Local and landscape effects of organic farming on butterfly species richness and abundance." *Journal of Applied Ecology* 45: 813–20.

Rusch, A., R. Chaplin-Kramer, M. M. Gardiner, V. Hawro, J. Holland, D. Landis, C. Thies, T. Tscharntke, W. W. Weisser, C. Winqvist, et al. 2016. "Agricultural landscape simplification reduces natural pest control: a quantitative synthesis." *Agriculture, Ecosystems and Environment* 221: 198–204.

Samways, M. J. 2020. *Insect Conservation: A Global Synthesis.* Wallingford, Oxon, UK: CABI.

Samways, M. J., P. S. Barton, K. Birkhofer, F. Chichorro, C. Deacon, T. Fartmann, P. Cardoso. 2020. "Solutions for humanity on how to conserve insects." *Biological Conservation* 242: 108427.

Schneider, M. K., G. Lüscher, P. Jeanneret, M. Arndorfer, Y. Ammari, D. Bailey, K. Balázs, A. Báldi, J.-P. Choisis, P. Dennis, et al. 2014. "Gains to species diversity in organically farmed fields are not propagated at the farm level." *Nature Communications* 5: 4151.

Simaika, J. P., and M. J. Samways. 2018. "Insect conservation psychology." *Journal of Insect Conservation* 22: 635–642.

Stanley, D. A., D. Gunning, and J. C. Stout. 2013. "Pollinators and pollination of oilseed rape crops (*Brassica napus* L.) in Ireland: ecological and economic incentives for pollinator conservation." *Journal of Insect Conservation* 17: 1181–9.

Thornton, I. 1996. *Krakatau: The Destruction and Reassembly of an Island Ecosystem.* Cambridge, Mass.: Harvard University Press.

Tilman, D., J. Fargione, B. Wolff, C. D'Antonio, A. Dobson, R. Howarth, D. Schindler, W. H. Schlesinger, D. Simberloff, and D. Swackhamer. 2001. "Forecasting agriculturally driven global environmental change." *Science* 292: 281–4.

Tuck, S. L., C. Winqvist, F. Mota, J. Ahnström, L. A. Turnbull, and J. Bengtsson. 2014. "Land-use intensity and the effects of organic farming on biodiversity: a hierarchical meta-analysis." *Journal of Applied Ecology* 51: 746–55.

United Nations. 2017. *Report of the Special Rapporteur on the Right to Food.* Human Rights Council, 34th Session, A/HRC/34/48.

van Huis, A. 2013. "Potential of insects as food and feed in assuring food security." *Annual Review of Entomology* 58: 563–83.

Vanbergen, A. J., and the Insect Pollination Initiative. 2013. "Threats to an ecosystem service: pressures on pollinators." *Frontiers in Ecology and the Environment* 11: 251–9.

Vickruck, J. L., L. R. Best, M. P. Gavin, J. H. Devries, and P. Galpern. 2019. "Pothole wetlands provide reservoir habitat for native bees in prairie croplands." *Biological Conservation* 232: 43–50.

Winter, S., T. Bauer, P. Strauss, S. Kratschmer, D. Paredes, D. Popescu, B. Landa, G. Guzmán, J. A. Gómez, M. Guernion, et al. 2018. "Effects of vegetation management intensity on biodiversity and ecosystem services in vineyards: a meta-analysis." *Journal of Applied Ecology* 55: 2484–95.

Wyckhuys, K. A. G., K. L. Heong, F. Sachez-Bayo, F. J. J. A. Bianchi, J. G. Lundgren, and J. W. Bentley. 2019. "Ecological illiteracy can deepen farmers' pesticide dependency." *Environmental Research Letters* 14: 093004.12

Chapter 12

Conclusions

Nicoletta Batini

World hunger. Pandemics. Cardiovascular diseases. Cancer. Obesity. Diabetes. Antimicrobial resistance. Climate change. Ocean dead zones. Fishery depletion. Species extinction. Deforestation. Income and wealth inequality. Low labor productivity. Public and private debt. Deruralization. The list goes on. There is one issue at the heart of all these problems that is too often overlooked by economists and policymakers: the global food system.

Although food systems are essential to people and economies because they provide the energy we need to live, work, and prosper, they are rarely the focus of macroeconomic policy. Our lack of action and even discussion about reform reflects a widespread belief that the agri-food industry—now highly mechanized, subsidized, and globally concentrated—offers all we could wish for when it comes to food.

The COVID-19 outbreak, believed to have originated in a live food market in China at the end of 2019, offered a brutal reality check. In a matter of months, the food sector turned from economics' ugly duckling to a world economy's white swan.[1]

COVID-19, a severe respiratory syndrome, became a pandemic and resulted in harsh lockdowns in most parts of the world. With cases spreading fast, many people flocked to grocery stores to stock up, and images of long lines and empty shelves suddenly reminded us of how important food systems are in our lives. At the same time, food relief organizations all around the world struggled to meet surging demand from those hit hard by mass layoffs and informal job losses caused by the pandemic.

Bare shelves and spikes in the price of staple food do not just reflect the human instinct to hoard at uncertain times or the emergent food insecurity of the "new needy," however. They are evidence that the global food supply chain—highly centralized and operating on a just-in-time supply basis—is prone to falter and fail during systemic events such as pandemics and natural disasters. In some developed countries, for example, the outbreak made it impossible to harvest or package food as key processing plants closed in the face of mounting COVID-19 cases, and seasonal migrant workers could not cross borders to reach the fields. Elsewhere, food stocks reached historic highs, and farmers dumped milk and destroyed eggs and produce, because most of their largest buyers, such as restaurants, cafeterias, and bars, were closed. At the time of this writing, the virus has struck mostly developed nations, but in developing countries food shortages of biblical proportions have been predicted by the United Nations Food and Agriculture Organization (FAO) and the World Food Program. These could lead to a hunger pandemic that would eclipse the coronavirus unless measures are taken fast to protect the most vulnerable and keep global food supply chains functional.

The Great Lockdown is simply deepening cracks in the global food system's long, fragile facade. According to the FAO, already in 2018 billions of people were undernourished while billions were overweight or obese, because the food they ate was high in calories but low in nutritional content, which unintentionally promoted obesity, diabetes, cancer, and cardiovascular diseases, all of which compromise immune health. Today, citizens with weak immune systems and the hundreds of undernourished people worldwide are suffering disproportionally the lethal consequences of COVID-19. In all these cases, the human toll comes with huge tolls on productivity and public spending.

The limitations of the food system go beyond failing to feed the world well. Food produced through the overuse of chemicals, genetic modification, monoculture cropping systems, and intensive animal farming on land and at sea is fundamentally unhealthy for the planet and ultimately for the system according to which we produce food. Industrial animal farming operations that rear large numbers of animals in confined spaces breed bacteria and viruses such as *Salmonella*, *Escherichia coli*, and bird and swine flus such as H1N1 and H5N1, and they are behind the spread of antibiotic-resistant superbugs. At the same time, our relentless disturbance of pristine habitats to farm and hunt has allowed deadly pathogens such as SARS, Zika, HIV, Ebola, and now, possibly, COVID-19, to jump species, infecting ours.

To avoid the worst, immediate actions are needed to keep the global food supply chains moving. Past the emergency, the human and financial damages of the coronavirus crisis will require a rebuilding of economies across the world.

This offers a unique opportunity to invest in the transformation necessary to nourish all people, regenerate the environment, and enable the flourishing of local communities depressed by the crisis. Food system reforms tailored to individual country circumstances can help mitigate future shocks from pandemics and climate change, bringing about multiple, long-lasting health, economic, and environmental benefits.

In the previous pages of this book, we have examined diverse strategies for bringing about a health–economy–environment win–win–win transformation in the global food system. Although, as discussed, economic policies must be tailored to individual countries' level of wealth and development, three main policy areas generally emerged as central to successful reform of our food system:

- *Healthy and sustainable diets.* If people currently following Western diets would eat more plant-based, minimally processed foods in line with scientific recommendations, they would improve their health, increase land use efficiency, make healthy food more affordable globally, and slash global emissions. This can be achieved by repurposing agricultural subsidies to support the global supply of plant-based proteins both on land and at sea and align procurement practices, education programs, and healthcare systems toward better dietary choices. Levies on unhealthy foods, like taxes on carbon for fossil fuels, can help reflect the true cost of these foods in their prices. In turn, better diets can reduce healthcare costs globally, strengthen public and private balance sheets, reduce income inequality, and help us weather the next pandemic with healthier people and stronger immune systems.
- *Regenerative land and sea farming.* A shift toward agroecology and regenerative ocean farming based on strong local and regional food systems can heal our soils, air, and water; increase economic resilience;

and boost local jobs. Economic policies to make this happen include government support for sustainable farming and fishing; leveling the financial and regulatory playing field for smaller, polycultural farming operations relative to large intensive farms; and instituting collective procurement practices that support foods sourced locally and regionally.

- *Conservation.* Reducing the environmental burden created by our current food system can restore biodiversity, bolster carbon sequestration, and lower the risk of future pandemics. This calls for policies to rapidly align national regulations with recent proposals by the UN Convention on Biological Diversity for a global framework to protect Earth's wildlife and set the right economic incentives and markets for conservation. Also needed are measures to eradicate the trade of wild animals for human consumption and traditional medicine, which are contributing to the extinction of key species and threatening entire ecosystems.

Food systems are at the crossroads of human, animal, economic, and environmental health. The coronavirus crisis has clearly shown that ignoring this fact condemns the world economy to unprecedented human and financial shocks, which are bound to become more severe and frequent as climate changes and global population grows. By prioritizing food system reforms in our build-forward agenda, we can bring renewed energy to our quest for a more inclusive and sustainable global economy and have a good chance to secure both the UN Sustainable Development Goals and the Paris Climate Agreement. As Arundhati Roy recently held, "Historically, pandemics have forced humans to break with the past and imagine their world anew. This one is no different. It is a portal, a gateway between one world and the next" (Roy 2020). If we can muster the will before it is too late, we can have our nutritious food, thriving economies, and a habitable planet too.

References

Roy, A. 2020. "The pandemic is a portal." *Financial Times*, April 3. https://www.ft.com/content/10d8f5e8-74eb-11ea-95fe-fcd274e920ca

Taleb, N. N. 2010. *The Black Swan: Second Edition: The Impact of the Highly Improbable: With a New Section: "On Robustness and Fragility" (Incerto).* New York: Random House Trade Paperbacks.

Endnote

1. A white swan event, a term popularized by finance professor, writer, and former Wall Street trader Nassim Nicholas Taleb, is a variation of black and gray swan event (Taleb 2010). It is defined as an event that is highly certain (contrary to black and gray swans that are either unpredictable—black swan—or somewhat predictable but not certain—gray swan). All these events carry extreme impacts and can be explained rationally after they have occurred.

ACKNOWLEDGMENTS

This book began with an economic awakening. After the global financial crisis, while studying data on fiscal spending for major advanced economies, I began delving into public health issues such as pathology statistics and the economic burden of diseases. Doing that, I became increasingly aware of the strong and causal connection between diets and the macroeconomy. By serendipity, I was dragged into more readings and documentary viewings of the environmental impact of modern food systems. I became convinced that many social, economic, and environmental woes could probably be solved or at least alleviated by redressing food systems to make them sustainable for people and planet, and I realized that this could have vastly beneficial consequences for economies as well, from both a public finance and an employment, productivity, and income distribution point of view. Crucially, I discovered that although the challenges of modern food systems had been widely investigated by either nutritionists or environmentalists, a less sectorial and more general economic policy "theory" of the problem, and of its economic solutions, had never been developed. As an economist, I felt this was too juicy to be left alone; I could not think of any economic subjects that are more complex and controversial than our food choices and the climate crisis they contribute to. I thus decided, with a mix of excitement and trepidation, to embark on an analysis that could derive such a transformative economic theory.

At the start, the journey of shaping the book was very solitary. But as my desire to learn and understand grew stronger, I slowly began weaving a web of communication with numerous climate science, economic policy, biology, ecology, and public health experts. Some of them have become authors of this book; some have not but have contributed directly or indirectly to its contents through either their writings or direct conversations. I am thankful for all the time, information, and knowledge they shared. Working with the book's chapter authors has been a wonderful and particularly educational experience for me, and I thank all of them for their energy, vision, and dedication in making this book come alive. Each of them possesses a unique wealth of both scientific and policy experience; it is no chance that they feature here. Their great professionalism, passion, and hands-on knowledge have allowed us to produce a novel and truly multidisciplinary and kaleidoscopic representation of the problems vexing current food systems. It has also allowed us to pinpoint the ills behind the economic and structural policies that shape them, enabling us to identify a set of practical, economical, and viable steps to fix them.

In this process, Emily Turner has been our first reader and ultimately a collaborator. The book owes much to her thoughtfulness and care throughout the writing and production process. I also owe much to David Miller and all the Editorial Board at Island Press for believing in this project from the beginning. Patty Loo, Jim Beardow, Jeff Haynes, and Josh Park have been key partners in supporting collaboration from the International Monetary Fund side, and Liliana Zerpa has offered patient assistance on the Fund HR side. Colleagues at the fund's IEO have been wonderful at cheerleading my efforts, and particular thanks goes to Charles Collyns and Prakash Loungani, for blessing this external activity, and to Monse Acosta, Ralph Chami, Tamar Gutner, Michael Kell, Helen Oxenbridge, Caterina Ruggeri-Laderchi, Philip Lymbery, and Ann Tutwiler for reading and offering valuable comments on different sections of the preliminary manuscript. Qihao Tang has generously and speedily helped me multiple times with graphic issues.

Of course, I would not have been able to work on this project without the optimism and patience of my children, Lina and Jehanne, who coped cheerfully and well with my long hours in front of the computer on evenings and weekends, in both summer and winter. Like my mother, Maria Pia, they believe that this book may help make a difference and thus had to be written. For them, and for us all, failure is not an option.

Nicoletta Batini is a scholar of innovative monetary and fiscal policy practices and a leading expert in the design of macroeconomic strategies to deal with the climate change–public health nexus, with a focus on land use and food systems. She has published extensively in all these fields and since 2019 works for the Fund's Independent Evaluation Office. Before the IMF, she was advisor of the Bank of England's Monetary Policy Committee, professor of economics at the University of Surrey, and director of the International Economics and Policy Office of the Treasury in Italy. She has handled extensive consultancy roles internationally. She holds a PhD in international finance (Scuola Superiore S. Anna) and a PhD in monetary economics (University of Oxford).

Martin W. Bloem is the Robert S. Lawrence Professor of Environmental Health Sciences in the Johns Hopkins Bloomberg School of Public Health and director of the Johns Hopkins Center for a Livable Future since December 2017. He spent twelve years at the United Nations World Food Programme (WFP) and as the WFP's Global Coordinator for UNAIDS, the Joint United Nations Programme on HIV/AIDS. Martin has more than three decades of experience in research on public health, nutrition, emergencies, and food systems. From 1985 to 2005, he worked and lived in Thailand, Bangladesh, Indonesia, and Singapore before he moved to Rome, working at the United Nations global level. Martin holds a medical degree from the University of Utrecht and a doctorate from the University of Maastricht.

Patty Cantrell is a community organizer focused on linking rural assets to market opportunities through development of values-based supply chains. She leads the New Growth community development corporation in west central Missouri. She spent the bulk of her career in the food system arena. Patty led development of northwest Michigan's Taste the Local Difference and Food and Farming Network initiatives and chaired the Michigan Good Food Charter infrastructure task force. Patty holds a master's degree in business administration and bachelor's degrees in economics and political science. She is a 1987 Fulbright Scholar and 2007–2009 Kellogg Food and Society Fellow.

Ivon Cuadros-Casanova is a doctoral student within the framework of Inspire4Nature, a training network at the science–policy interface, where she is exploring synergies between biodiversity conservation and the achievement of the Sustainable Development Goals. She worked internationally for scientific institutions and nongovernment organizations, which enriched her understanding of the biological and socioeconomic aspects influencing biodiversity conservation outcomes. Through field-base experience, she has advanced knowledge in the design of ecological assessment studies and long-term monitoring programs and understands the key role of ecological-based science to achieve socioeconomic sustainability. She pursues a deeper understanding of the significance of biodiversity and ecosystem services as a pathway to influence environmental policy and law enforcement.

Charl Deacon is a postdoctoral research fellow affiliated with the Department of Conservation Ecology and Entomology, Stellenbosch University, South Africa. Charl specializes in freshwater insect ecology (particularly Odonata, Hemiptera, and Coleoptera), aquatic ecosystem conservation, and insect biogeography. He also has strong interest in terrestrial insect ecology and biogeography, especially for how they relate to the management of agroecosystems.

Ruth DeFries is a professor of ecology and sustainable development at Columbia University in New York. Her research quantifies how land use change affects climate, biodiversity, and other ecosystem services, as well as human development, in the tropics with particular focus in India. DeFries was elected as a member of the U.S. National Academy of Sciences and received a MacArthur Fellowship and other honors for her scientific research. Her books for popular audiences include *The Big Ratchet: How Humanity Thrives in the Face of Natural Crisis* (2014) and *What Would Nature Do? A Guide for Our Uncertain Times* (2021).

Saskia de Pee is senior technical advisor for nutrition at the United Nations World Food Programme (WFP), where she leads the Systems Analysis for Nutrition team and is adjunct associate professor at the Friedman School of Nutrition Science and Policy, Tufts University, Boston and at Human Nutrition, Wageningen University, the Netherlands. She has worked in public health nutrition for more than twenty years, focusing on science as well as practical applications, policies, and strategies. Before joining WFP in 2007 she worked for Helen Keller International in the Asia Pacific region for ten years. She has coauthored more than 150 scientific publications and holds a PhD in nutrition from Wageningen University, the Netherlands.

Dickson Despommier, PhD, is professor emeritus of Public Health and Microbiology at Columbia University and is an adjunct professor at Fordham University, where he teaches a course, "Ecology for Designers." Despommier authored *The Vertical Farm* (St. Martin's Press) and writes on integrating farming into the cityscape. His interest focuses on reinventing the built environment. Vertical farming is the linchpin concept enabling cities to eventually exist independent of the natural landscape. His vision also includes rainwater harvesting, construction using cross-laminated timber technology, and renewable energy generation based on clear photovoltaic glass laminates that function as windows.

Jessica C. Fanzo, PhD is the Bloomberg Distinguished Professor of Global Food Policy and Ethics at the Berman Institute of Bioethics, the Bloomberg School of Public Health, and the Nitze School of Advanced International Studies at Johns Hopkins University. She also serves as the director of Hopkins's Global Food Policy and Ethics Program and as director of food and nutrition security at the JHU Alliance for a Healthier World. From 2017 to 2019, Jessica served as the cochair of the Global Nutrition Report and the UN High Level Panel of Experts on Food Systems and Nutrition. Before coming to Hopkins, she held positions at Columbia University, the Earth Institute, the Food and Agriculture Organization of the United Nations, the World Food Programme, Bioversity International, and the Millennium Development Goal Centre at the World Agroforestry Center in Kenya. Jessica has a PhD in nutrition from the University of Arizona.

Luigi Fontana, MD, PhD, FRACP is a professor of medicine and the Leonard P. Ullmann Chair of Translational Metabolic Health at the University of Sydney, where he directs the Healthy Longevity Research and Clinical Program. He is also a clinical academic in the Department of Endocrinology at the Royal Prince Alfred Hospital. He is an internationally recognized physician scientist and one of the world's leaders in the field of nutrition and healthy longevity. His pioneering studies on the effects of dietary restriction in humans have opened a new area of nutrition-related research that holds tremendous promise for the prevention of age-related chronic diseases.

Bruce Friedrich is cofounder and executive director of the Good Food Institute (GFI). With branches in the United States, India, Israel, Brazil, Europe, and Asia-Pacific, GFI is accelerating the production of plant-based and cultivated meat in order to bolster the global protein supply while protecting our environment, promoting global health, and preventing food insecurity. Bruce oversees GFI's global strategy, working with directors and international managing directors to ensure that GFI is maximally effective at delivering mission-focused results. Bruce graduated magna cum laude from Georgetown Law and also holds degrees from Johns Hopkins University and the London School of Economics.

John Ikerd holds BS, MS, and PhD degrees in agricultural economics and is professor emeritus of Agricultural Economics, University of Missouri–Columbia. He had a thirty-year academic career on faculties of North Carolina State University, Oklahoma State University, the University of Georgia, and the University of Missouri. Since retiring in 2000, he spends most of his time on issues related to agricultural sustainability. In 2014, Ikerd was commissioned by the Food and Agricultural Organization of the United Nations to write the regional report "Family Farms of North America," in recognition for the International Year of the Family Farming. He has written six books and numerous book chapters, journal articles, and professional papers.

Stephen R. Kaufman, MD, is an ophthalmologist in northeast Ohio. He is an assistant professor at Case Western Reserve University. He is chair of the Christian Vegetarian Association, and his writings include *Good News for All Creation* and *Guided by the Faith of Christ: Seeking to Stop Violence and Scapegoating*.

Charles Knirsch is vice president of Pfizer Vaccines Research and Development and adjunct assistant professor of medicine at Columbia University. He is a widely published researcher and has cotaught Parasitic Diseases with Dr. Despommier. He has worked in a number of partnerships and codevelopment programs on neglected tropical diseases with the National Institutes of Health, the Centers for Disease Control and Prevention, and the World Health Organization, the latter in a program with the International Trachoma Initiative to eliminate blinding trachoma by the year 2020.

Divya Mehra serves as a strategic partnerships adviser in the Strategic Partnerships Division at the World Food Program (WFP). Divya joined the WFP in 2012 and has held several positions in Rome and New York, including in Nutrition, Supply Chain and Partnerships. Her expertise lies in system approaches and solutions for development, focusing on food security, nutrition, and health. Divya's experiences have been multidisciplinary. Trained in health policy and environmental health, she obtained her master's and doctoral degrees in public health from Columbia University.

Philippe Pointereau is an agronomist. He leads the Agro-Environment department of SOLAGRO and coordinates European projects and studies with the Joint Research Centre–Institute for Environment and Sustainability of the European Commission and the European Environment Agency. His research interests cover agroecology, environmental assessment of farming systems, and agri-food chains. He coordinates the scientific committee of the prospective Afterres2050 for a sustainable food system and agriculture in France and participates in the research project BioNutriNet, measuring the impact of organic diets on environment and health.

Carlo Rondinini is a research scientist at Sapienza University of Rome and Coordinator of the Global Mammal Assessment, an initiative in partnership with the International Union for Conservation of Nature to maintain the information on mammal extinction risk on the Red List. He has worked with government and nongovernment organizations, including the Intergovernmental Science-Policy Platform on Biodiversity and Ecosystem Services and the Convention on Biological Diversity to map species distributions, assess species extinction risk, set conservation targets, identify conservation priorities, develop scenarios of biodiversity change, and identify solutions for species conservation at the national, regional, and global scale.

Michael J. Samways is distinguished professor in the Department of Conservation Ecology & Entomology, Stellenbosch University, South Africa, fellow of the Royal Society of South Africa, and member of the Academy of Science of South Africa. He focuses on all aspects of insect conservation, nationally and internationally. Michael has received several major awards, including the John Herschel Medal of the Royal Society of South Africa, the Gold Medal of the South African Academy of Science and Arts, the Gold Medal of the Academy of Science of South Africa, and the Marsh Award of the Royal Entomological Society.

Geeta Sethi is the advisor and global lead for food systems at the World Bank. She is the lead architect of the World Bank's Food System Transformation agenda, a food system that addresses the triple bottom line: prosperity, sustainability, and healthy people. She also manages the World Bank's program on Food Loss and Waste Reduction. She has worked extensively on fragile low- and middle-income economies, focusing and publishing academic work on rural development, service delivery, and intergovernmental fiscal policies. She has delivered many lending programs to the World Bank Board. Previously, she was chief of staff to the climate change vice president and special envoy and the operations and strategy manager for climate change and worked as program manager for the Global Agriculture and Food Security Program. She has an MBA and PhD in economics.

Bren Smith, GreenWave executive director and owner of Thimble Island Ocean Farm, pioneered the development of regenerative ocean farming. A lifelong commercial fisherman, he was named one of *Rolling Stone* magazine's "25 People Shaping the Future" and featured in *TIME* magazine's "Best Inventions of 2017." Bren is the winner of the Buckminster Fuller Prize and has been profiled by *60 Minutes*, CNN, *The New Yorker*, *The Wall Street Journal*, *National Geographic*, and elsewhere. He is an Ashoka, Castanea, and Echoing Green Climate Fellow and author of *Eat Like a Fish: My Adventures Farming the Ocean to Fight Climate Change.*

Rodolfo Werner is a marine biologist and a wildlife conservationist who has devoted his professional career to study and work toward the conservation of the Patagonian Sea, the Southern Ocean, and Antarctica. He is an advisor to The Pew Charitable Trusts, the Antarctic & Southern Ocean Coalition, and the Antarctic Wildlife Research Fund and is a senior delegate on meetings of the Convention for the Conservation of Antarctic Marine Living Resources and the Antarctic Treaty. He has published extensively in scientific journals and participated in Antarctic expeditions and documentaries. He also works as a naturalist and lecturer on tourist vessels traveling to Antarctica, South Georgia, and the Malvinas and Falkland Islands, mainly on board the *NG-Explorer* (Lindblad Expeditions).

Hanna Wernerson is an MSc student at Stockholm Resilience Center and course coordinator at the Center for Environment and Development Studies at Uppsala University, Sweden. Wernerson worked for a year and a half as an agricultural marketing specialist for the U.S. Foreign Agricultural Service in Canada before returning to graduate school. Wernerson is currently researching animal–human relationships in commercial cattle farming, exploring how our interactions with nonhumans influence the way we think and act. Wernerson also engages with nonacademic spheres of action, including her work with local food sovereignty through the Ottawa Good Food Box in Canada and the Swedish civil society organization Stadsmissionen.

INDEX

Page numbers followed by "b", "f" and "t" indicate boxes, figures and tables.